SHERLOCK

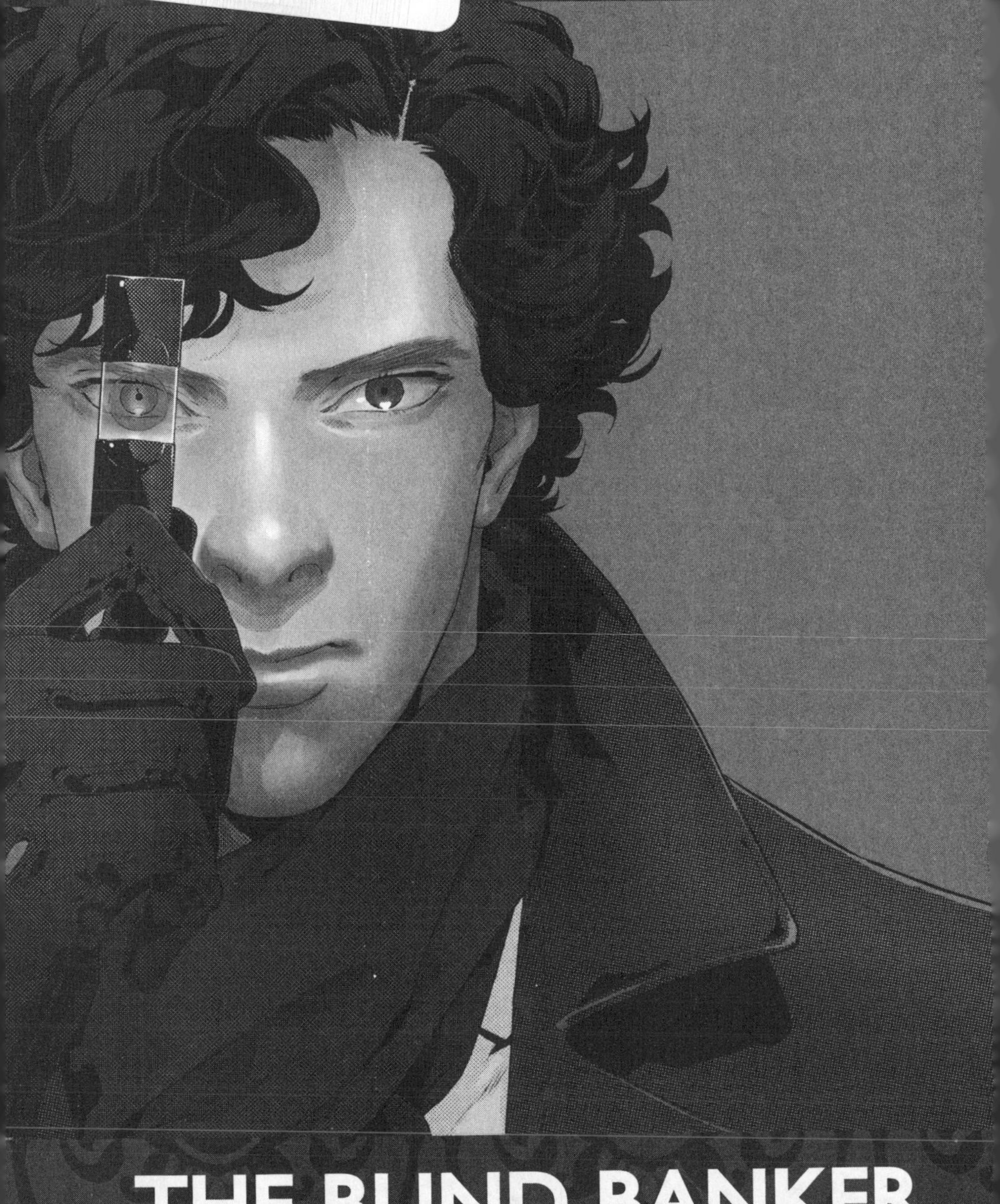

THE BLIND BANKER

SHERLOCK

THE BLIND BANKER

SCRIPT
STEVE THOMPSON

ADAPTATION/ART
JAY.

LETTERING
AMOONA SAOHIN

Originally published in Japanese by Kadokawa.
This manga is presented in its original right-to-left reading format.

Based on the TV series **SHERLOCK**
co-created by **STEVEN MOFFAT** & **MARK GATISS**
and adapting Episode Two: The Blind Banker.

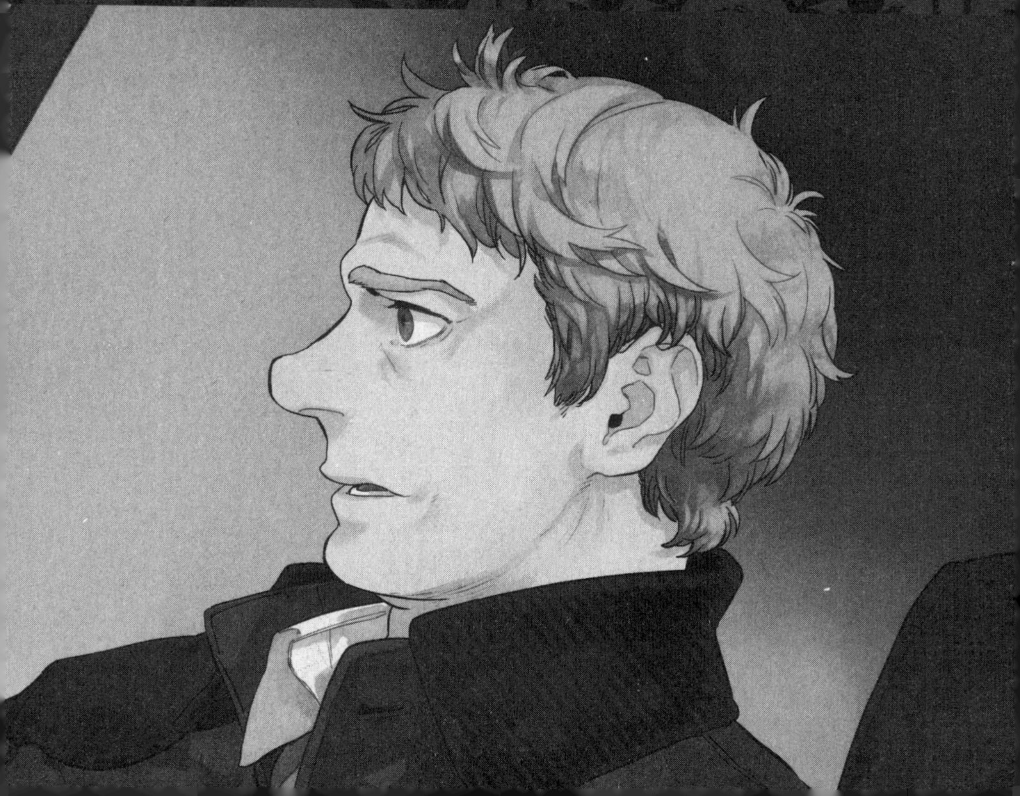

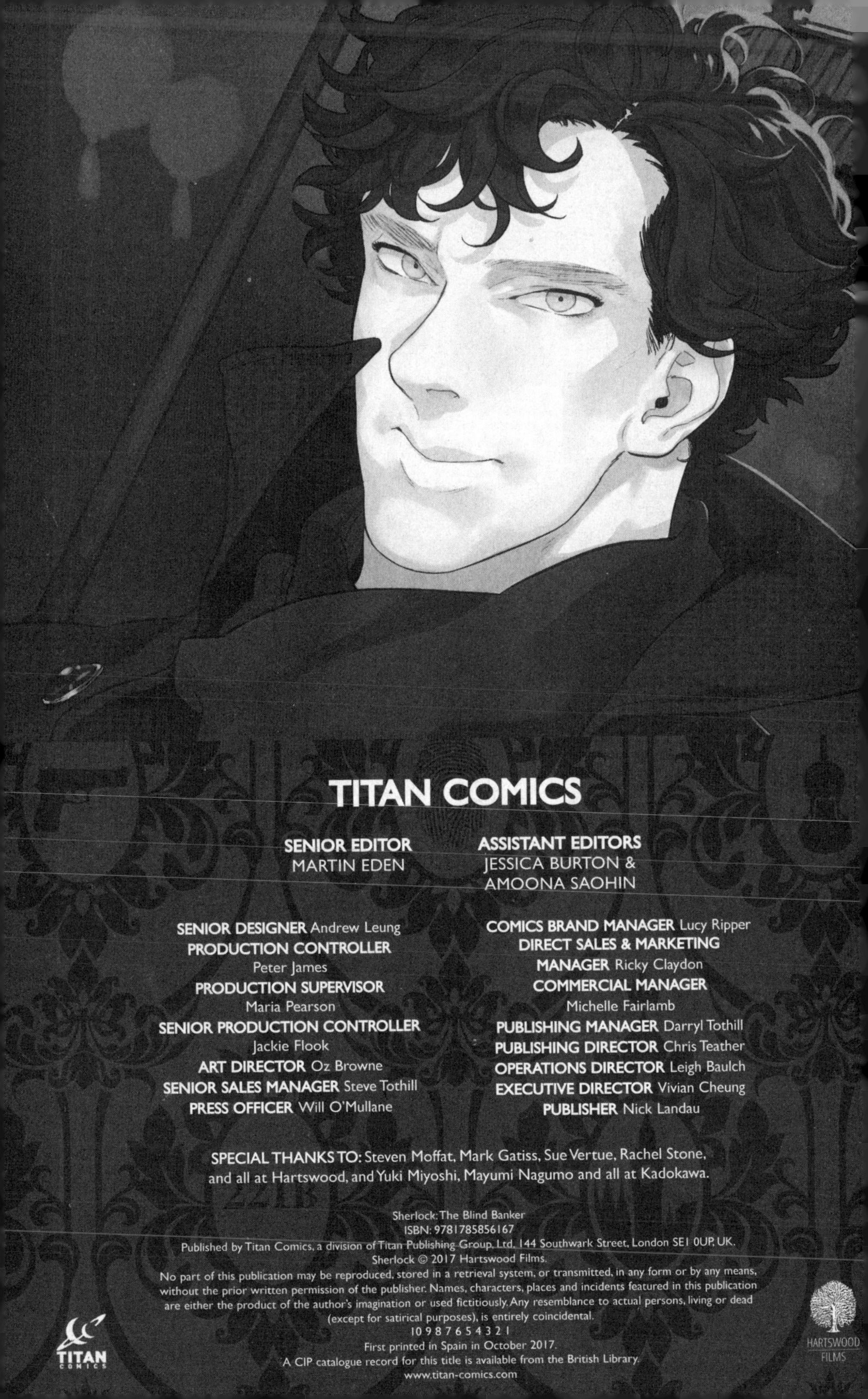

TITAN COMICS

SENIOR EDITOR
MARTIN EDEN

ASSISTANT EDITORS
JESSICA BURTON &
AMOONA SAOHIN

SENIOR DESIGNER Andrew Leung
PRODUCTION CONTROLLER
Peter James
PRODUCTION SUPERVISOR
Maria Pearson
SENIOR PRODUCTION CONTROLLER
Jackie Flook
ART DIRECTOR Oz Browne
SENIOR SALES MANAGER Steve Tothill
PRESS OFFICER Will O'Mullane

COMICS BRAND MANAGER Lucy Ripper
DIRECT SALES & MARKETING MANAGER Ricky Claydon
COMMERCIAL MANAGER
Michelle Fairlamb
PUBLISHING MANAGER Darryl Tothill
PUBLISHING DIRECTOR Chris Teather
OPERATIONS DIRECTOR Leigh Baulch
EXECUTIVE DIRECTOR Vivian Cheung
PUBLISHER Nick Landau

SPECIAL THANKS TO: Steven Moffat, Mark Gatiss, Sue Vertue, Rachel Stone, and all at Hartswood, and Yuki Miyoshi, Mayumi Nagumo and all at Kadokawa.

Sherlock: The Blind Banker
ISBN: 9781785856167
Published by Titan Comics, a division of Titan Publishing Group, Ltd. 144 Southwark Street, London SE1 0UP, UK.

10 9 8 7 6 5 4 3 2 1
First printed in Spain in October 2017.
A CIP catalogue record for this title is available from the British Library.
www.titan-comics.com

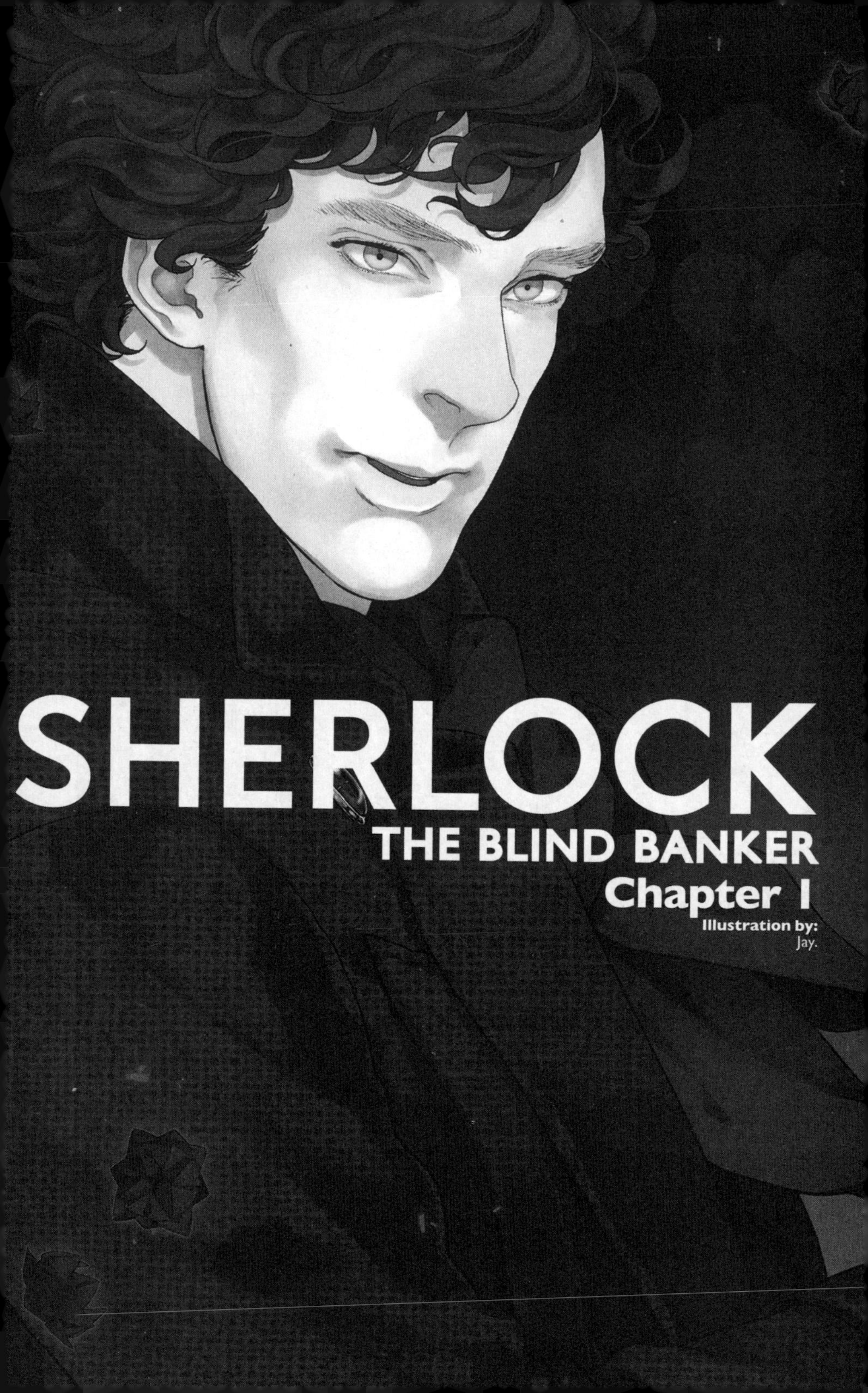

SHERLOCK

THE BLIND BANKER

Chapter 1

Illustration by:
Jay.

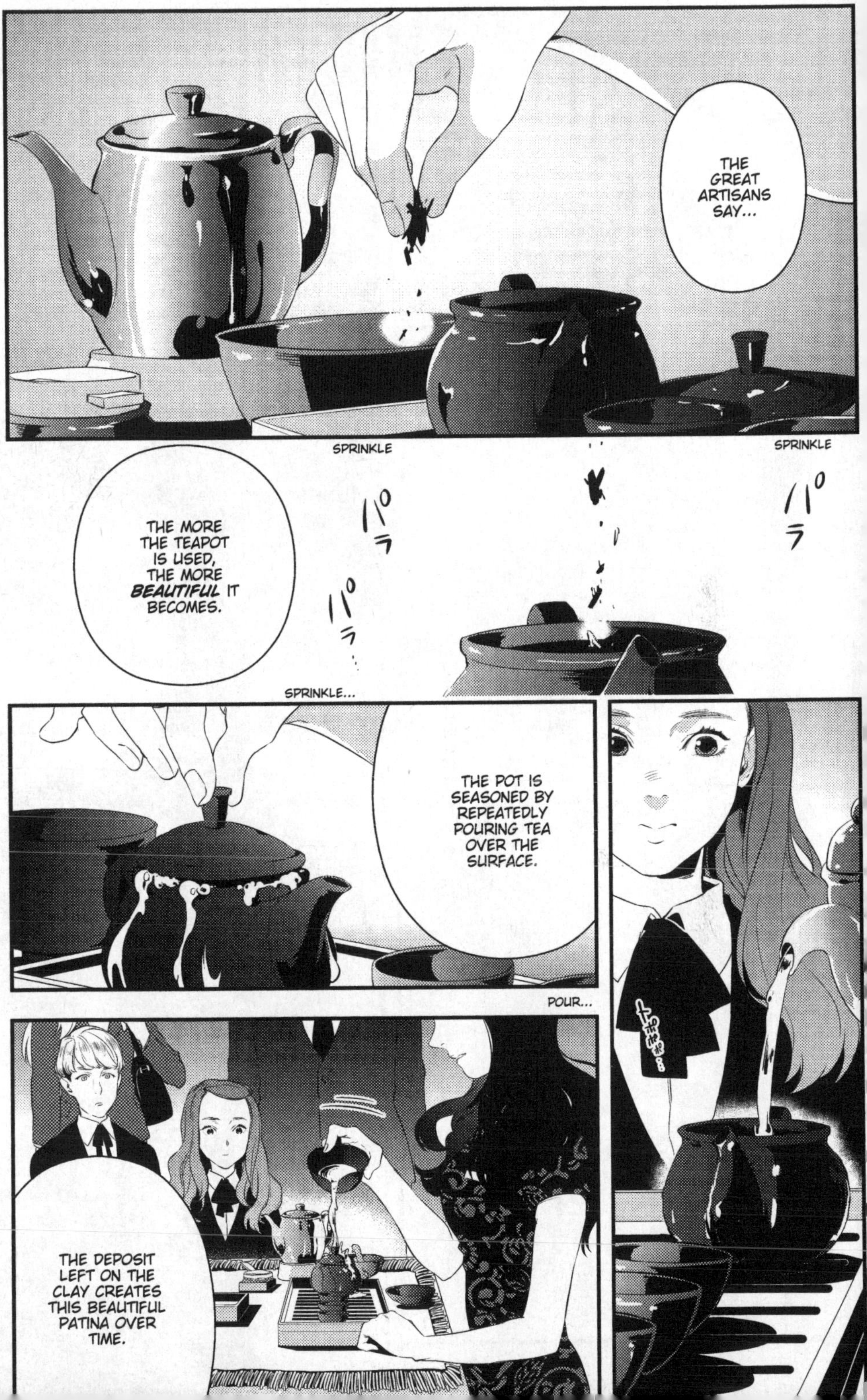
THE GREAT ARTISANS SAY...
SPRINKLE
SPRINKLE
パラ
パラ
パラ...
THE MORE THE TEAPOT IS USED, THE MORE **BEAUTIFUL** IT BECOMES.
SPRINKLE...
トポポポ...
POUR...
THE POT IS SEASONED BY REPEATEDLY POURING TEA OVER THE SURFACE.
THE DEPOSIT LEFT ON THE CLAY CREATES THIS BEAUTIFUL PATINA OVER TIME.

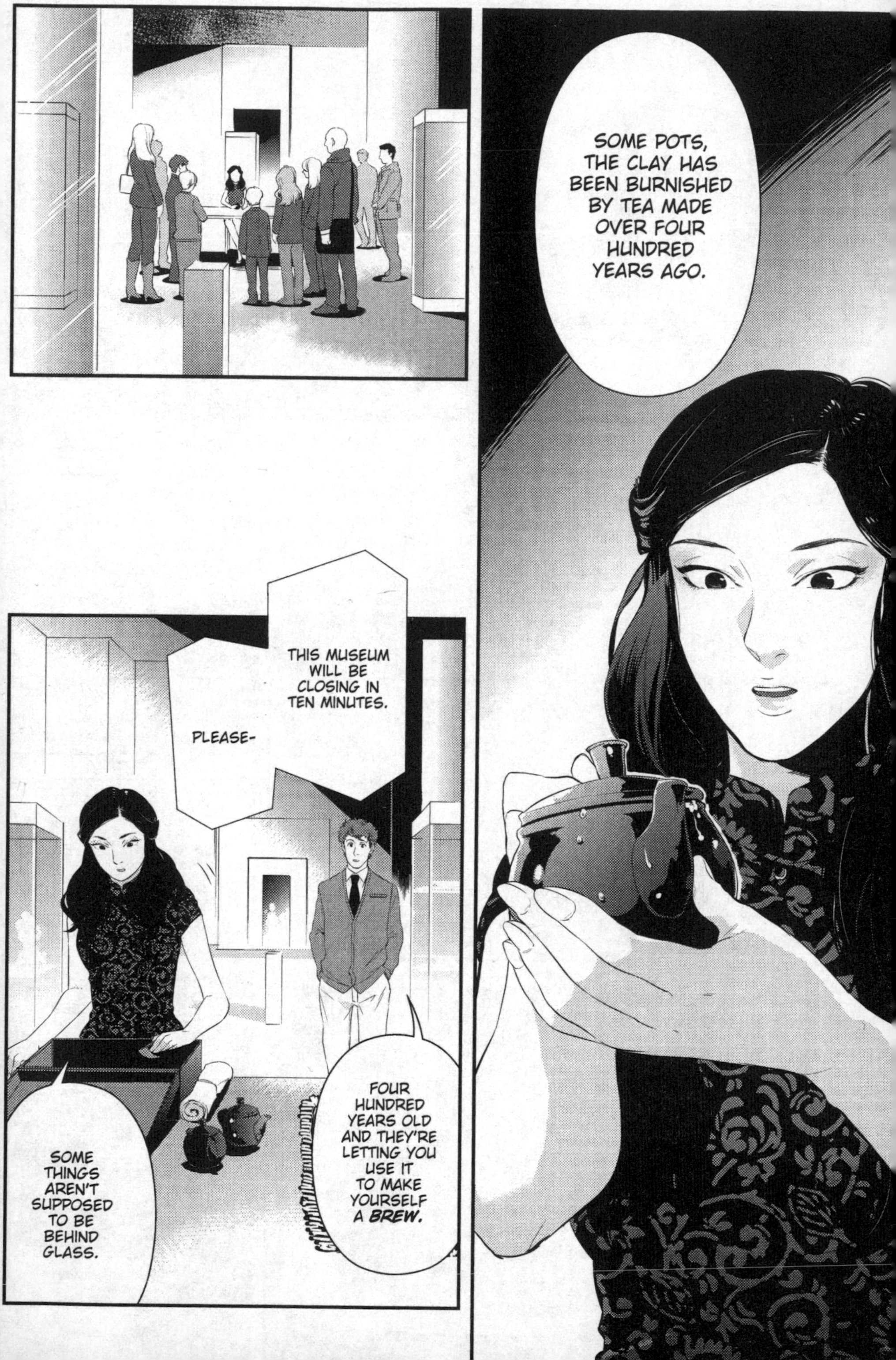
SOME POTS, THE CLAY HAS BEEN BURNISHED BY TEA MADE OVER FOUR HUNDRED YEARS AGO.
THIS MUSEUM WILL BE CLOSING IN TEN MINUTES.
PLEASE-
FOUR HUNDRED YEARS OLD AND THEY'RE LETTING YOU USE IT TO MAKE YOURSELF A *BREW.*
SOME THINGS AREN'T SUPPOSED TO BE BEHIND GLASS.

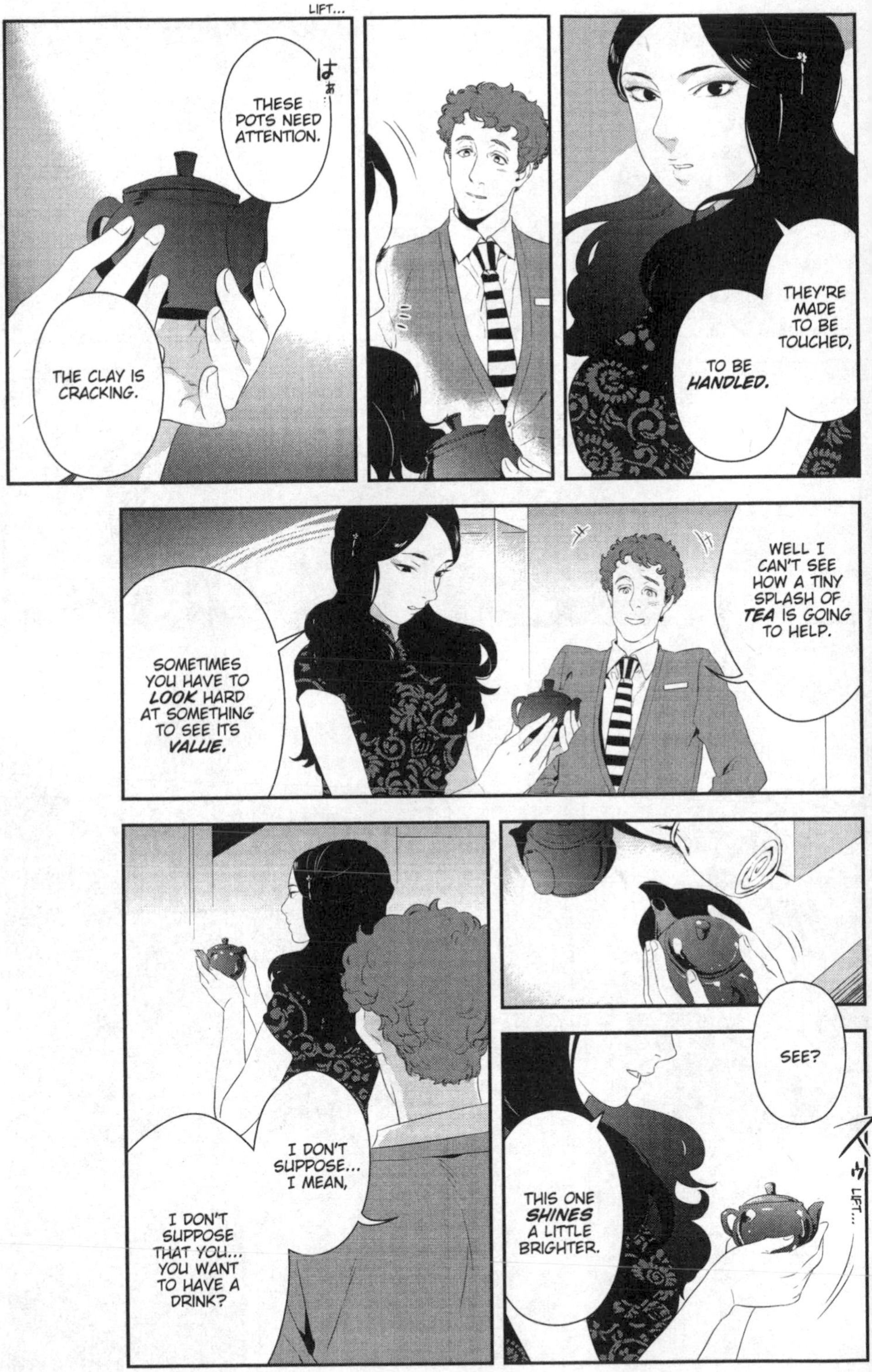

THEY'RE MADE TO BE TOUCHED,
TO BE **HANDLED.**
LIFT...
はぁ…
THESE POTS NEED ATTENTION.
THE CLAY IS CRACKING.
WELL I CAN'T SEE HOW A TINY SPLASH OF **TEA** IS GOING TO HELP.
SOMETIMES YOU HAVE TO **LOOK** HARD AT SOMETHING TO SEE ITS **VALUE.**
SEE?
LIFT...
THIS ONE **SHINES** A LITTLE BRIGHTER.
I DON'T SUPPOSE... I MEAN,
I DON'T SUPPOSE THAT YOU... YOU WANT TO HAVE A DRINK?

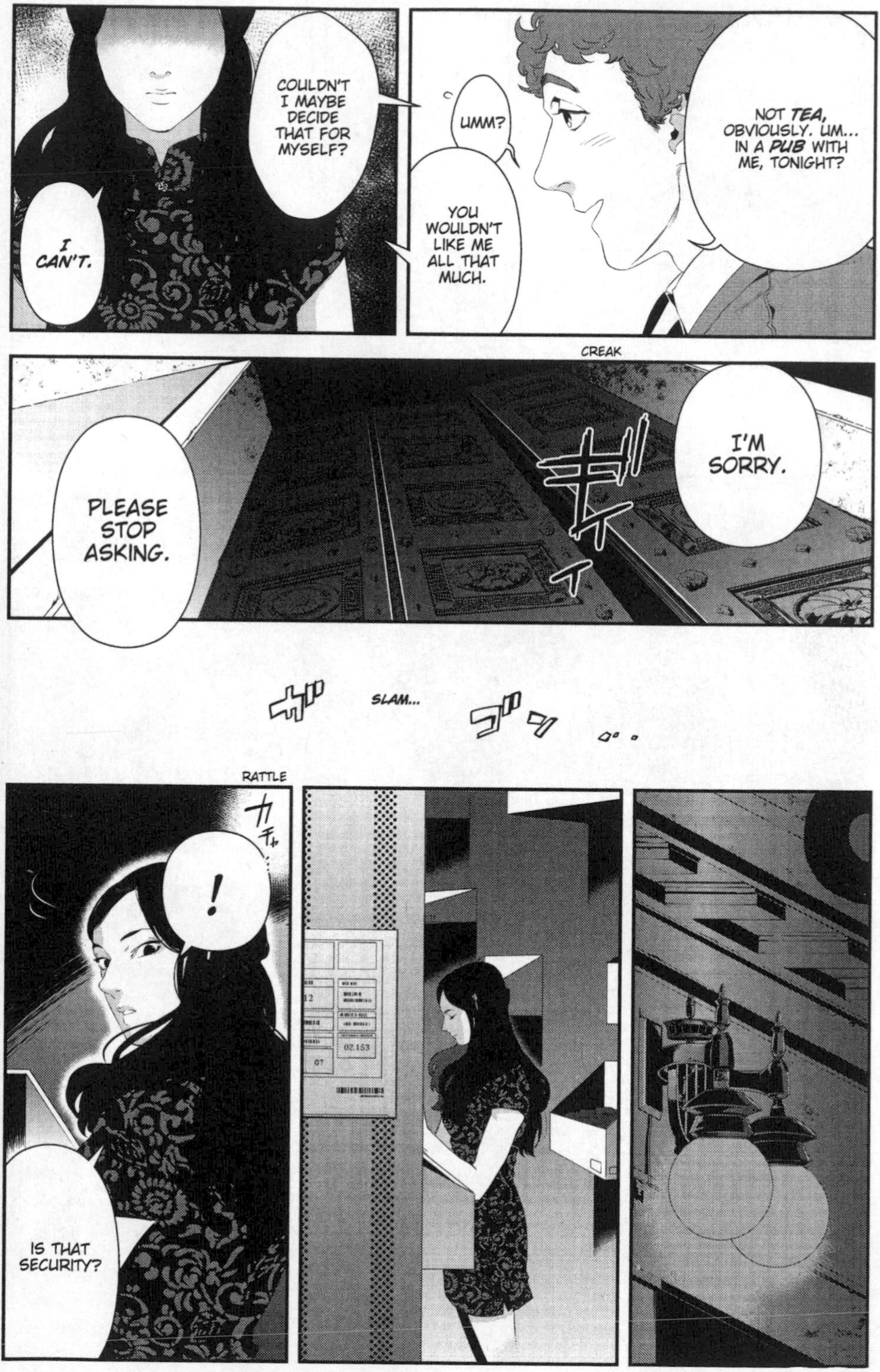
NOT TEA, OBVIOUSLY. UM... IN A PUB WITH ME, TONIGHT?
UMM?
YOU WOULDN'T LIKE ME ALL THAT MUCH.
COULDN'T I MAYBE DECIDE THAT FOR MYSELF?
I CAN'T.
CREAK
I'M SORRY.
PLEASE STOP ASKING.
SLAM...
RATTLE
!
IS THAT SECURITY?

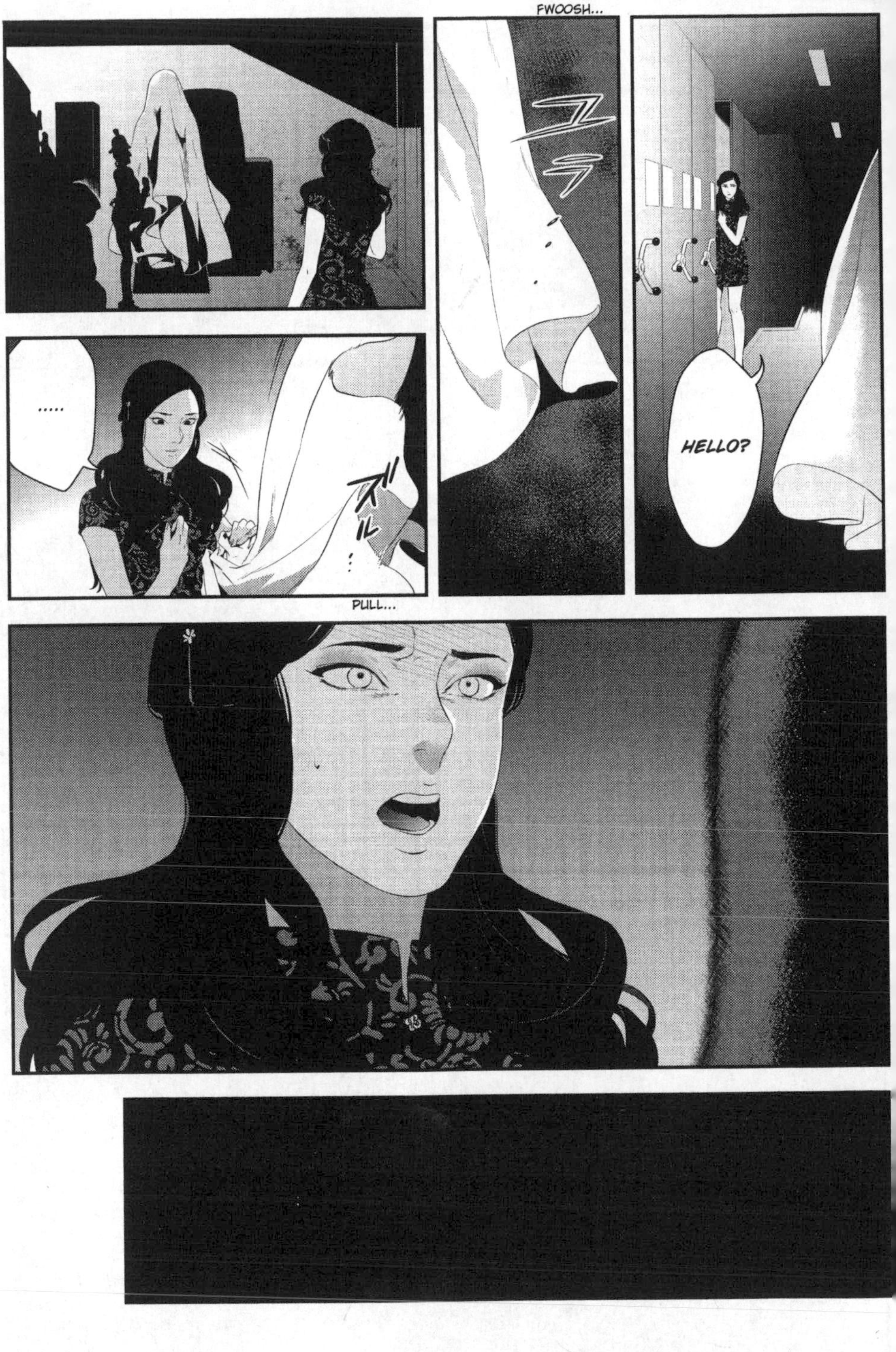
HELLO?
FWOOSH...
.....
PULL...

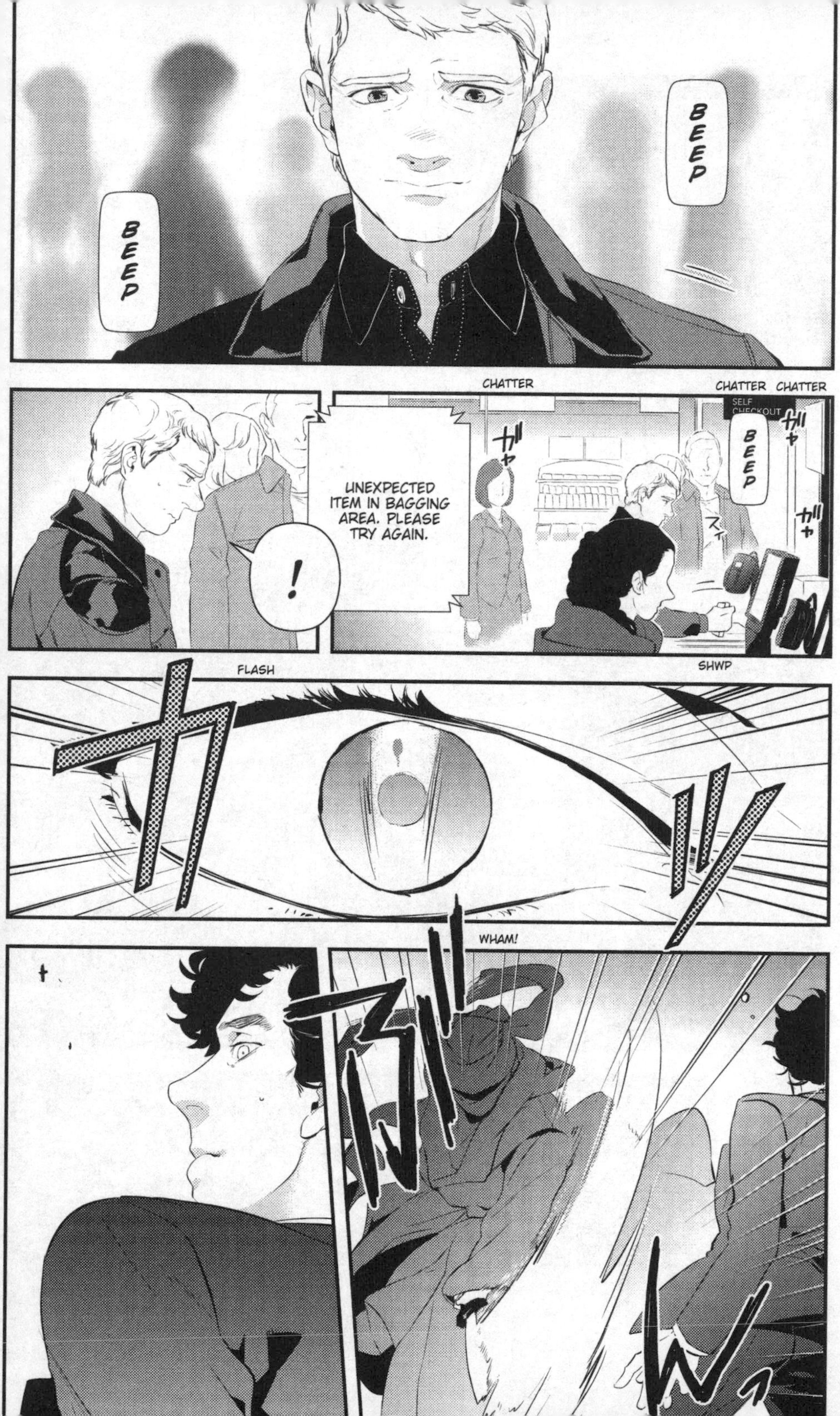
BEEP
BEEP
CHATTER CHATTER
SELF CHECKOUT
BEEP
CHATTER
UNEXPECTED ITEM IN BAGGING AREA. PLEASE TRY AGAIN.
SHWP
!
FLASH
WHAM!

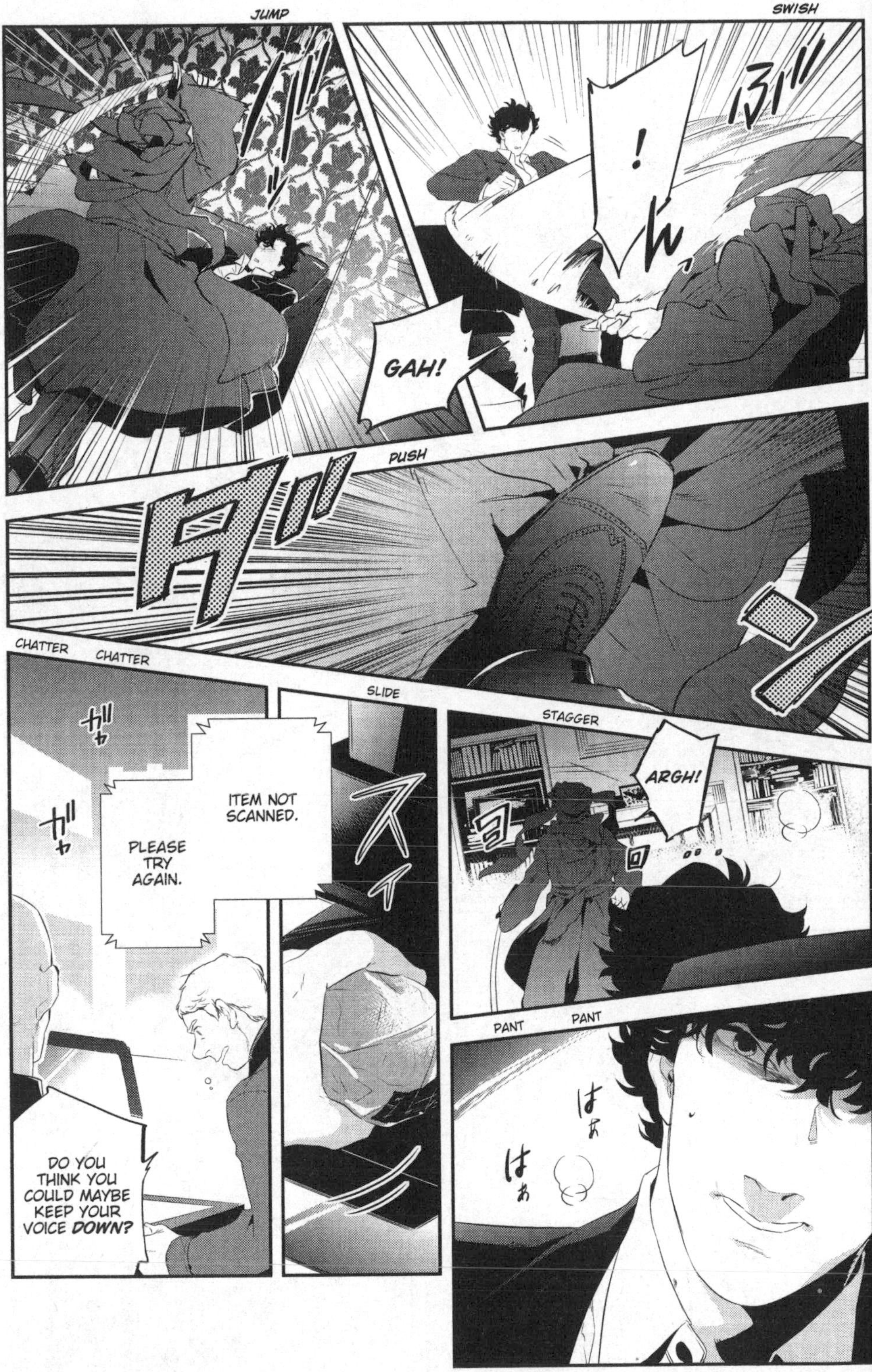
SWISH
!
GAH!
JUMP
PUSH
STAGGER
ARGH!
PANT PANT
SLIDE
CHATTER CHATTER
ITEM NOT SCANNED.
PLEASE TRY AGAIN.
DO YOU THINK YOU COULD MAYBE KEEP YOUR VOICE **DOWN**?

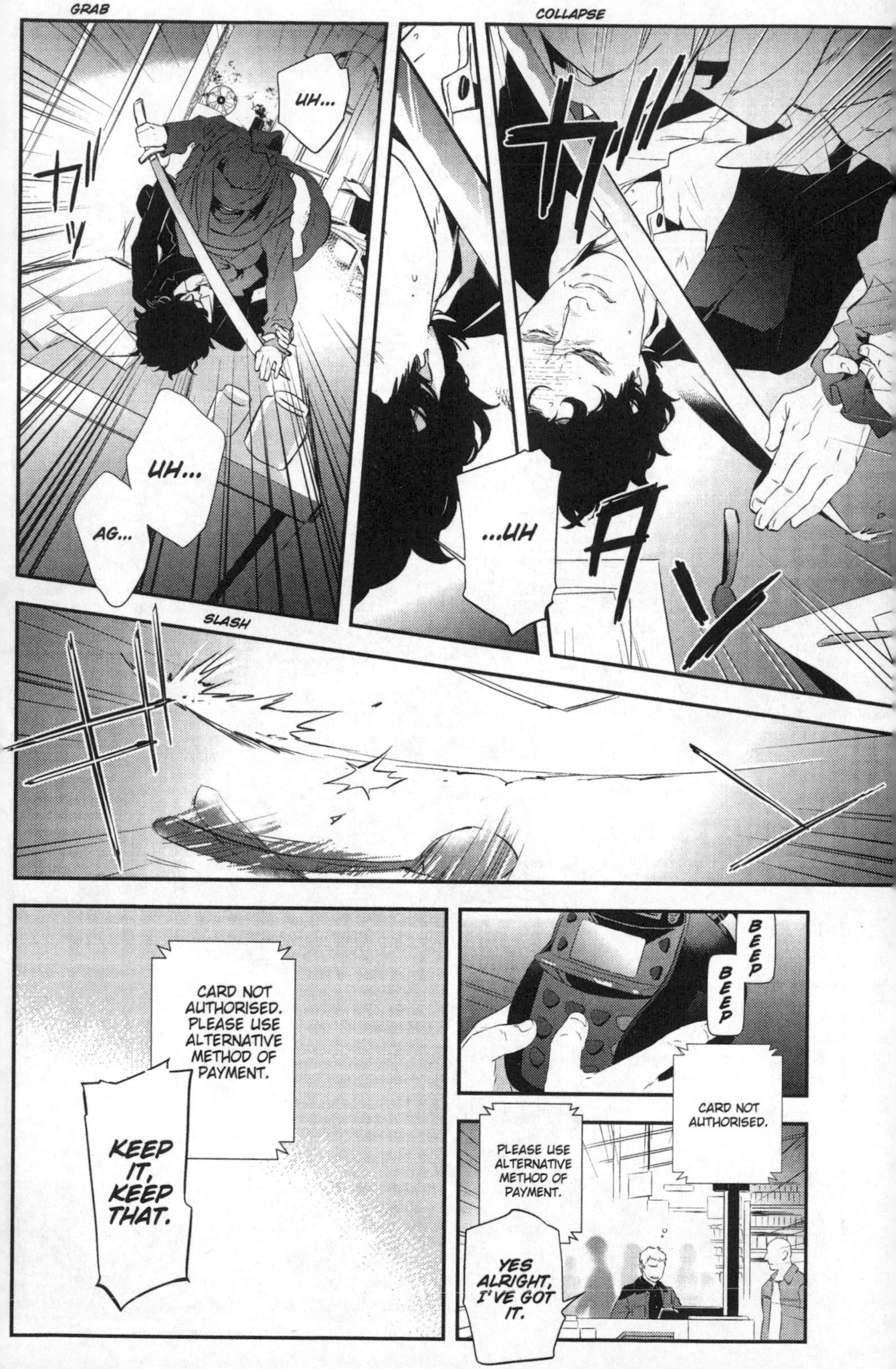
COLLAPSE
...UH
GRAB
UH...
UH...
AG...
SLASH
BEEP
BEEP
CARD NOT AUTHORISED.
PLEASE USE ALTERNATIVE METHOD OF PAYMENT.
YES ALRIGHT, I'VE GOT IT.
CARD NOT AUTHORISED. PLEASE USE ALTERNATIVE METHOD OF PAYMENT.
KEEP IT, KEEP THAT.

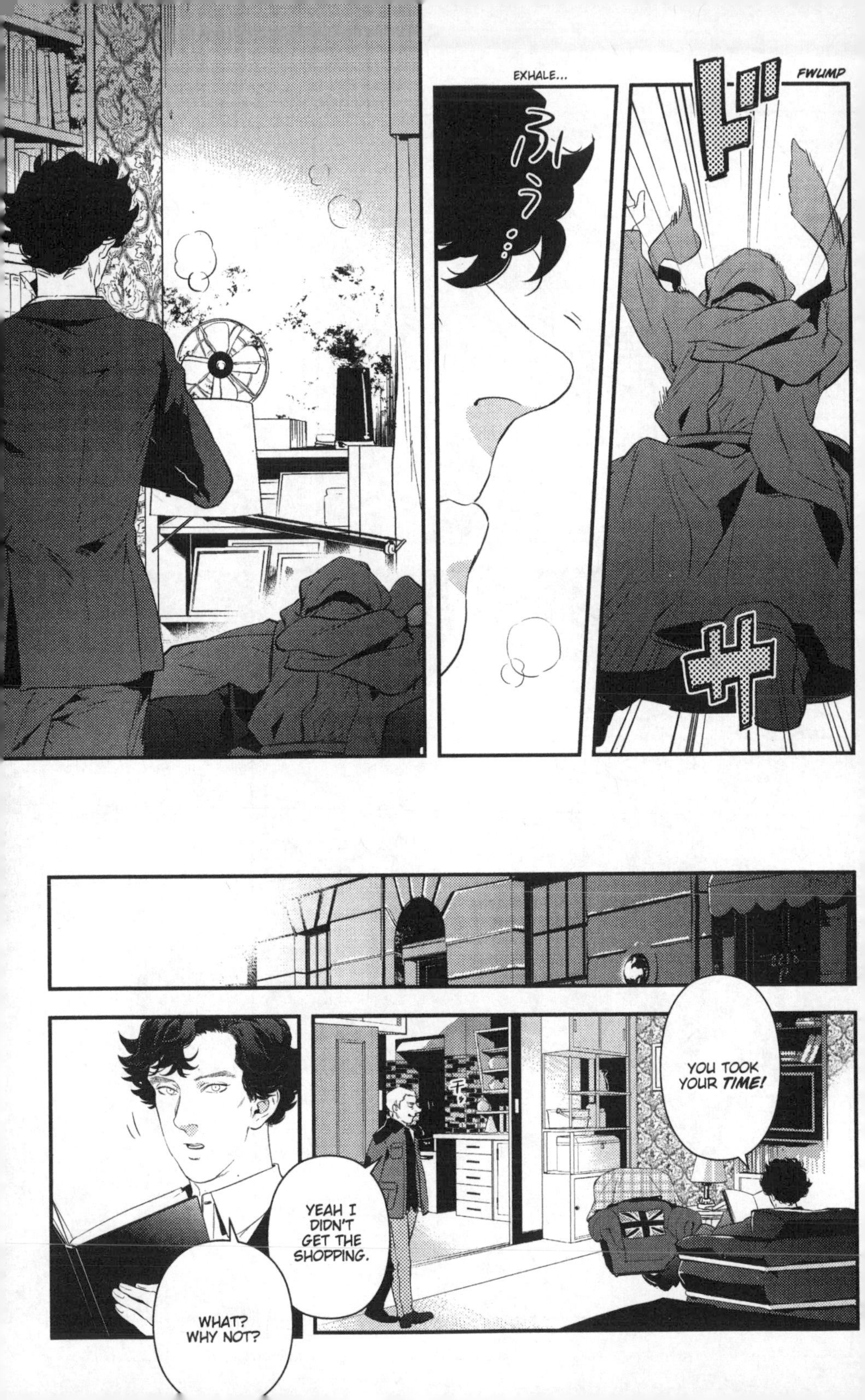
FWUMP
ドッ
EXHALE...
ふぅ...
YOU TOOK YOUR *TIME!*
YEAH I DIDN'T GET THE SHOPPING.
WHAT? WHY NOT?

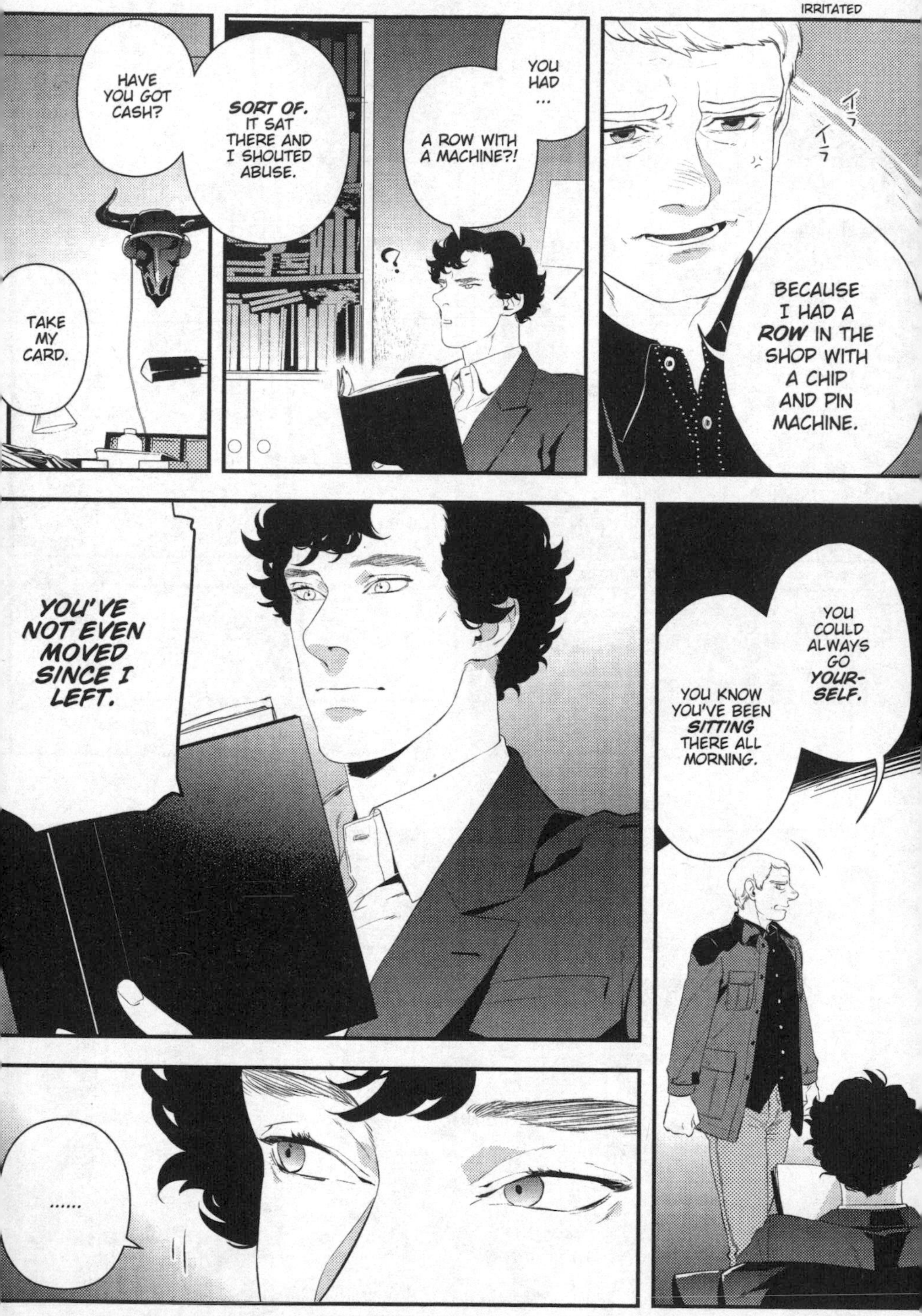
IRRITATED
BECAUSE I HAD A ROW IN THE SHOP WITH A CHIP AND PIN MACHINE.
YOU HAD ...
A ROW WITH A MACHINE?!
SORT OF. IT SAT THERE AND I SHOUTED ABUSE.
HAVE YOU GOT CASH?
TAKE MY CARD.
YOU COULD ALWAYS GO YOURSELF.
YOU KNOW YOU'VE BEEN SITTING THERE ALL MORNING.
YOU'VE NOT EVEN MOVED SINCE I LEFT.
......

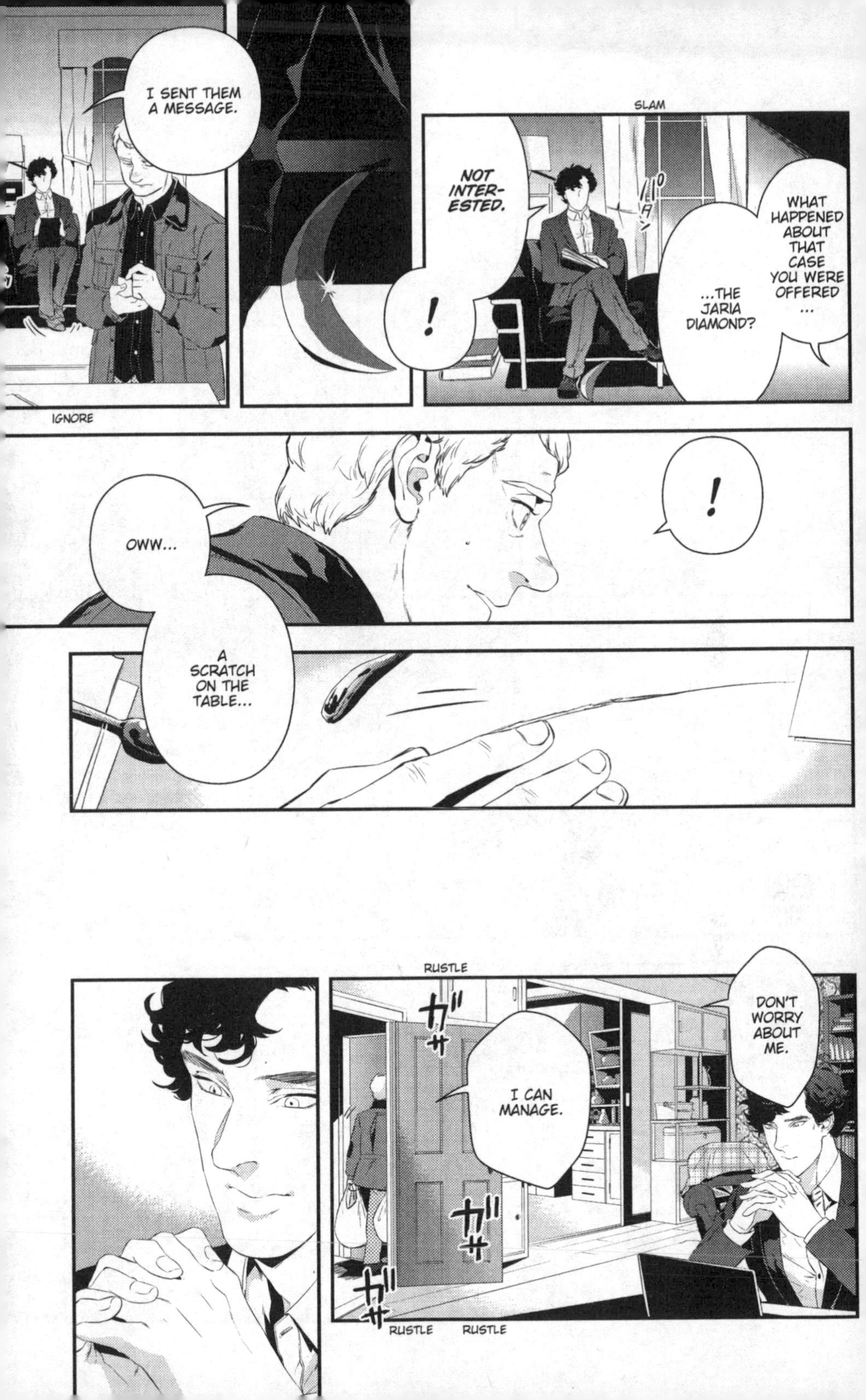
SLAM
WHAT HAPPENED ABOUT THAT CASE YOU WERE OFFERED ...
...THE JARIA DIAMOND?
NOT INTERESTED.
!
I SENT THEM A MESSAGE.
IGNORE
!
OWW...
A SCRATCH ON THE TABLE...
RUSTLE
DON'T WORRY ABOUT ME.
I CAN MANAGE.
RUSTLE
RUSTLE

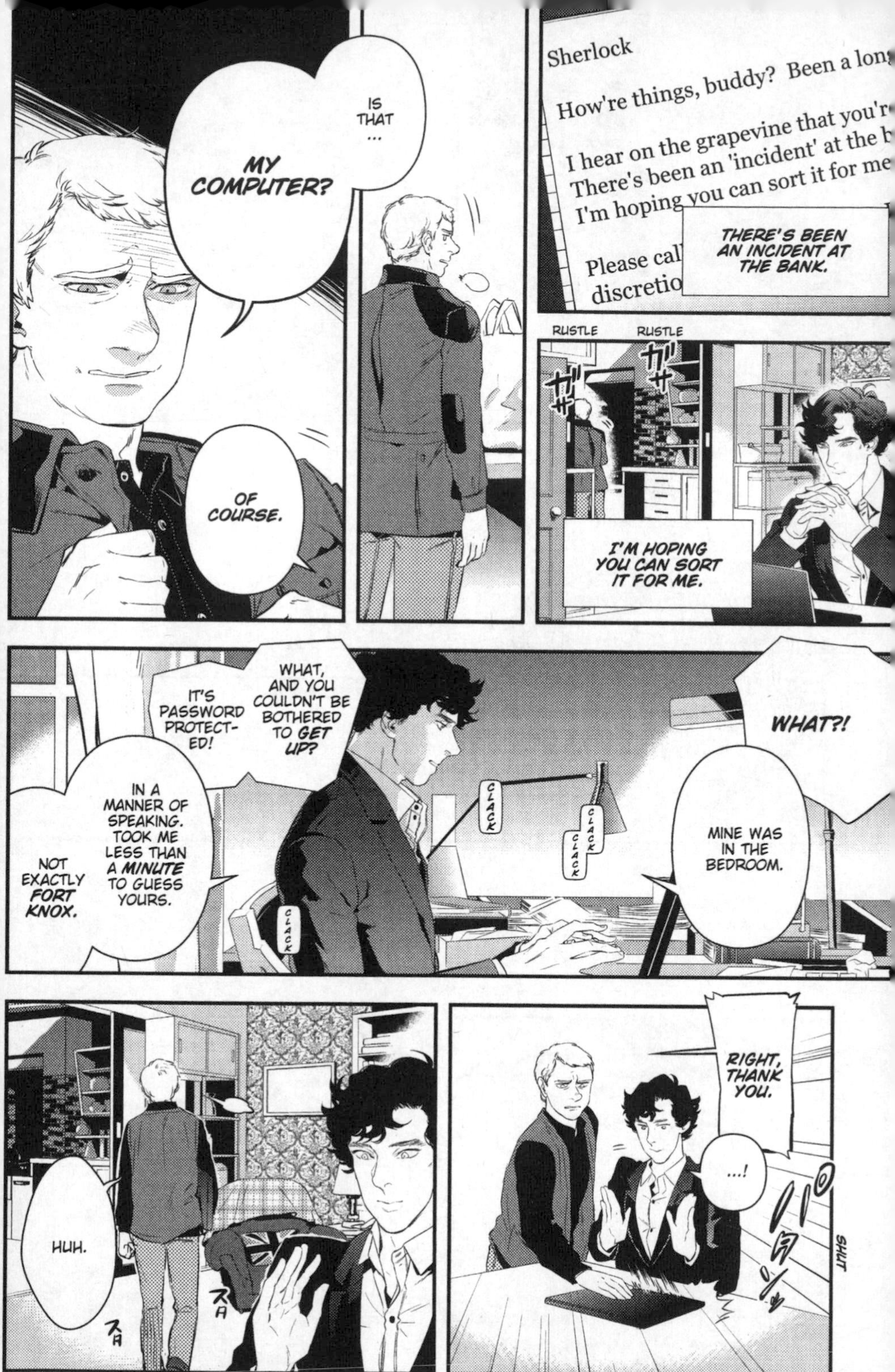

Sherlock
How're things, buddy? Been a long
I hear on the grapevine that you'r
There's been an 'incident' at the b
I'm hoping you can sort it for me
Please cal
discretio
THERE'S BEEN AN INCIDENT AT THE BANK.
RUSTLE RUSTLE
I'M HOPING YOU CAN SORT IT FOR ME.
IS THAT ... MY COMPUTER?
OF COURSE.
WHAT?!
MINE WAS IN THE BEDROOM.
CLACK CLACK CLACK
WHAT, AND YOU COULDN'T BE BOTHERED TO GET UP?
IT'S PASSWORD PROTECT-ED!
CLACK
IN A MANNER OF SPEAKING. TOOK ME LESS THAN A MINUTE TO GUESS YOURS.
NOT EXACTLY FORT KNOX.
RIGHT, THANK YOU.
...!
SHUT
HUH.
THUD THUD

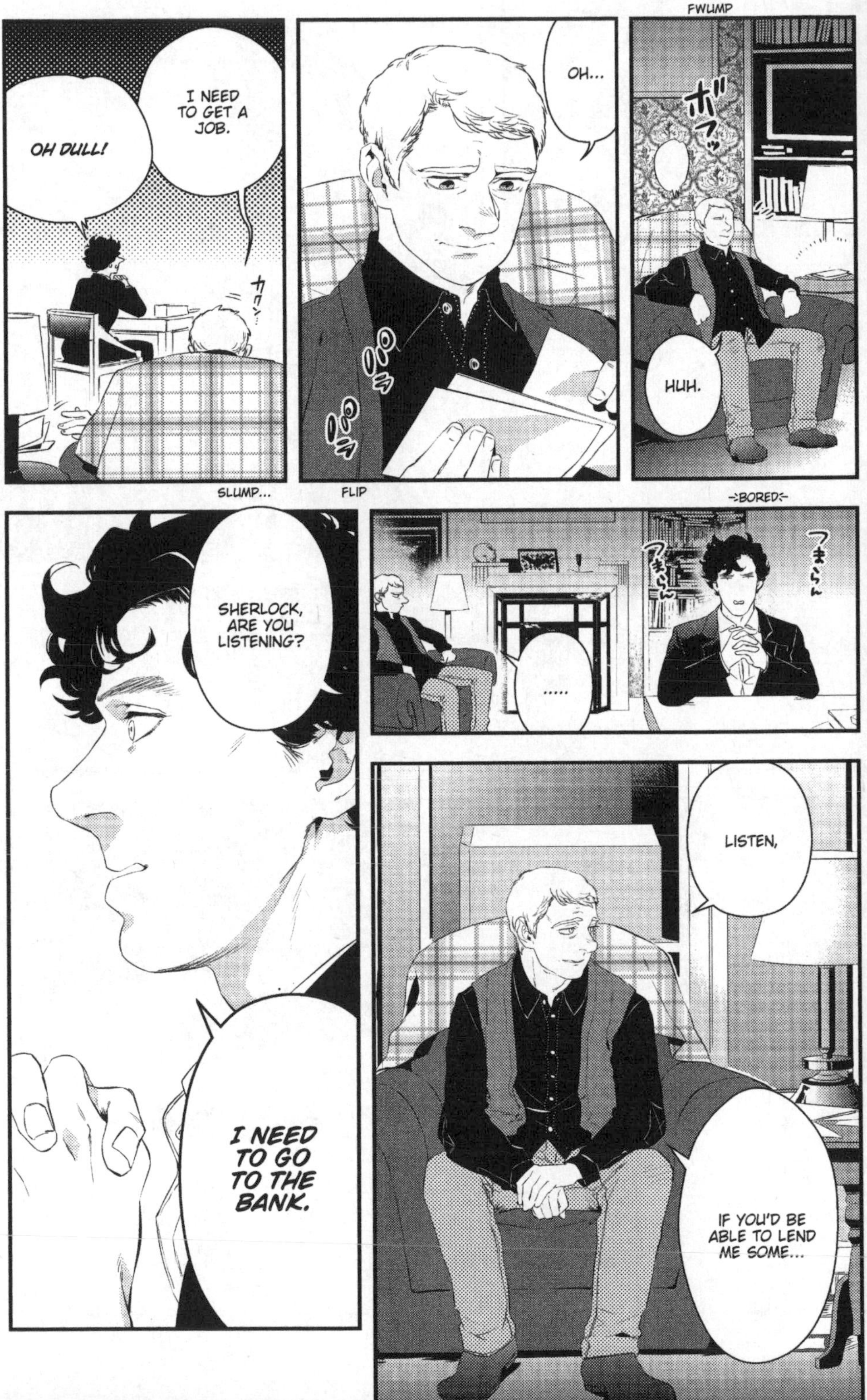
FWUMP
ボフッ
HUH.
OH...
パラ パラ
FLIP
I NEED TO GET A JOB.
OH DULL!
カクン…
SLUMP...
-BORED-
つまらん
つまらん
.....
LISTEN,
IF YOU'D BE ABLE TO LEND ME SOME...
SHERLOCK, ARE YOU LISTENING?
I NEED TO GO TO THE BANK.

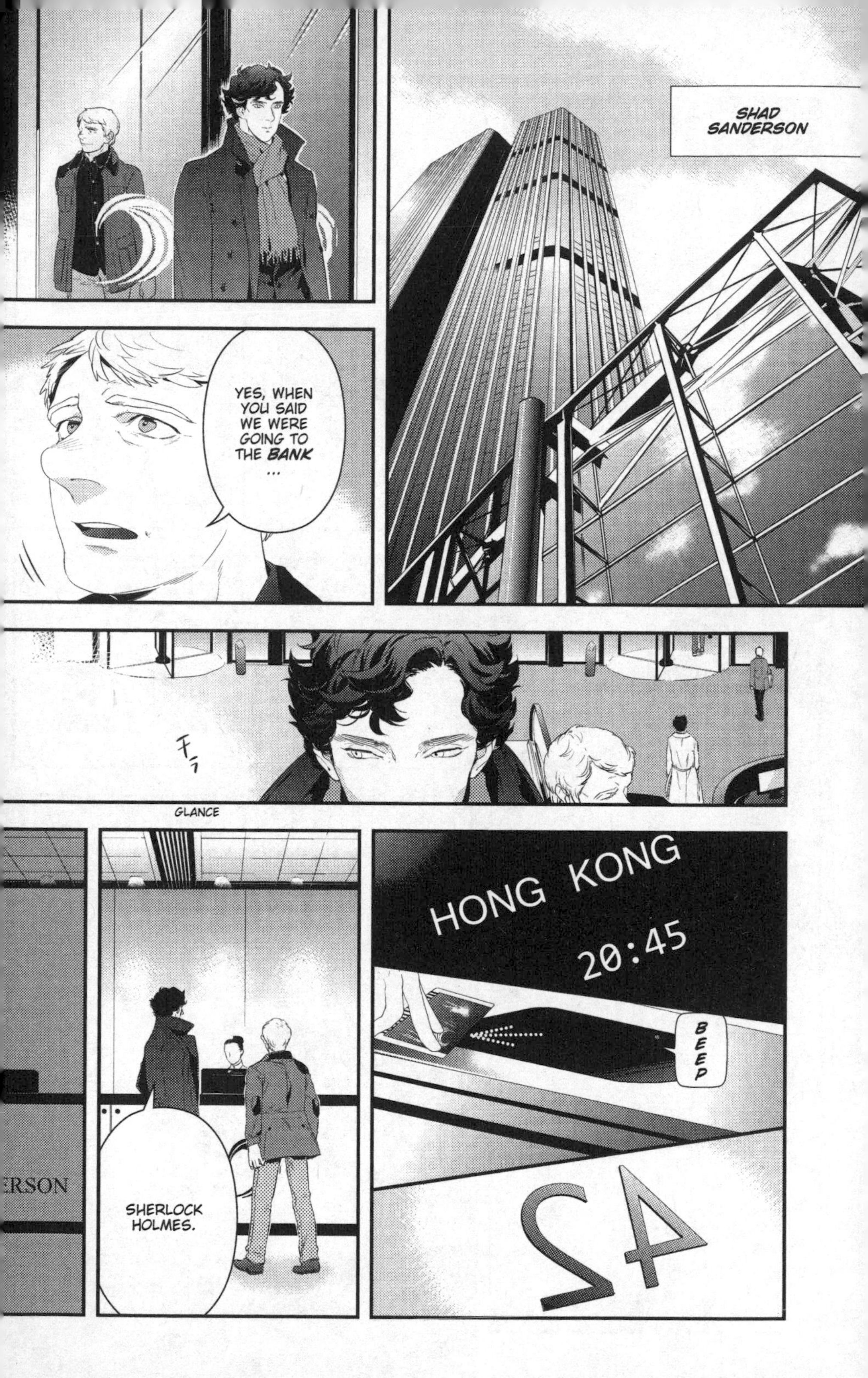
SHAD SANDERSON
YES, WHEN YOU SAID WE WERE GOING TO THE *BANK* ...
チラ
GLANCE
HONG KONG
20:45
BEEP
42
SHERLOCK HOLMES.
ERSON

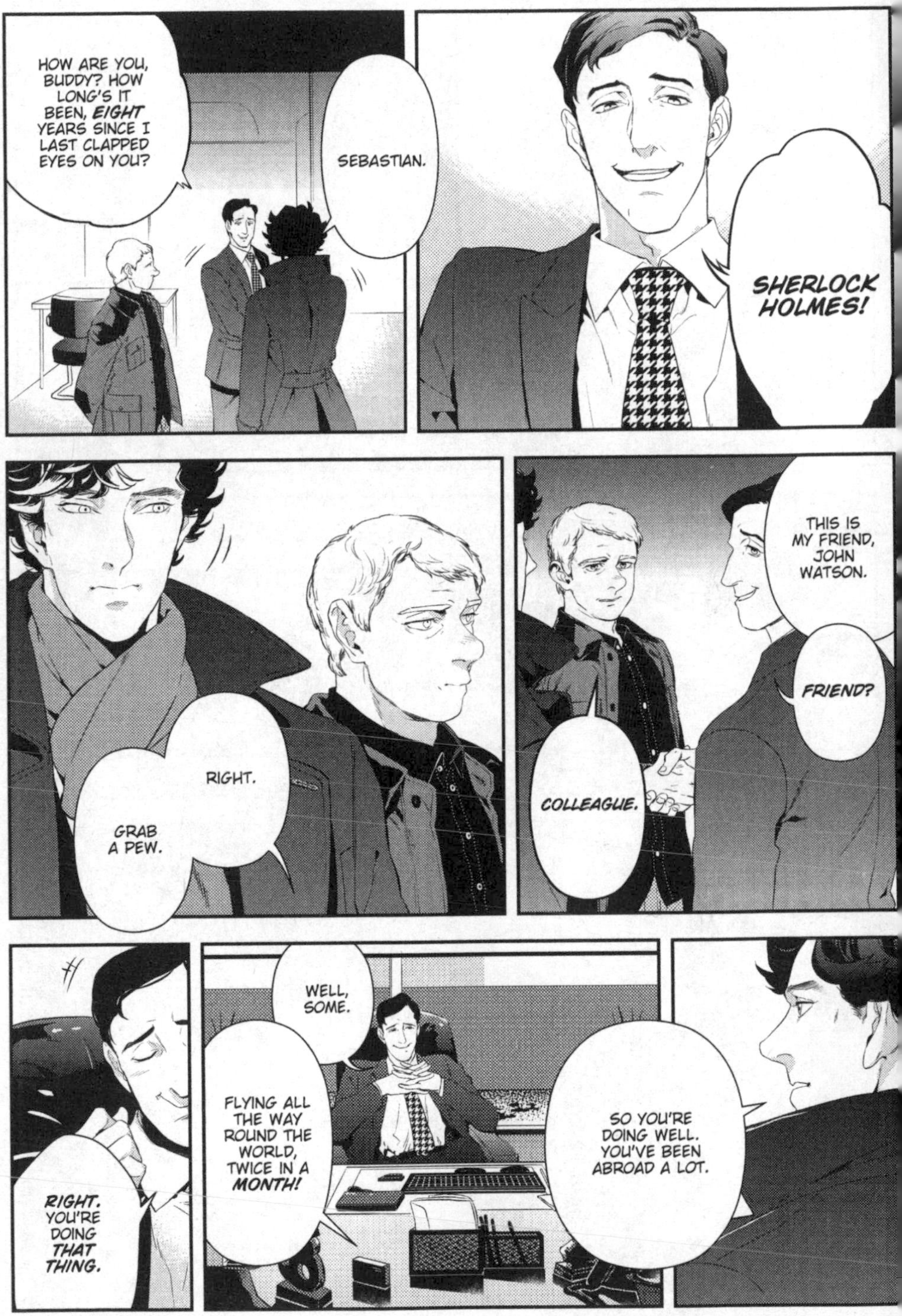
SHERLOCK HOLMES!
SEBASTIAN.
HOW ARE YOU, BUDDY? HOW LONG'S IT BEEN, *EIGHT* YEARS SINCE I LAST CLAPPED EYES ON YOU?
THIS IS MY FRIEND, JOHN WATSON.
FRIEND?
COLLEAGUE.
RIGHT.
GRAB A PEW.
SO YOU'RE DOING WELL. YOU'VE BEEN ABROAD A LOT.
WELL, SOME.
FLYING ALL THE WAY ROUND THE WORLD, TWICE IN A *MONTH!*
RIGHT. YOU'RE DOING *THAT* THING.

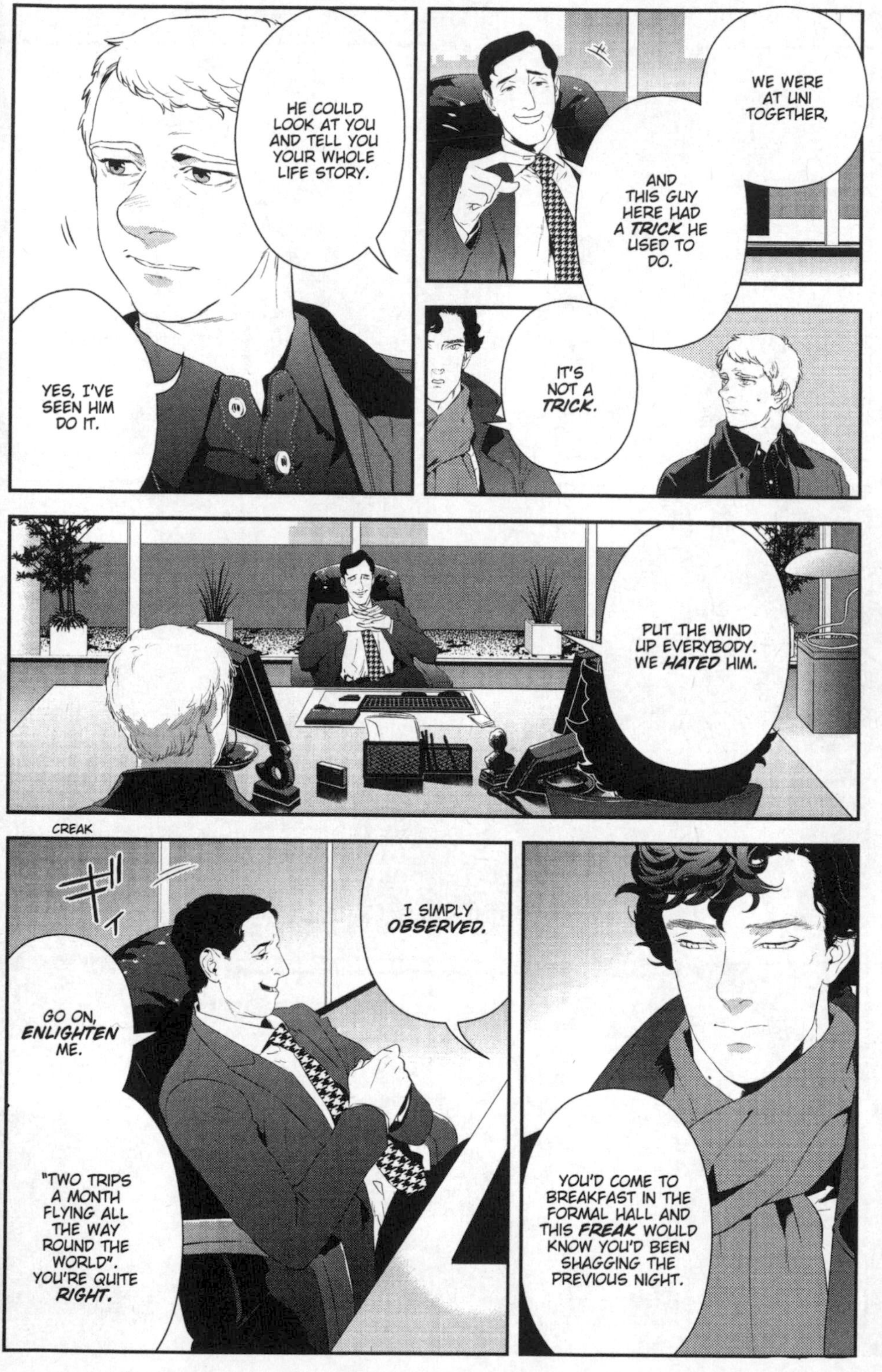
WE WERE AT UNI TOGETHER,
AND THIS GUY HERE HAD A *TRICK* HE USED TO DO.
IT'S NOT A *TRICK*.
HE COULD LOOK AT YOU AND TELL YOU YOUR WHOLE LIFE STORY.
YES, I'VE SEEN HIM DO IT.
PUT THE WIND UP EVERYBODY. WE *HATED* HIM.
YOU'D COME TO BREAKFAST IN THE FORMAL HALL AND THIS *FREAK* WOULD KNOW YOU'D BEEN SHAGGING THE PREVIOUS NIGHT.
CREAK
ギィ
I SIMPLY *OBSERVED.*
GO ON, *ENLIGHTEN* ME.
"TWO TRIPS A MONTH FLYING ALL THE WAY ROUND THE WORLD". YOU'RE QUITE *RIGHT*.

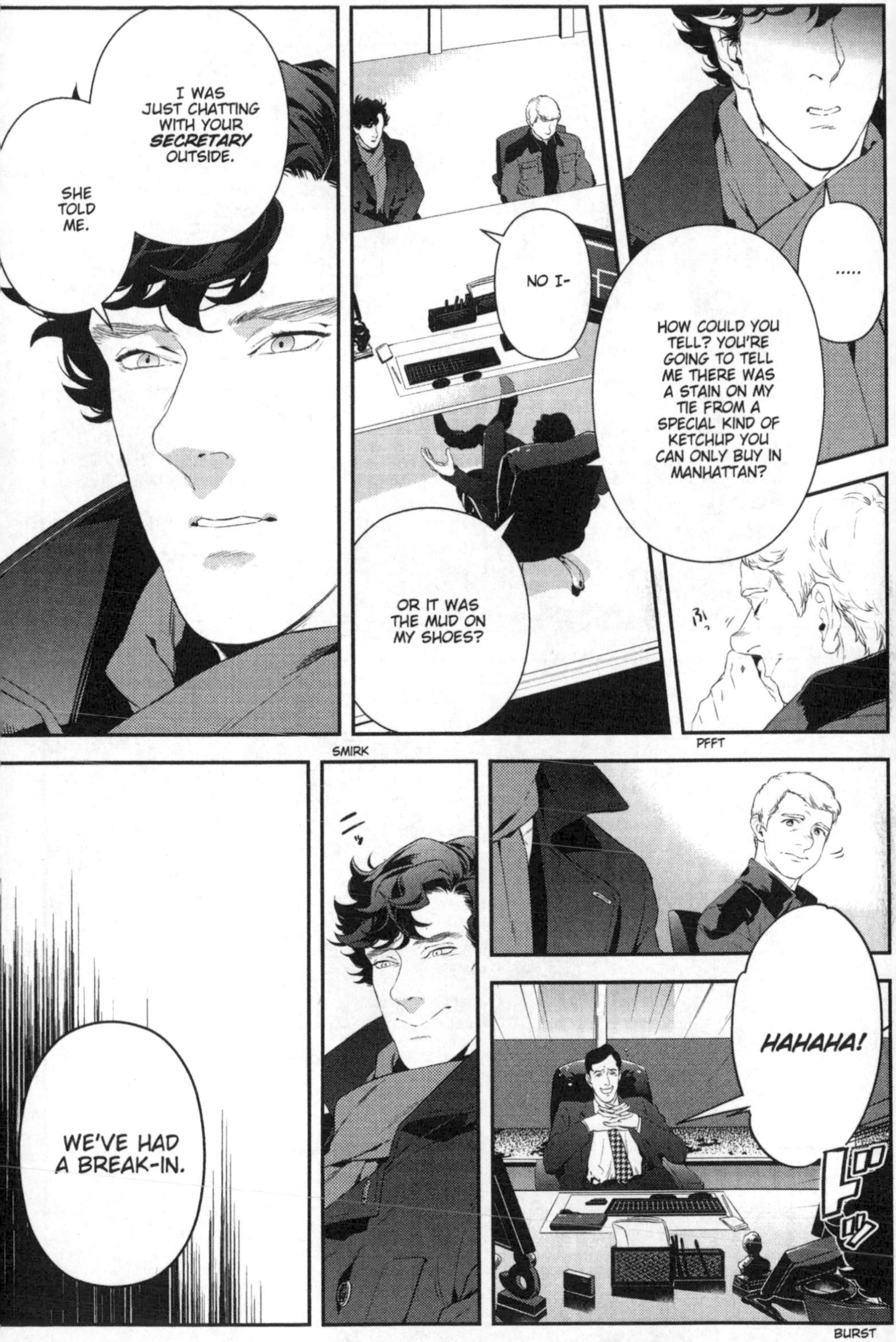
.....
HOW COULD YOU TELL? YOU'RE GOING TO TELL ME THERE WAS A STAIN ON MY TIE FROM A SPECIAL KIND OF KETCHUP YOU CAN ONLY BUY IN MANHATTAN?
PFFT
NO I-
OR IT WAS THE MUD ON MY SHOES?
I WAS JUST CHATTING WITH YOUR **SECRETARY** OUTSIDE.
SHE TOLD ME.
HAHAHA!
BURST
SMIRK
WE'VE HAD A BREAK-IN.

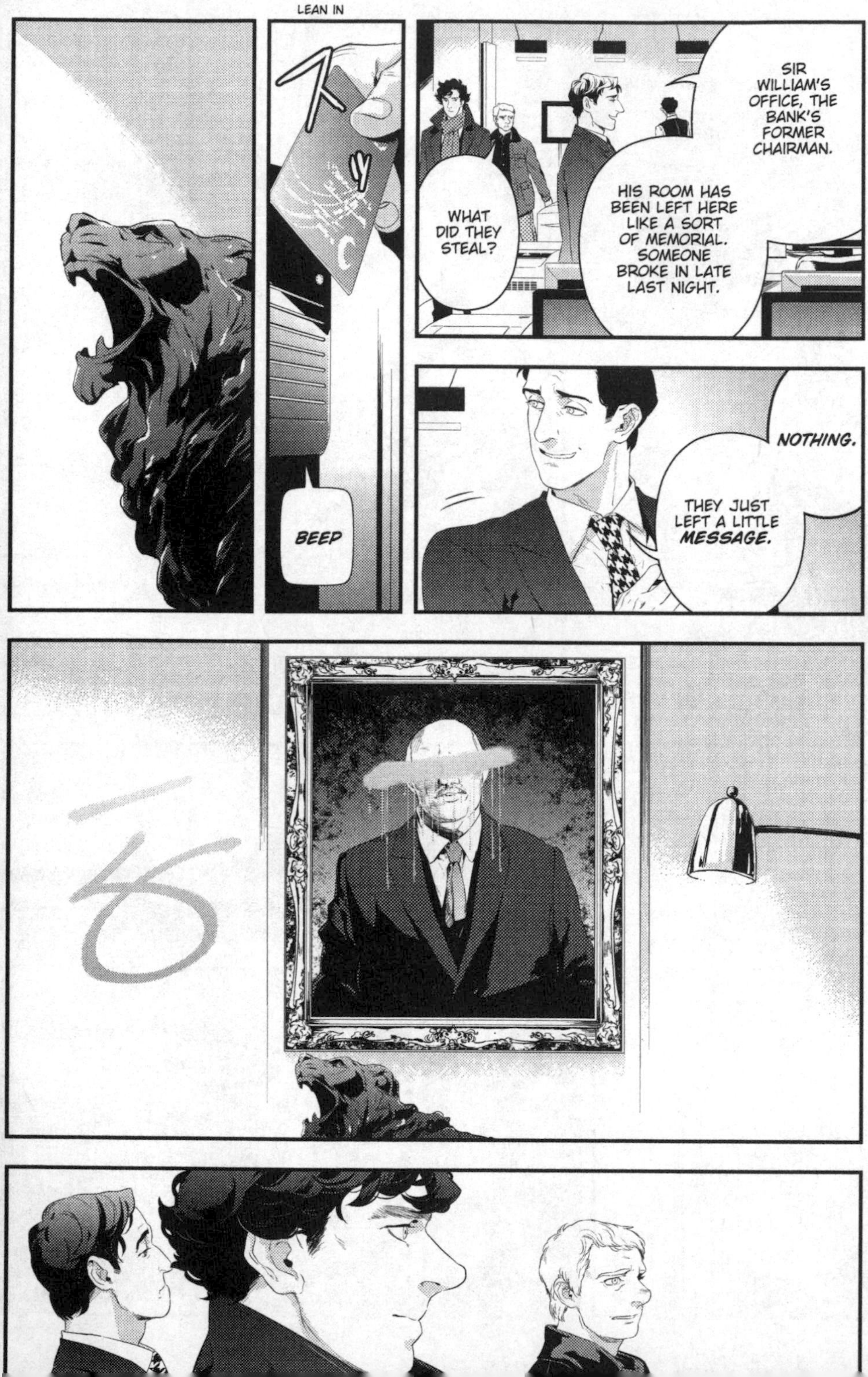
SIR WILLIAM'S OFFICE, THE BANK'S FORMER CHAIRMAN.
HIS ROOM HAS BEEN LEFT HERE LIKE A SORT OF MEMORIAL. SOMEONE BROKE IN LATE LAST NIGHT.
WHAT DID THEY STEAL?
NOTHING.
THEY JUST LEFT A LITTLE MESSAGE.
LEAN IN
BEEP

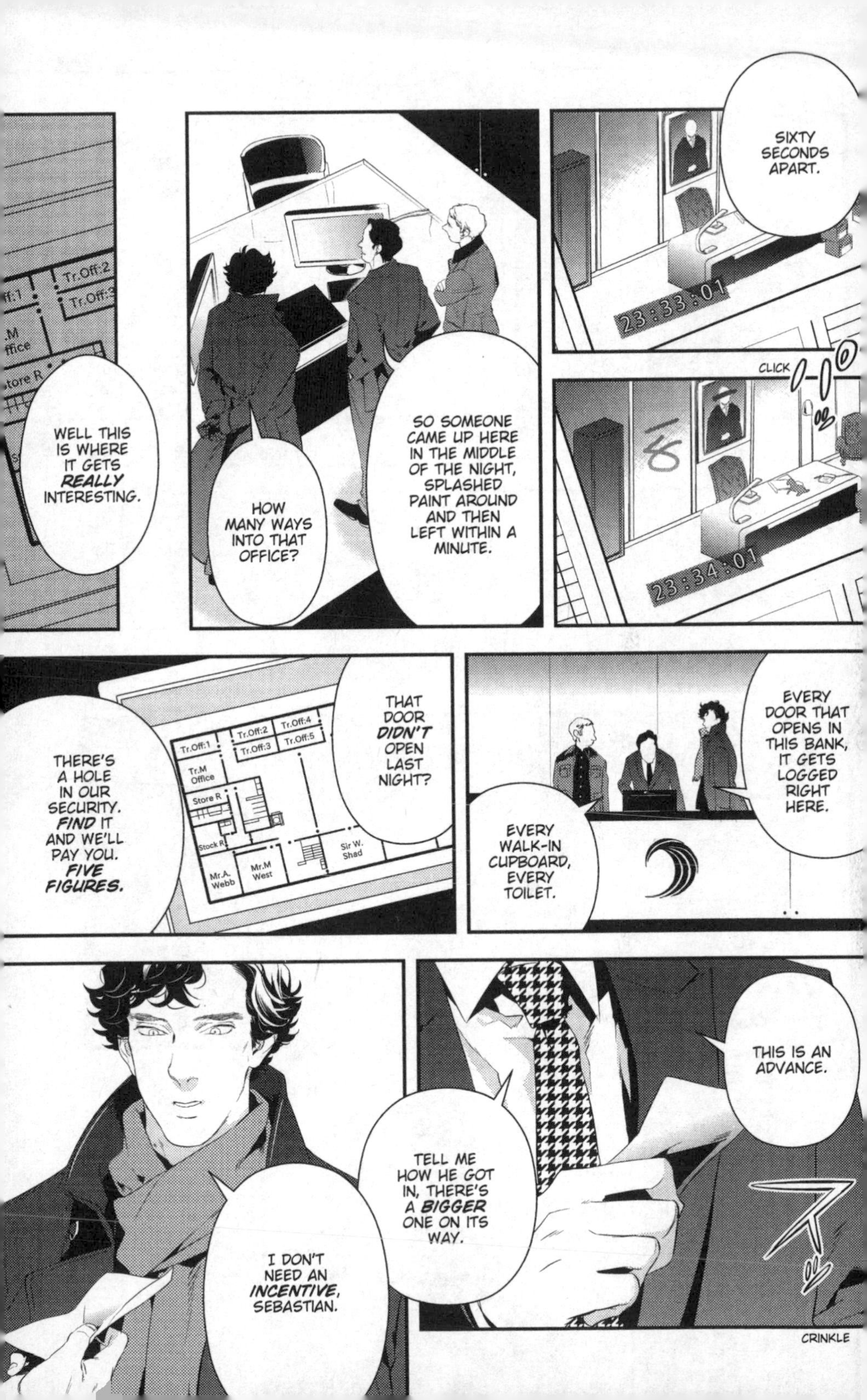
SIXTY SECONDS APART.
23:33:01
CLICK
23:34:01
SO SOMEONE CAME UP HERE IN THE MIDDLE OF THE NIGHT, SPLASHED PAINT AROUND AND THEN LEFT WITHIN A MINUTE.
HOW MANY WAYS INTO THAT OFFICE?
WELL THIS IS WHERE IT GETS ***REALLY*** INTERESTING.
EVERY DOOR THAT OPENS IN THIS BANK, IT GETS LOGGED RIGHT HERE.
EVERY WALK-IN CUPBOARD, EVERY TOILET.
THAT DOOR ***DIDN'T*** OPEN LAST NIGHT?
Tr.Off:1
Tr.Off:2
Tr.Off:3
Tr.Off:4
Tr.Off:5
Tr.M Office
Store R
Stock R
Sir W. Shad
Mr.A. Webb
Mr.M West
THERE'S A HOLE IN OUR SECURITY. ***FIND*** IT AND WE'LL PAY YOU. ***FIVE FIGURES.***
THIS IS AN ADVANCE.
TELL ME HOW HE GOT IN, THERE'S A ***BIGGER*** ONE ON ITS WAY.
CRINKLE
I DON'T NEED AN ***INCENTIVE,*** SEBASTIAN.

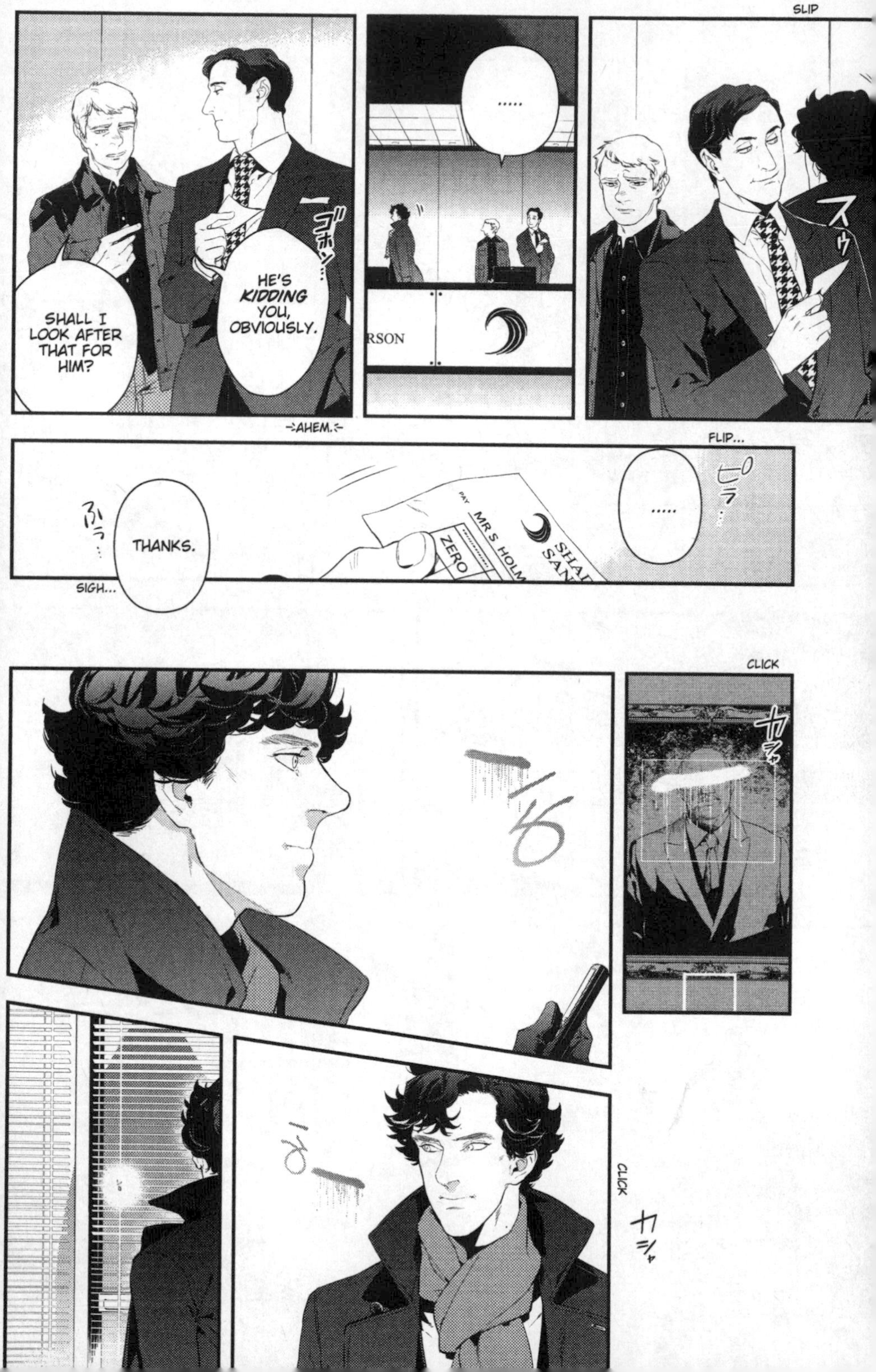

SLIP
スゥ
.....
ゴホッ…
AHEM.
HE'S *KIDDING* YOU, OBVIOUSLY.
SHALL I LOOK AFTER THAT FOR HIM?
FLIP...
ピラ…
.....
PAY
MR S HOLM
ZERO
THANKS.
ふぅ…
SIGH...
CLICK
カシャ
CLICK
カシャ

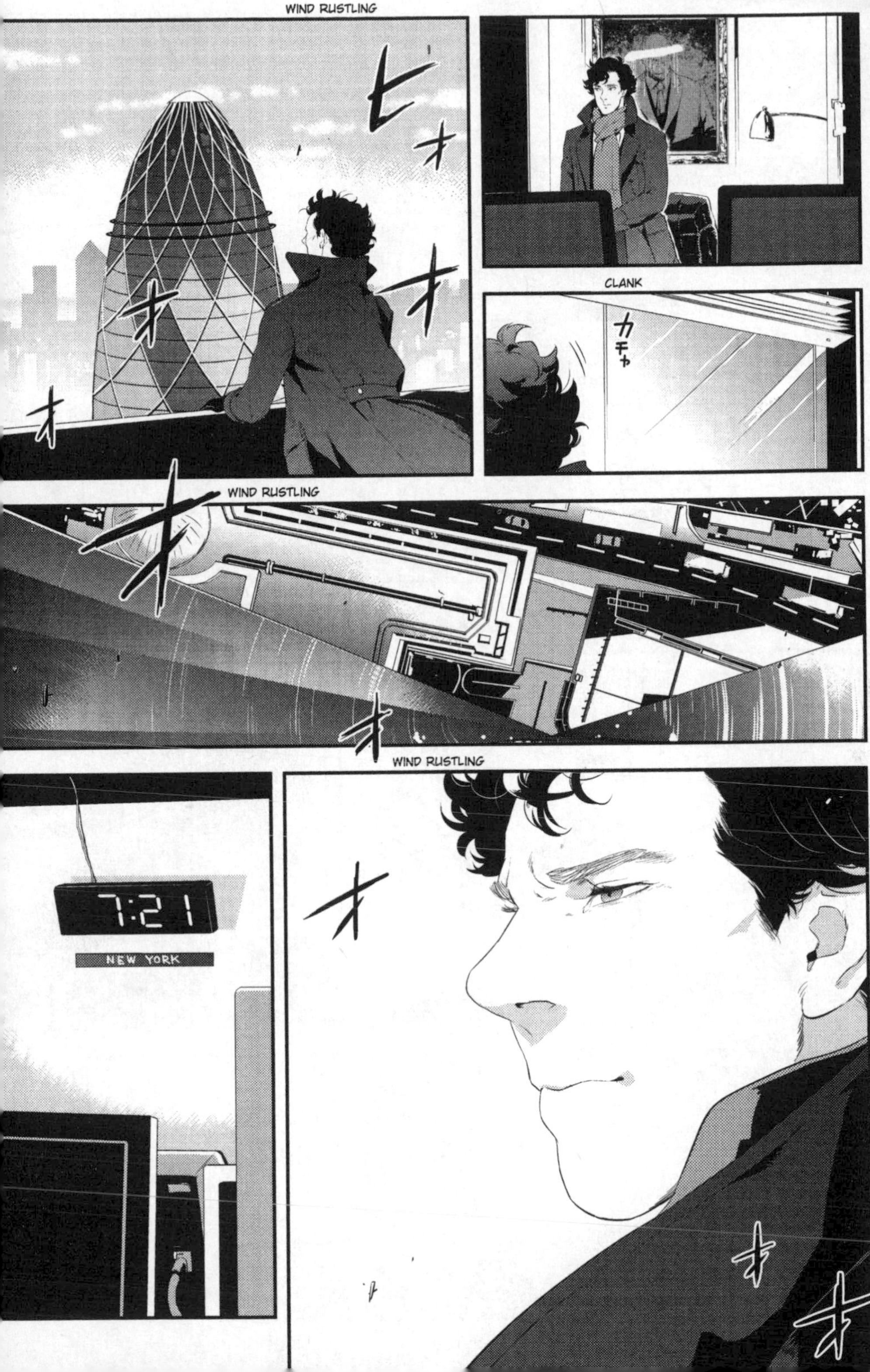
CLANK
カチャ
WIND RUSTLING
WIND RUSTLING
WIND RUSTLING
7:21
NEW YORK

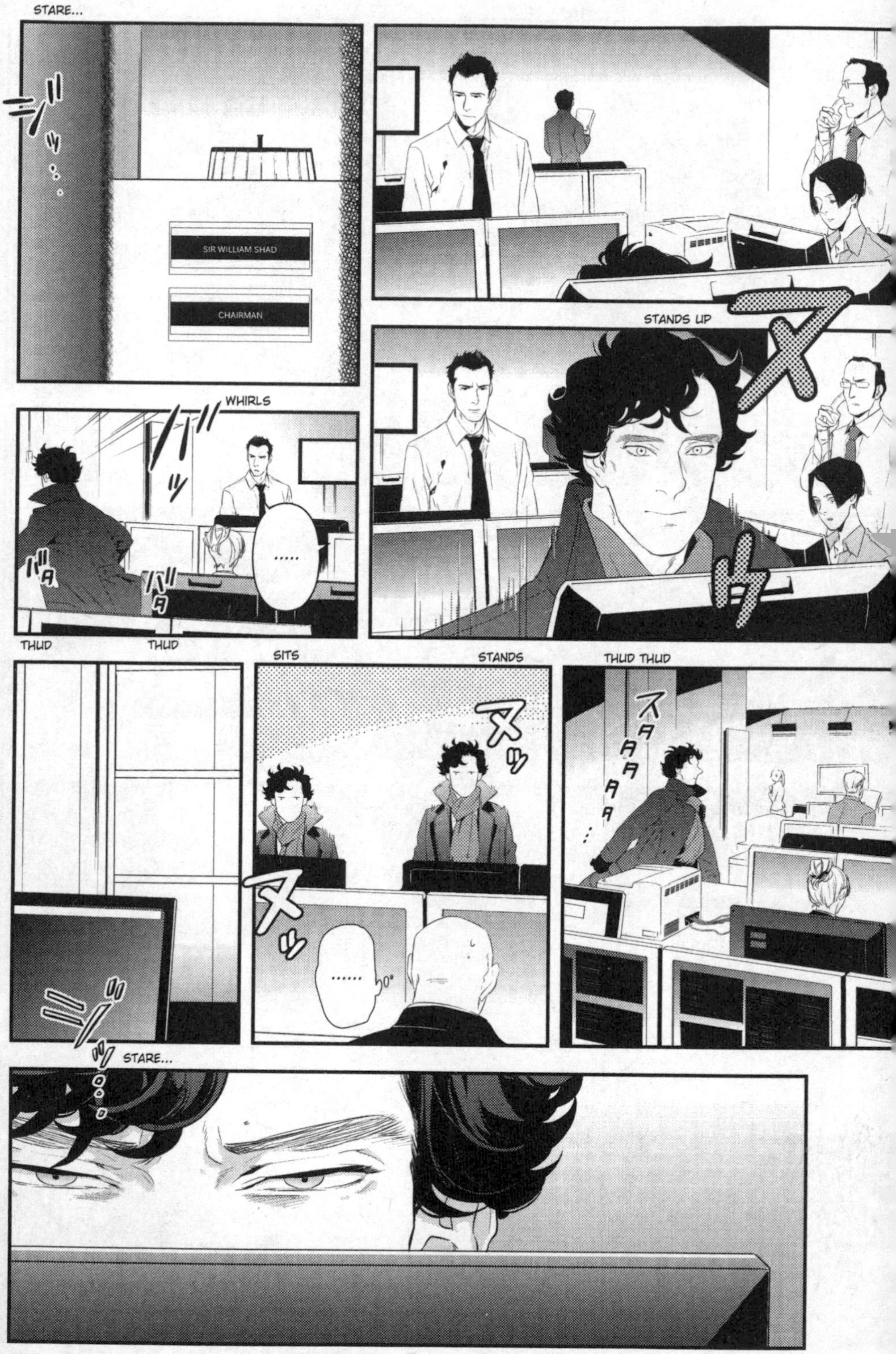

STARE...
SIR WILLIAM SHAD
CHAIRMAN
STANDS UP
WHIRLS
.....
THUD
THUD
THUD THUD
STANDS
SITS
......
STARE...

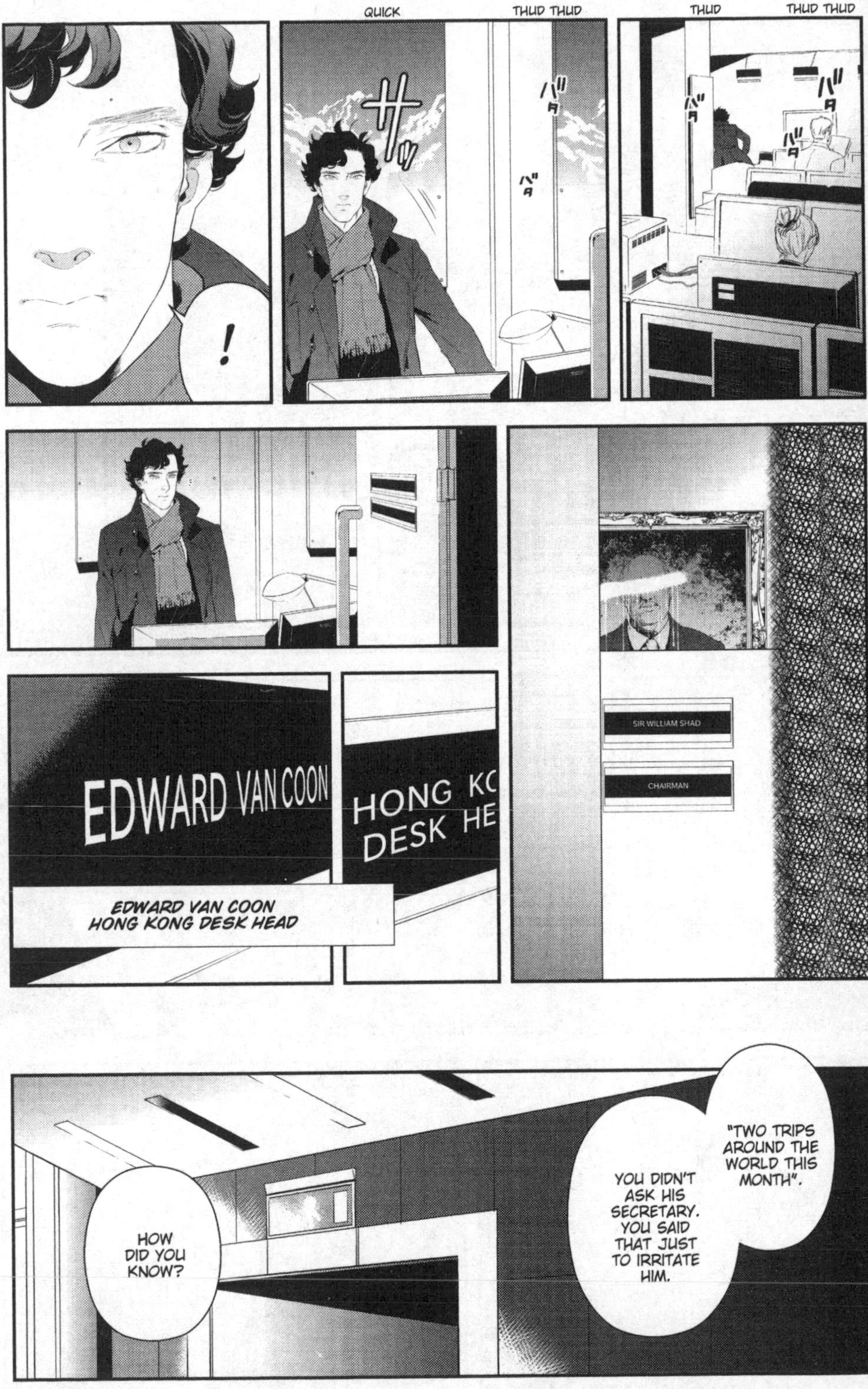
THUD
THUD THUD
QUICK
THUD THUD
!
SIR WILLIAM SHAD
CHAIRMAN
HONG KC
DESK HE
EDWARD VAN COON
EDWARD VAN COON
HONG KONG DESK HEAD
"TWO TRIPS AROUND THE WORLD THIS MONTH".
YOU DIDN'T ASK HIS SECRETARY. YOU SAID THAT JUST TO IRRITATE HIM.
HOW DID YOU KNOW?

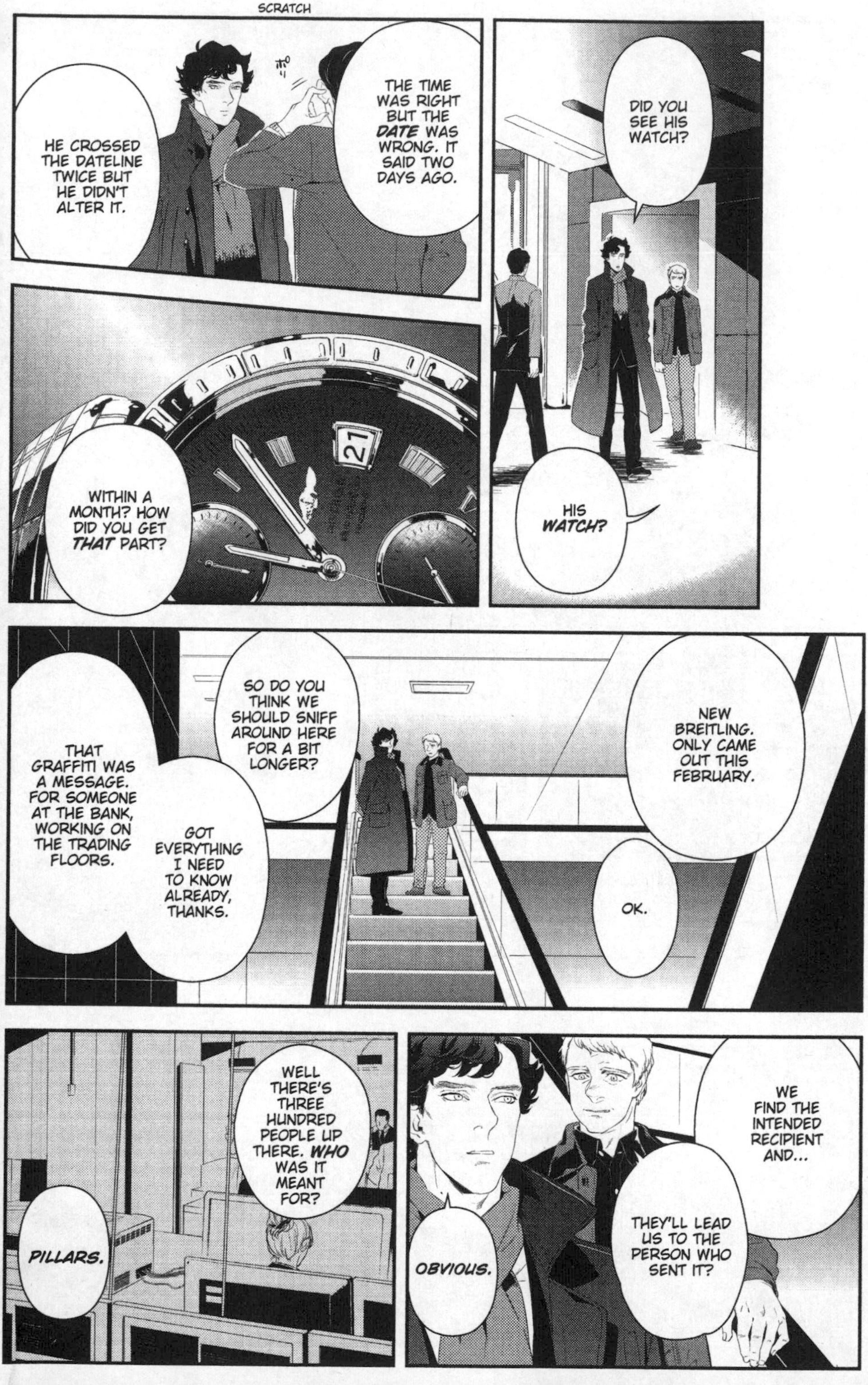
DID YOU SEE HIS WATCH?
HIS *WATCH?*
SCRATCH
THE TIME WAS RIGHT BUT THE *DATE* WAS WRONG. IT SAID TWO DAYS AGO.
HE CROSSED THE DATELINE TWICE BUT HE DIDN'T ALTER IT.
WITHIN A MONTH? HOW DID YOU GET *THAT* PART?
NEW BREITLING. ONLY CAME OUT THIS FEBRUARY.
OK.
SO DO YOU THINK WE SHOULD SNIFF AROUND HERE FOR A BIT LONGER?
GOT EVERYTHING I NEED TO KNOW ALREADY, THANKS.
THAT GRAFFITI WAS A MESSAGE. FOR SOMEONE AT THE BANK, WORKING ON THE TRADING FLOORS.
WE FIND THE INTENDED RECIPIENT AND...
THEY'LL LEAD US TO THE PERSON WHO SENT IT?
OBVIOUS.
WELL THERE'S THREE HUNDRED PEOPLE UP THERE. *WHO* WAS IT MEANT FOR?
PILLARS.

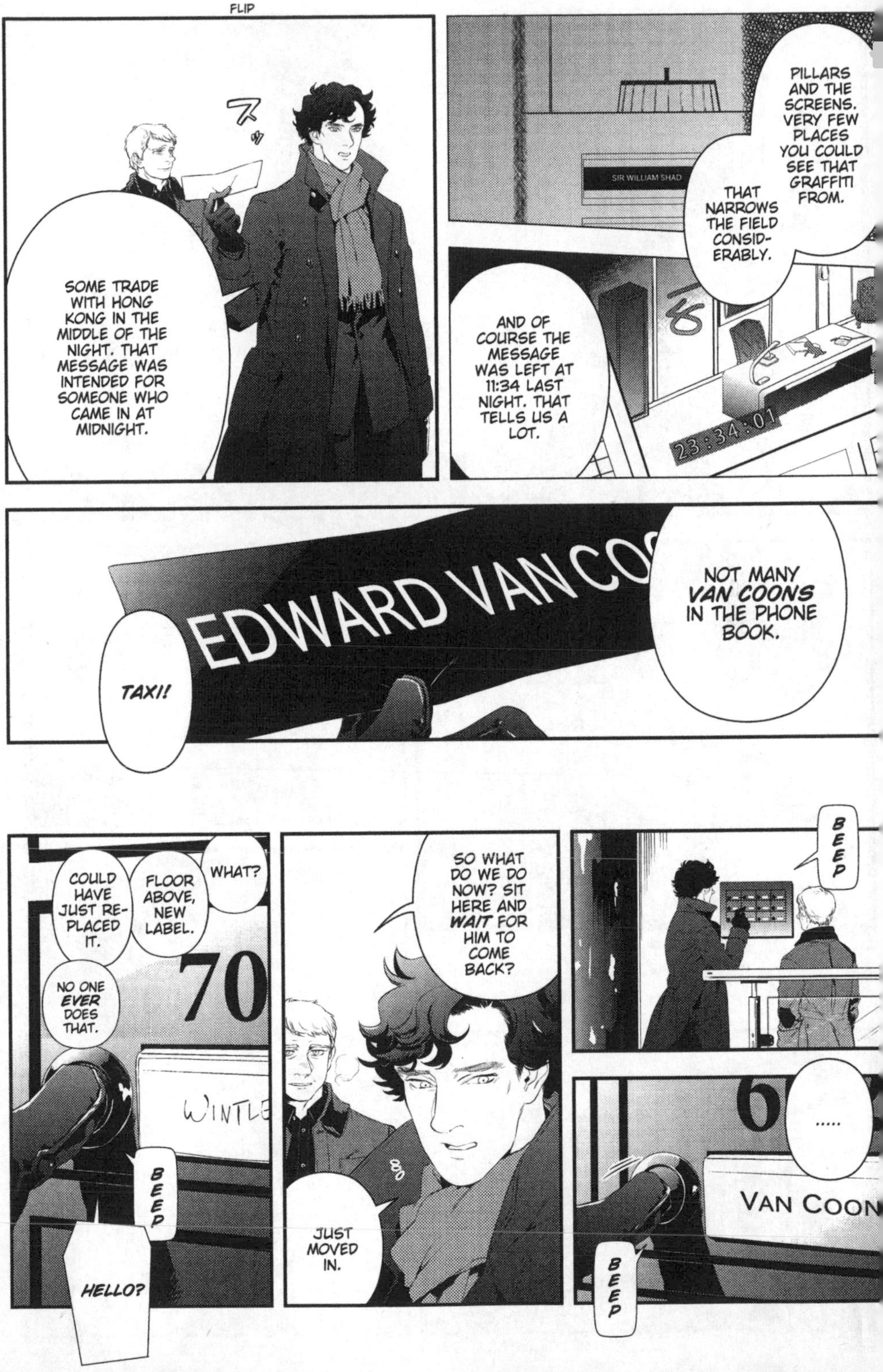
PILLARS AND THE SCREENS. VERY FEW PLACES YOU COULD SEE THAT GRAFFITI FROM.
THAT NARROWS THE FIELD CONSID-ERABLY.
SIR WILLIAM SHAD
AND OF COURSE THE MESSAGE WAS LEFT AT 11:34 LAST NIGHT. THAT TELLS US A LOT.
23:34:01
FLIP
ズッ
SOME TRADE WITH HONG KONG IN THE MIDDLE OF THE NIGHT. THAT MESSAGE WAS INTENDED FOR SOMEONE WHO CAME IN AT MIDNIGHT.
NOT MANY *VAN COONS* IN THE PHONE BOOK.
EDWARD VAN CO
TAXI!
BEEP
.....
VAN COON
BEEP
SO WHAT DO WE DO NOW? SIT HERE AND *WAIT* FOR HIM TO COME BACK?
JUST MOVED IN.
WHAT?
FLOOR ABOVE, NEW LABEL.
COULD HAVE JUST RE-PLACED IT.
NO ONE *EVER* DOES THAT.
70
WINTLE
BEEP
HELLO?

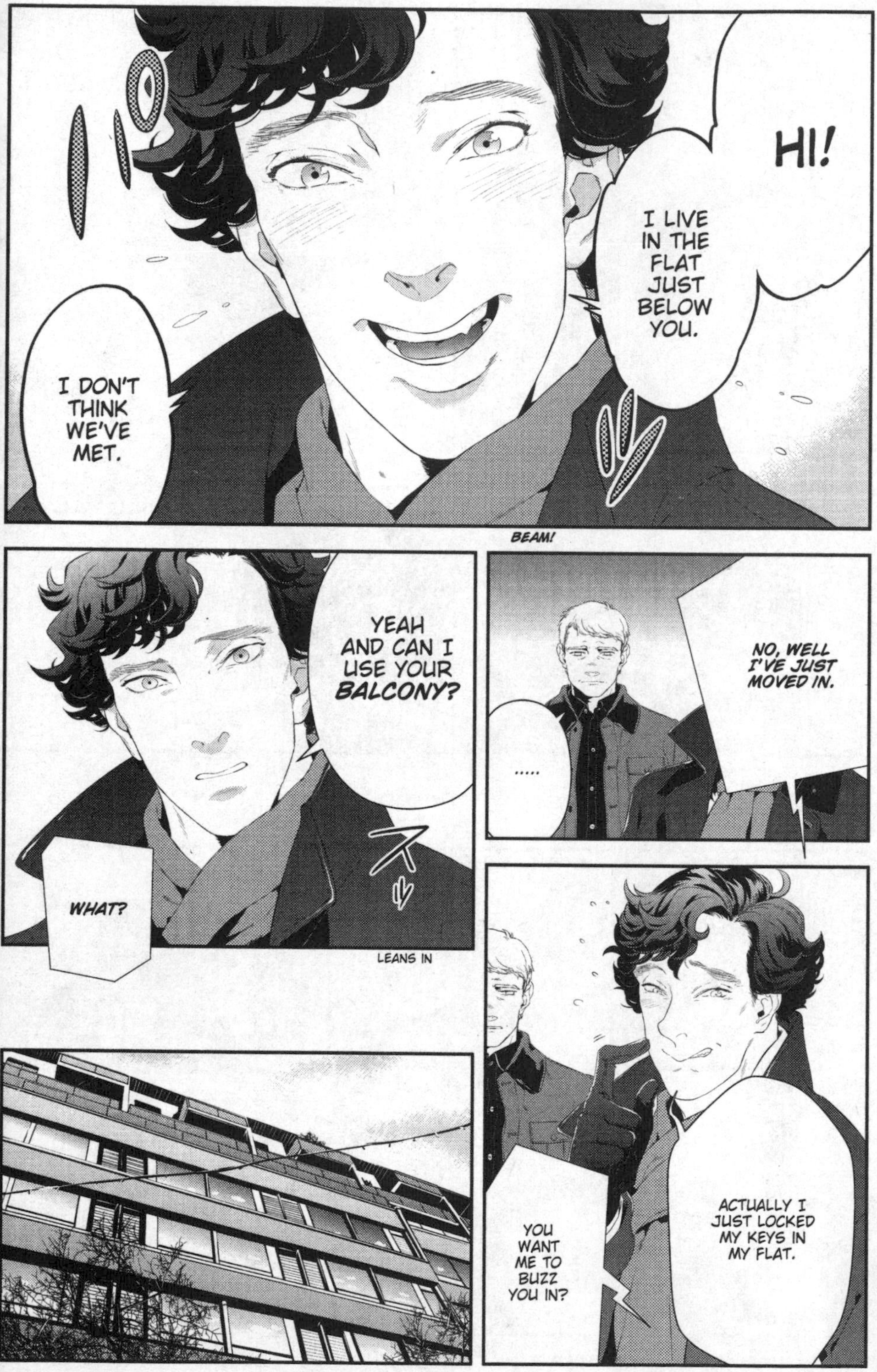
HI!
I LIVE IN THE FLAT JUST BELOW YOU.
I DON'T THINK WE'VE MET.
BEAM!
NO, WELL I'VE JUST MOVED IN.
.....
ACTUALLY I JUST LOCKED MY KEYS IN MY FLAT.
YOU WANT ME TO BUZZ YOU IN?
YEAH AND CAN I USE YOUR BALCONY?
WHAT?
LEANS IN

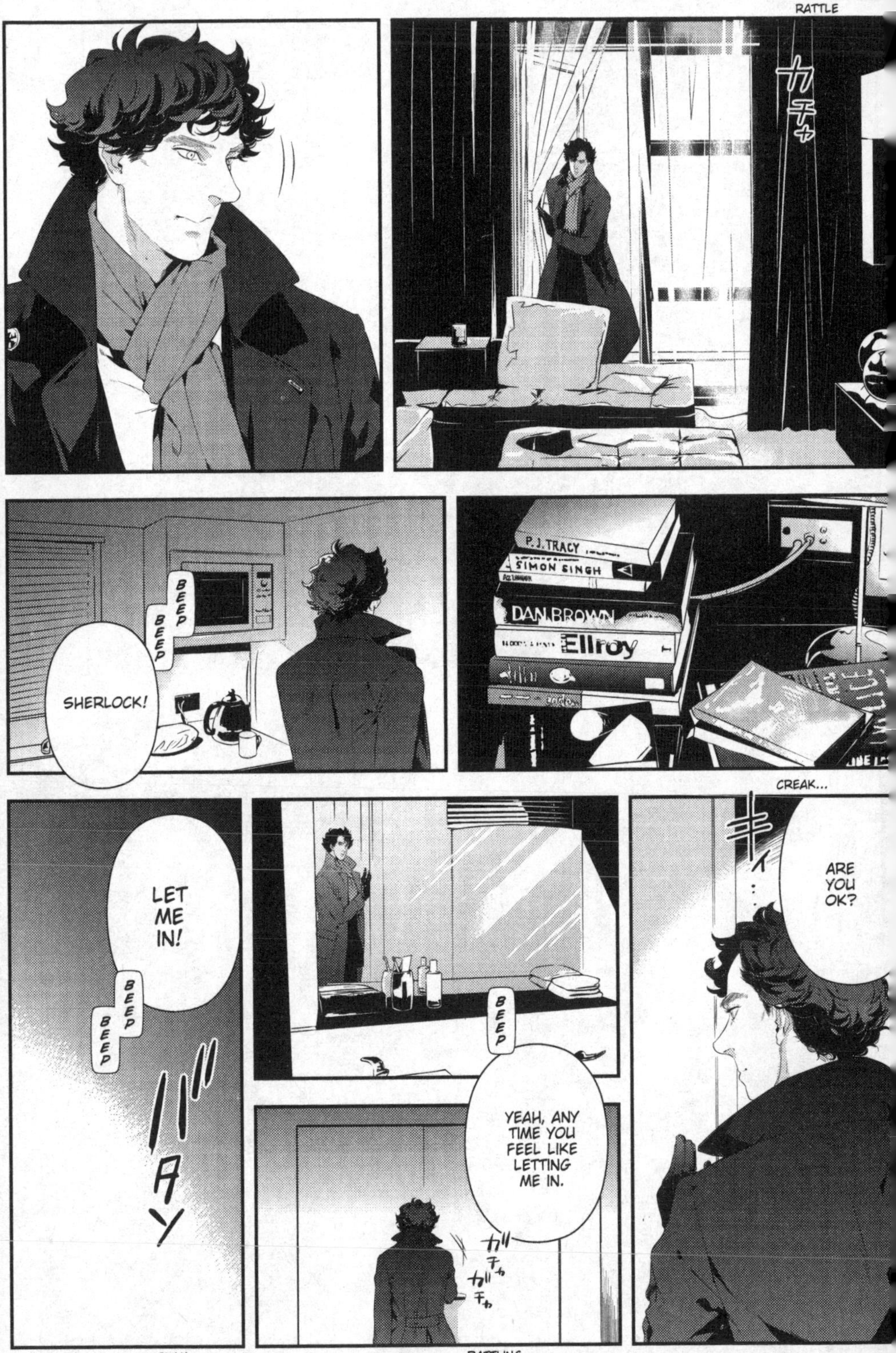
RATTLE
カチャ
P.J. TRACY
SIMON SINGH
DAN BROWN
Ellroy
BEEP BEEP
SHERLOCK!
CREAK...
キイ…
ARE YOU OK?
BEEP
YEAH, ANY TIME YOU FEEL LIKE LETTING ME IN.
ガチャ ガチャ
RATTLING
LET ME IN!
BEEP BEEP
バタン
SLAM

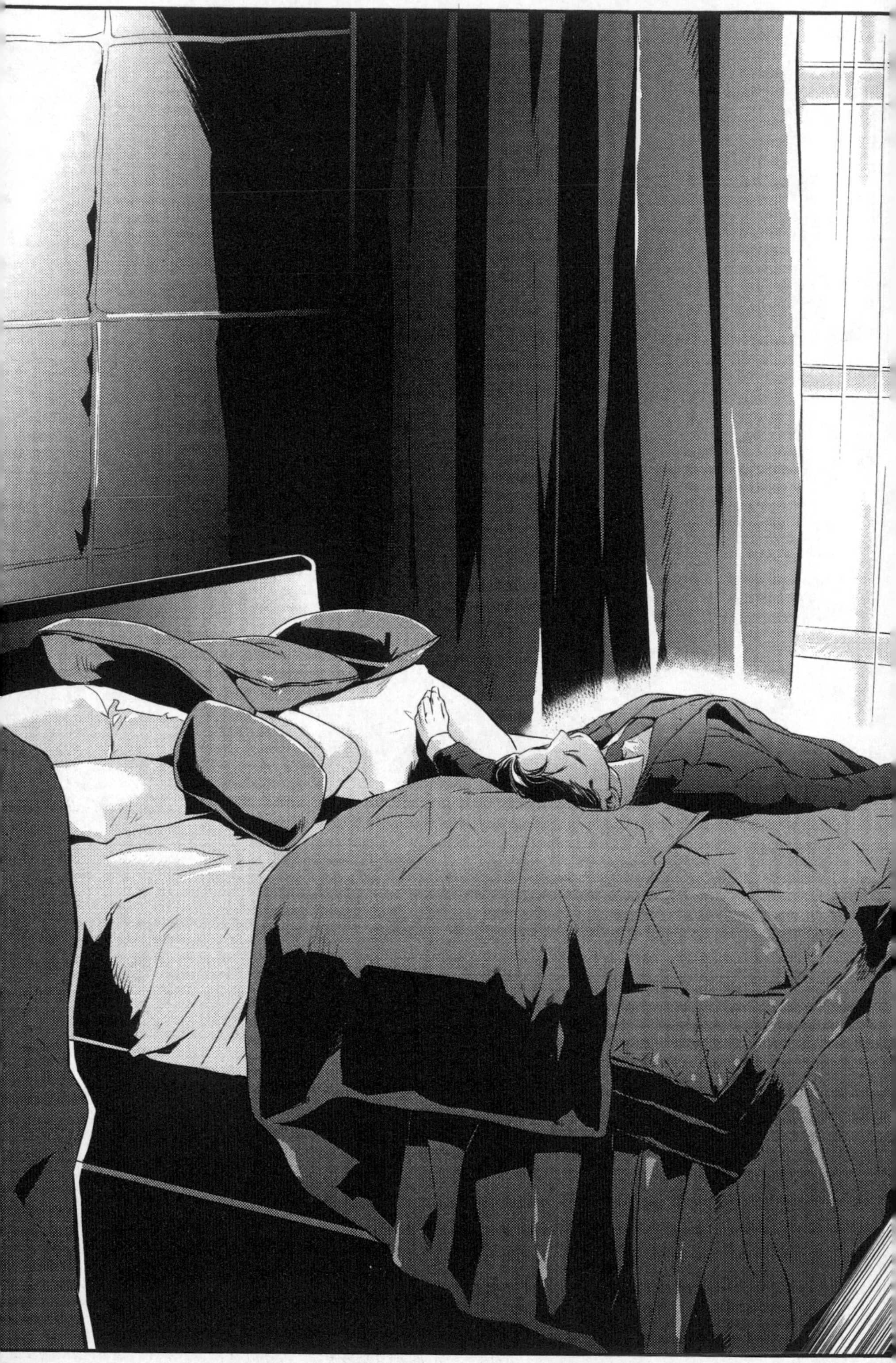

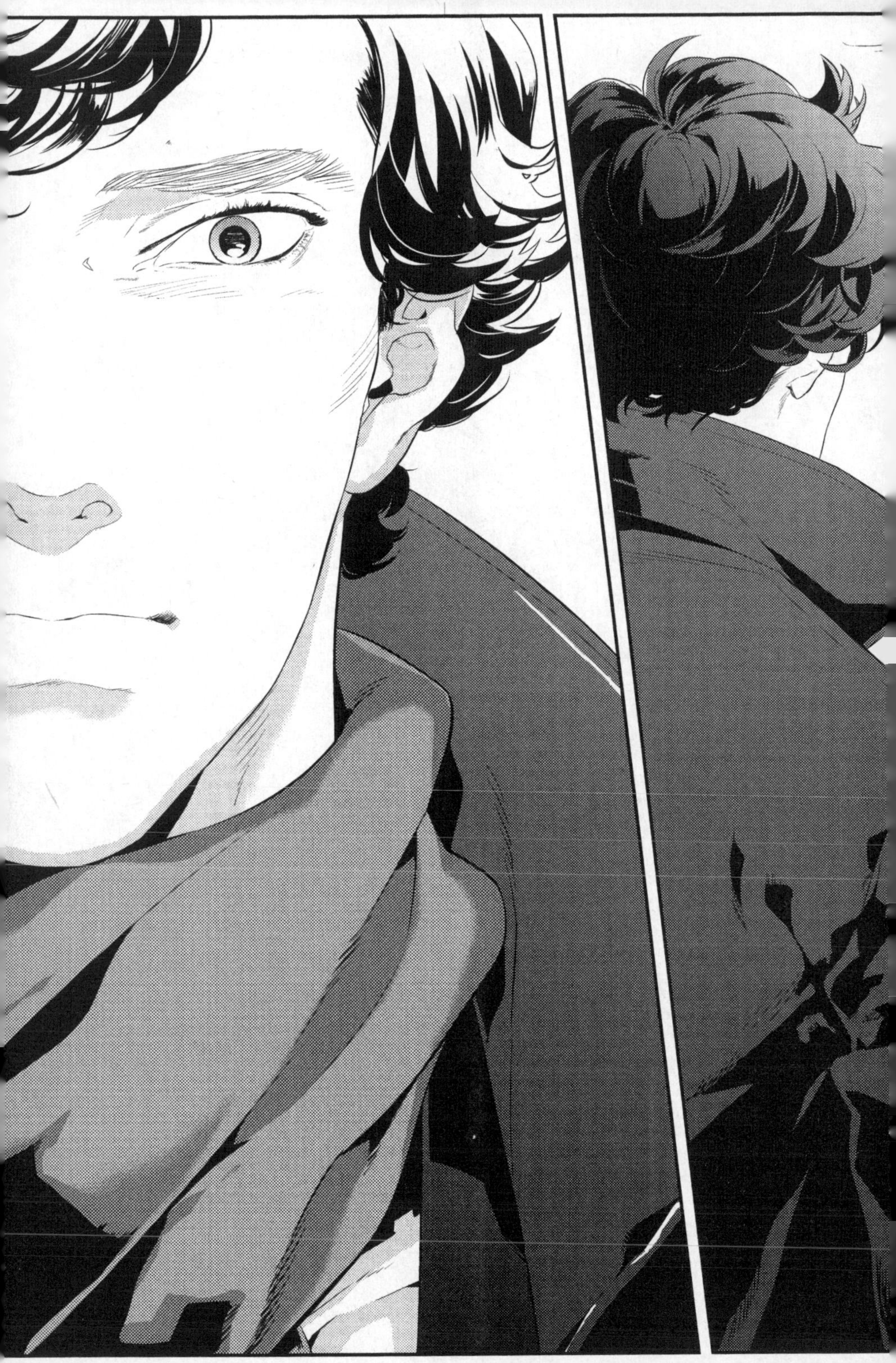

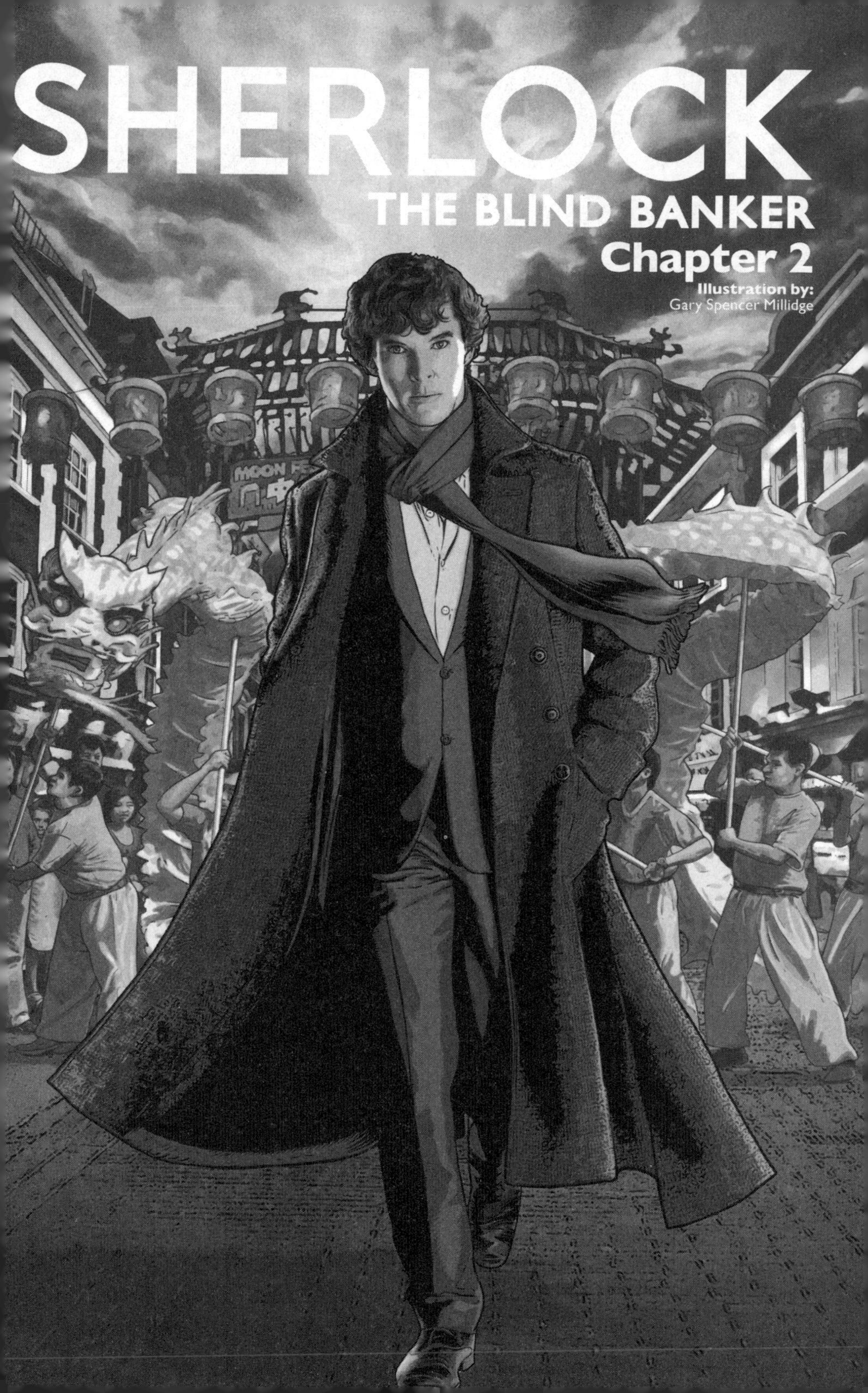
SHERLOCK
THE BLIND BANKER
Chapter 2
Illustration by:
Gary Spencer Millidge

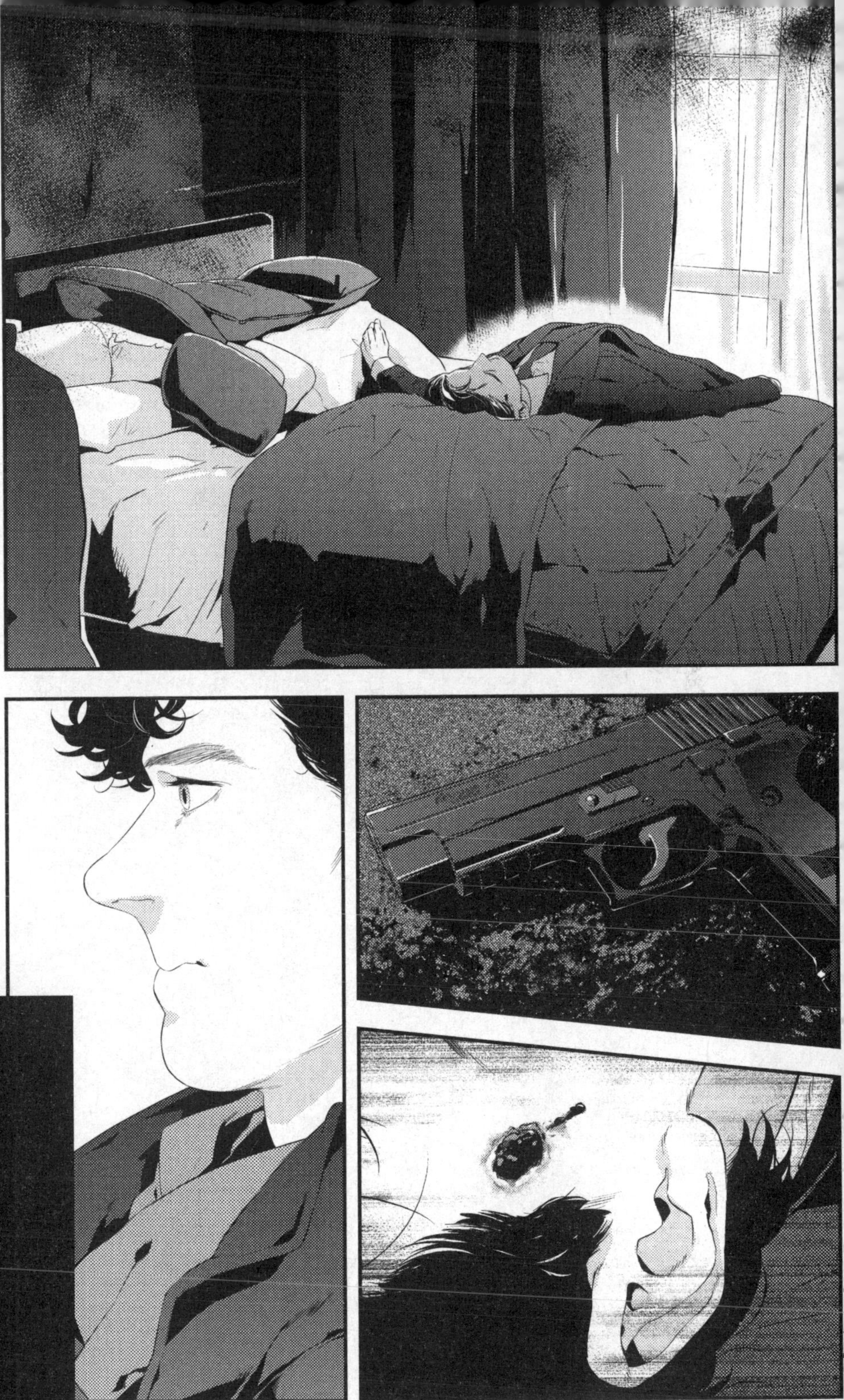

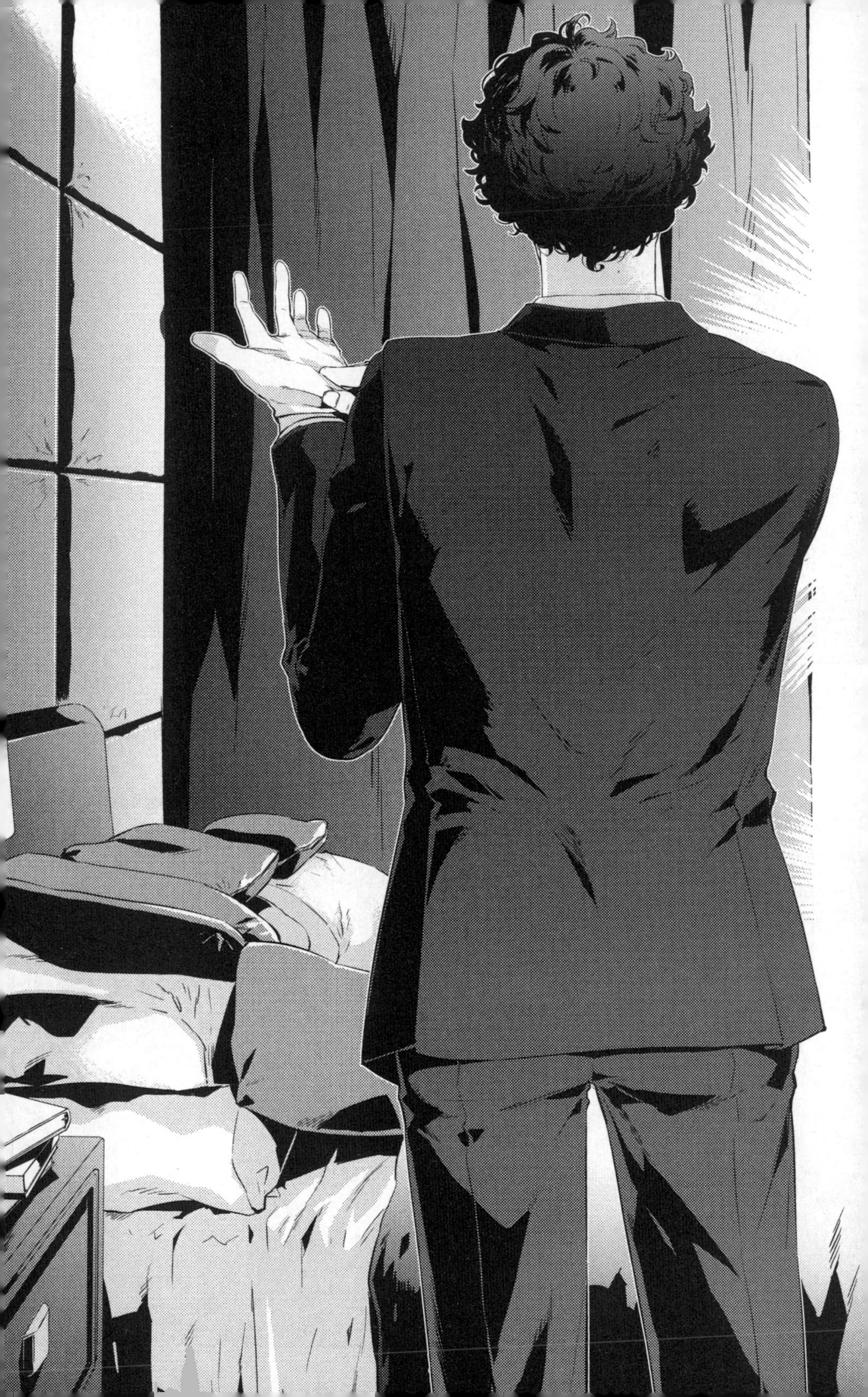

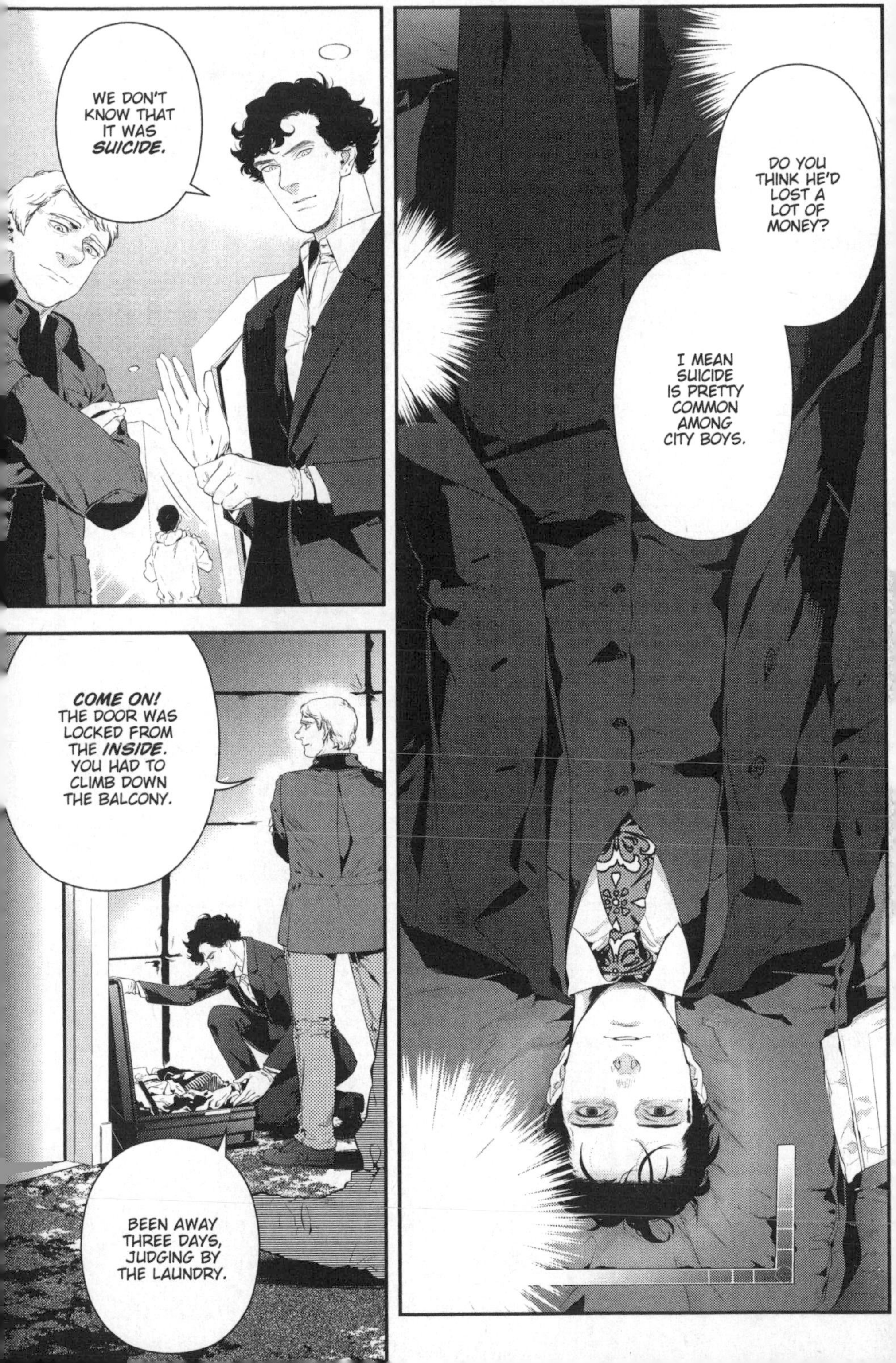
DO YOU THINK HE'D LOST A LOT OF MONEY?
I MEAN SUICIDE IS PRETTY COMMON AMONG CITY BOYS.
WE DON'T KNOW THAT IT WAS *SUICIDE.*
COME ON! THE DOOR WAS LOCKED FROM THE *INSIDE*. YOU HAD TO CLIMB DOWN THE BALCONY.
BEEN AWAY THREE DAYS, JUDGING BY THE LAUNDRY.

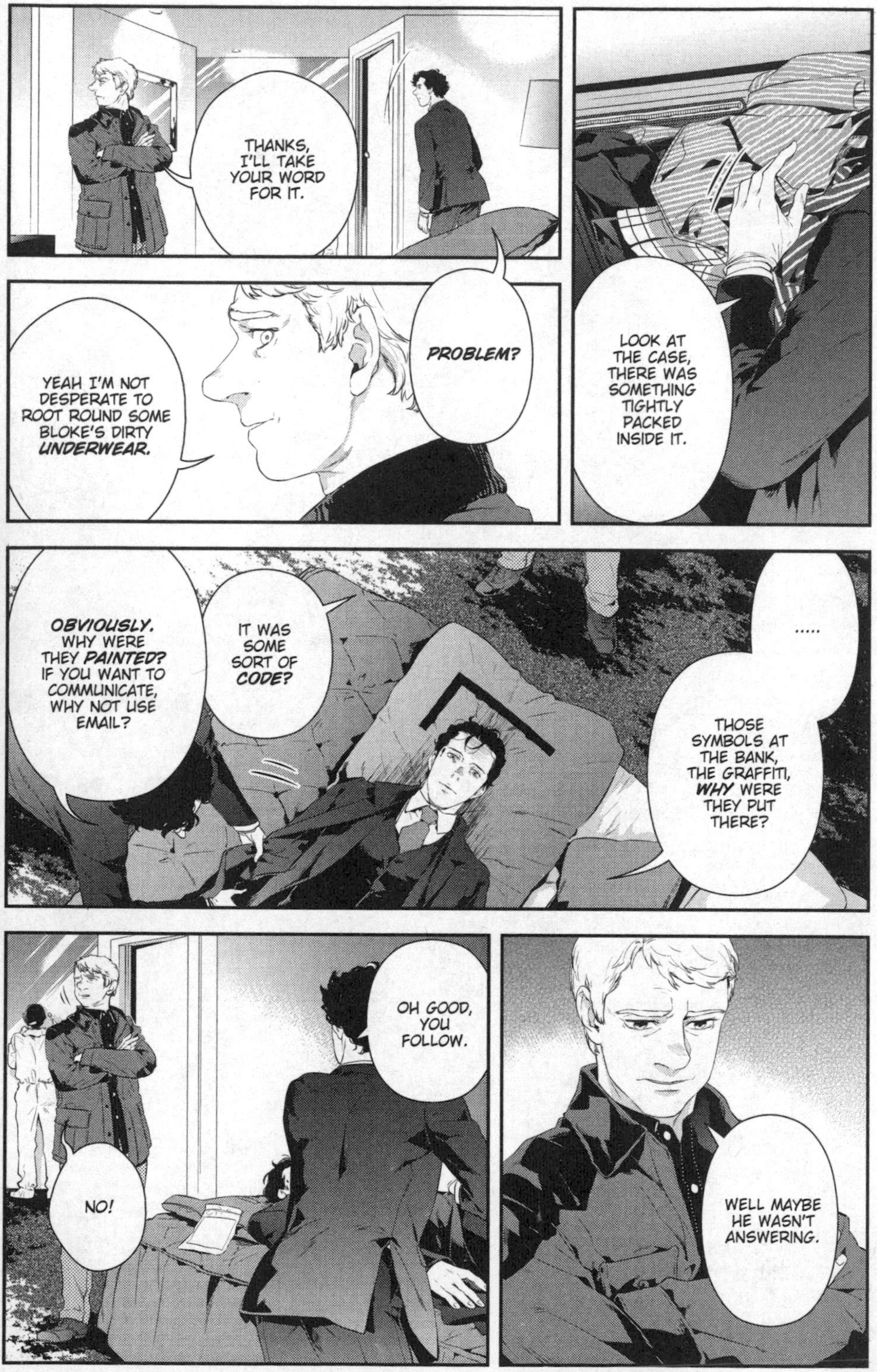
LOOK AT THE CASE, THERE WAS SOMETHING TIGHTLY PACKED INSIDE IT.
THANKS, I'LL TAKE YOUR WORD FOR IT.
PROBLEM?
YEAH I'M NOT DESPERATE TO ROOT ROUND SOME BLOKE'S DIRTY UNDERWEAR.
.....
THOSE SYMBOLS AT THE BANK, THE GRAFFITI, WHY WERE THEY PUT THERE?
IT WAS SOME SORT OF CODE?
OBVIOUSLY. WHY WERE THEY PAINTED? IF YOU WANT TO COMMUNICATE, WHY NOT USE EMAIL?
WELL MAYBE HE WASN'T ANSWERING.
OH GOOD, YOU FOLLOW.
NO!

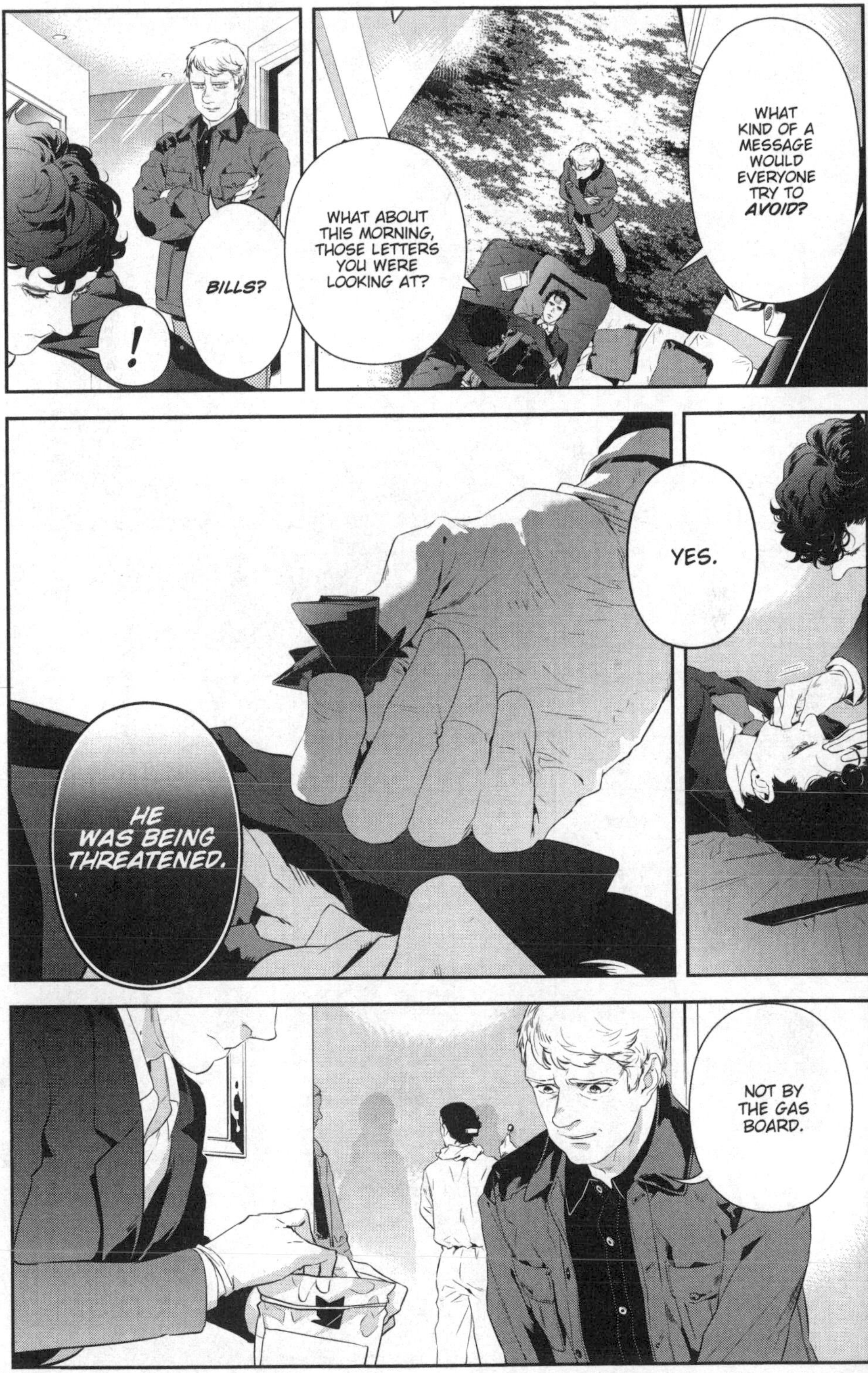
WHAT KIND OF A MESSAGE WOULD EVERYONE TRY TO *AVOID?*
WHAT ABOUT THIS MORNING, THOSE LETTERS YOU WERE LOOKING AT?
BILLS?
!
YES.
HE WAS BEING THREATENED.
NOT BY THE GAS BOARD.

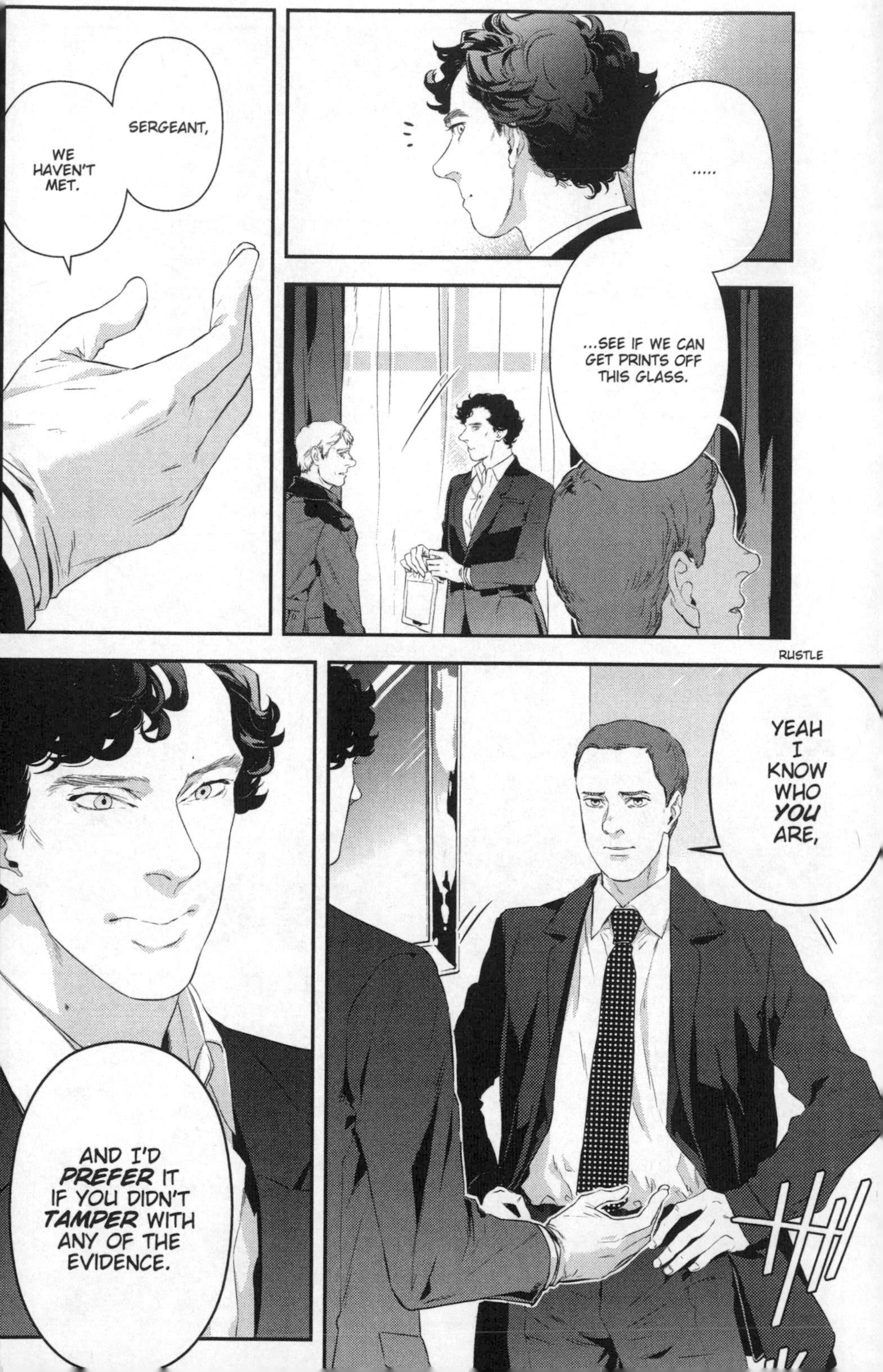
.....
...SEE IF WE CAN GET PRINTS OFF THIS GLASS.
SERGEANT,
WE HAVEN'T MET.
RUSTLE
YEAH I KNOW WHO YOU ARE,
AND I'D PREFER IT IF YOU DIDN'T TAMPER WITH ANY OF THE EVIDENCE.

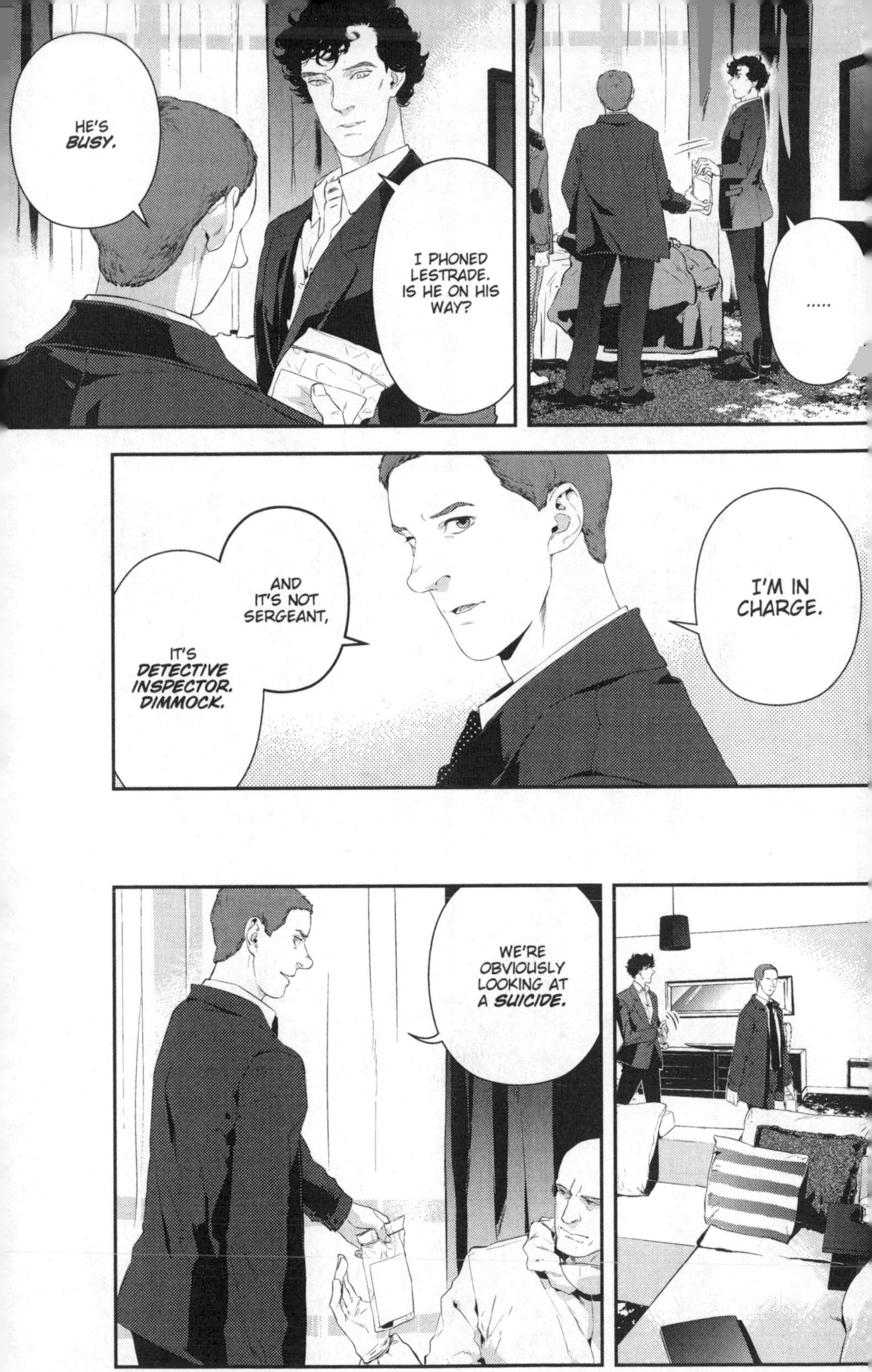
.....
I PHONED LESTRADE. IS HE ON HIS WAY?
HE'S BUSY.
I'M IN CHARGE.
AND IT'S NOT SERGEANT,
IT'S DETECTIVE INSPECTOR. DIMMOCK.
WE'RE OBVIOUSLY LOOKING AT A SUICIDE.

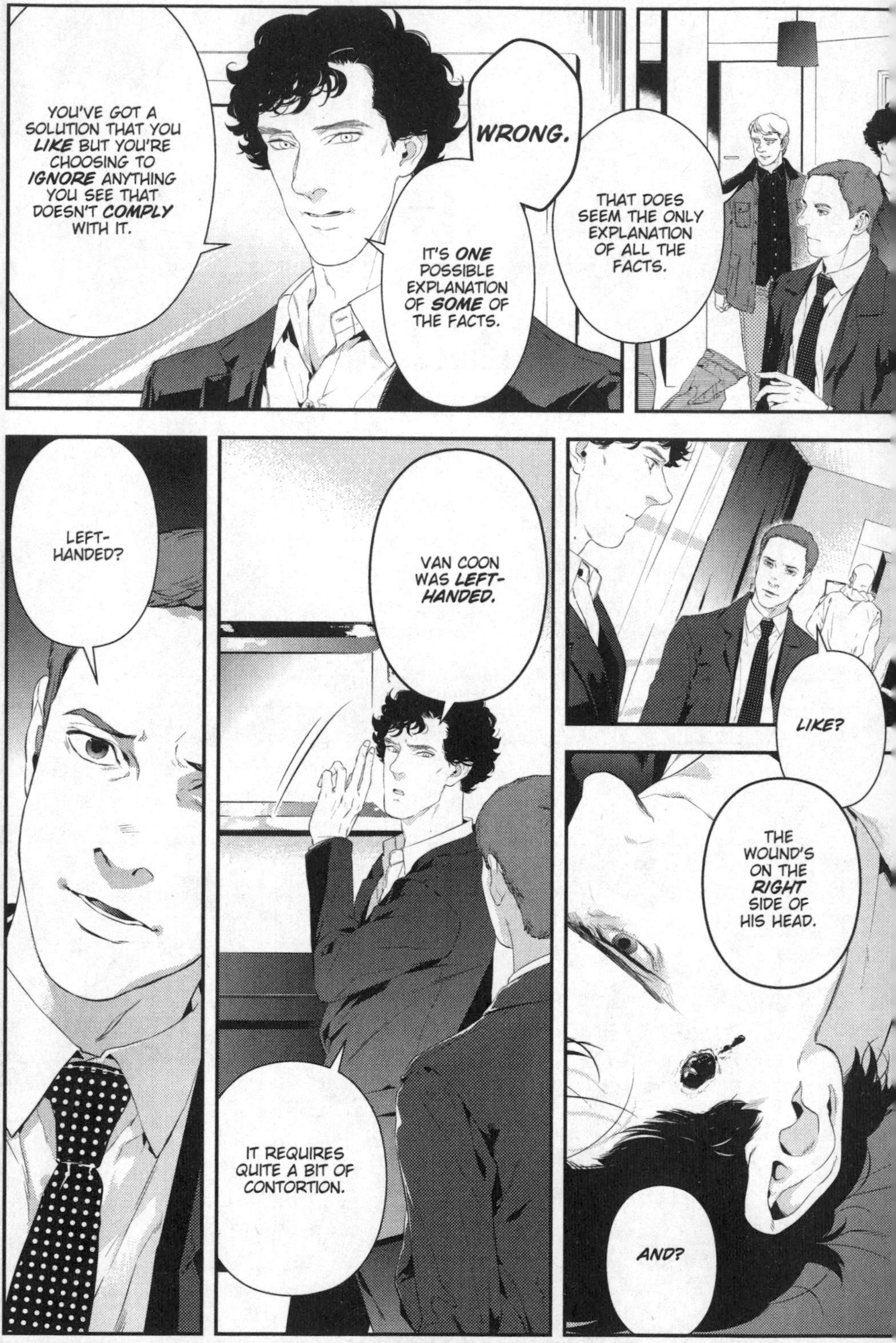
THAT DOES SEEM THE ONLY EXPLANATION OF ALL THE FACTS.
WRONG.
IT'S ONE POSSIBLE EXPLANATION OF SOME OF THE FACTS.
YOU'VE GOT A SOLUTION THAT YOU LIKE BUT YOU'RE CHOOSING TO IGNORE ANYTHING YOU SEE THAT DOESN'T COMPLY WITH IT.
LIKE?
THE WOUND'S ON THE RIGHT SIDE OF HIS HEAD.
AND?
VAN COON WAS LEFT-HANDED.
IT REQUIRES QUITE A BIT OF CONTORTION.
LEFT-HANDED?

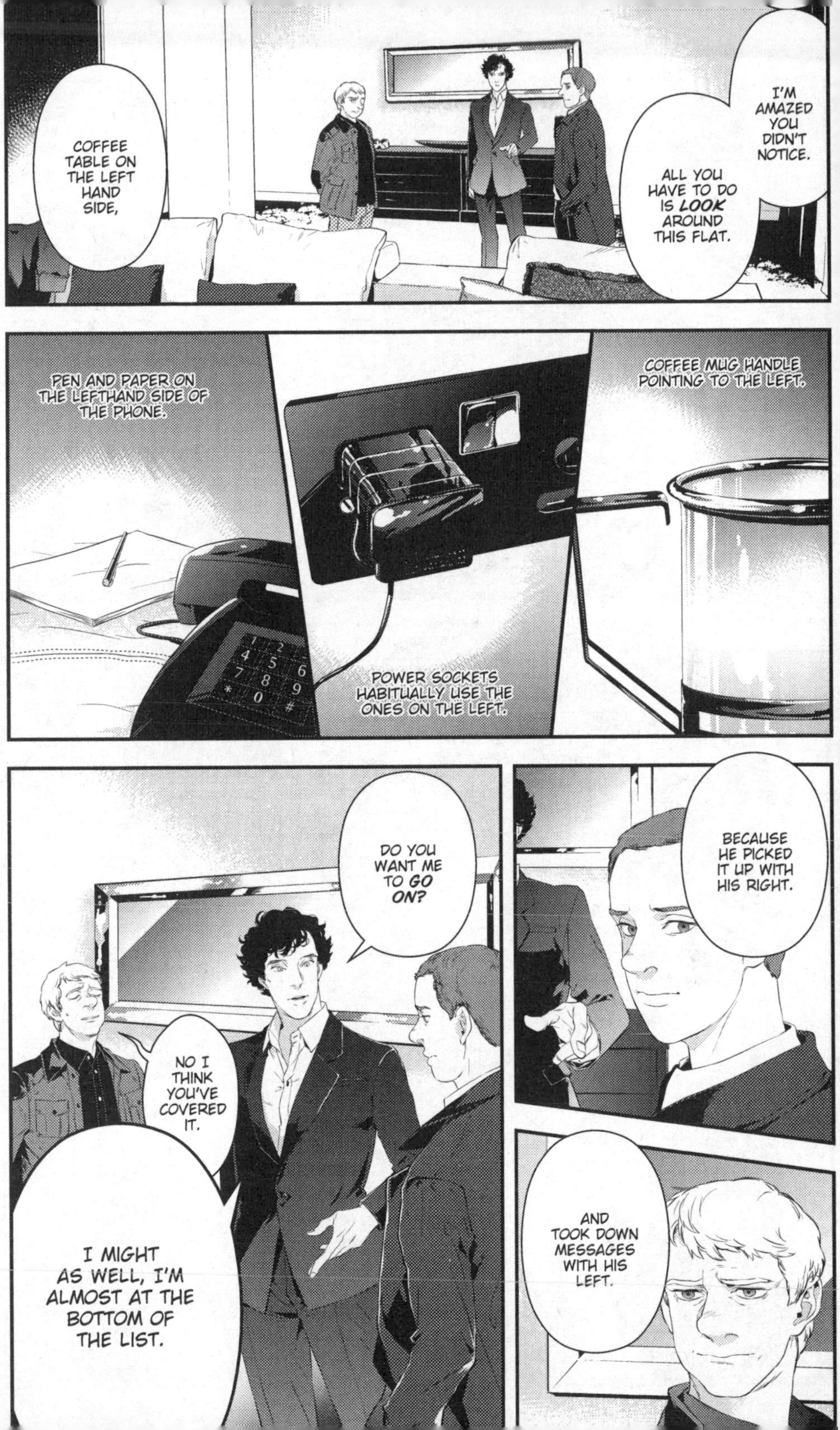
I'M AMAZED YOU DIDN'T NOTICE.
ALL YOU HAVE TO DO IS ***LOOK*** AROUND THIS FLAT.
COFFEE TABLE ON THE LEFT HAND SIDE,
COFFEE MUG HANDLE POINTING TO THE LEFT.
POWER SOCKETS HABITUALLY USE THE ONES ON THE LEFT.
PEN AND PAPER ON THE LEFTHAND SIDE OF THE PHONE.
BECAUSE HE PICKED IT UP WITH HIS RIGHT.
AND TOOK DOWN MESSAGES WITH HIS LEFT.
DO YOU WANT ME TO ***GO ON?***
NO I THINK YOU'VE COVERED IT.
I MIGHT AS WELL, I'M ALMOST AT THE BOTTOM OF THE LIST.

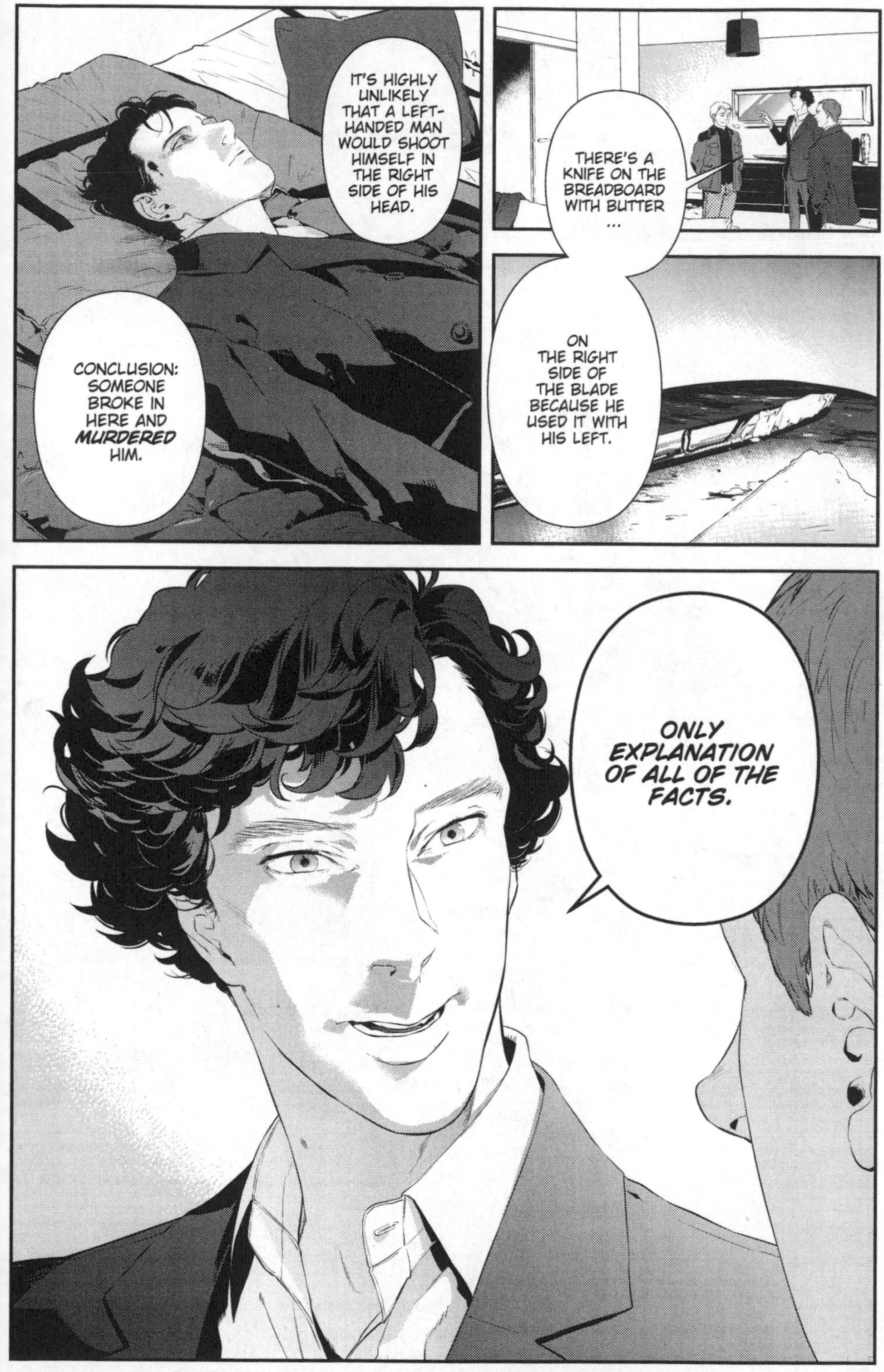
THERE'S A KNIFE ON THE BREADBOARD WITH BUTTER ...
ON THE RIGHT SIDE OF THE BLADE BECAUSE HE USED IT WITH HIS LEFT.
IT'S HIGHLY UNLIKELY THAT A LEFT-HANDED MAN WOULD SHOOT HIMSELF IN THE RIGHT SIDE OF HIS HEAD.
CONCLUSION: SOMEONE BROKE IN HERE AND *MURDERED* HIM.
ONLY EXPLANATION OF ALL OF THE FACTS.

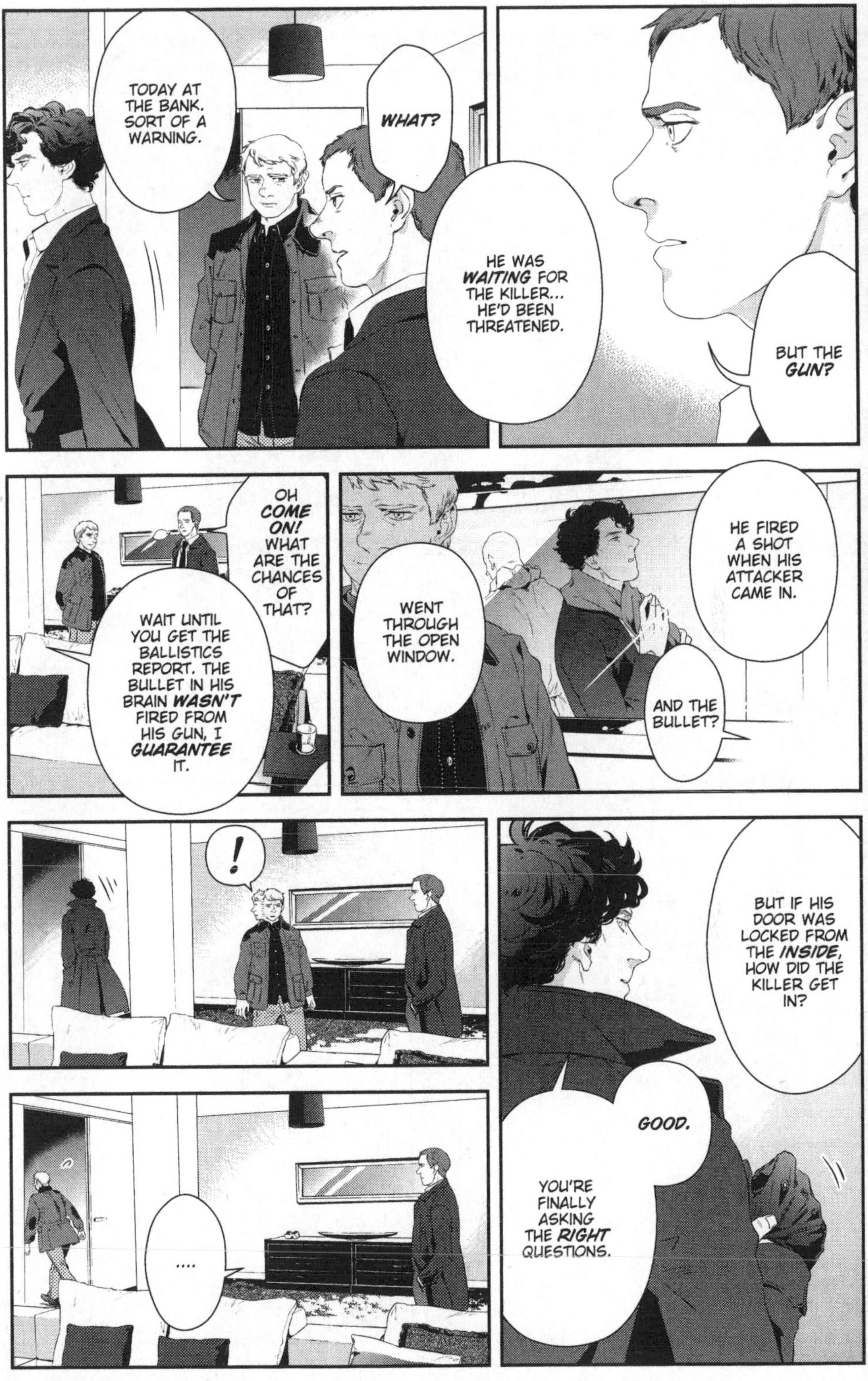
BUT THE *GUN?*
WHAT?
TODAY AT THE BANK. SORT OF A WARNING.
HE WAS *WAITING* FOR THE KILLER... HE'D BEEN THREATENED.
HE FIRED A SHOT WHEN HIS ATTACKER CAME IN.
AND THE BULLET?
WENT THROUGH THE OPEN WINDOW.
OH *COME ON!* WHAT ARE THE CHANCES OF THAT?
WAIT UNTIL YOU GET THE BALLISTICS REPORT. THE BULLET IN HIS BRAIN *WASN'T* FIRED FROM HIS GUN, I *GUARANTEE* IT.
BUT IF HIS DOOR WAS LOCKED FROM THE *INSIDE*, HOW DID THE KILLER GET IN?
GOOD.
YOU'RE FINALLY ASKING THE *RIGHT* QUESTIONS.
!
....

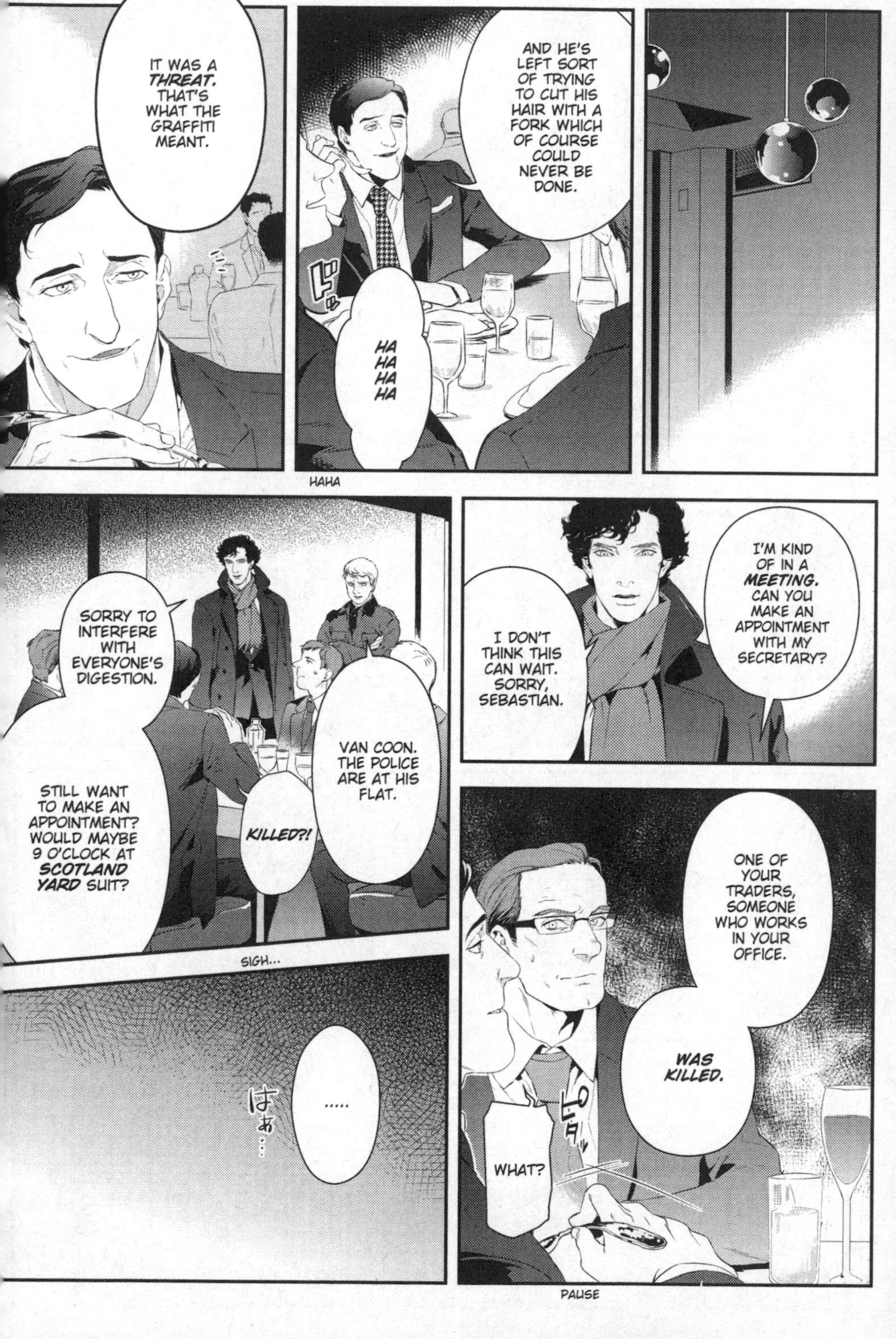
AND HE'S LEFT SORT OF TRYING TO CUT HIS HAIR WITH A FORK WHICH OF COURSE COULD NEVER BE DONE.
ドッ
HA HA HA HA
HAHA
IT WAS A THREAT. THAT'S WHAT THE GRAFFITI MEANT.
I'M KIND OF IN A MEETING. CAN YOU MAKE AN APPOINTMENT WITH MY SECRETARY?
I DON'T THINK THIS CAN WAIT. SORRY, SEBASTIAN.
ONE OF YOUR TRADERS, SOMEONE WHO WORKS IN YOUR OFFICE.
WAS KILLED.
ピタッ
WHAT?
PAUSE
KILLED?!
VAN COON. THE POLICE ARE AT HIS FLAT.
SORRY TO INTERFERE WITH EVERYONE'S DIGESTION.
STILL WANT TO MAKE AN APPOINTMENT? WOULD MAYBE 9 O'CLOCK AT SCOTLAND YARD SUIT?
SIGH...
.....
はぁ…

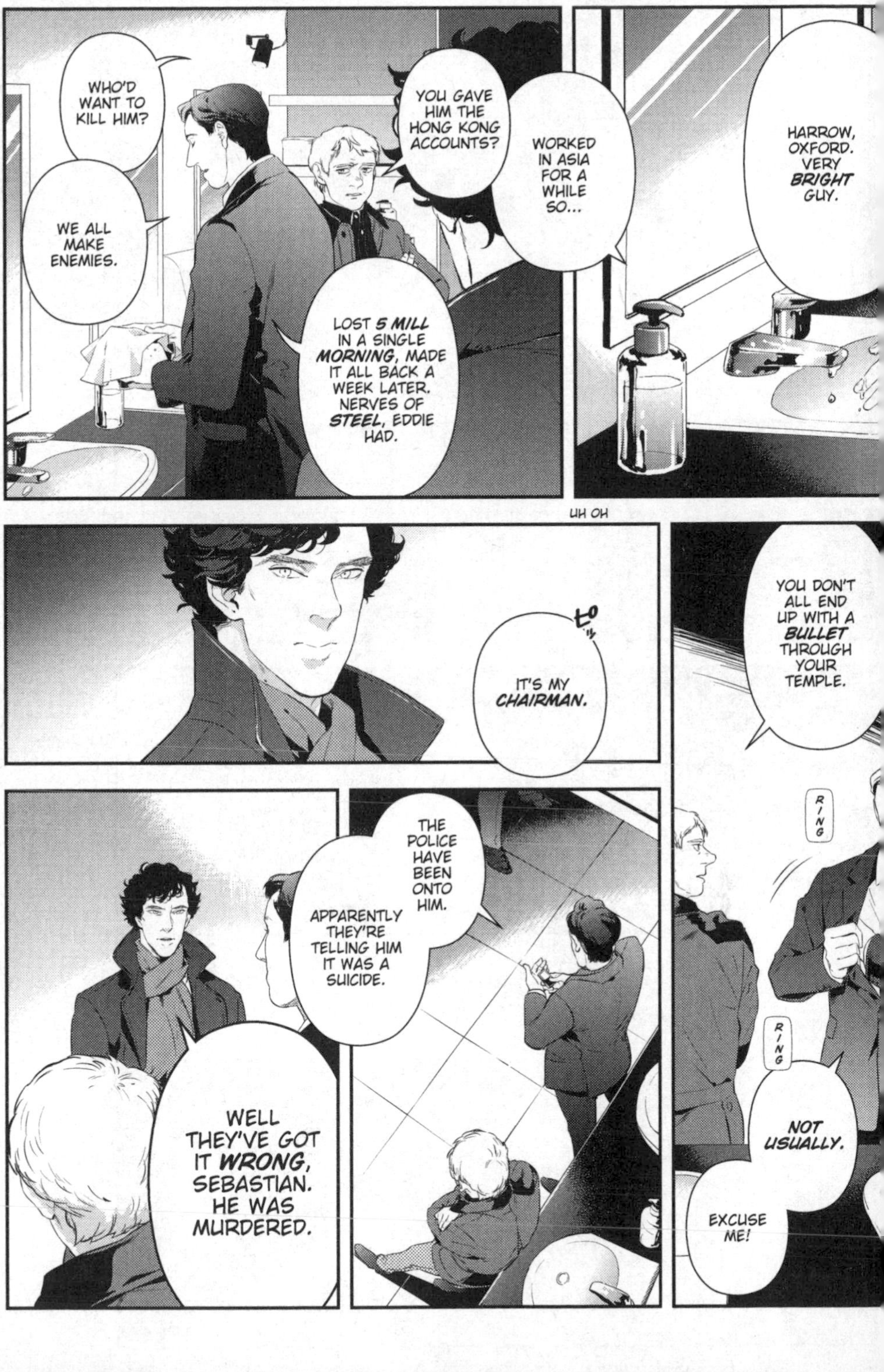
HARROW, OXFORD. VERY **BRIGHT** GUY.
WORKED IN ASIA FOR A WHILE SO...
YOU GAVE HIM THE HONG KONG ACCOUNTS?
LOST **5 MILL** IN A SINGLE **MORNING**, MADE IT ALL BACK A WEEK LATER. NERVES OF **STEEL**, EDDIE HAD.
WHO'D WANT TO KILL HIM?
WE ALL MAKE ENEMIES.
UH OH
YOU DON'T ALL END UP WITH A **BULLET** THROUGH YOUR TEMPLE.
RING
RING
NOT USUALLY.
EXCUSE ME!
ピッ
IT'S MY **CHAIRMAN.**
THE POLICE HAVE BEEN ONTO HIM.
APPARENTLY THEY'RE TELLING HIM IT WAS A SUICIDE.
WELL THEY'VE GOT IT **WRONG**, SEBASTIAN. HE WAS MURDERED.

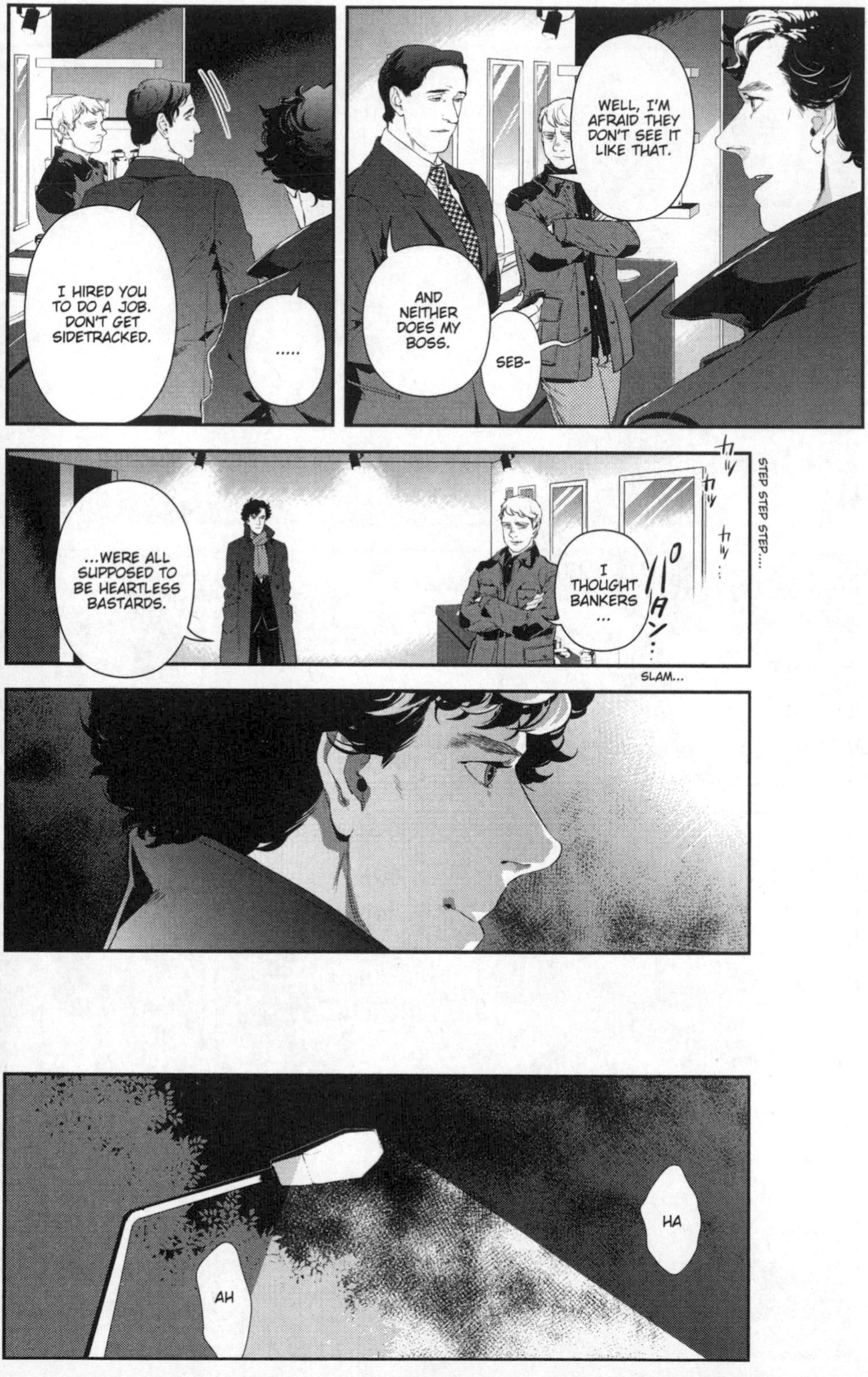
WELL, I'M AFRAID THEY DON'T SEE IT LIKE THAT.
AND NEITHER DOES MY BOSS.
SEB-
I HIRED YOU TO DO A JOB. DON'T GET SIDETRACKED.
.....
STEP STEP STEP...
I THOUGHT BANKERS ...
...WERE ALL SUPPOSED TO BE HEARTLESS BASTARDS.
SLAM...
HA
AH

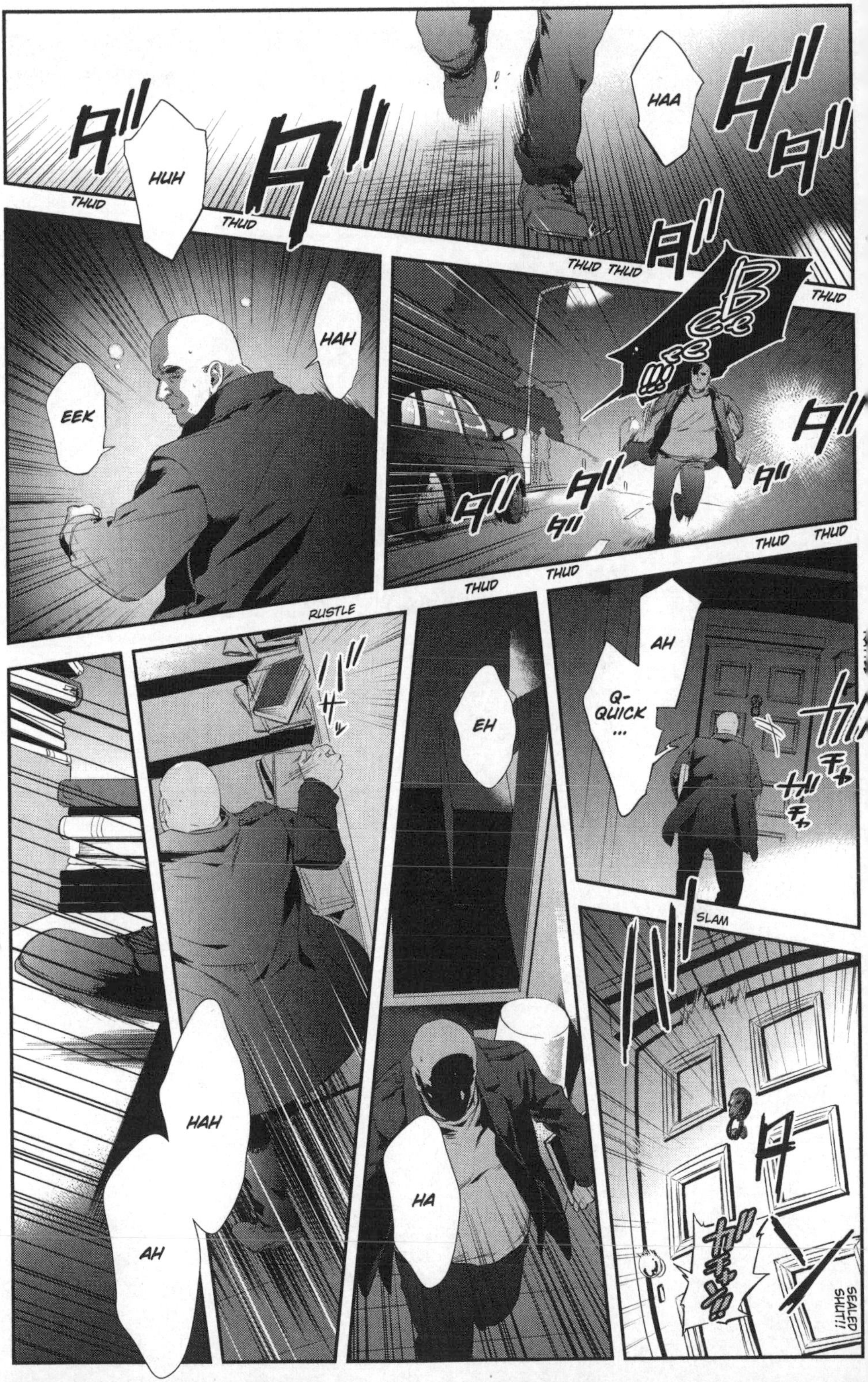
HAA
HUH
THUD
THUD
THUD THUD
THUD
Beeee!!!
THUD THUD
THUD
THUD
HAH
EEK
RUSTLE
AH
Q-QUICK...
SLAM
SEALED SHUT!!
EH
HA
HAH
AH

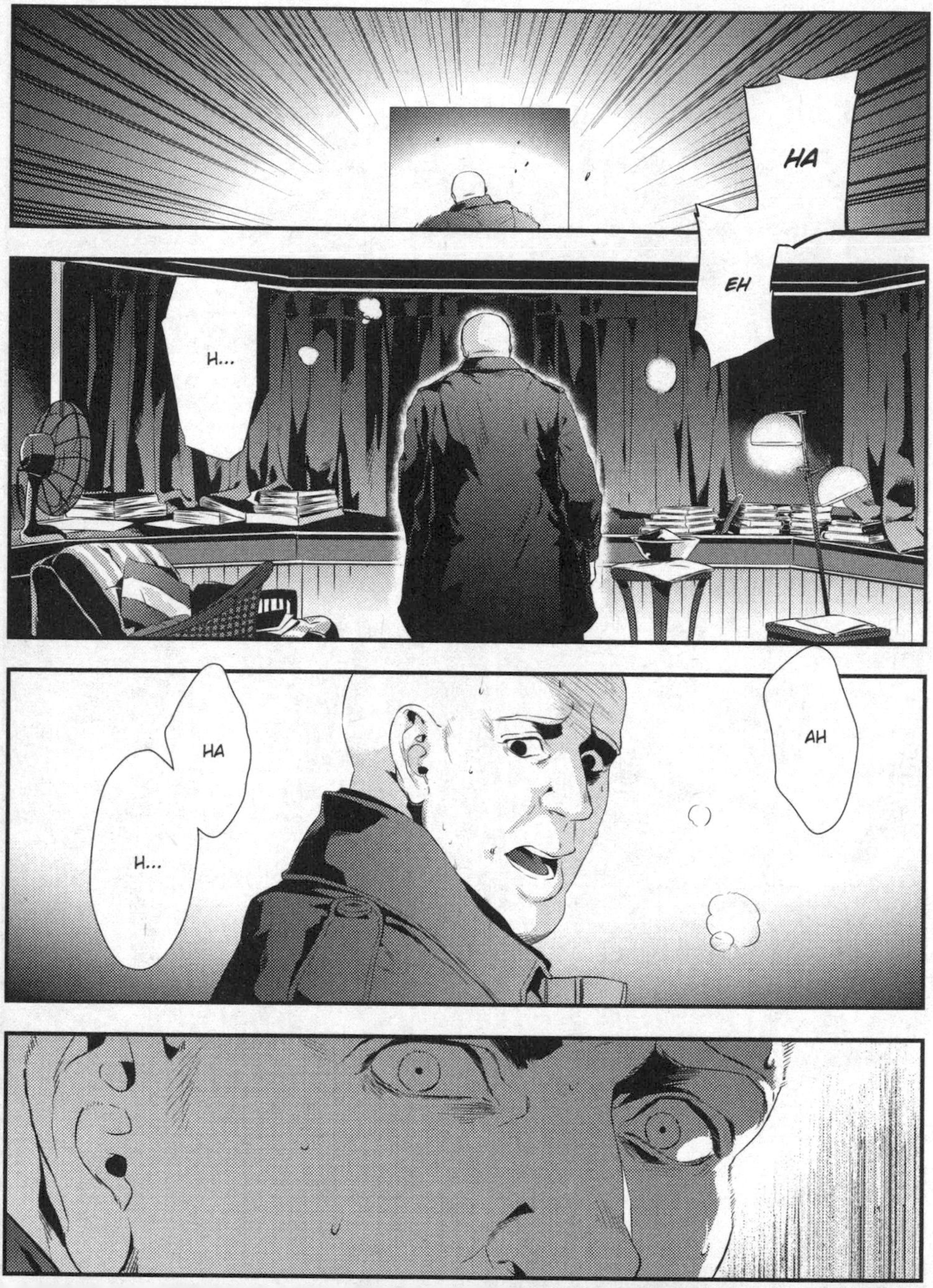
HA
EH
H...
AH
HA
H...

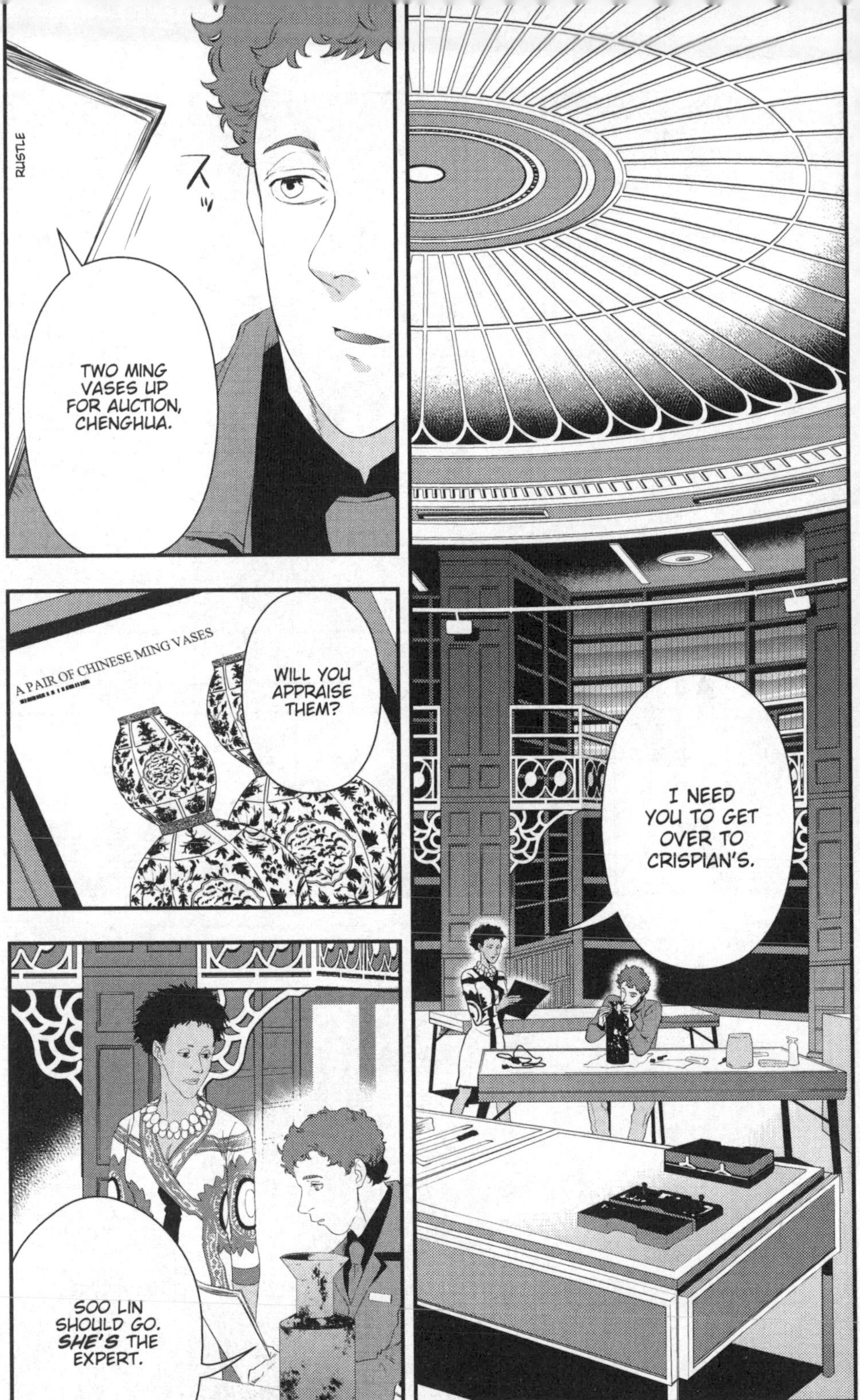
I NEED YOU TO GET OVER TO CRISPIAN'S.
RUSTLE
スッ
TWO MING VASES UP FOR AUCTION, CHENGHUA.
A PAIR OF CHINESE MING VASES
WILL YOU APPRAISE THEM?
SOO LIN SHOULD GO. ***SHE'S*** THE EXPERT.

SOO LIN HAS *RESIGNED* HER JOB.

I NEED YOU.

.....

BUZZ

BUZZ

Soo Lin yao

SOO LIN YAO'S FLAT.

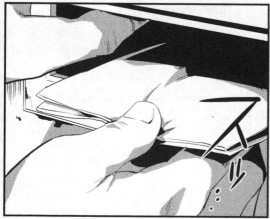

CRINKLE...

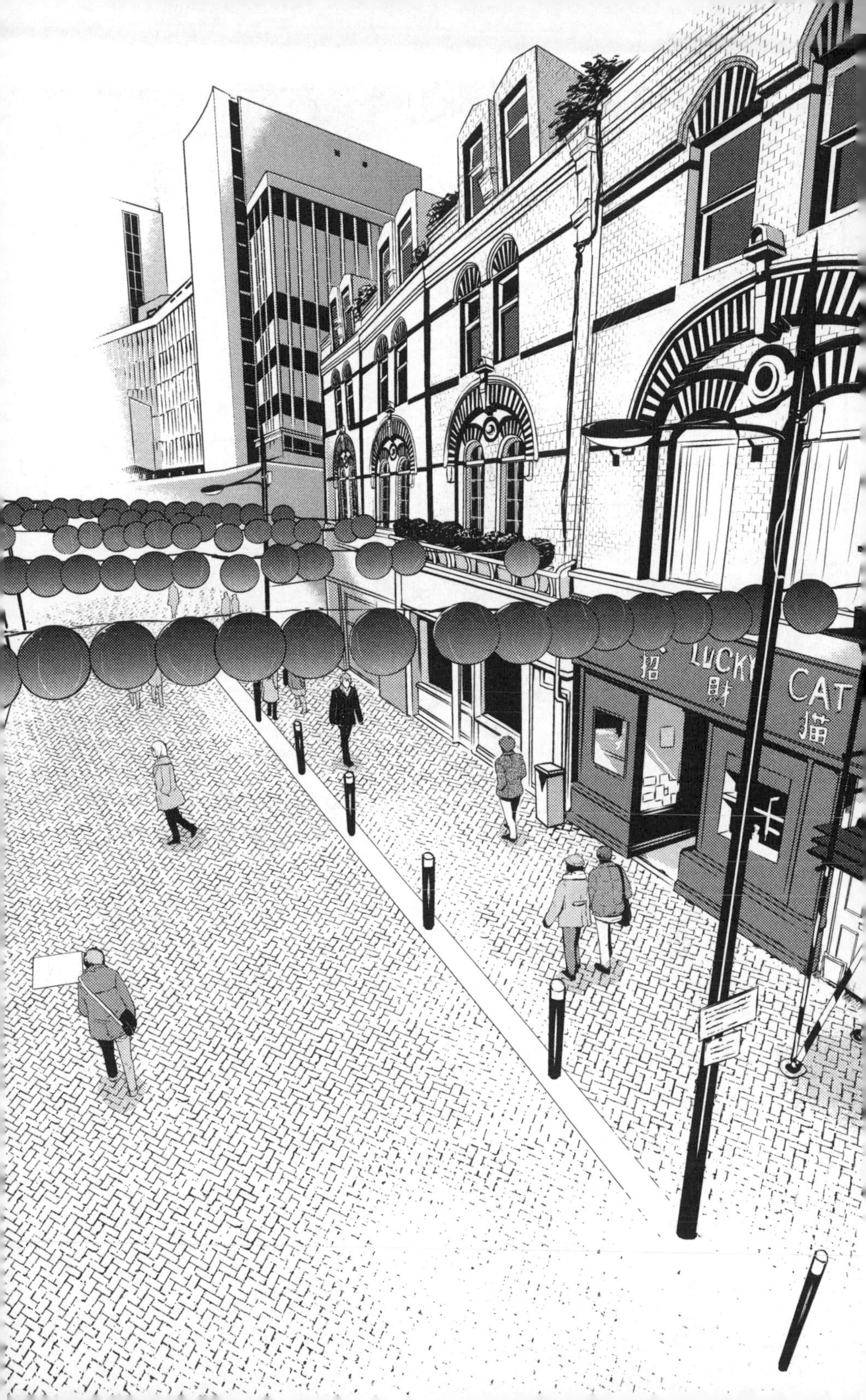
LUCKY CAT
招財猫

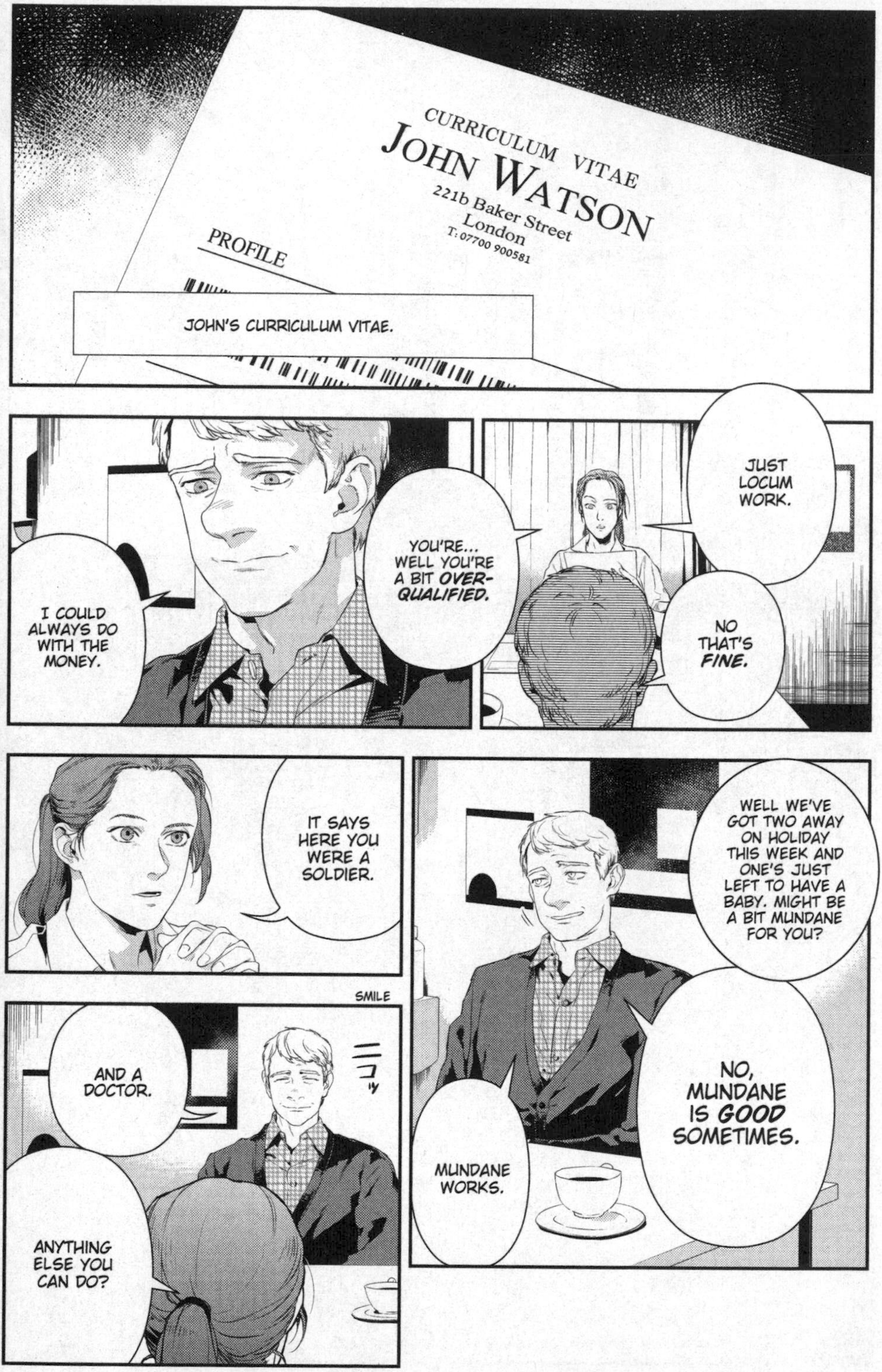
CURRICULUM VITAE
JOHN WATSON
221b Baker Street
London
T: 07700 900581
PROFILE
JOHN'S CURRICULUM VITAE.
JUST LOCUM WORK.
NO THAT'S FINE.
YOU'RE... WELL YOU'RE A BIT OVER-QUALIFIED.
I COULD ALWAYS DO WITH THE MONEY.
WELL WE'VE GOT TWO AWAY ON HOLIDAY THIS WEEK AND ONE'S JUST LEFT TO HAVE A BABY. MIGHT BE A BIT MUNDANE FOR YOU?
NO, MUNDANE IS GOOD SOMETIMES.
MUNDANE WORKS.
IT SAYS HERE YOU WERE A SOLDIER.
SMILE
ニコッ
AND A DOCTOR.
ANYTHING ELSE YOU CAN DO?

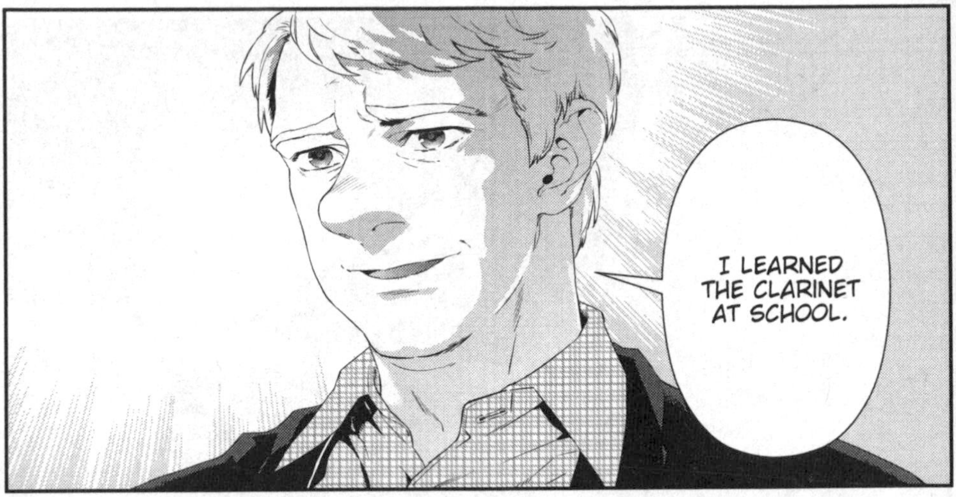
I LEARNED THE CLARINET AT SCHOOL.
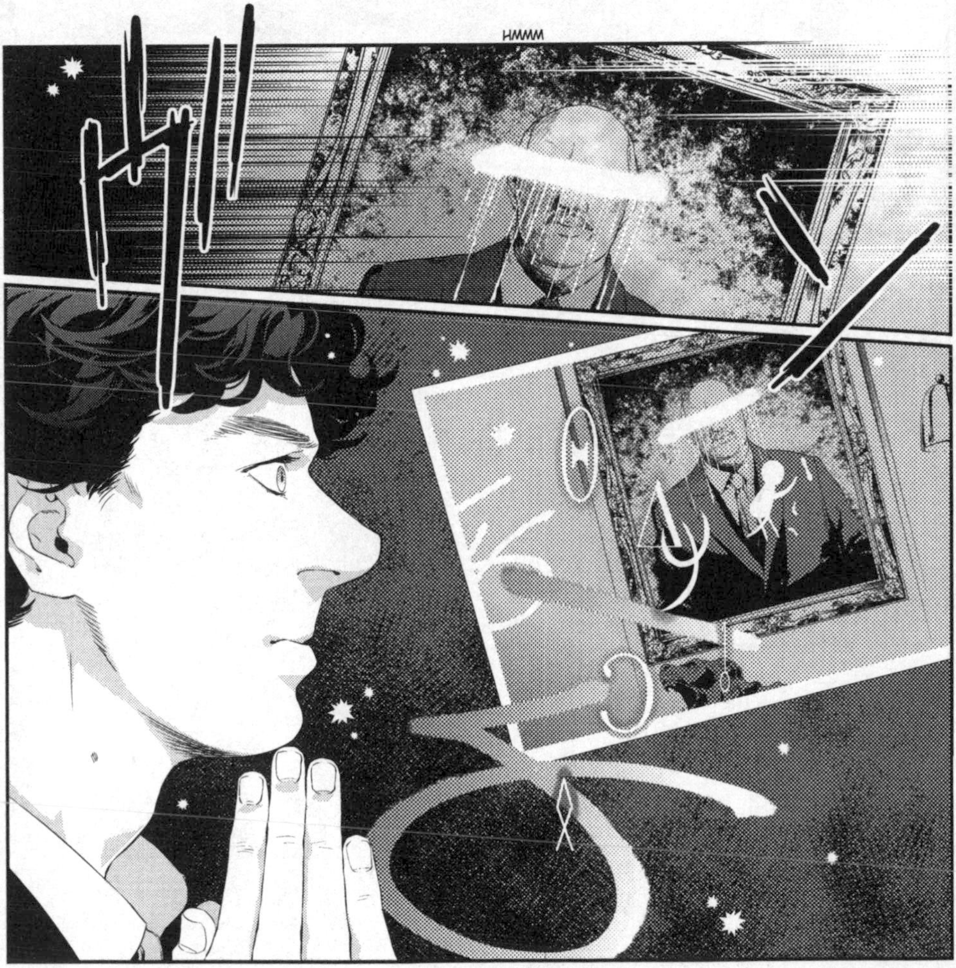
HMMM

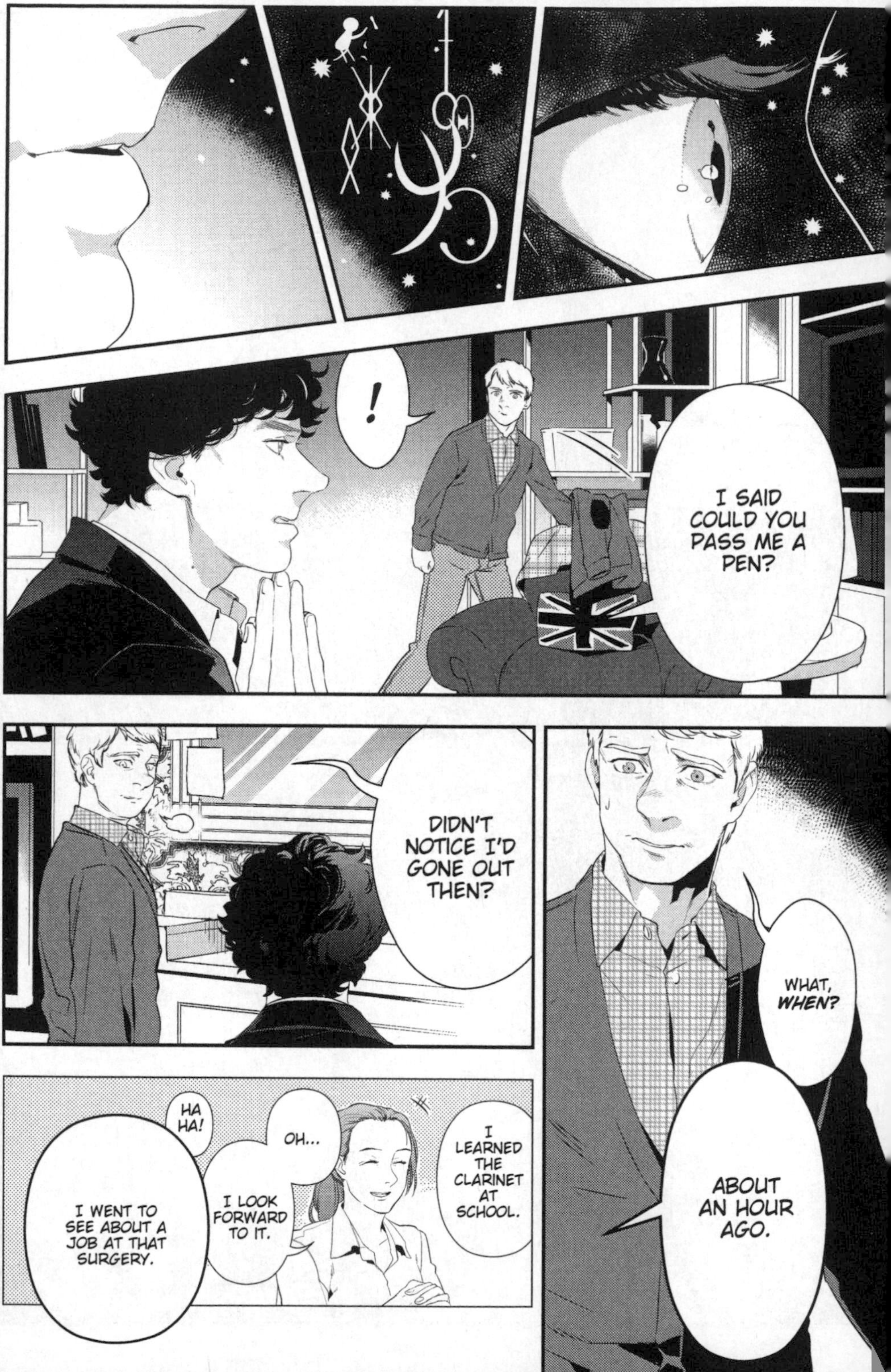
I SAID COULD YOU PASS ME A PEN?
!
WHAT, *WHEN?*
ABOUT AN HOUR AGO.
DIDN'T NOTICE I'D GONE OUT THEN?
I LEARNED THE CLARINET AT SCHOOL.
HA HA!
OH...
I LOOK FORWARD TO IT.
I WENT TO SEE ABOUT A JOB AT THAT SURGERY.

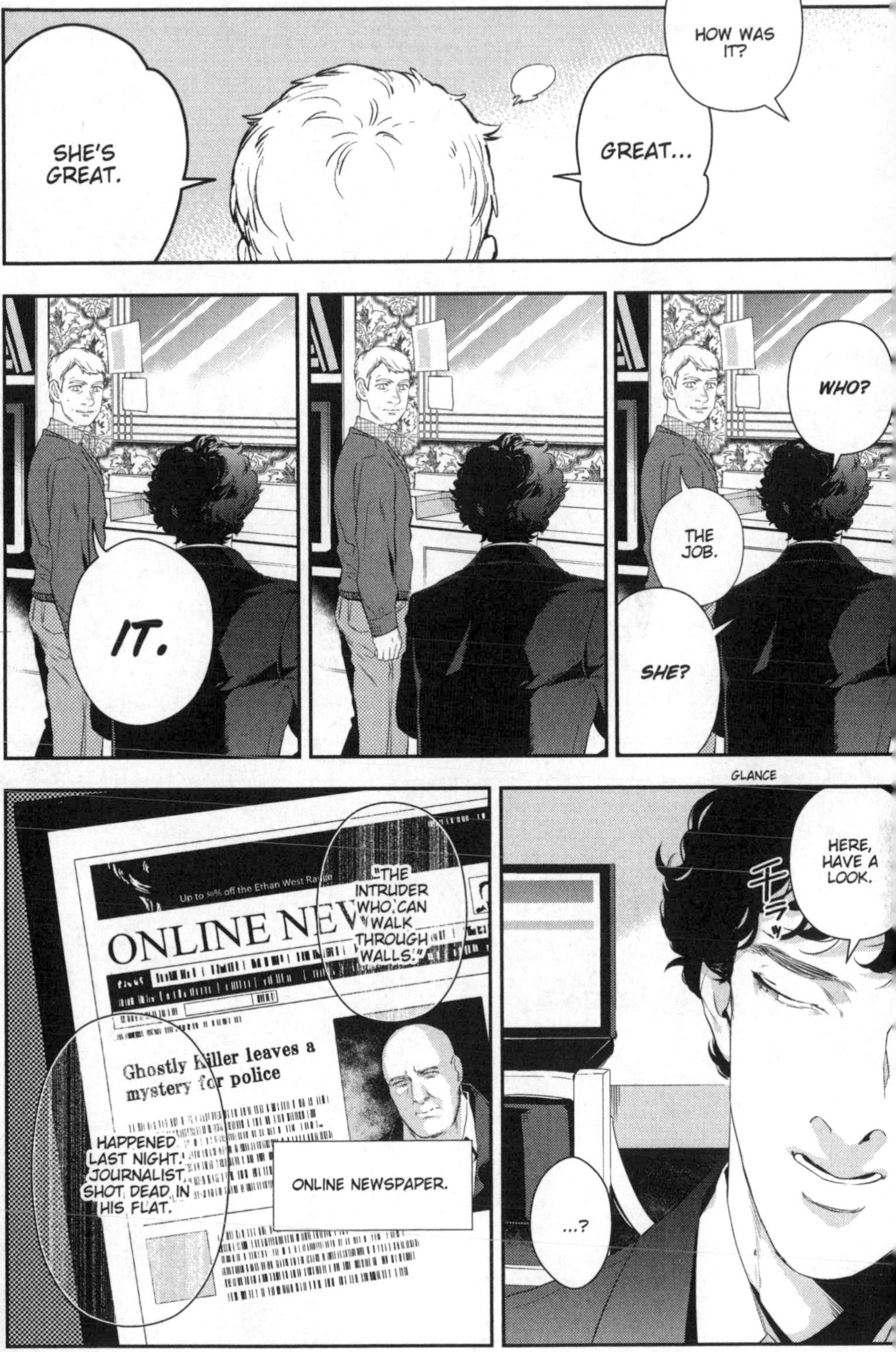
HOW WAS IT?
GREAT...
SHE'S GREAT.
WHO?
THE JOB.
SHE?
IT.
GLANCE
HERE, HAVE A LOOK.
...?
"THE INTRUDER WHO CAN WALK THROUGH WALLS."
Ghostly Killer leaves a mystery for police
HAPPENED LAST NIGHT. JOURNALIST SHOT DEAD IN HIS FLAT.
ONLINE NEWSPAPER.

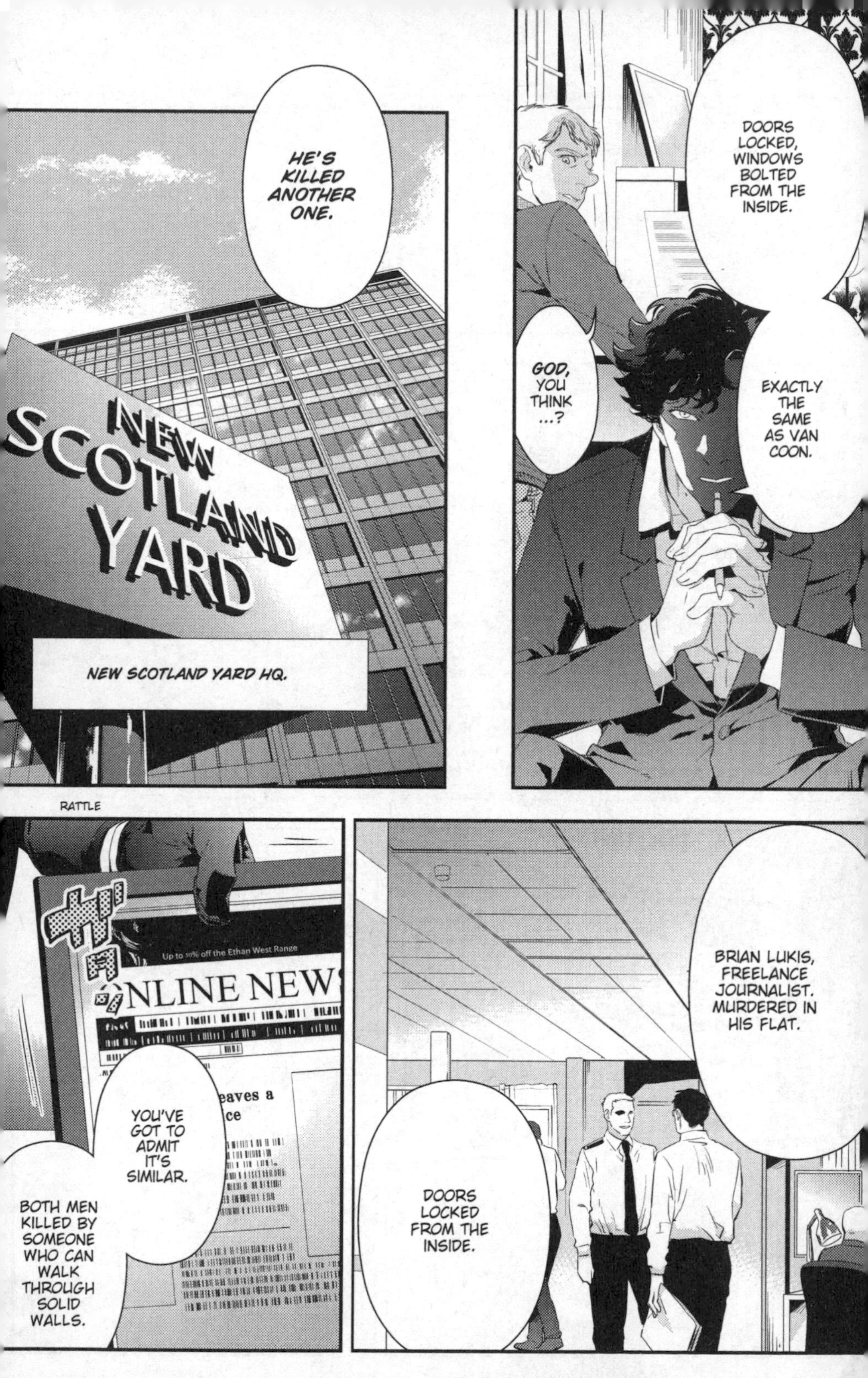

DOORS LOCKED, WINDOWS BOLTED FROM THE INSIDE.
GOD, YOU THINK ...?
EXACTLY THE SAME AS VAN COON.
HE'S KILLED ANOTHER ONE.
NEW SCOTLAND YARD
NEW SCOTLAND YARD HQ.
BRIAN LUKIS, FREELANCE JOURNALIST. MURDERED IN HIS FLAT.
DOORS LOCKED FROM THE INSIDE.
RATTLE
Up to 50% off the Ethan West Range
ONLINE NEWS
YOU'VE GOT TO ADMIT IT'S SIMILAR.
BOTH MEN KILLED BY SOMEONE WHO CAN WALK THROUGH SOLID WALLS.

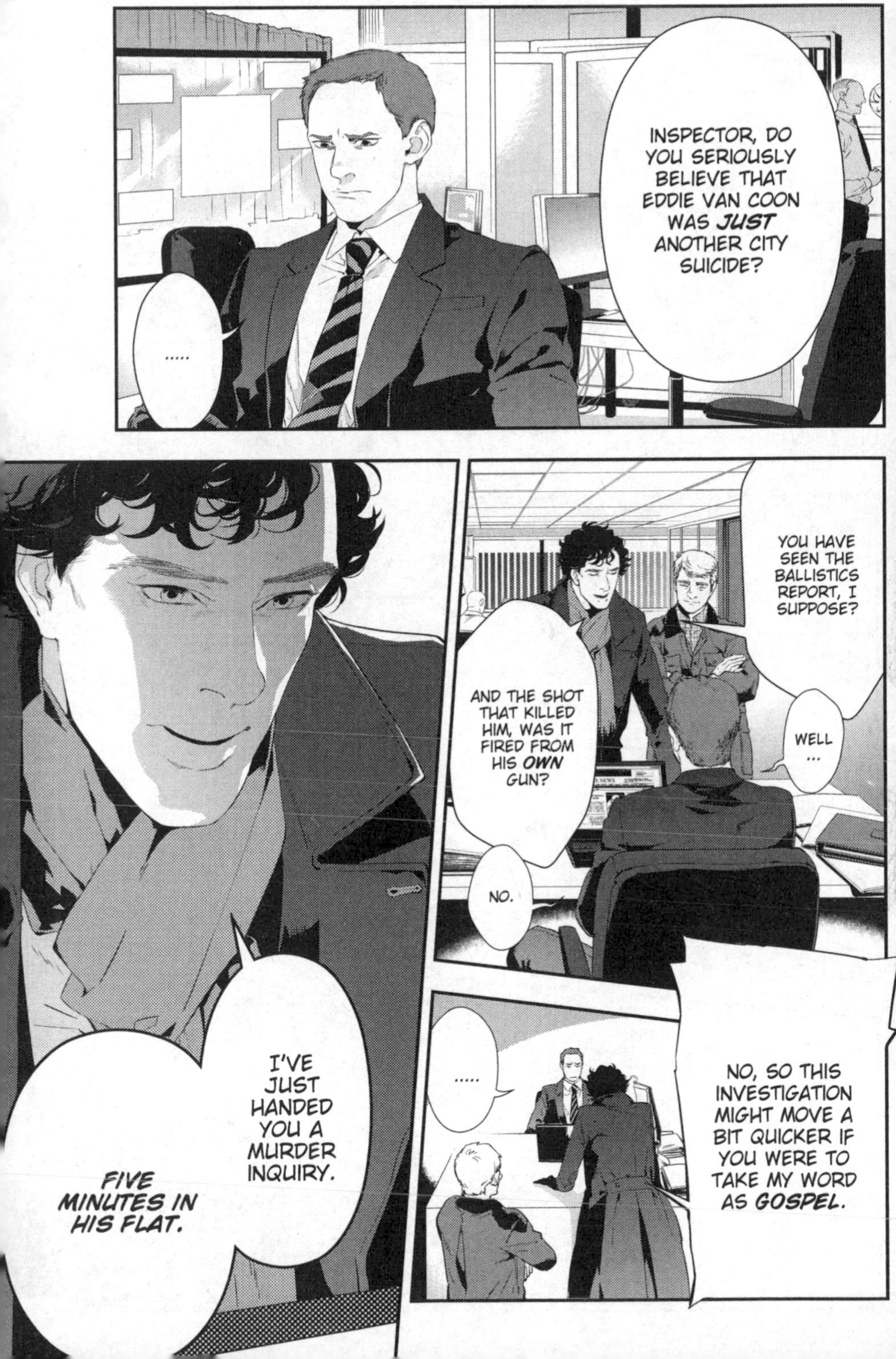
INSPECTOR, DO YOU SERIOUSLY BELIEVE THAT EDDIE VAN COON WAS *JUST* ANOTHER CITY SUICIDE?
.....
YOU HAVE SEEN THE BALLISTICS REPORT, I SUPPOSE?
WELL ...
AND THE SHOT THAT KILLED HIM, WAS IT FIRED FROM HIS *OWN* GUN?
NO.
NO, SO THIS INVESTIGATION MIGHT MOVE A BIT QUICKER IF YOU WERE TO TAKE MY WORD AS ***GOSPEL***.
.....
I'VE JUST HANDED YOU A MURDER INQUIRY.
FIVE MINUTES IN HIS FLAT.

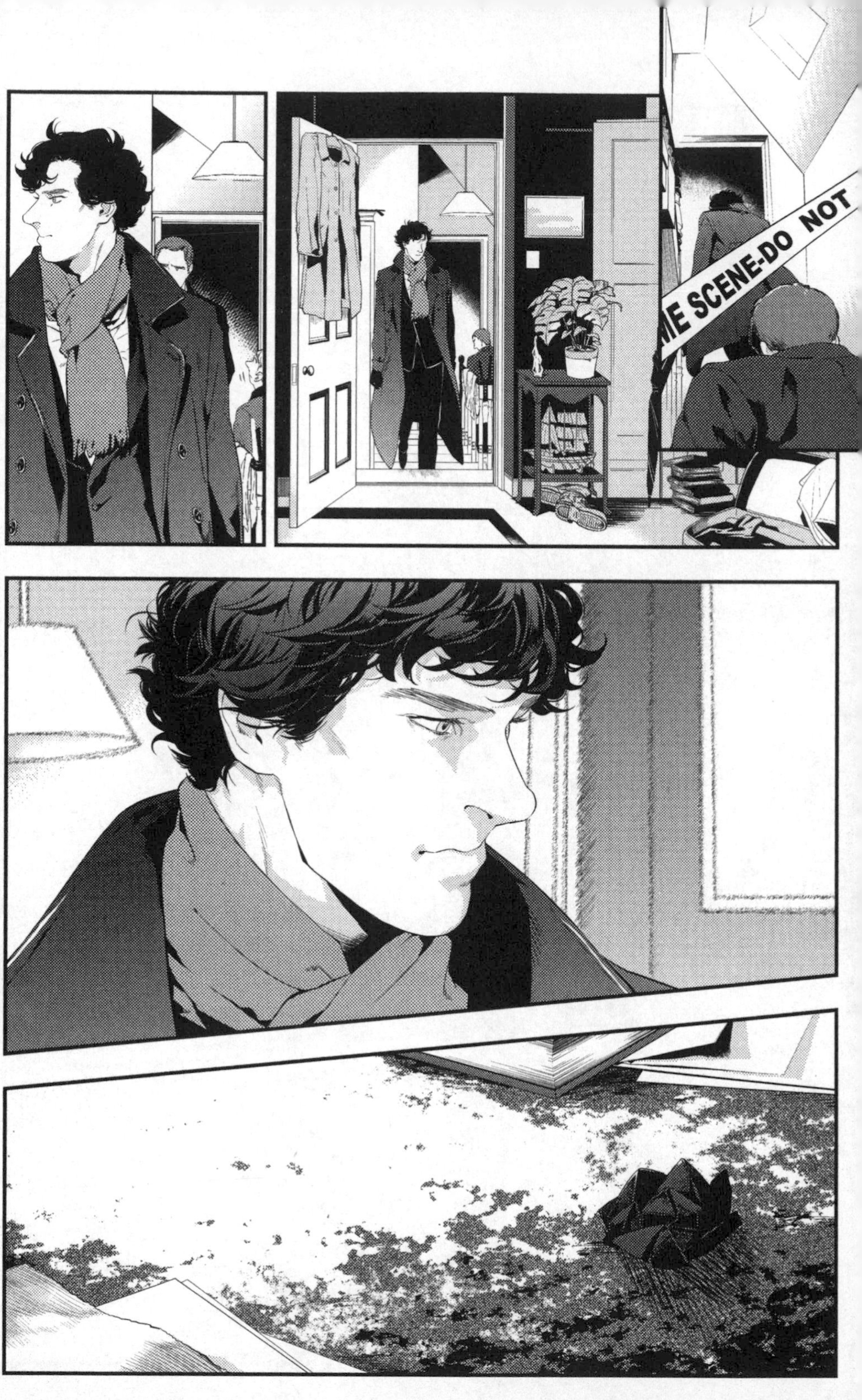
ME SCENE-DO NOT

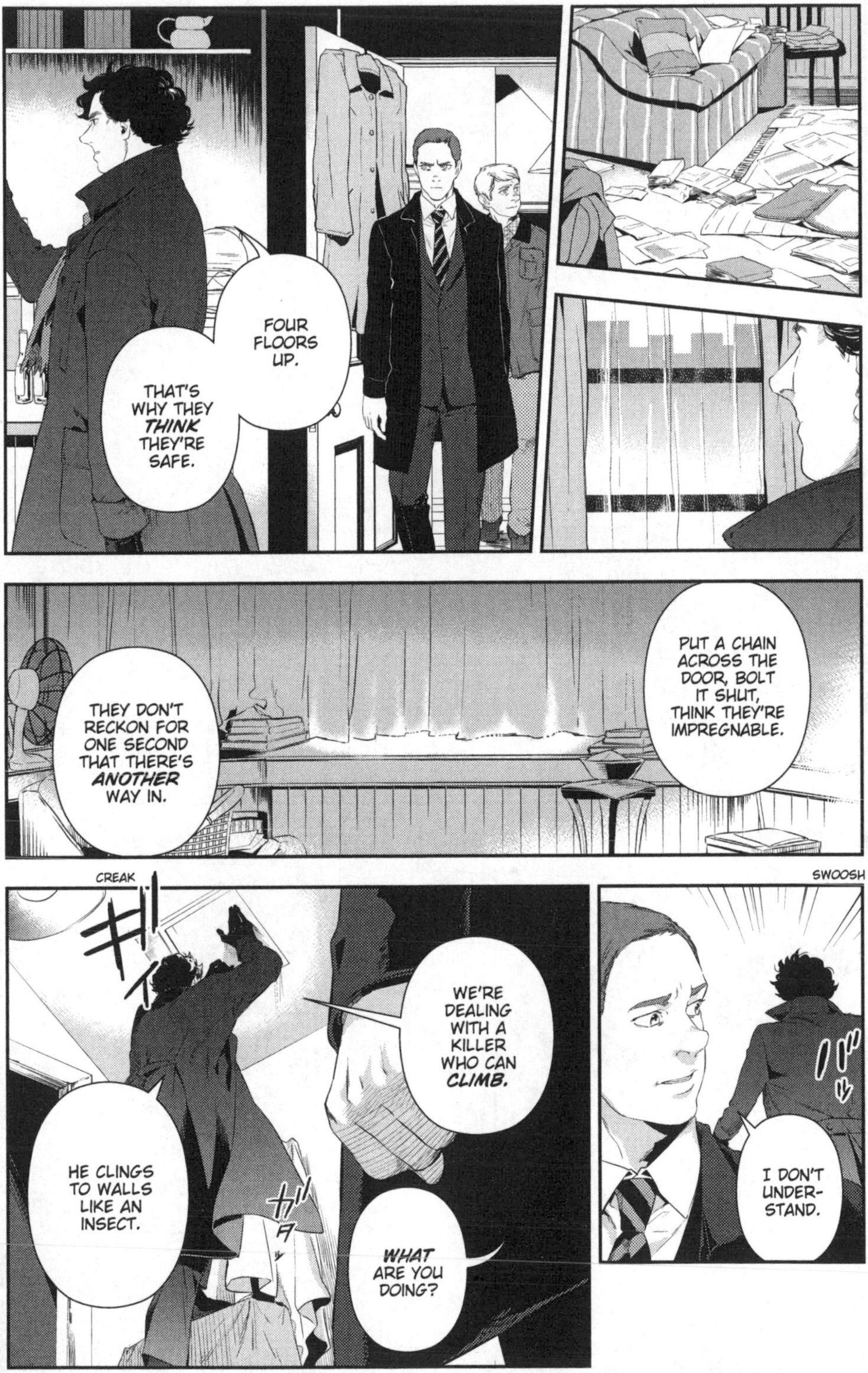
FOUR FLOORS UP.
THAT'S WHY THEY ***THINK*** THEY'RE SAFE.
PUT A CHAIN ACROSS THE DOOR, BOLT IT SHUT, THINK THEY'RE IMPREGNABLE.
THEY DON'T RECKON FOR ONE SECOND THAT THERE'S ***ANOTHER*** WAY IN.
SWOOSH
I DON'T UNDER-STAND.
CREAK
WE'RE DEALING WITH A KILLER WHO CAN ***CLIMB.***
HE CLINGS TO WALLS LIKE AN INSECT.
WHAT ARE YOU DOING?
CLATTER

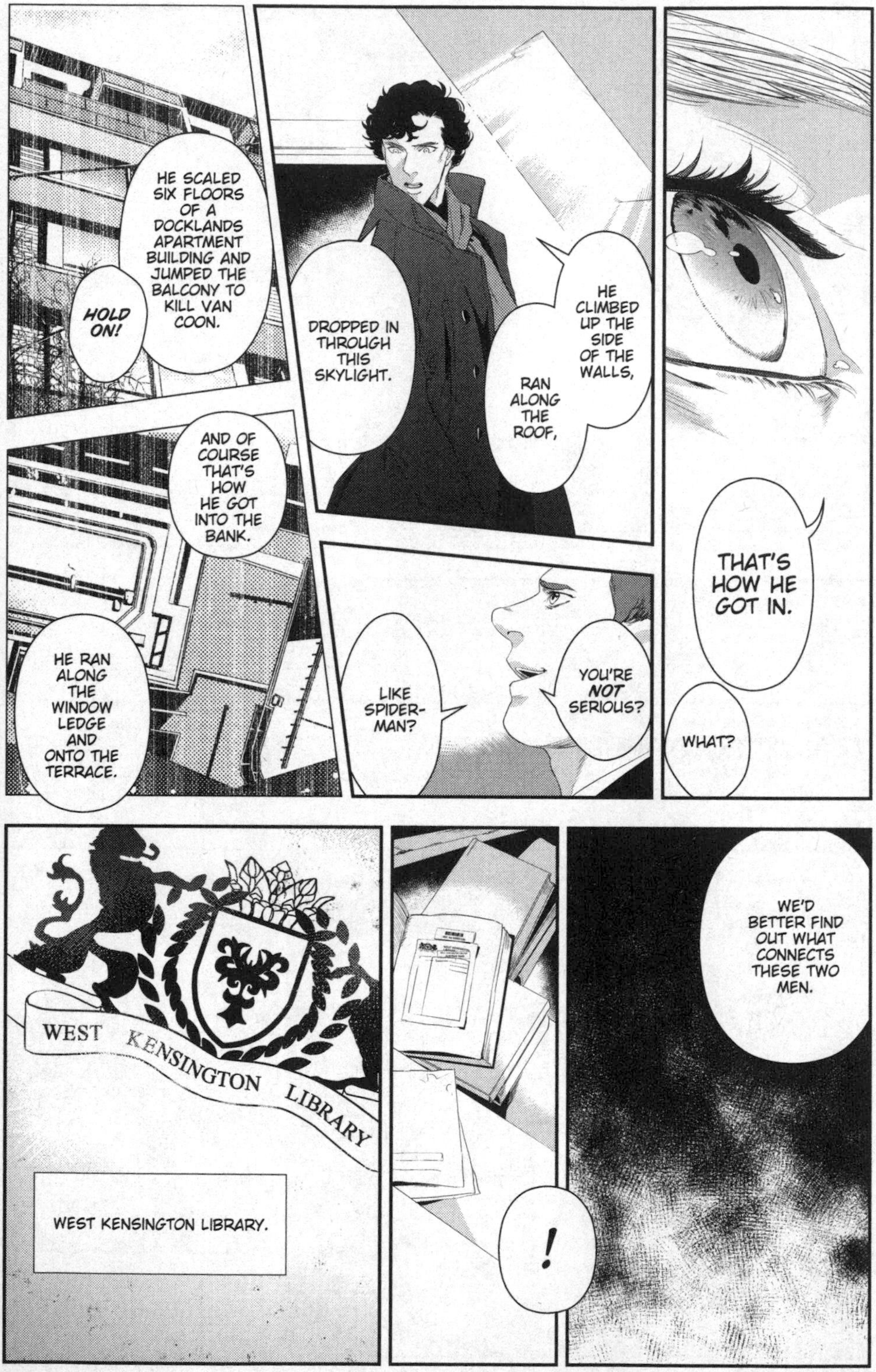
THAT'S HOW HE GOT IN.
WHAT?
HE CLIMBED UP THE SIDE OF THE WALLS,
RAN ALONG THE ROOF,
DROPPED IN THROUGH THIS SKYLIGHT.
YOU'RE *NOT* SERIOUS?
LIKE SPIDER-MAN?
HE SCALED SIX FLOORS OF A DOCKLANDS APARTMENT BUILDING AND JUMPED THE BALCONY TO KILL VAN COON.
HOLD ON!
AND OF COURSE THAT'S HOW HE GOT INTO THE BANK.
HE RAN ALONG THE WINDOW LEDGE AND ONTO THE TERRACE.
WE'D BETTER FIND OUT WHAT CONNECTS THESE TWO MEN.
!
WEST KENSINGTON LIBRARY
WEST KENSINGTON LIBRARY.

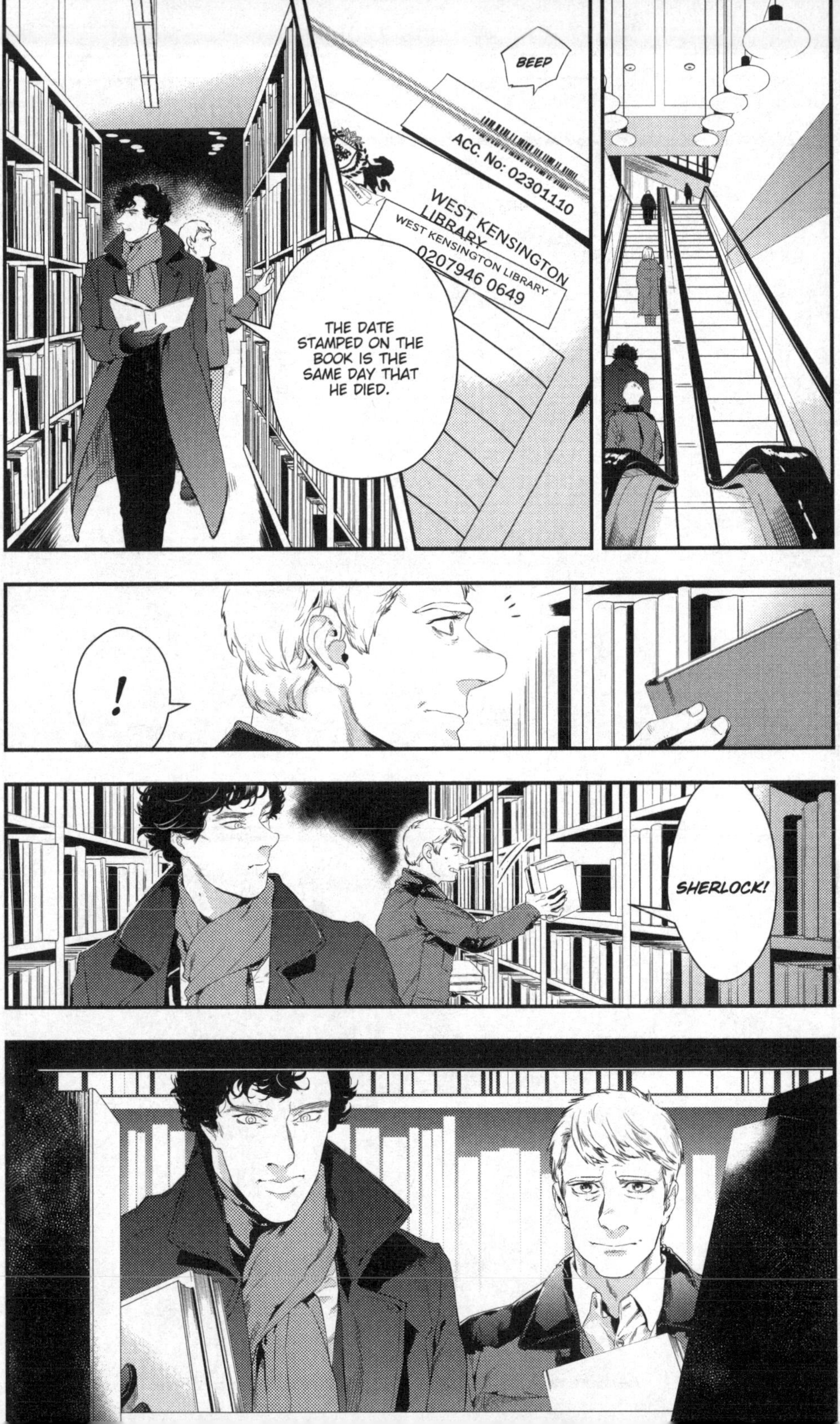
BEEP
ACC. No: 02301110
WEST KENSINGTON LIBRARY
WEST KENSINGTON LIBRARY
0207946 0649
THE DATE STAMPED ON THE BOOK IS THE SAME DAY THAT HE DIED.
!
SHERLOCK!

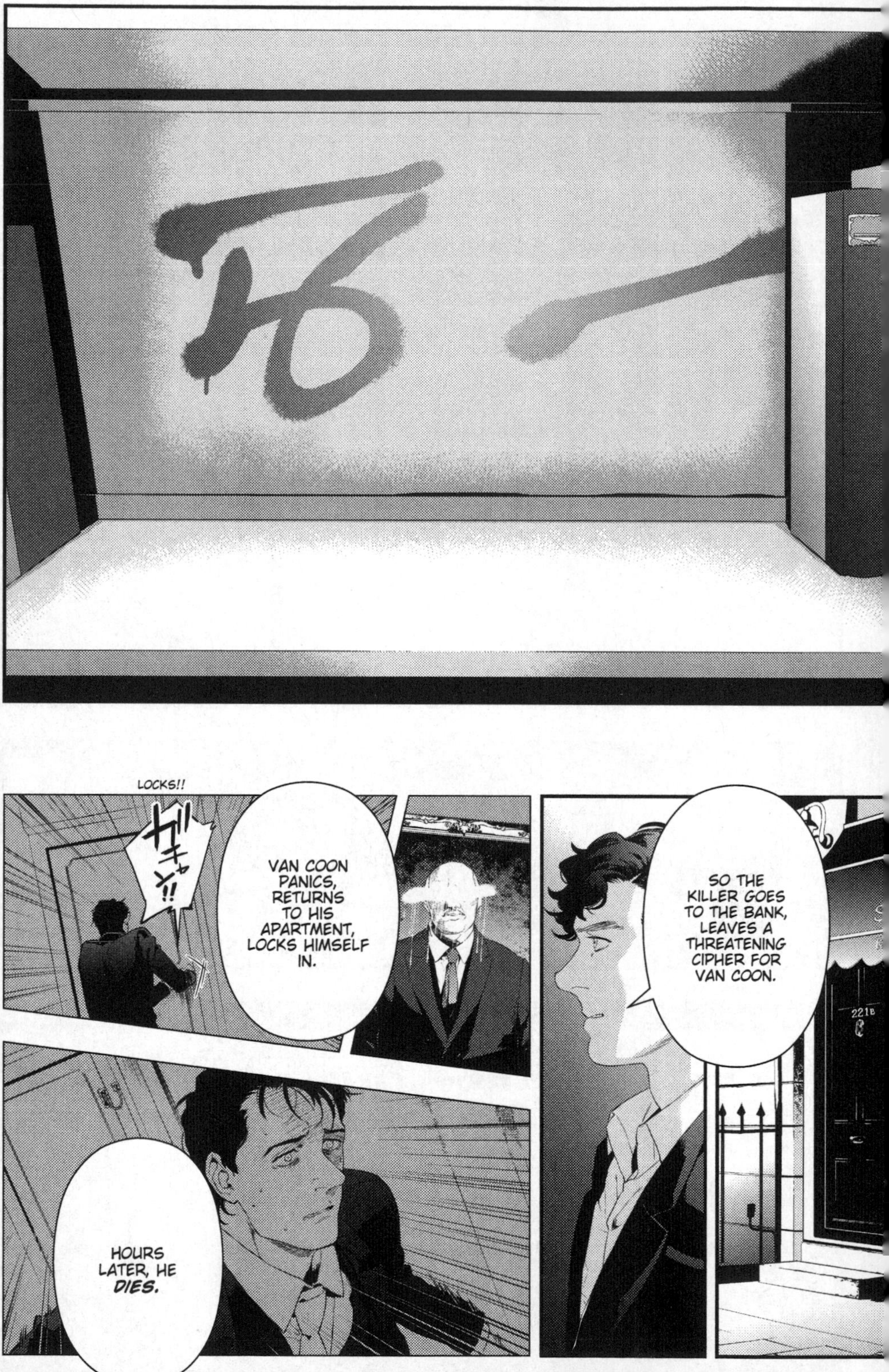
SO THE KILLER GOES TO THE BANK, LEAVES A THREATENING CIPHER FOR VAN COON.
LOCKS!!
VAN COON PANICS, RETURNS TO HIS APARTMENT, LOCKS HIMSELF IN.
HOURS LATER, HE *DIES.*

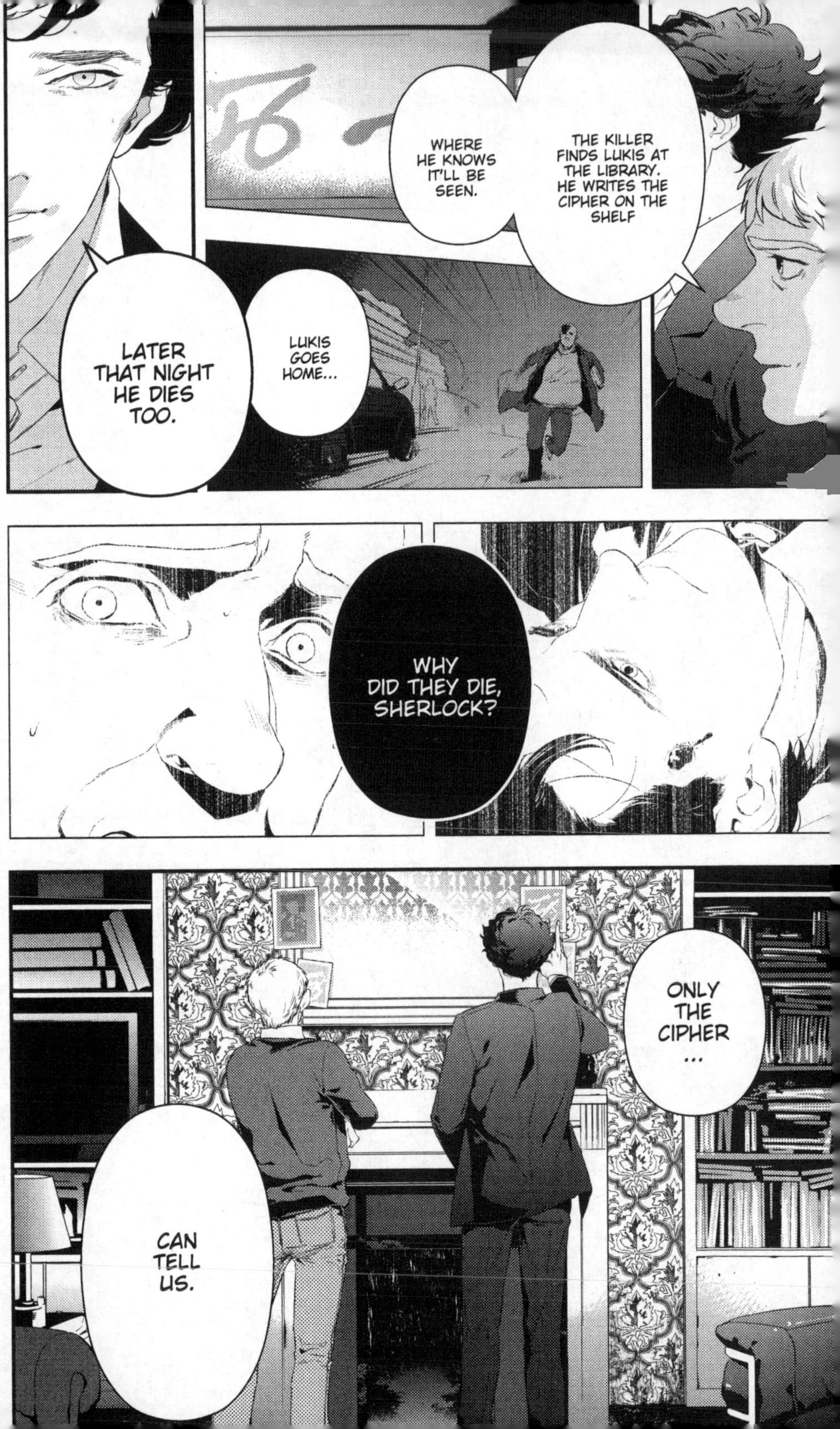
THE KILLER FINDS LUKIS AT THE LIBRARY. HE WRITES THE CIPHER ON THE SHELF
WHERE HE KNOWS IT'LL BE SEEN.
LUKIS GOES HOME...
LATER THAT NIGHT HE DIES TOO.
WHY DID THEY DIE, SHERLOCK?
ONLY THE CIPHER ...
CAN TELL US.

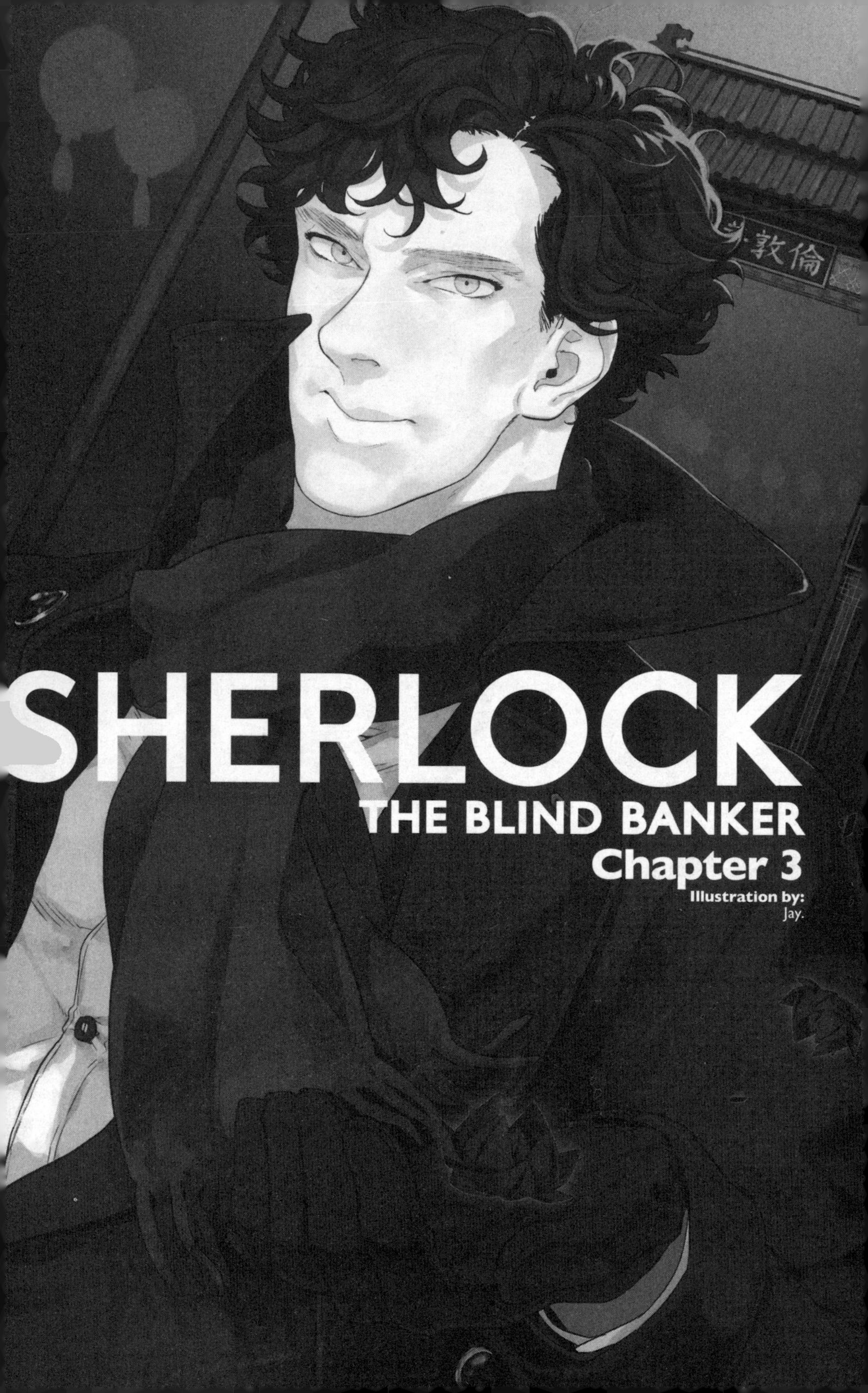

SHERLOCK

THE BLIND BANKER

Chapter 3

Illustration by:
Jay.

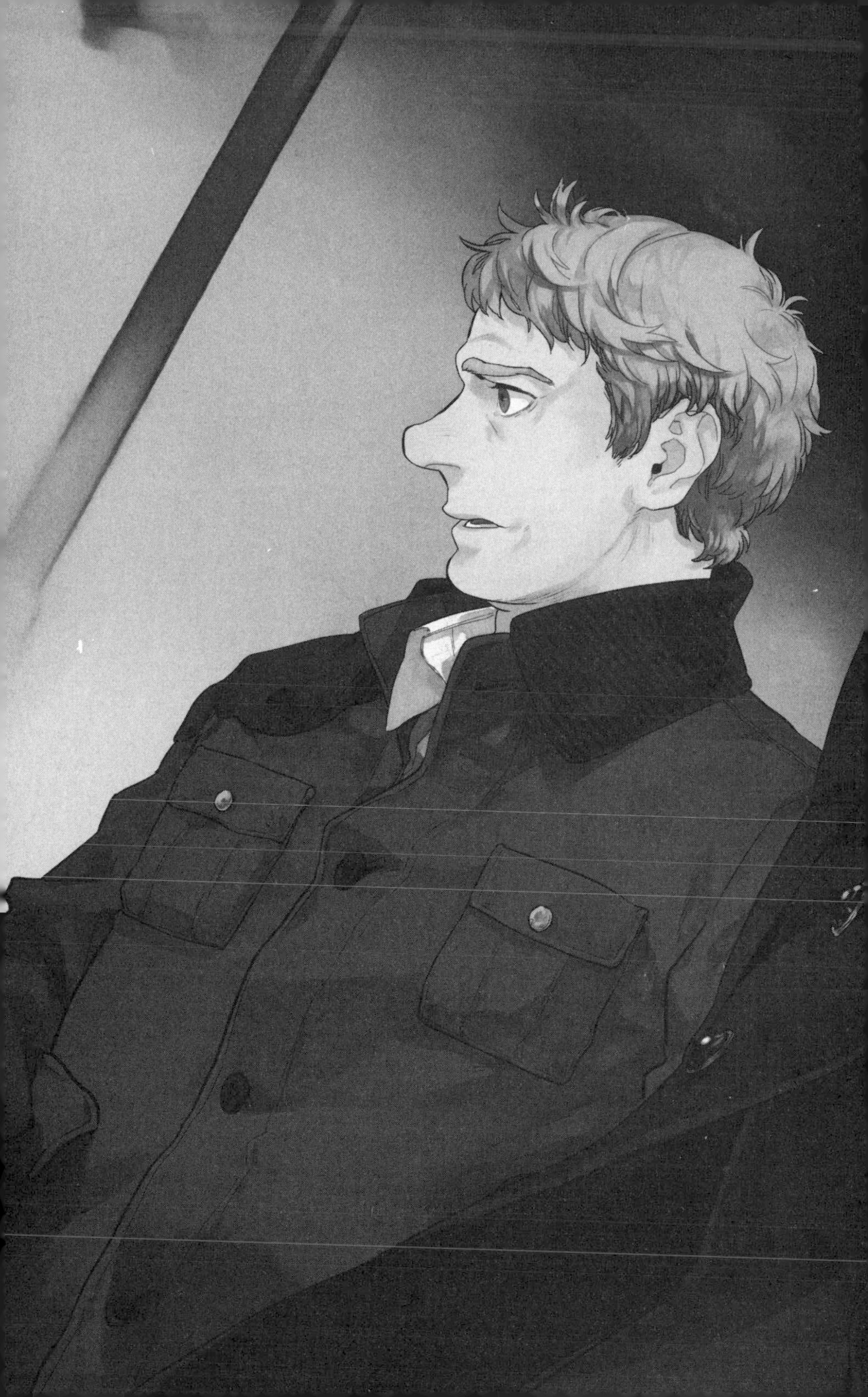

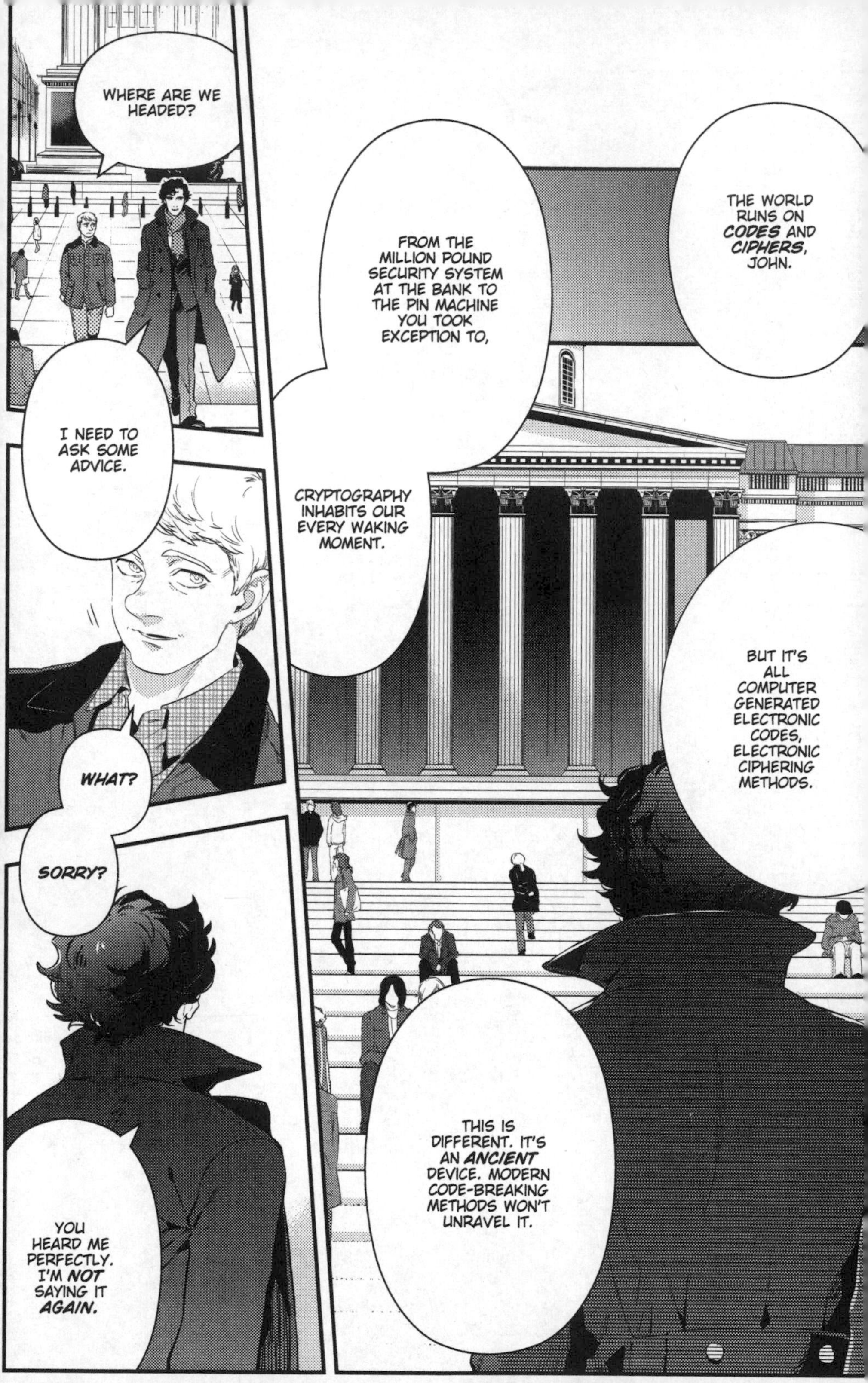
THE WORLD RUNS ON ***CODES*** AND ***CIPHERS***, JOHN.
FROM THE MILLION POUND SECURITY SYSTEM AT THE BANK TO THE PIN MACHINE YOU TOOK EXCEPTION TO,
CRYPTOGRAPHY INHABITS OUR EVERY WAKING MOMENT.
BUT IT'S ALL COMPUTER GENERATED ELECTRONIC CODES, ELECTRONIC CIPHERING METHODS.
THIS IS DIFFERENT. IT'S AN ***ANCIENT*** DEVICE. MODERN CODE-BREAKING METHODS WON'T UNRAVEL IT.
WHERE ARE WE HEADED?
I NEED TO ASK SOME ADVICE.
WHAT?
SORRY?
YOU HEARD ME PERFECTLY. I'M ***NOT*** SAYING IT ***AGAIN.***

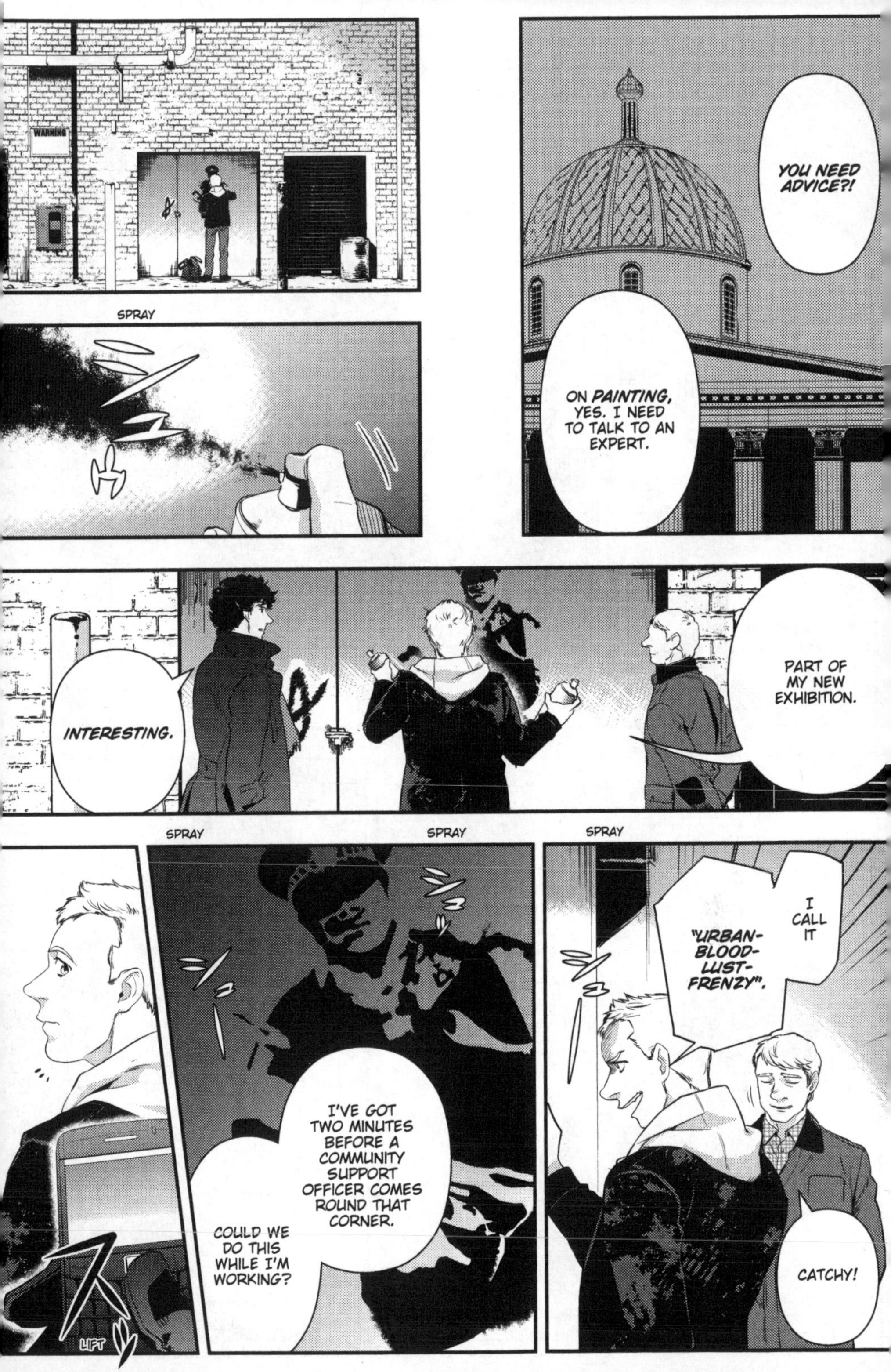
YOU NEED ADVICE?!
ON PAINTING, YES. I NEED TO TALK TO AN EXPERT.
WARNING
SPRAY
PART OF MY NEW EXHIBITION.
INTERESTING.
SPRAY
I CALL IT
"URBAN-BLOOD-LUST-FRENZY".
CATCHY!
SPRAY
SPRAY
I'VE GOT TWO MINUTES BEFORE A COMMUNITY SUPPORT OFFICER COMES ROUND THAT CORNER.
COULD WE DO THIS WHILE I'M WORKING?
LIFT

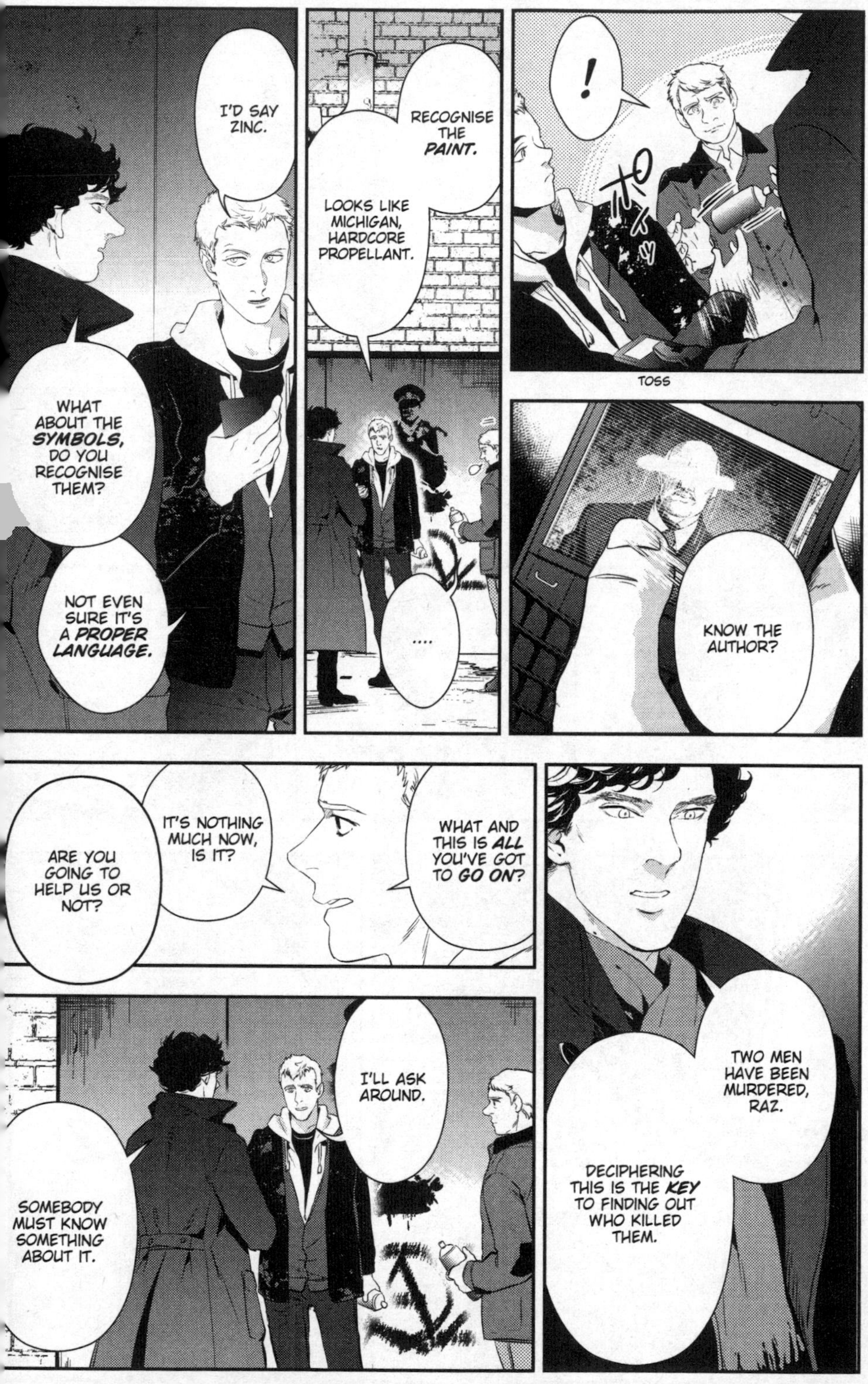
!
TOSS
KNOW THE AUTHOR?
RECOGNISE THE *PAINT.*
LOOKS LIKE MICHIGAN, HARDCORE PROPELLANT.
....
I'D SAY ZINC.
WHAT ABOUT THE *SYMBOLS,* DO YOU RECOGNISE THEM?
NOT EVEN SURE IT'S A *PROPER LANGUAGE.*
TWO MEN HAVE BEEN MURDERED, RAZ.
DECIPHERING THIS IS THE *KEY* TO FINDING OUT WHO KILLED THEM.
WHAT AND THIS IS *ALL* YOU'VE GOT TO *GO ON*?
IT'S NOTHING MUCH NOW, IS IT?
ARE YOU GOING TO HELP US OR NOT?
I'LL ASK AROUND.
SOMEBODY MUST KNOW SOMETHING ABOUT IT.

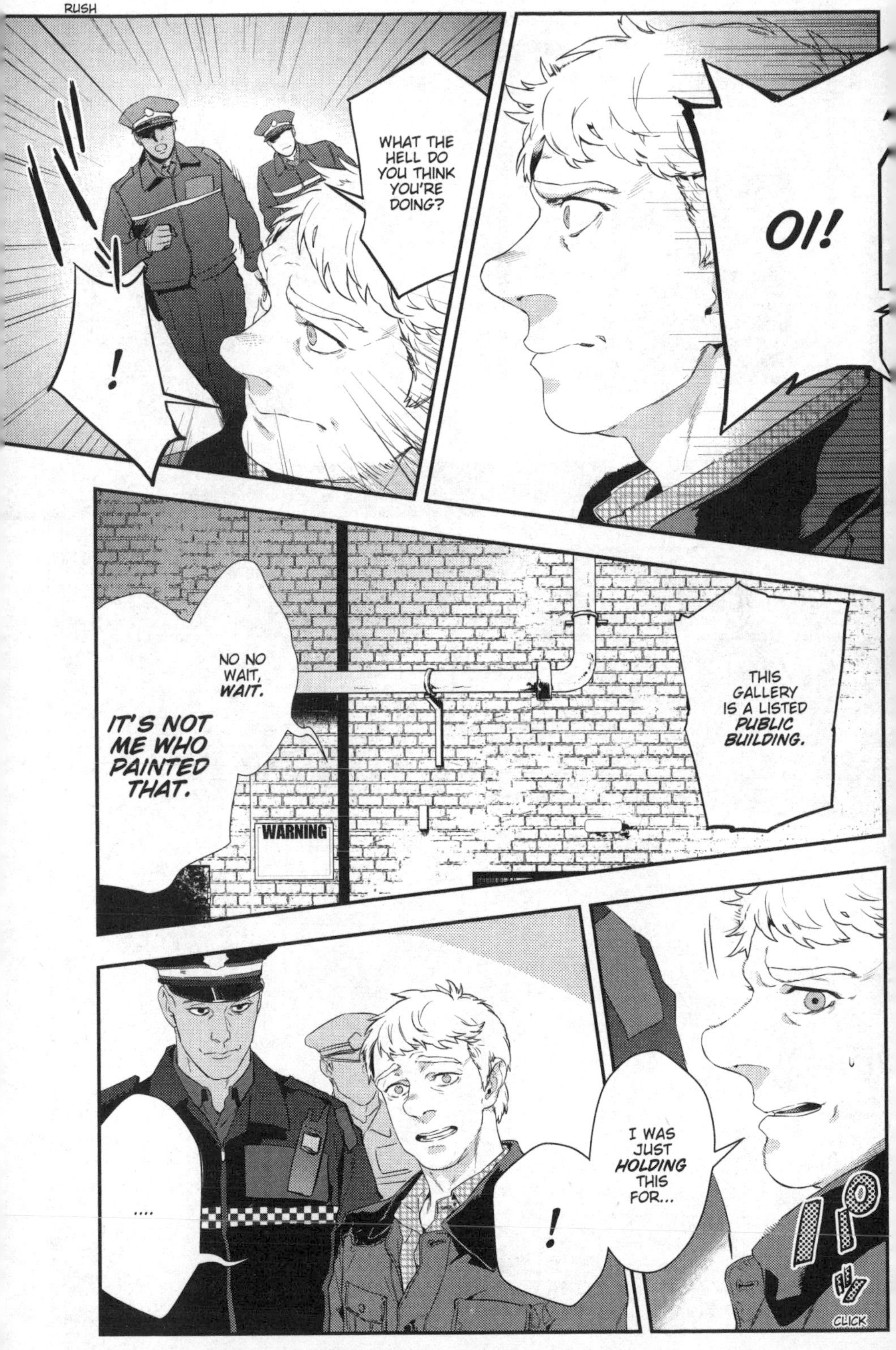

OI!
WHAT THE HELL DO YOU THINK YOU'RE DOING?
!
THIS GALLERY IS A LISTED PUBLIC BUILDING.
NO NO WAIT, WAIT.
IT'S NOT ME WHO PAINTED THAT.
WARNING
I WAS JUST HOLDING THIS FOR...
!?
CLICK
!
....

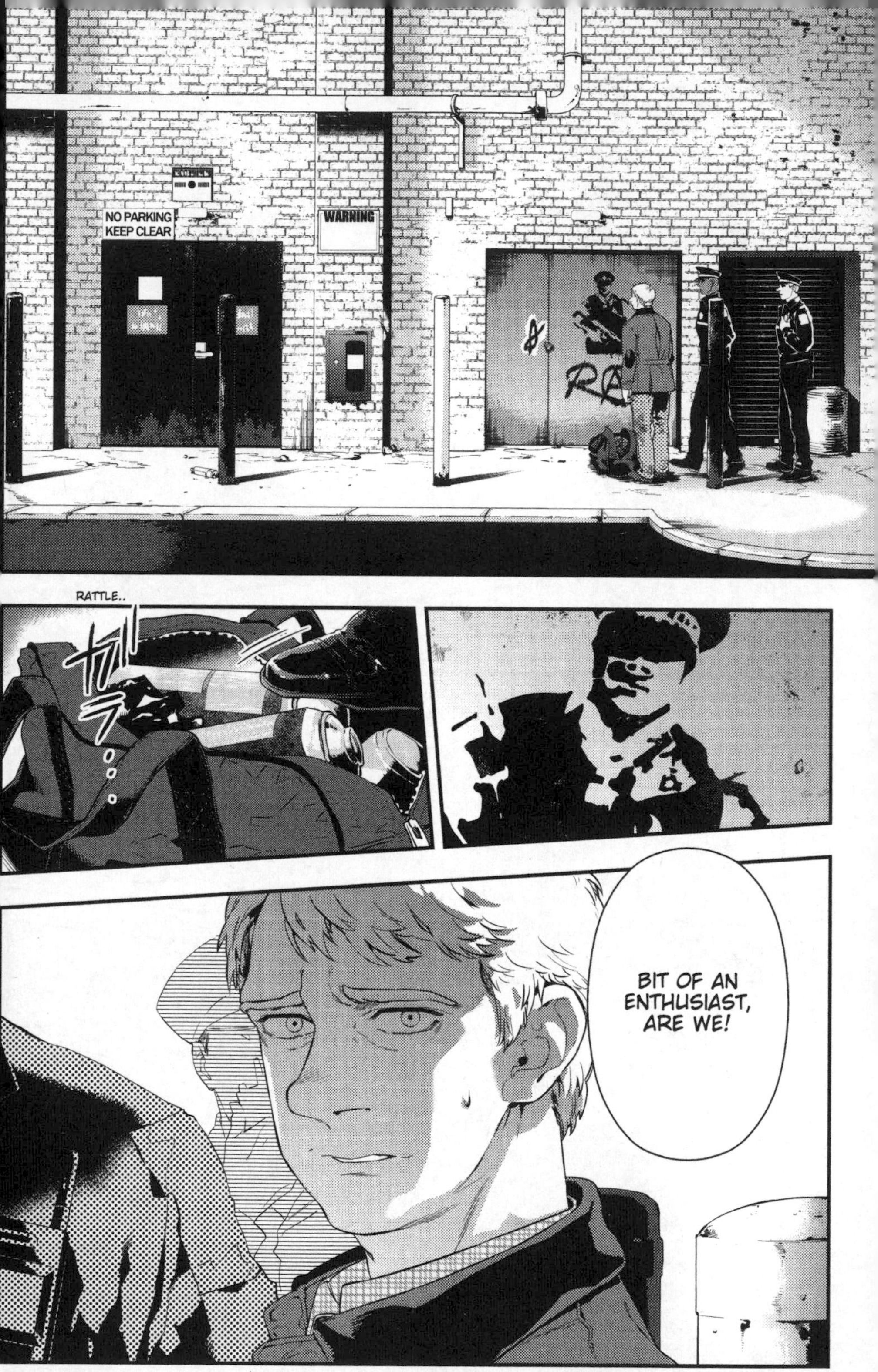
NO PARKING
KEEP CLEAR
WARNING
RATTLE..
BIT OF AN ENTHUSIAST, ARE WE!

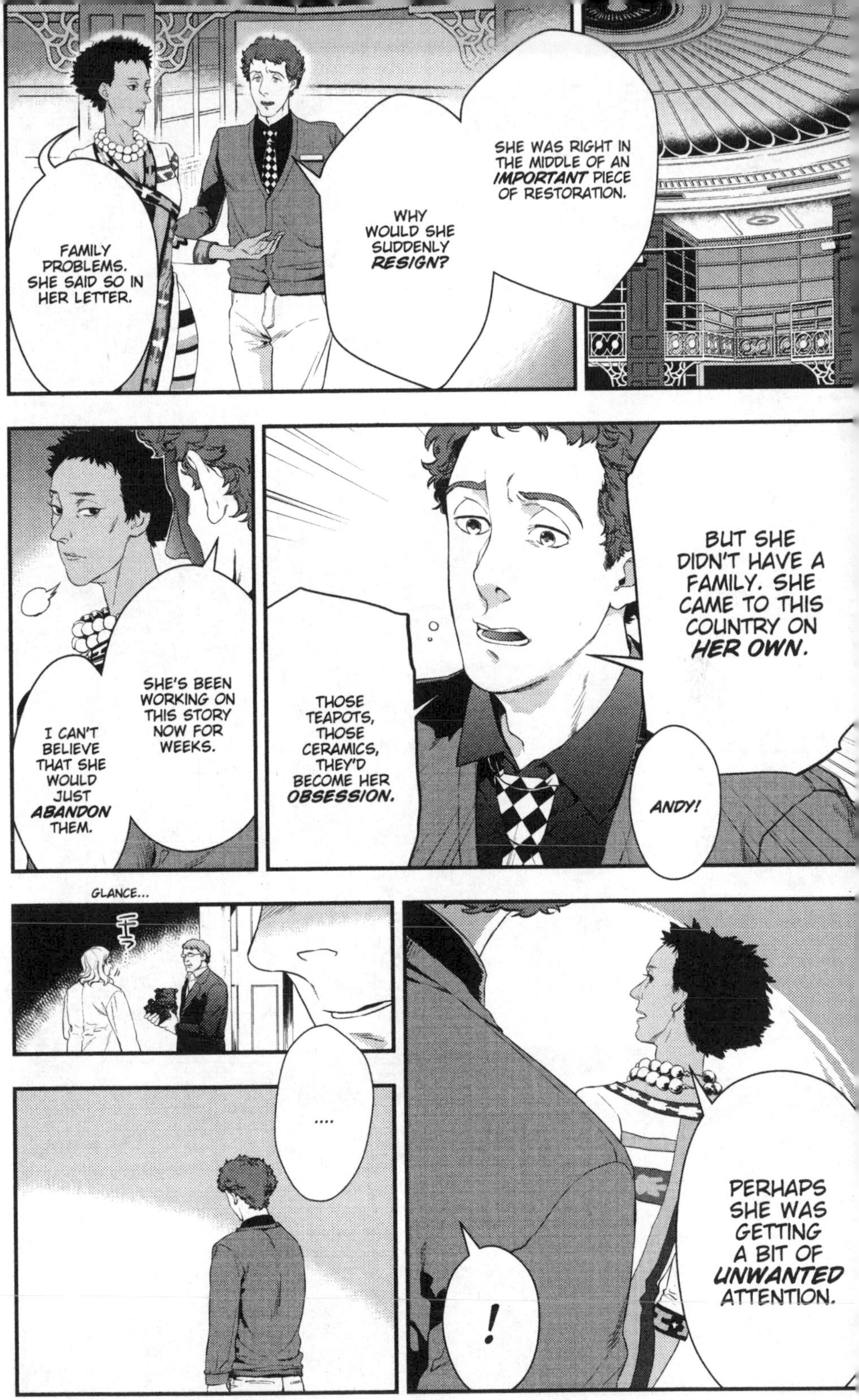
SHE WAS RIGHT IN THE MIDDLE OF AN *IMPORTANT* PIECE OF RESTORATION.
WHY WOULD SHE SUDDENLY *RESIGN?*
FAMILY PROBLEMS. SHE SAID SO IN HER LETTER.
BUT SHE DIDN'T HAVE A FAMILY. SHE CAME TO THIS COUNTRY ON *HER OWN.*
THOSE TEAPOTS, THOSE CERAMICS, THEY'D BECOME HER *OBSESSION.*
ANDY!
SHE'S BEEN WORKING ON THIS STORY NOW FOR WEEKS.
I CAN'T BELIEVE THAT SHE WOULD JUST *ABANDON* THEM.
PERHAPS SHE WAS GETTING A BIT OF *UNWANTED* ATTENTION.
!
GLANCE...
....

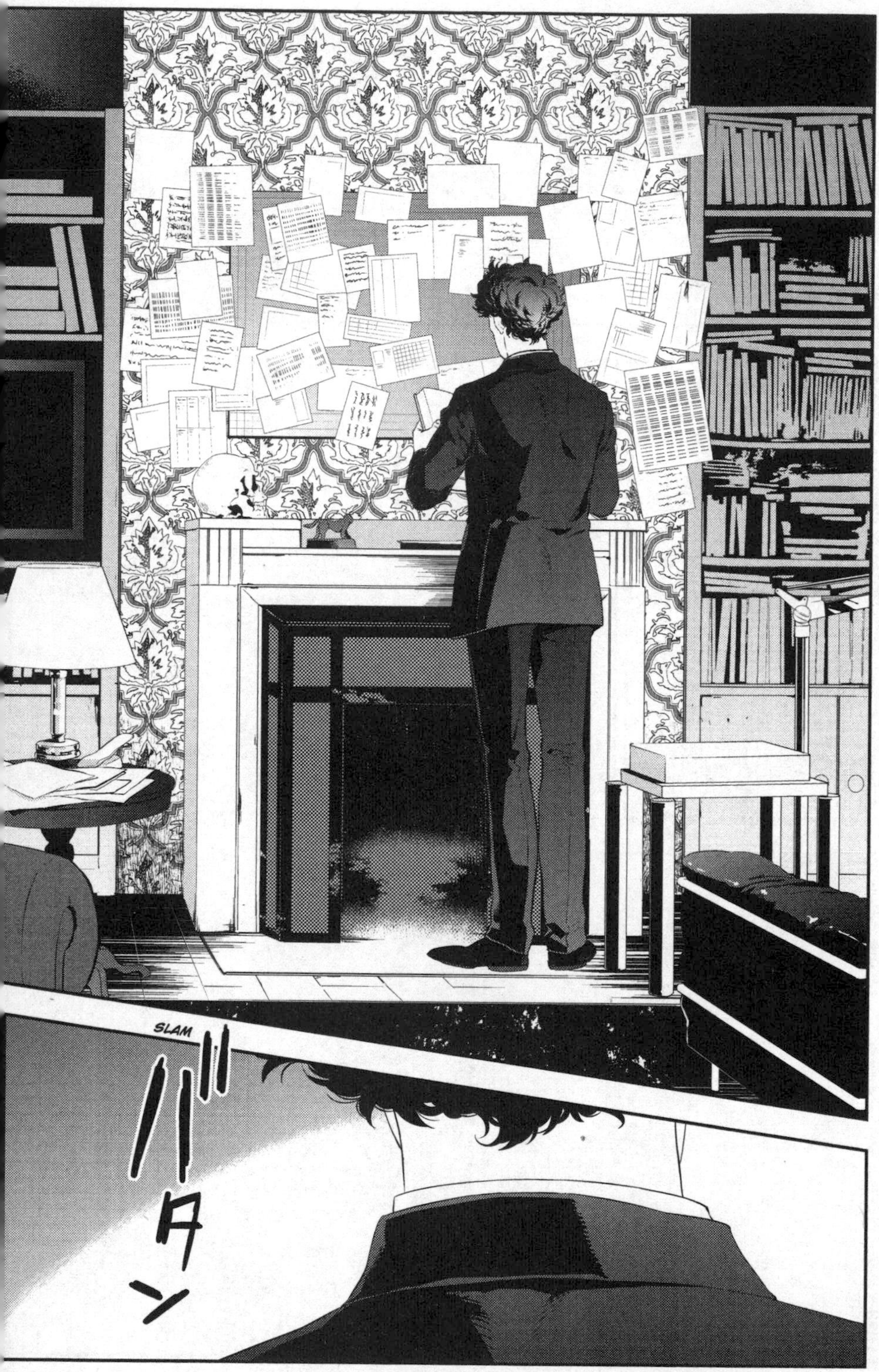
SLAM
バタン

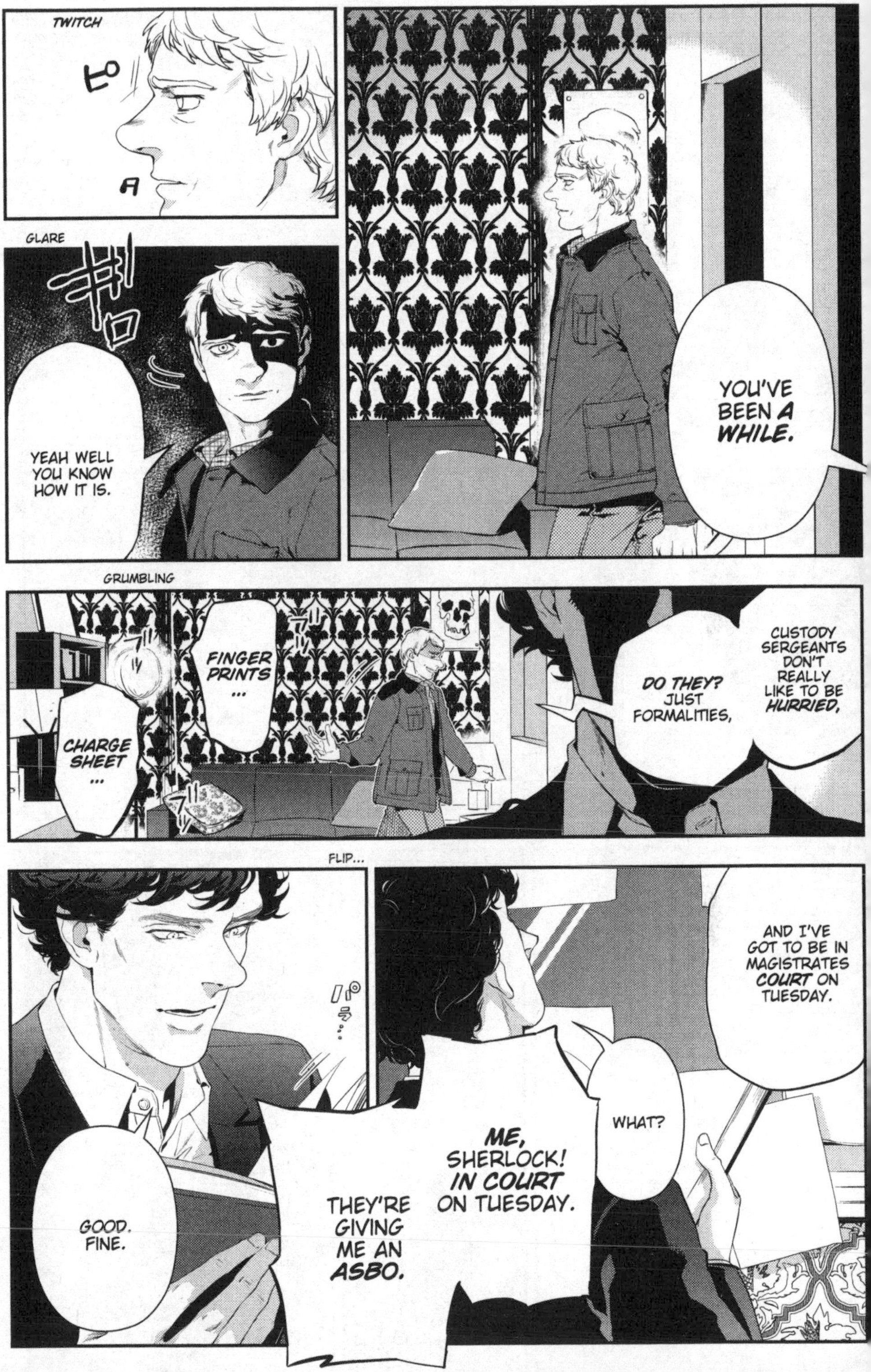
YOU'VE BEEN A WHILE.
TWITCH
GLARE
YEAH WELL YOU KNOW HOW IT IS.
GRUMBLING
CUSTODY SERGEANTS DON'T REALLY LIKE TO BE HURRIED,
DO THEY? JUST FORMALITIES,
FINGER PRINTS ...
CHARGE SHEET ...
AND I'VE GOT TO BE IN MAGISTRATES COURT ON TUESDAY.
WHAT?
ME, SHERLOCK! IN COURT ON TUESDAY.
THEY'RE GIVING ME AN ASBO.
FLIP...
GOOD. FINE.

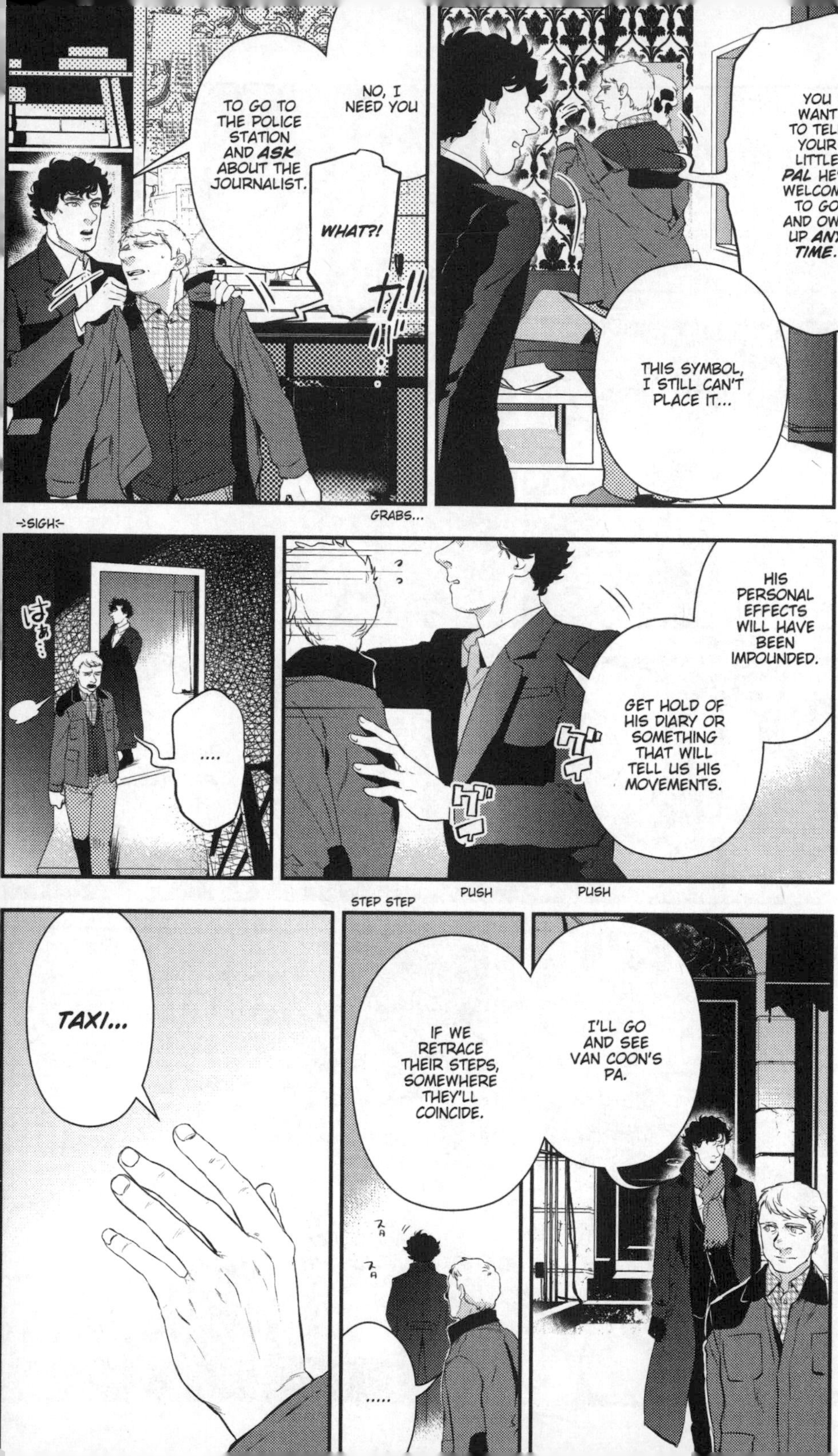
YOU WANT TO TELL YOUR LITTLE PAL HE'S WELCOME TO GO AND OWN UP ANY TIME.
THIS SYMBOL, I STILL CAN'T PLACE IT...
NO, I NEED YOU
TO GO TO THE POLICE STATION AND ASK ABOUT THE JOURNALIST.
WHAT?!
GRABS...
→SIGH←
HIS PERSONAL EFFECTS WILL HAVE BEEN IMPOUNDED.
GET HOLD OF HIS DIARY OR SOMETHING THAT WILL TELL US HIS MOVEMENTS.
グイ
グイ
PUSH
PUSH
はぁ…
....
I'LL GO AND SEE VAN COON'S PA.
IF WE RETRACE THEIR STEPS, SOMEWHERE THEY'LL COINCIDE.
.....
STEP STEP
TAXI...

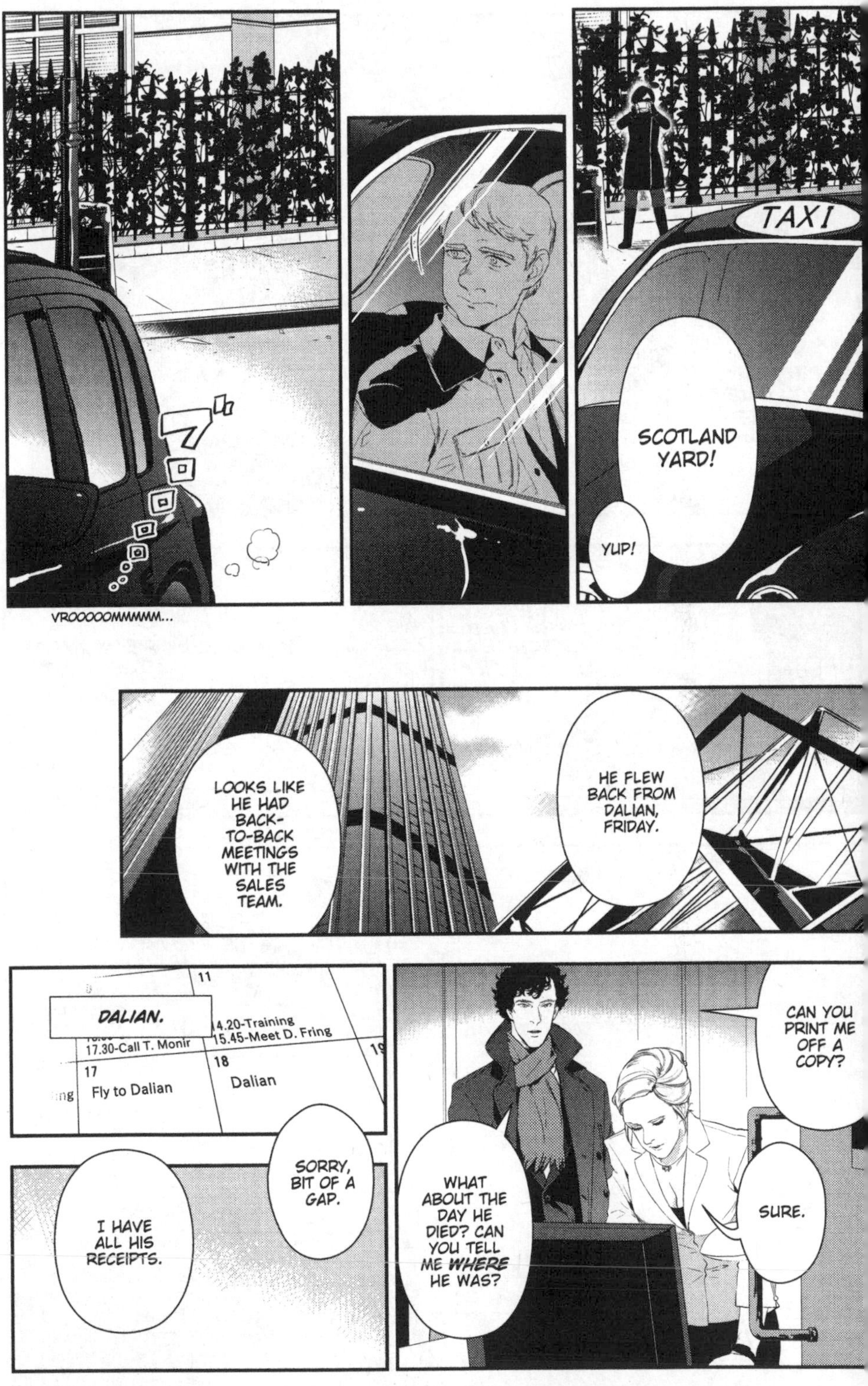
SCOTLAND YARD!
YUP!
VROOOOOMMMMM...
HE FLEW BACK FROM DALIAN, FRIDAY.
LOOKS LIKE HE HAD BACK-TO-BACK MEETINGS WITH THE SALES TEAM.
CAN YOU PRINT ME OFF A COPY?
SURE.
WHAT ABOUT THE DAY HE DIED? CAN YOU TELL ME *WHERE* HE WAS?
DALIAN.
11
14.20-Training
15.45-Meet D. Fring
17.30-Call T. Monir
17
Fly to Dalian
18
Dalian
SORRY, BIT OF A GAP.
I HAVE ALL HIS RECEIPTS.

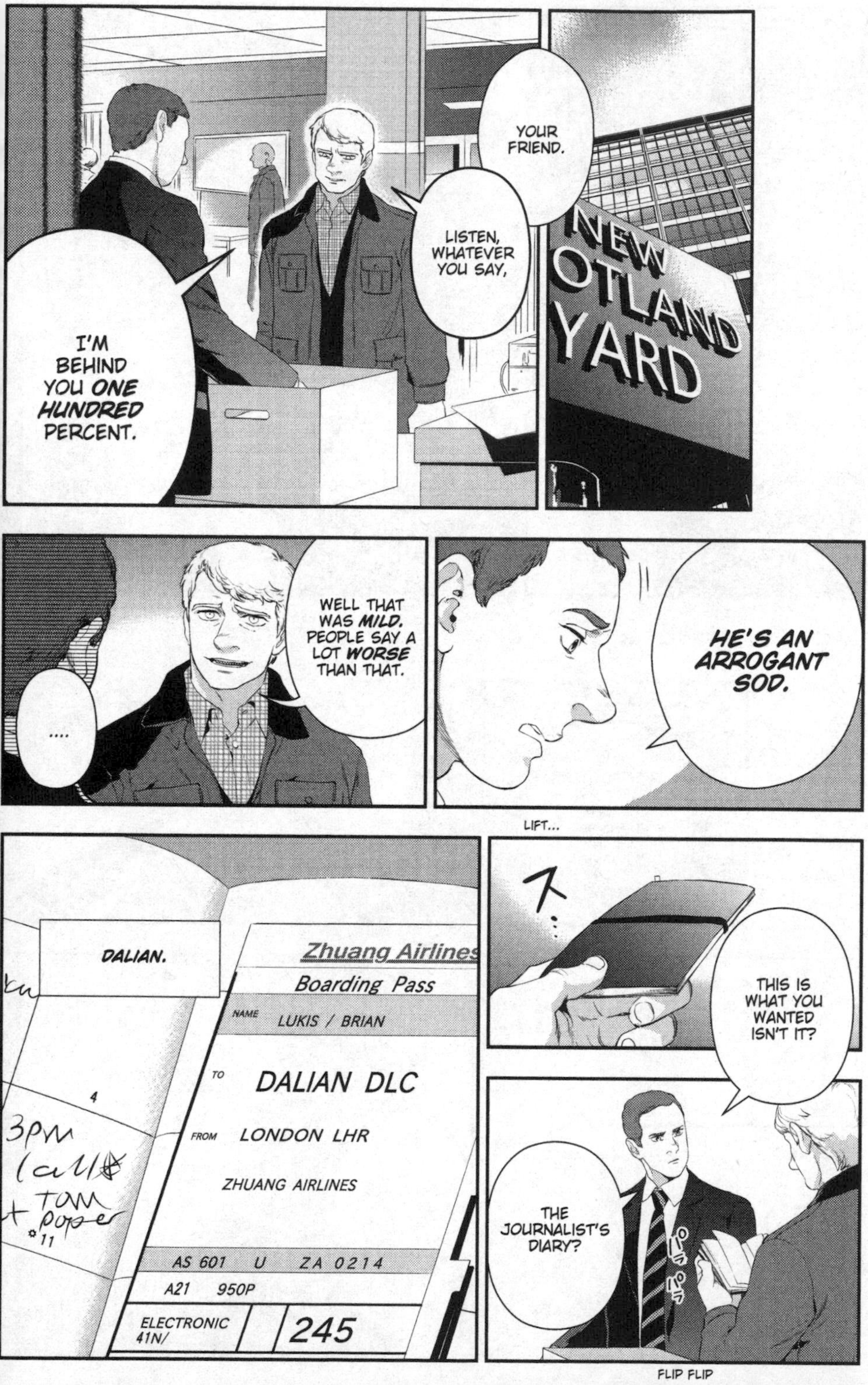

NEW
OTLAND
YARD
YOUR FRIEND.
LISTEN, WHATEVER YOU SAY,
I'M BEHIND YOU **ONE HUNDRED** PERCENT.
HE'S AN ARROGANT SOD.
WELL THAT WAS ***MILD.*** PEOPLE SAY A LOT ***WORSE*** THAN THAT.
....
LIFT...
ス
THIS IS WHAT YOU WANTED ISN'T IT?
THE JOURNALIST'S DIARY?
パラパラ
FLIP FLIP
DALIAN.
Zhuang Airlines
Boarding Pass
NAME LUKIS / BRIAN
TO DALIAN DLC
FROM LONDON LHR
ZHUANG AIRLINES
AS 601 U ZA 0214
A21 950P
ELECTRONIC 41N/
245
4
3pm
call
TOM
paper

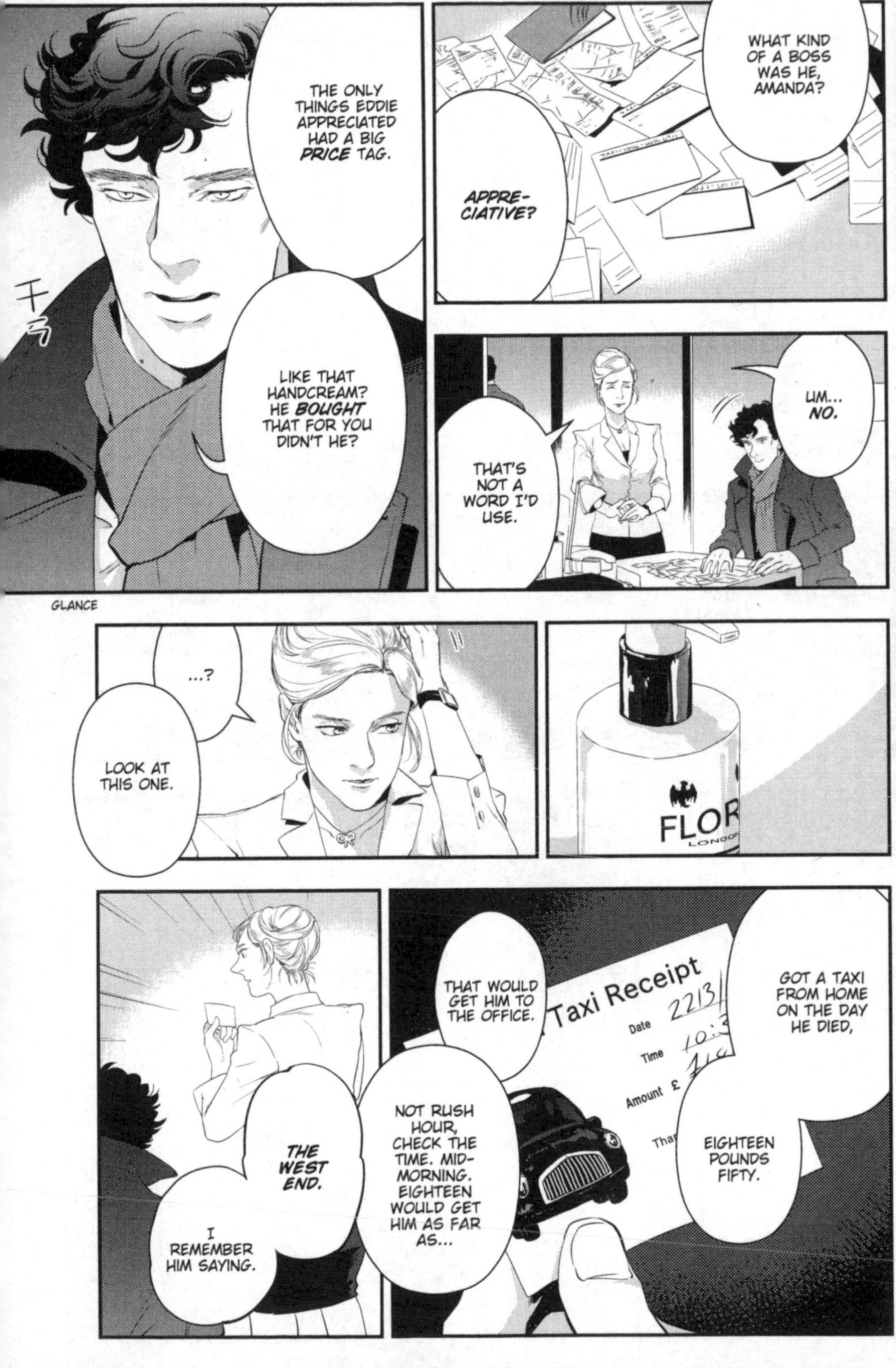
WHAT KIND OF A BOSS WAS HE, AMANDA?
APPRE-CIATIVE?
UM... NO.
THAT'S NOT A WORD I'D USE.
THE ONLY THINGS EDDIE APPRECIATED HAD A BIG PRICE TAG.
LIKE THAT HANDCREAM? HE BOUGHT THAT FOR YOU DIDN'T HE?
チラ
GLANCE
FLOR
...?
LOOK AT THIS ONE.
GOT A TAXI FROM HOME ON THE DAY HE DIED,
EIGHTEEN POUNDS FIFTY.
THAT WOULD GET HIM TO THE OFFICE.
Taxi Receipt
Date
Time
Amount £
NOT RUSH HOUR, CHECK THE TIME. MID-MORNING. EIGHTEEN WOULD GET HIM AS FAR AS...
THE WEST END.
I REMEMBER HIM SAYING.

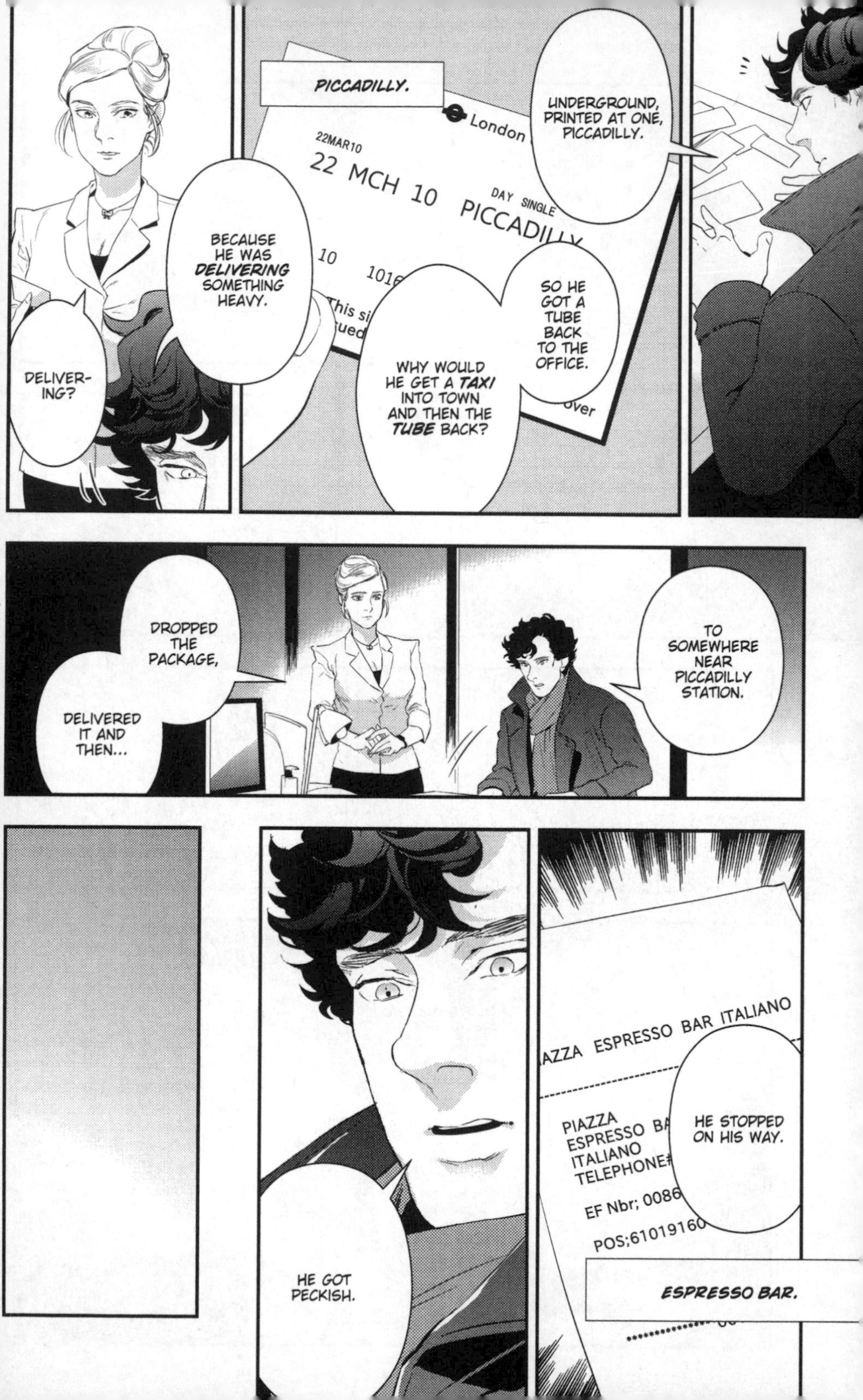
PICCADILLY.
London
22MAR10
22 MCH 10 PICCADILLY
DAY SINGLE
UNDERGROUND, PRINTED AT ONE, PICCADILLY.
SO HE GOT A TUBE BACK TO THE OFFICE.
WHY WOULD HE GET A *TAXI* INTO TOWN AND THEN THE *TUBE* BACK?
BECAUSE HE WAS *DELIVERING* SOMETHING HEAVY.
DELIVERING?
TO SOMEWHERE NEAR PICCADILLY STATION.
DROPPED THE PACKAGE,
DELIVERED IT AND THEN...
IAZZA ESPRESSO BAR ITALIANO
HE STOPPED ON HIS WAY.
PIAZZA
ESPRESSO BA
ITALIANO
TELEPHONE#
EF Nbr; 0086
POS;61019160
ESPRESSO BAR.
HE GOT PECKISH.

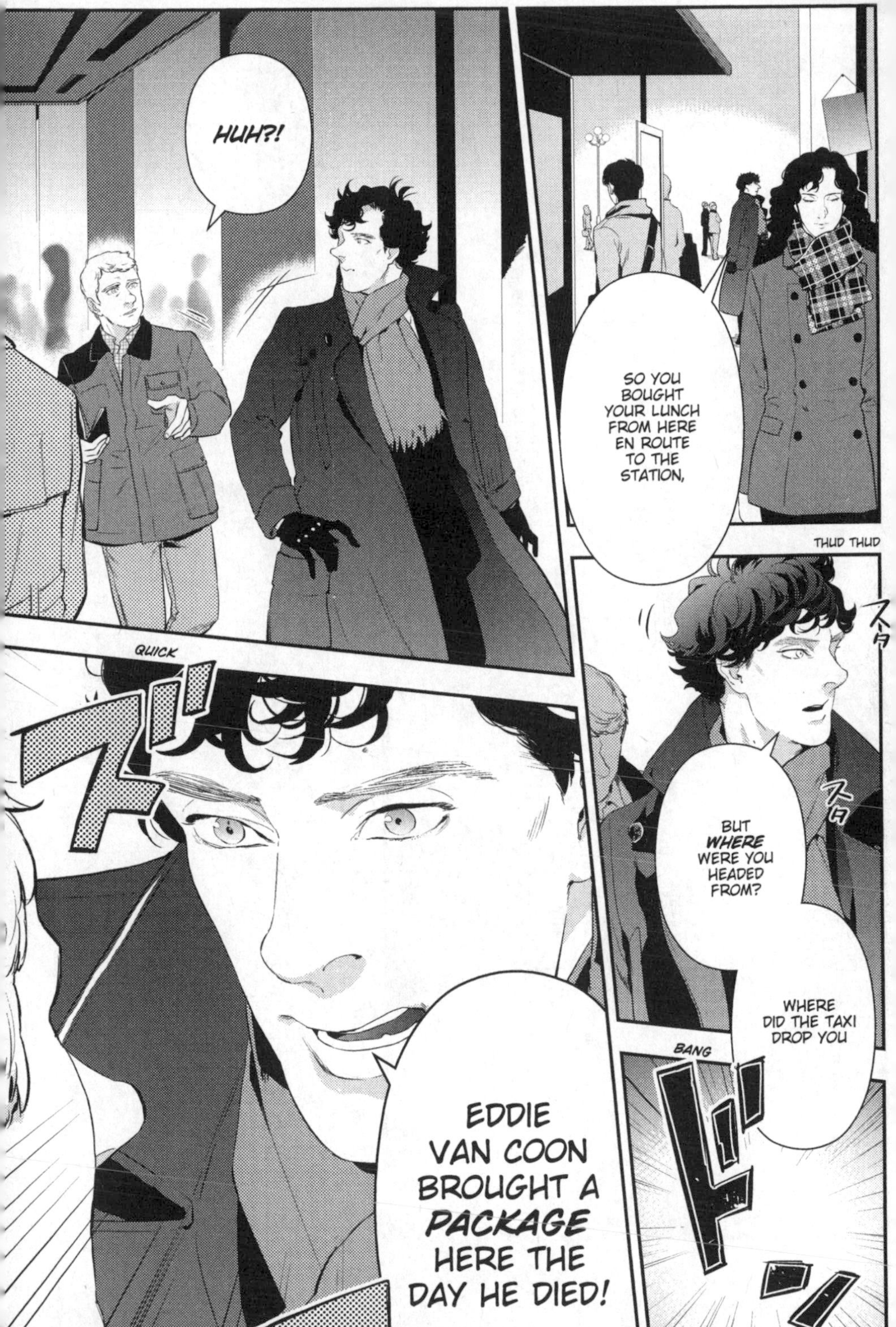
SO YOU BOUGHT YOUR LUNCH FROM HERE EN ROUTE TO THE STATION,
HUH?!
THUD THUD
BUT *WHERE* WERE YOU HEADED FROM?
WHERE DID THE TAXI DROP YOU
BANG
QUICK
EDDIE VAN COON BROUGHT A *PACKAGE* HERE THE DAY HE DIED!

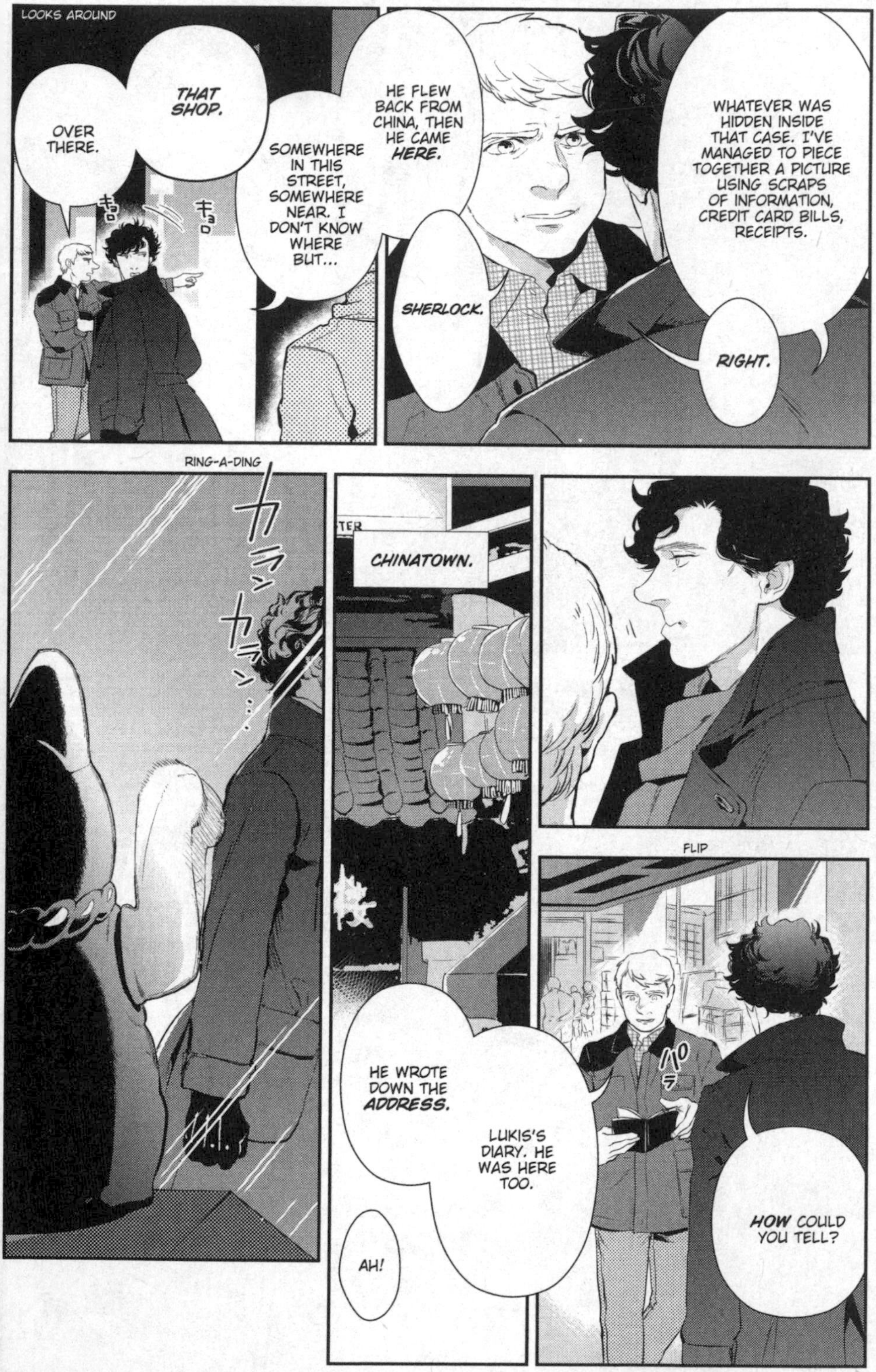
WHATEVER WAS HIDDEN INSIDE THAT CASE. I'VE MANAGED TO PIECE TOGETHER A PICTURE USING SCRAPS OF INFORMATION, CREDIT CARD BILLS, RECEIPTS.
HE FLEW BACK FROM CHINA, THEN HE CAME HERE.
RIGHT.
SHERLOCK.
SOMEWHERE IN THIS STREET, SOMEWHERE NEAR. I DON'T KNOW WHERE BUT...
THAT SHOP.
OVER THERE.
LOOKS AROUND
キョロキョロ
FLIP
パラ
HOW COULD YOU TELL?
LUKIS'S DIARY. HE WAS HERE TOO.
HE WROTE DOWN THE ADDRESS.
AH!
CHINATOWN.
RING-A-DING
カランカラン…

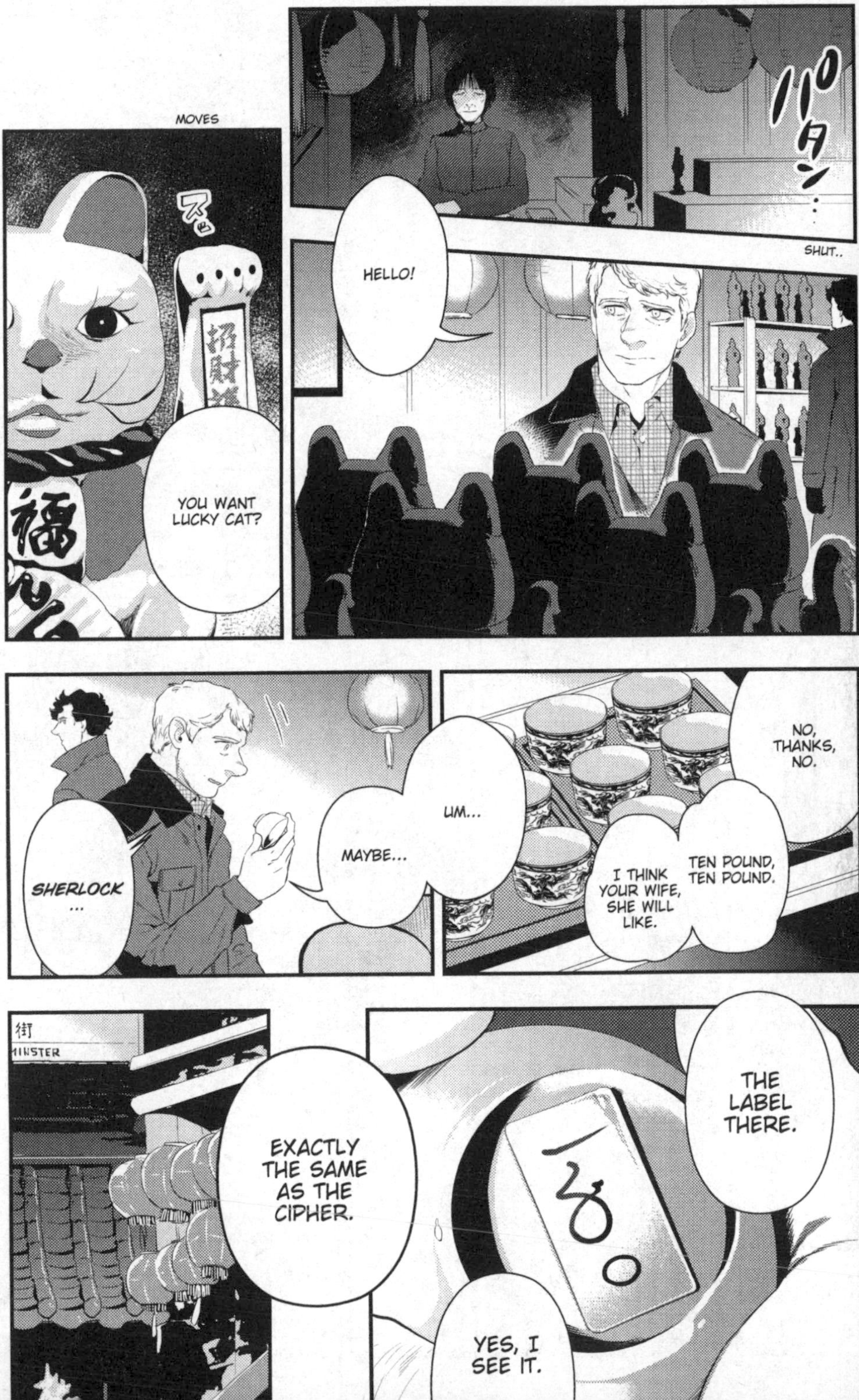
パタン…
SHUT..
HELLO!
MOVES
ス
YOU WANT LUCKY CAT?
NO, THANKS, NO.
TEN POUND, TEN POUND.
I THINK YOUR WIFE, SHE WILL LIKE.
UM...
MAYBE...
SHERLOCK...
THE LABEL THERE.
YES, I SEE IT.
EXACTLY THE SAME AS THE CIPHER.
街
MINSTER

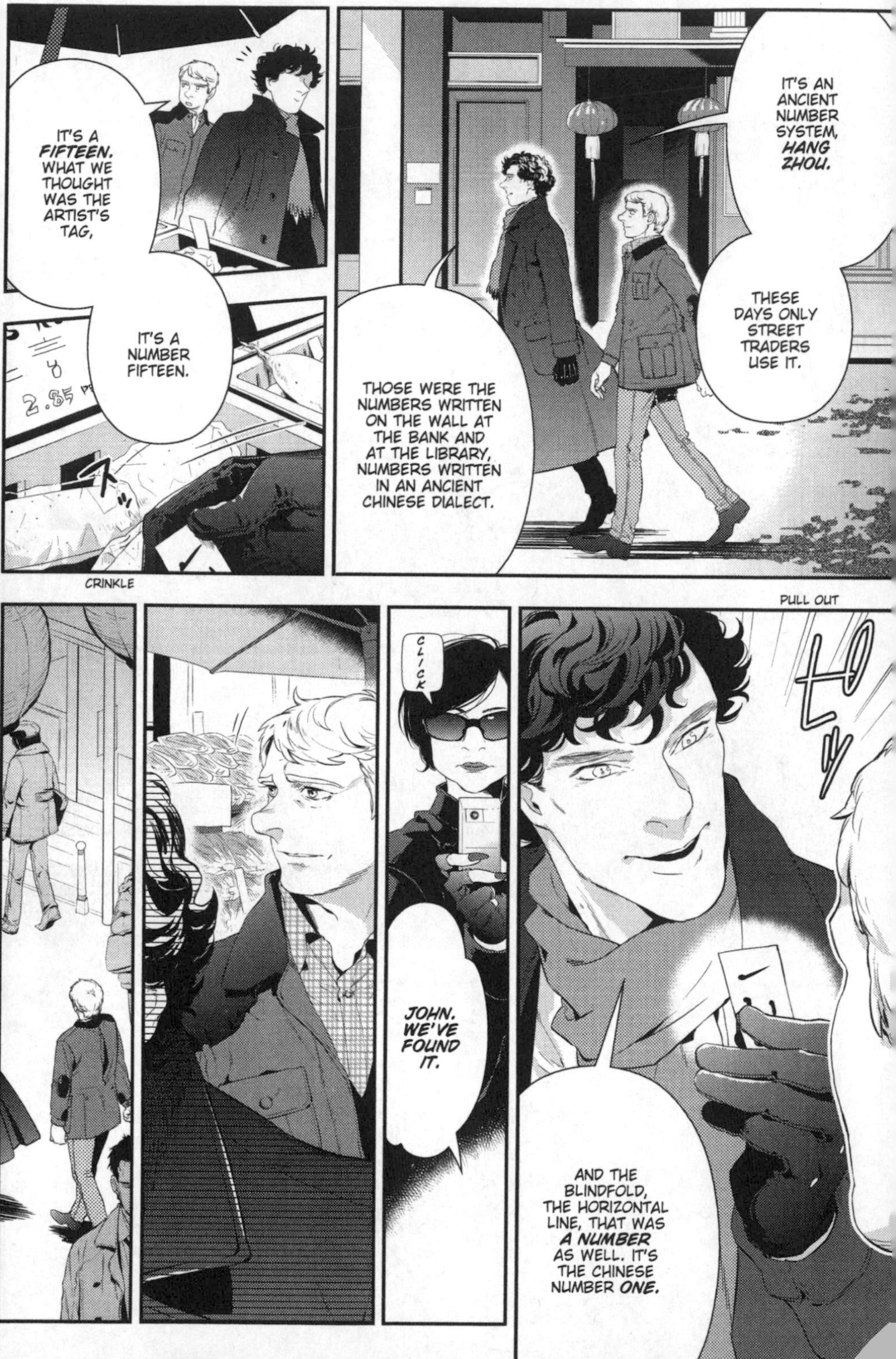
IT'S AN ANCIENT NUMBER SYSTEM, **HANG ZHOU.**
THESE DAYS ONLY STREET TRADERS USE IT.
THOSE WERE THE NUMBERS WRITTEN ON THE WALL AT THE BANK AND AT THE LIBRARY, NUMBERS WRITTEN IN AN ANCIENT CHINESE DIALECT.
IT'S A **FIFTEEN.** WHAT WE THOUGHT WAS THE ARTIST'S TAG,
IT'S A NUMBER FIFTEEN.
2.85
CRINKLE
PULL OUT
ピッ
AND THE BLINDFOLD, THE HORIZONTAL LINE, THAT WAS **A NUMBER** AS WELL. IT'S THE CHINESE NUMBER **ONE.**
CLICK
JOHN. WE'VE FOUND IT.

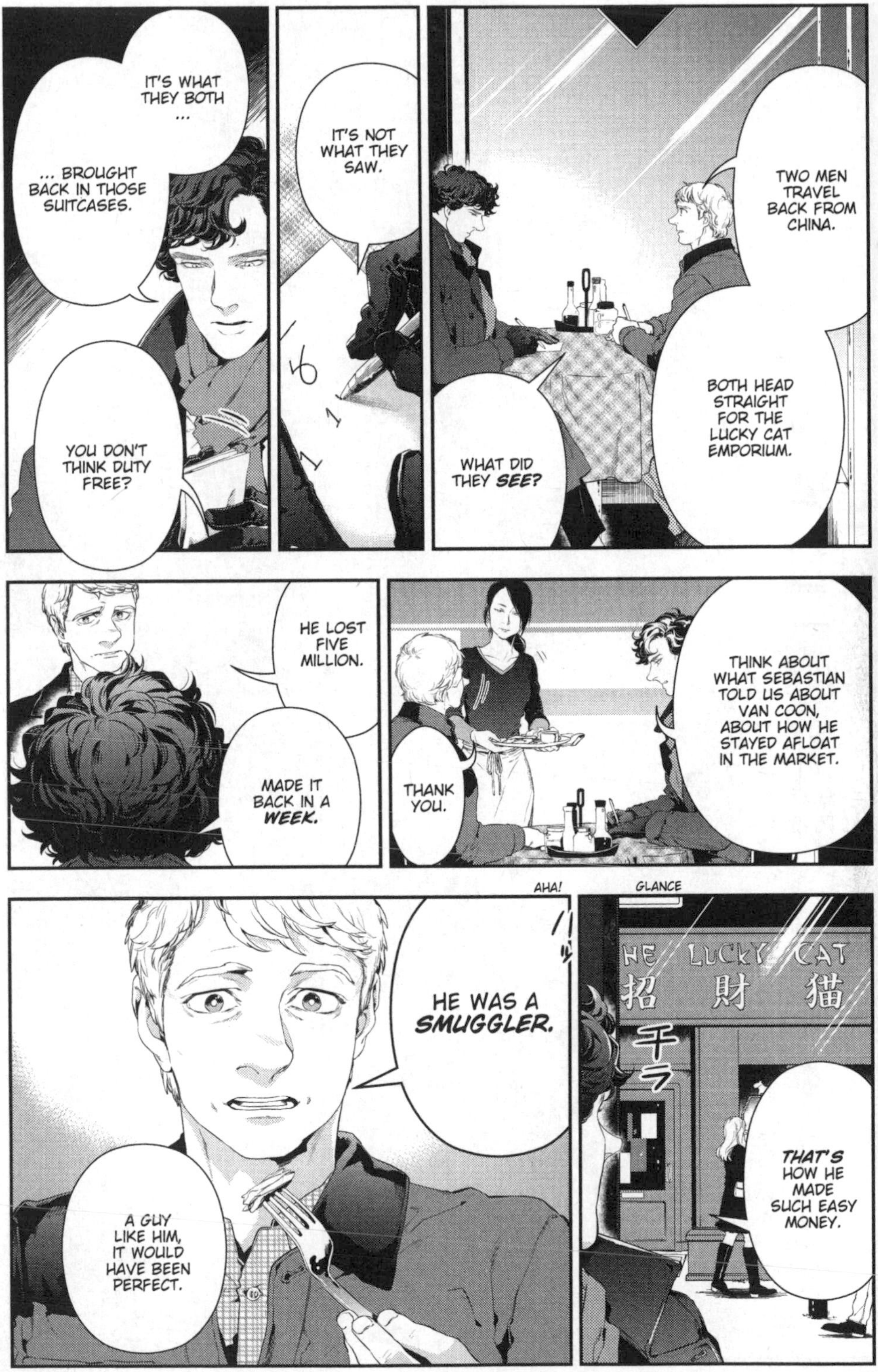
TWO MEN TRAVEL BACK FROM CHINA.
BOTH HEAD STRAIGHT FOR THE LUCKY CAT EMPORIUM.
WHAT DID THEY *SEE?*
IT'S NOT WHAT THEY SAW.
IT'S WHAT THEY BOTH ...
... BROUGHT BACK IN THOSE SUITCASES.
YOU DON'T THINK DUTY FREE?
THINK ABOUT WHAT SEBASTIAN TOLD US ABOUT VAN COON, ABOUT HOW HE STAYED AFLOAT IN THE MARKET.
THANK YOU.
HE LOST FIVE MILLION.
MADE IT BACK IN A *WEEK.*
GLANCE
HE LUCKY CAT
招財猫
チラ
THAT'S HOW HE MADE SUCH EASY MONEY.
AHA!
HE WAS A *SMUGGLER.*
A GUY LIKE HIM, IT WOULD HAVE BEEN PERFECT.

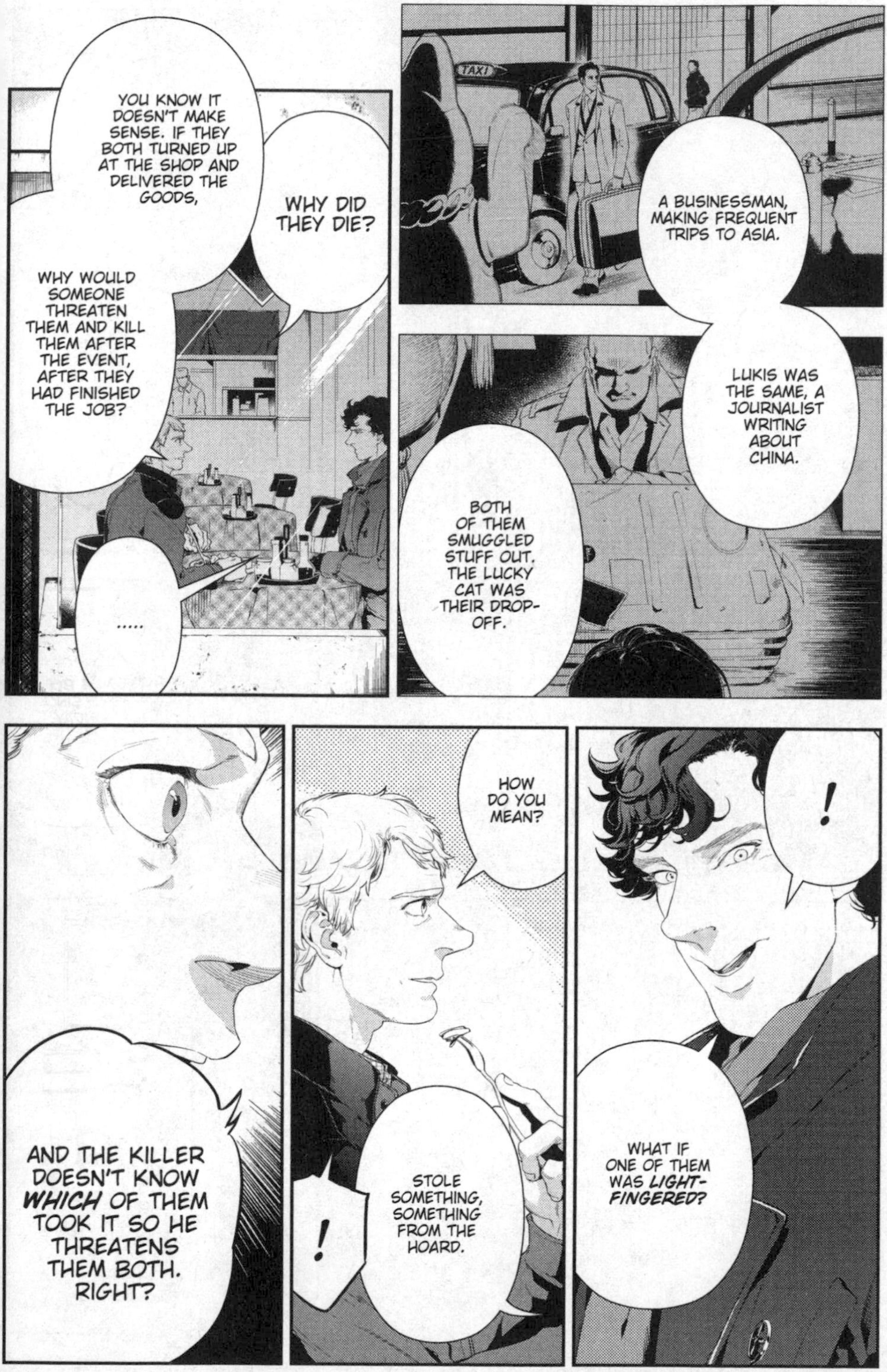
A BUSINESSMAN, MAKING FREQUENT TRIPS TO ASIA.
LUKIS WAS THE SAME, A JOURNALIST WRITING ABOUT CHINA.
BOTH OF THEM SMUGGLED STUFF OUT. THE LUCKY CAT WAS THEIR DROP-OFF.
YOU KNOW IT DOESN'T MAKE SENSE. IF THEY BOTH TURNED UP AT THE SHOP AND DELIVERED THE GOODS,
WHY DID THEY DIE?
WHY WOULD SOMEONE THREATEN THEM AND KILL THEM AFTER THE EVENT, AFTER THEY HAD FINISHED THE JOB?
.....
!
WHAT IF ONE OF THEM WAS *LIGHT-FINGERED?*
HOW DO YOU MEAN?
STOLE SOMETHING, SOMETHING FROM THE HOARD.
!
AND THE KILLER DOESN'T KNOW ***WHICH*** OF THEM TOOK IT SO HE THREATENS THEM BOTH. RIGHT?

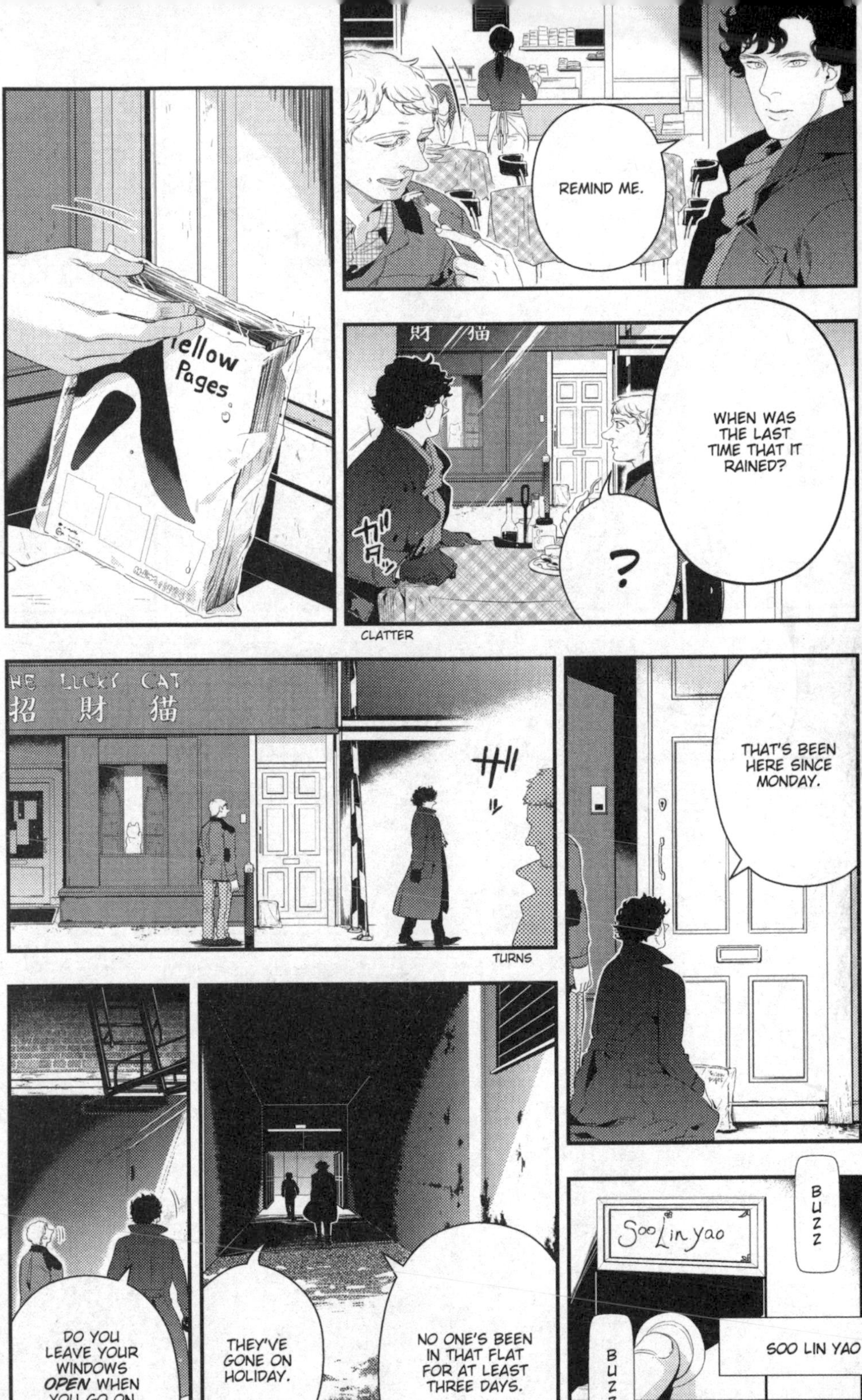
REMIND ME.
財 猫
WHEN WAS THE LAST TIME THAT IT RAINED?
?
ガタッ
CLATTER
Yellow Pages
THAT'S BEEN HERE SINCE MONDAY.
HE LUCKY CAT
招 財 猫
ザッ
TURNS
Soo Lin yao
BUZZ
BUZZ
SOO LIN YAO
NO ONE'S BEEN IN THAT FLAT FOR AT LEAST THREE DAYS.
THEY'VE GONE ON HOLIDAY.
DO YOU LEAVE YOUR WINDOWS *OPEN* WHEN YOU GO ON HOLIDAY?

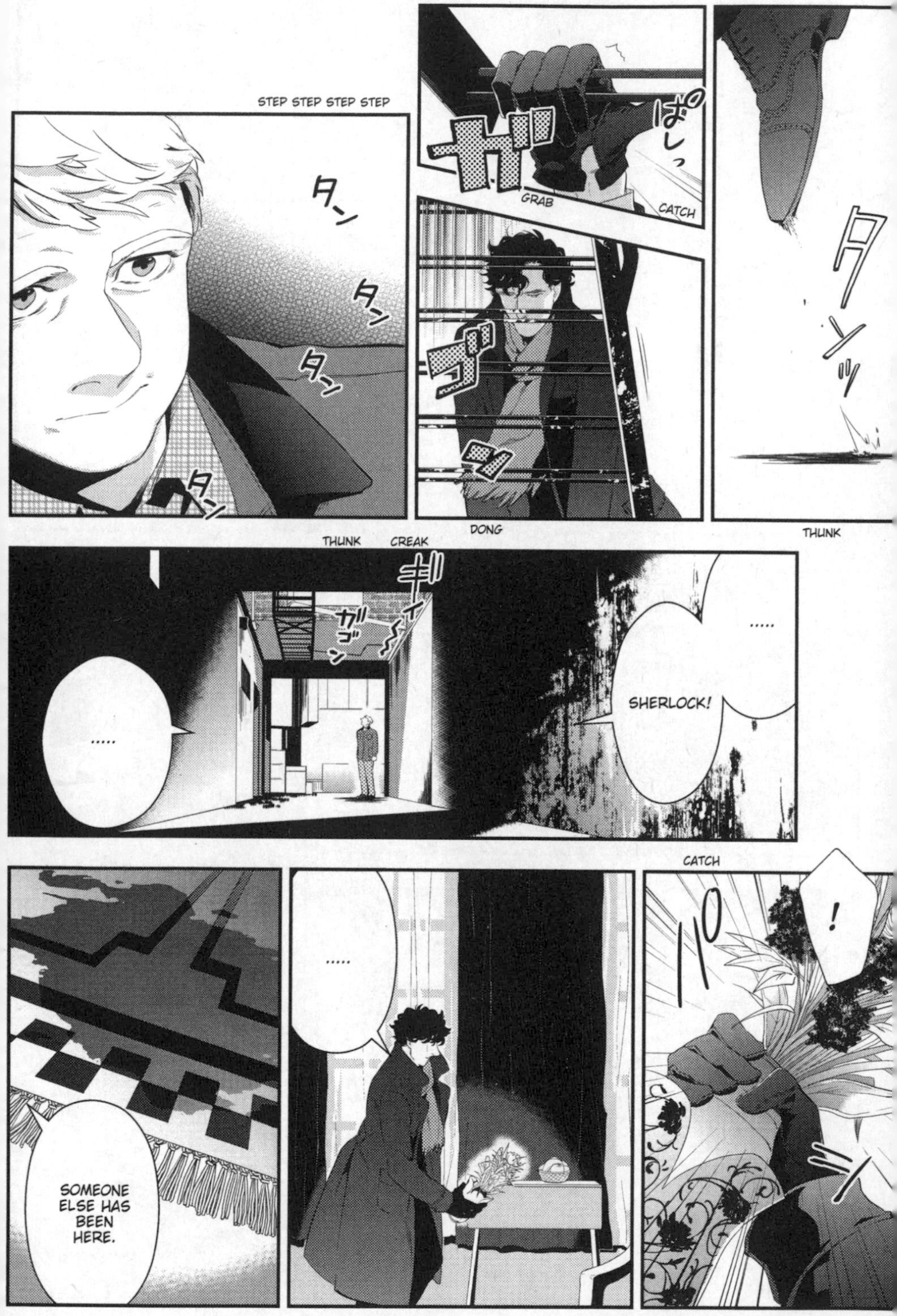
THUNK
CATCH
GRAB
DONG
STEP STEP STEP STEP
.....
SHERLOCK!
THUNK
CREAK
.....
CATCH
!
.....
SOMEONE ELSE HAS BEEN HERE.

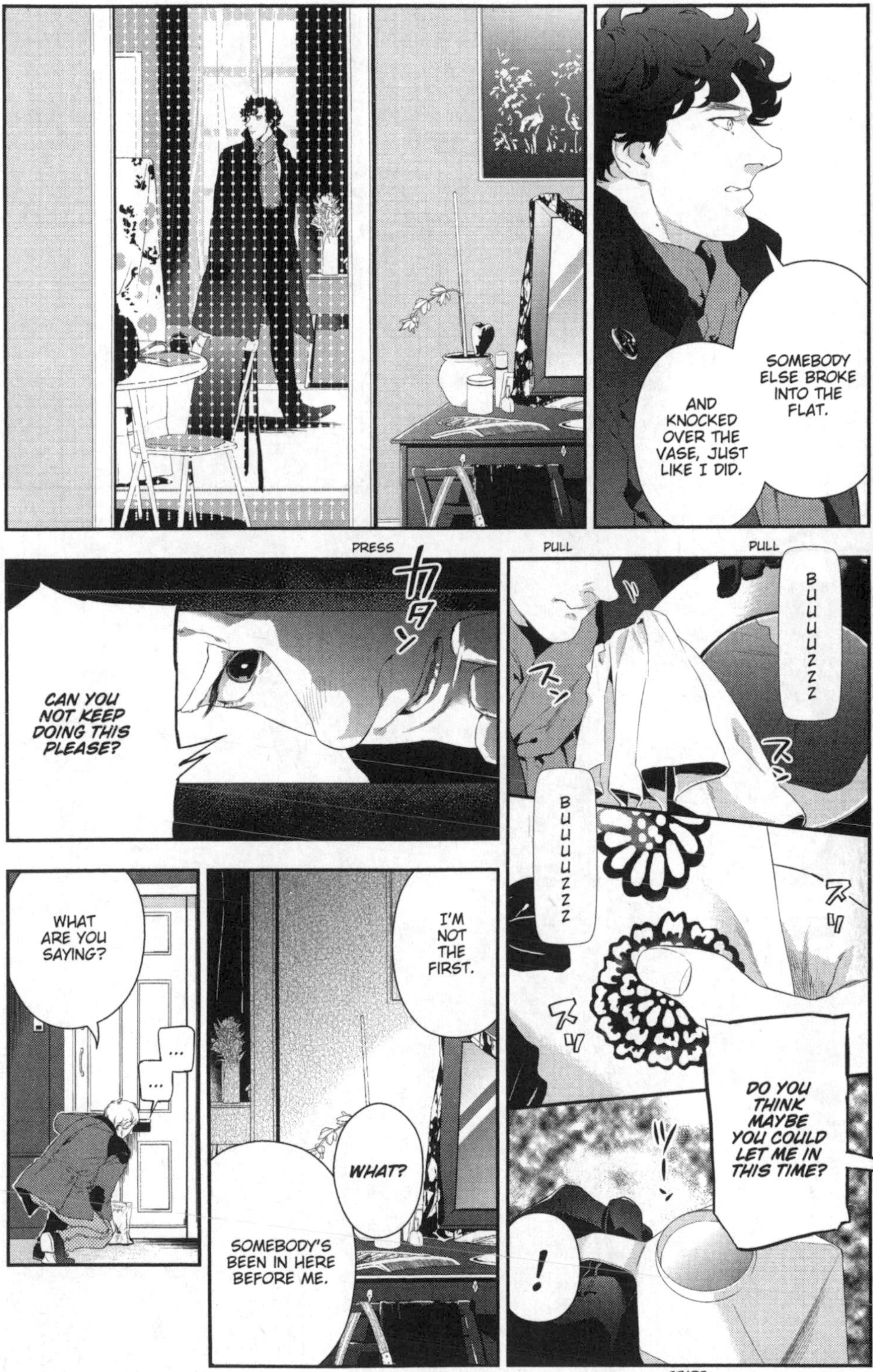
SOMEBODY ELSE BROKE INTO THE FLAT.
AND KNOCKED OVER THE VASE, JUST LIKE I DID.
PULL
PULL
BUUUUZZZ
BUUUUZZZ
DO YOU THINK MAYBE YOU COULD LET ME IN THIS TIME?
!
STARE
PRESS
CAN YOU NOT KEEP DOING THIS PLEASE?
I'M NOT THE FIRST.
WHAT?
SOMEBODY'S BEEN IN HERE BEFORE ME.
WHAT ARE YOU SAYING?
...
...

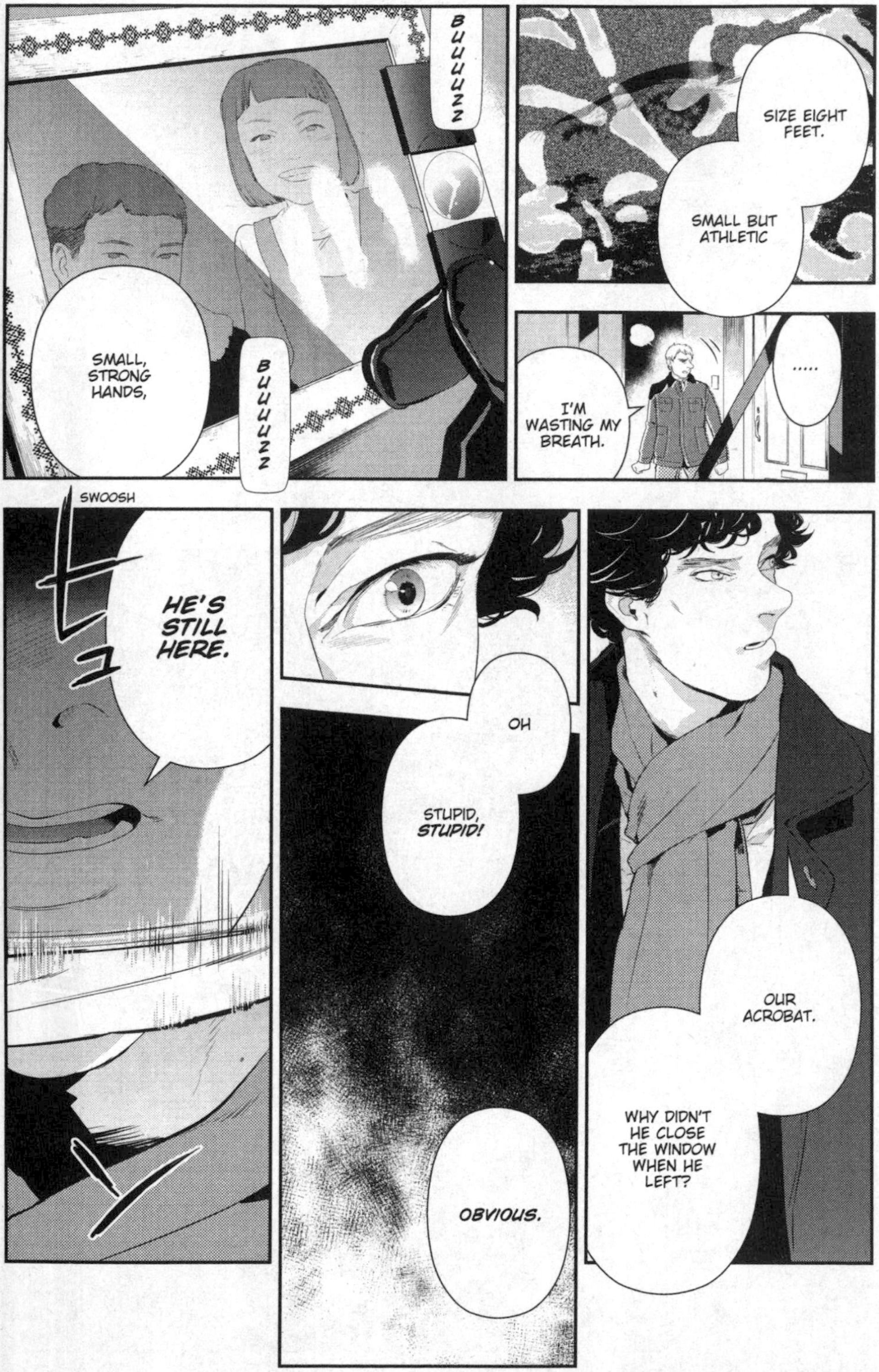
SIZE EIGHT FEET.
SMALL BUT ATHLETIC
.....
I'M WASTING MY BREATH.
BUUUUZZ
BUUUUZZ
SMALL, STRONG HANDS,
OUR ACROBAT.
WHY DIDN'T HE CLOSE THE WINDOW WHEN HE LEFT?
OH
STUPID, *STUPID!*
OBVIOUS.
SWOOSH
HE'S STILL HERE.

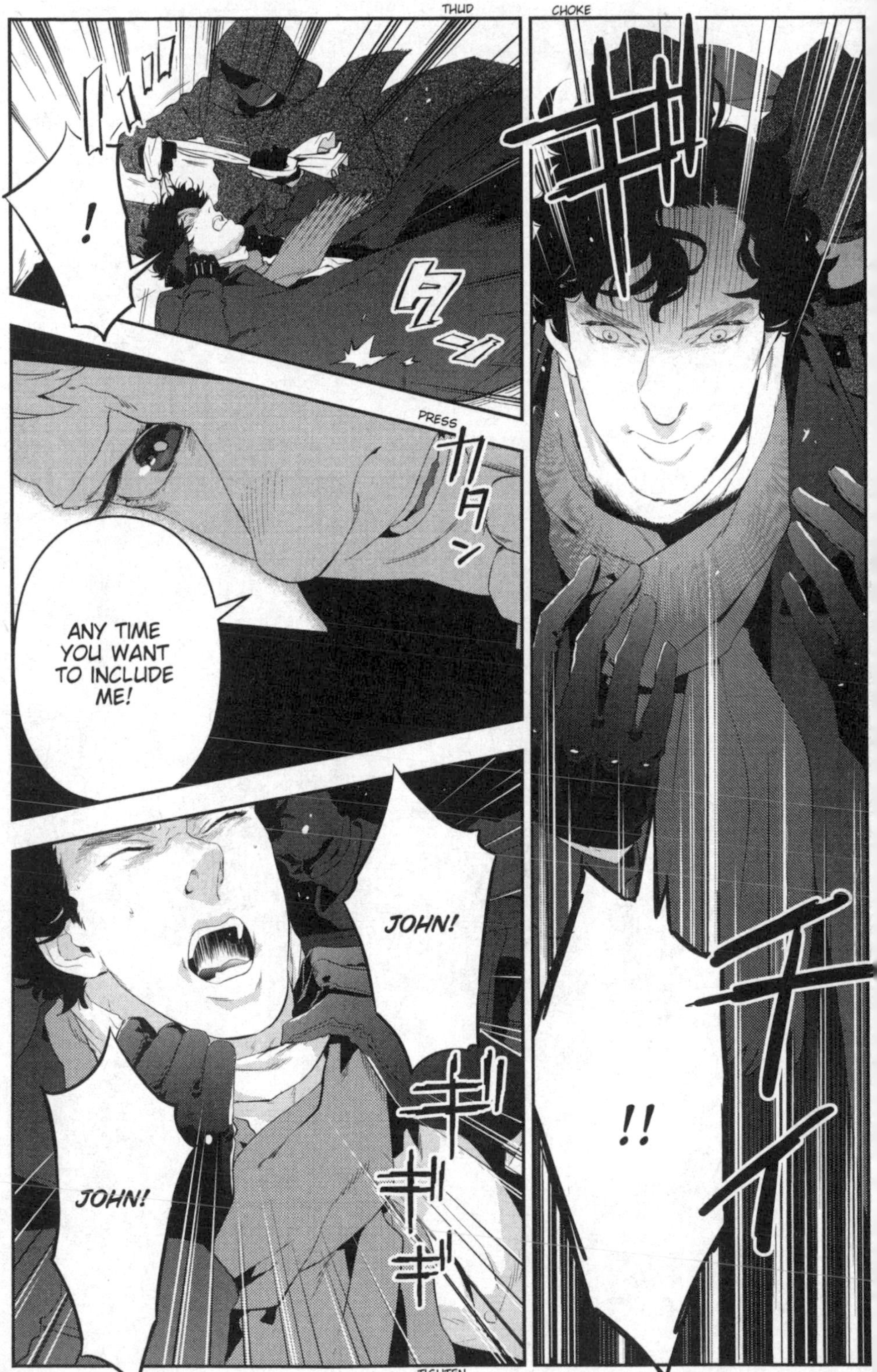
CHOKE
!!
THUD
!
PRESS
ANY TIME YOU WANT TO INCLUDE ME!
JOHN!
JOHN!
TIGHTEN

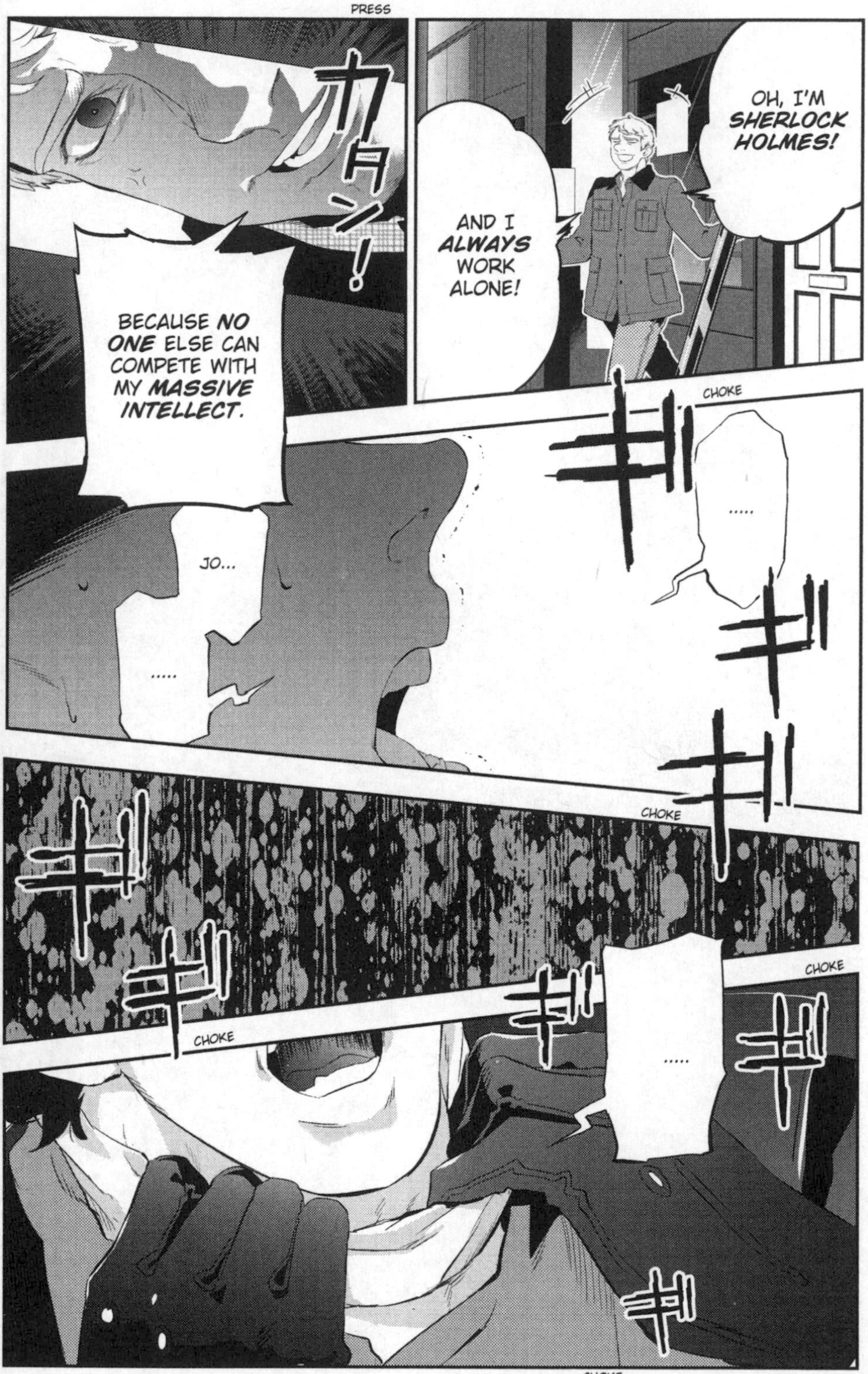
OH, I'M SHERLOCK HOLMES!
AND I ALWAYS WORK ALONE!
PRESS
BECAUSE NO ONE ELSE CAN COMPETE WITH MY MASSIVE INTELLECT.
CHOKE
.....
JO...
.....
CHOKE
CHOKE
.....
CHOKE
CHOKE

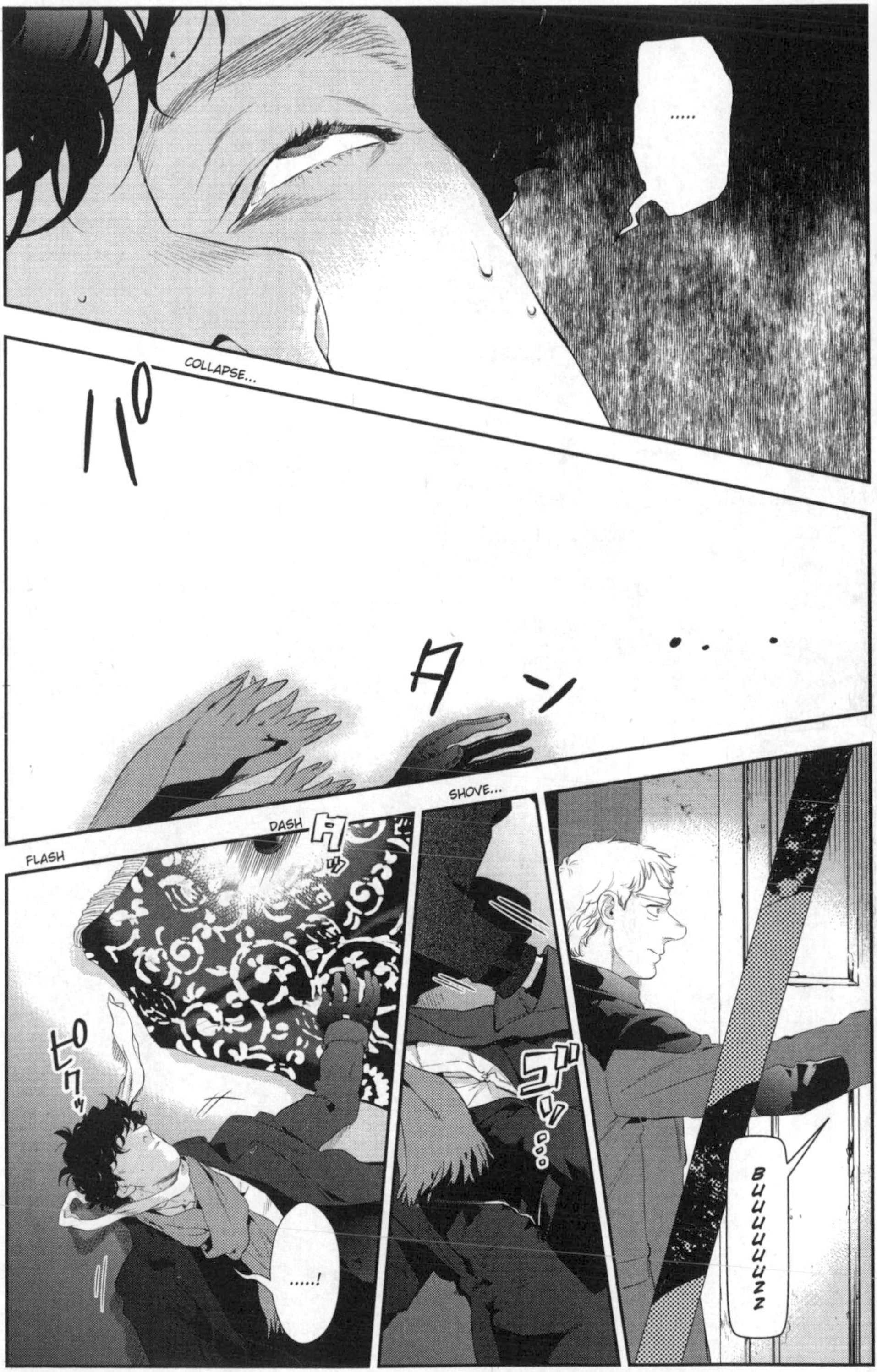
.....
COLLAPSE...
パ
タン
・・・
BUUUUUUZZ
SHOVE...
ゴソッ...
DASH
タッ
FLASH
ピクッ
......!

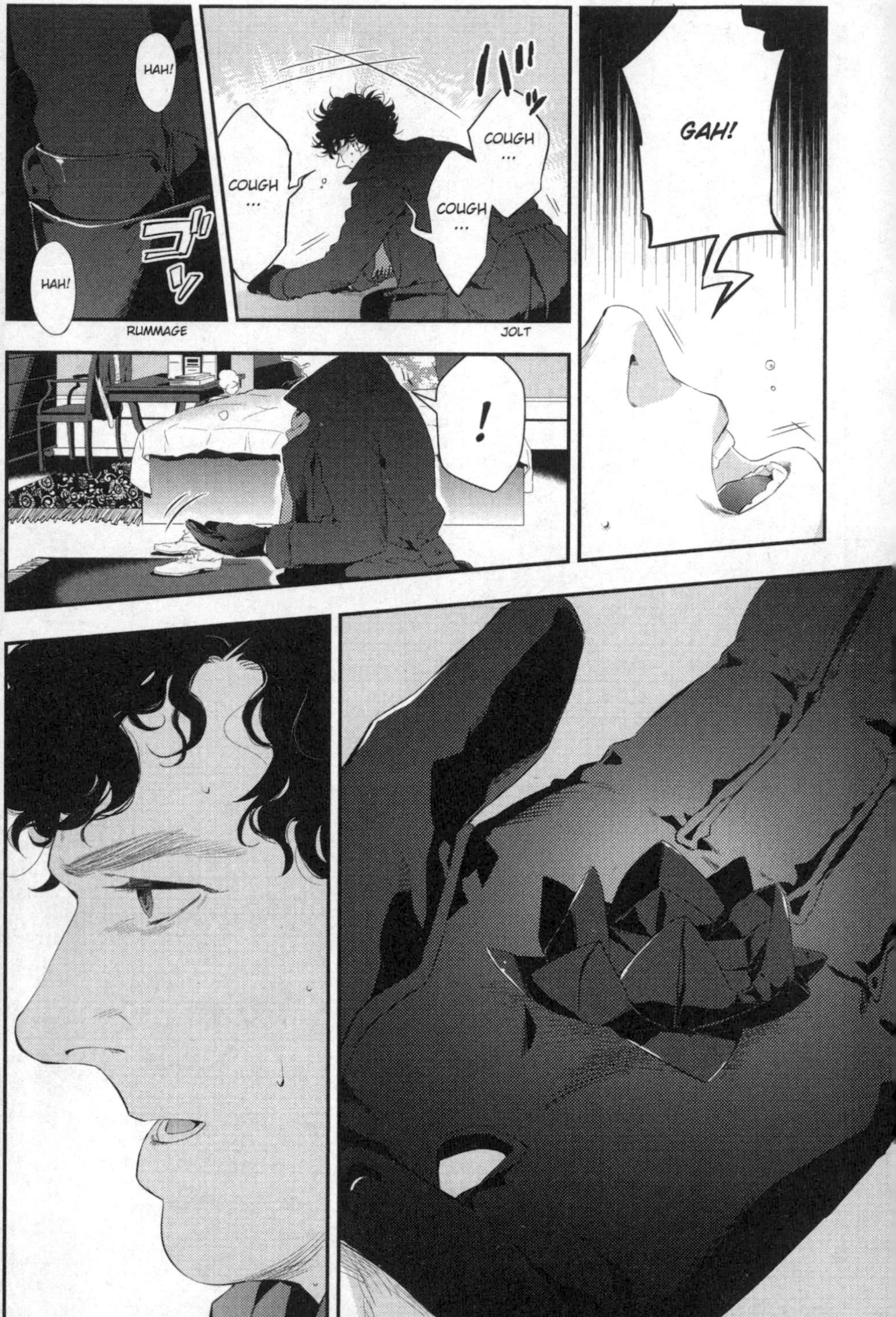
GAH!
バッ
COUGH...
COUGH...
COUGH...
JOLT
HAH!
HAH!
RUMMAGE
!

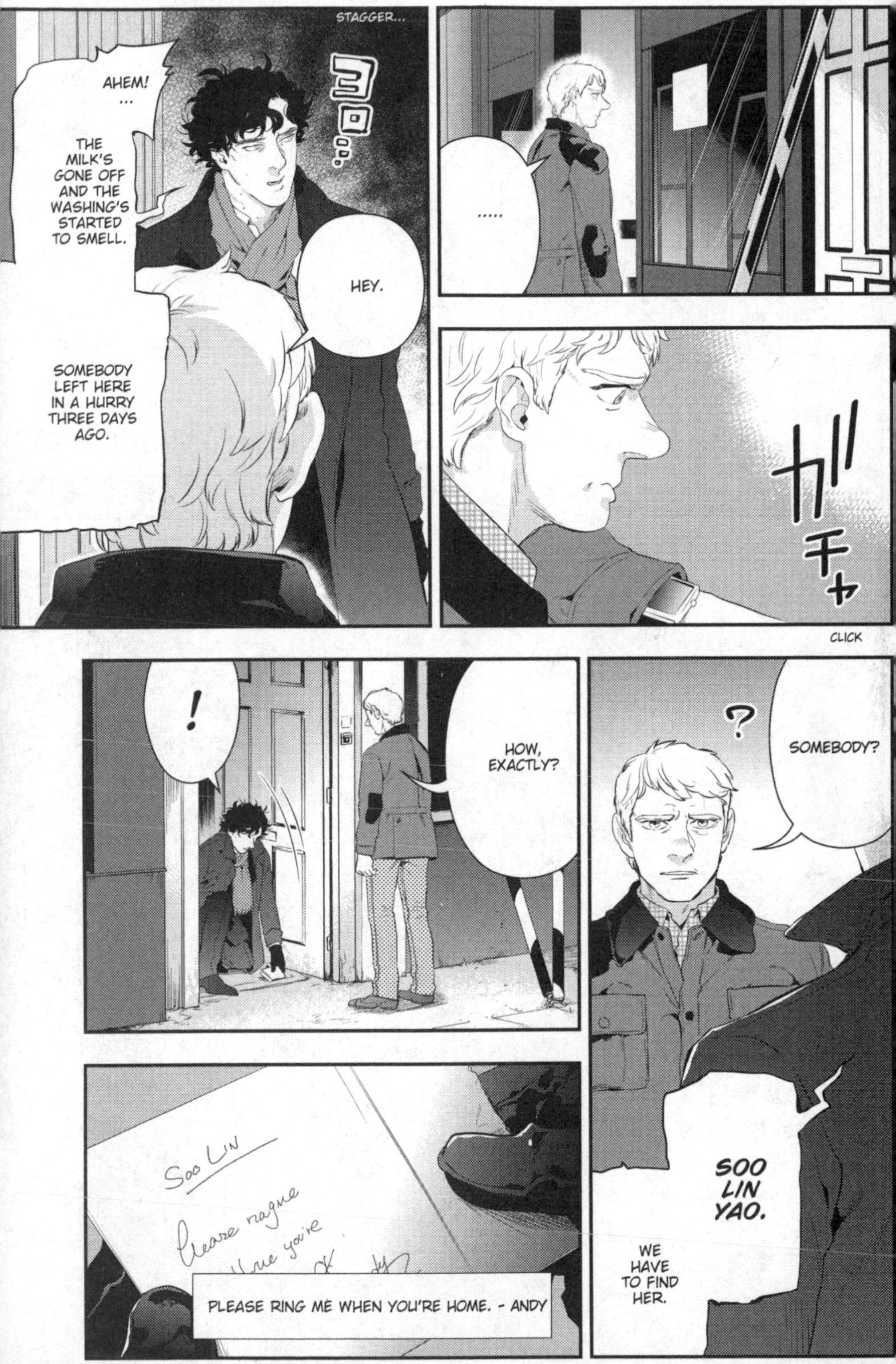
.....
ガチャ
CLICK
STAGGER...
ヨロ...
AHEM! ...
THE MILK'S GONE OFF AND THE WASHING'S STARTED TO SMELL.
HEY.
SOMEBODY LEFT HERE IN A HURRY THREE DAYS AGO.
?
SOMEBODY?
SOO LIN YAO.
WE HAVE TO FIND HER.
HOW, EXACTLY?
!
Soo LIN
PLEASE RING ME WHEN YOU'RE HOME. - ANDY

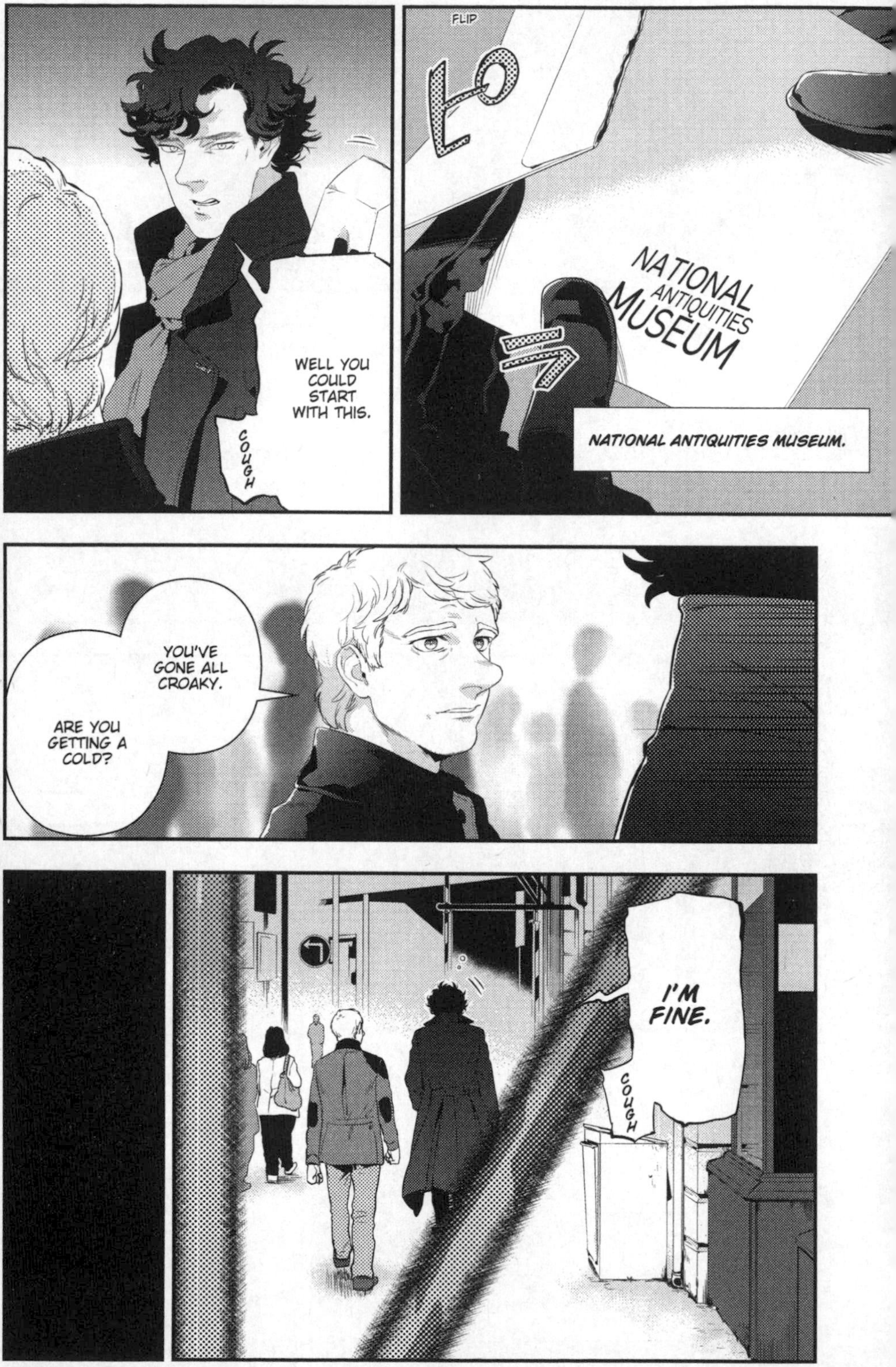
FLIP
NATIONAL ANTIQUITIES MUSEUM
NATIONAL ANTIQUITIES MUSEUM.
WELL YOU COULD START WITH THIS.
COUGH
YOU'VE GONE ALL CROAKY.
ARE YOU GETTING A COLD?
I'M FINE.
COUGH

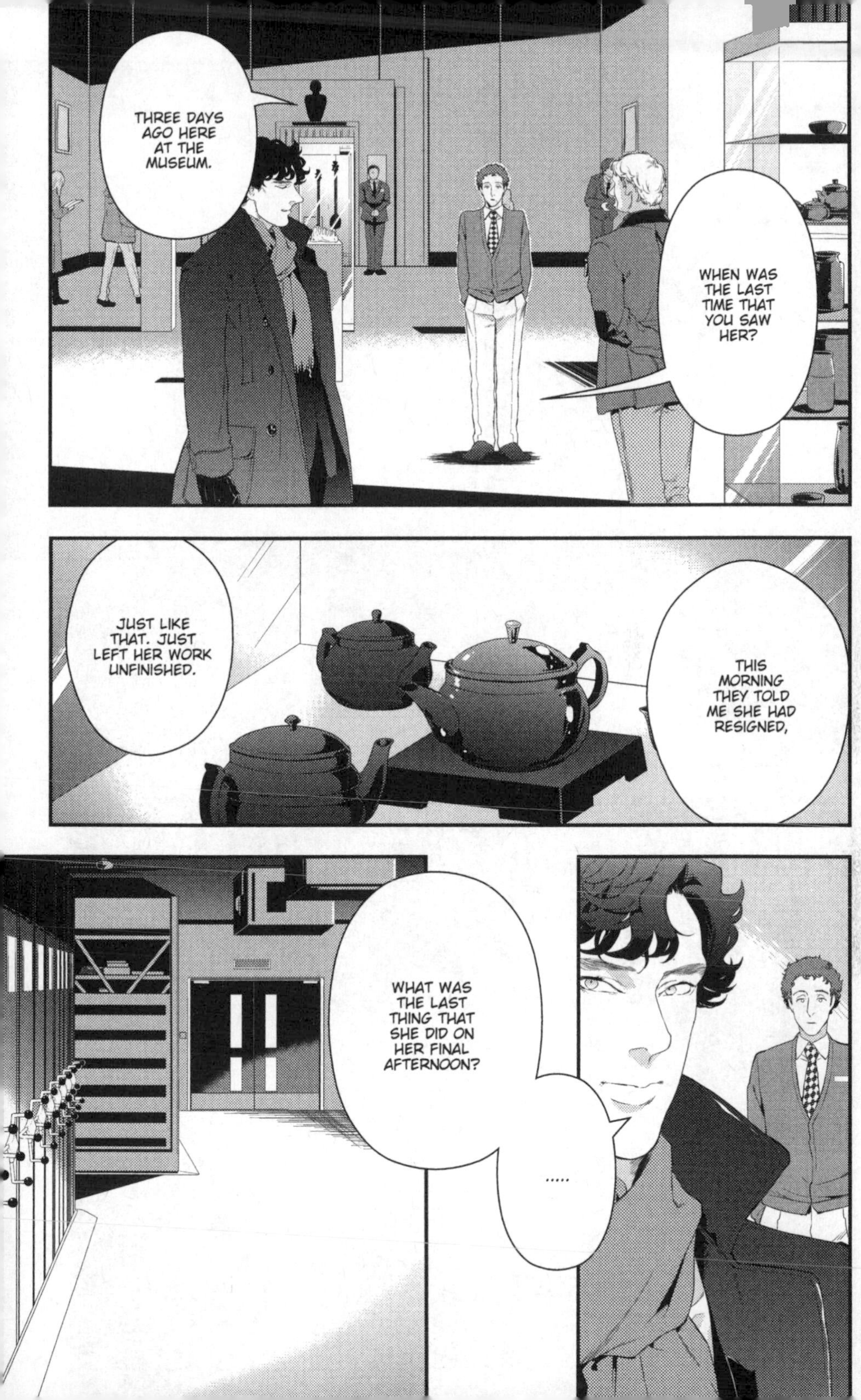
WHEN WAS THE LAST TIME THAT YOU SAW HER?
THREE DAYS AGO HERE AT THE MUSEUM.
THIS MORNING THEY TOLD ME SHE HAD RESIGNED,
JUST LIKE THAT. JUST LEFT HER WORK UNFINISHED.
WHAT WAS THE LAST THING THAT SHE DID ON HER FINAL AFTERNOON?
.....

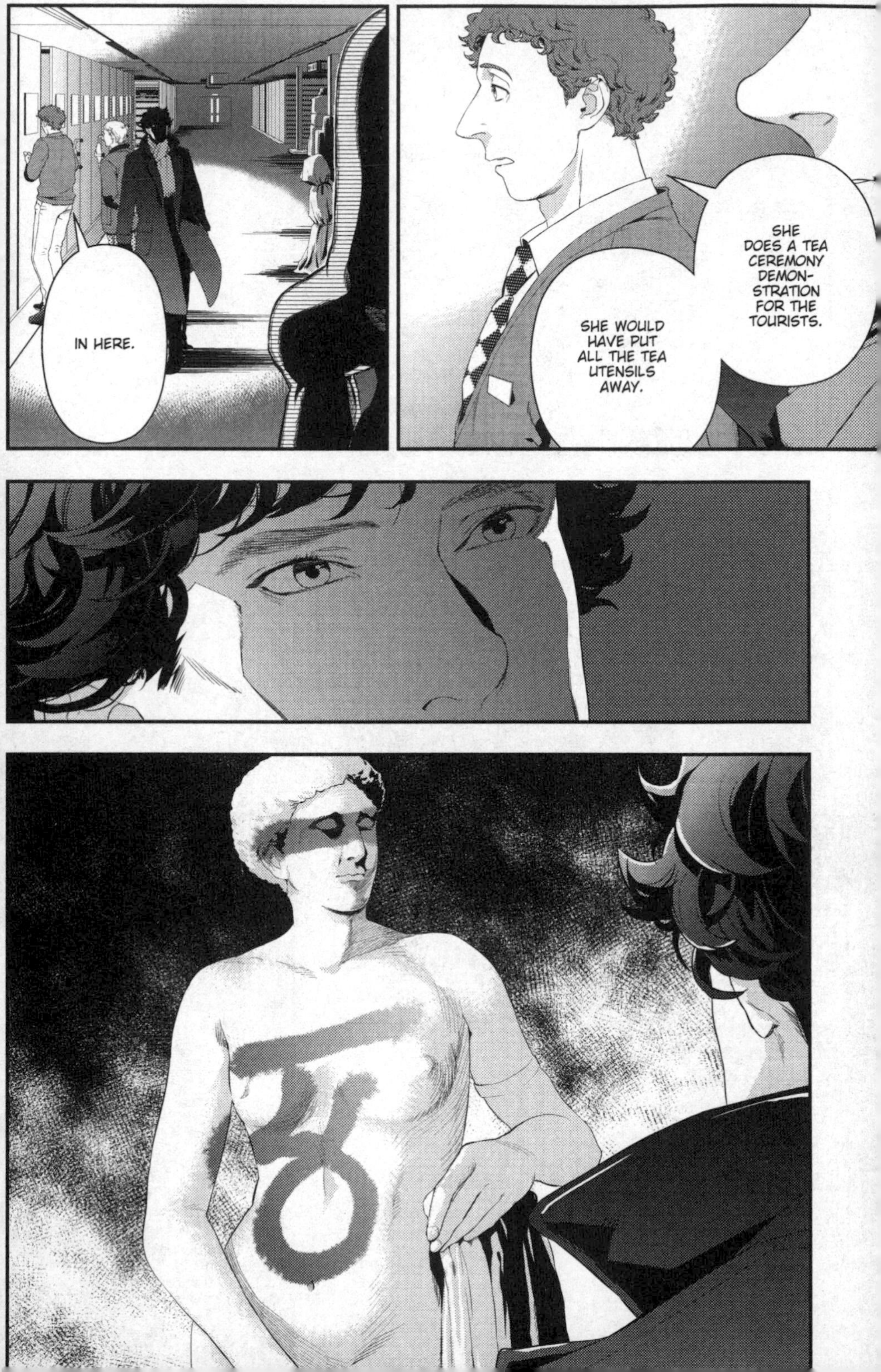
SHE DOES A TEA CEREMONY DEMON-STRATION FOR THE TOURISTS.
SHE WOULD HAVE PUT ALL THE TEA UTENSILS AWAY.
IN HERE.

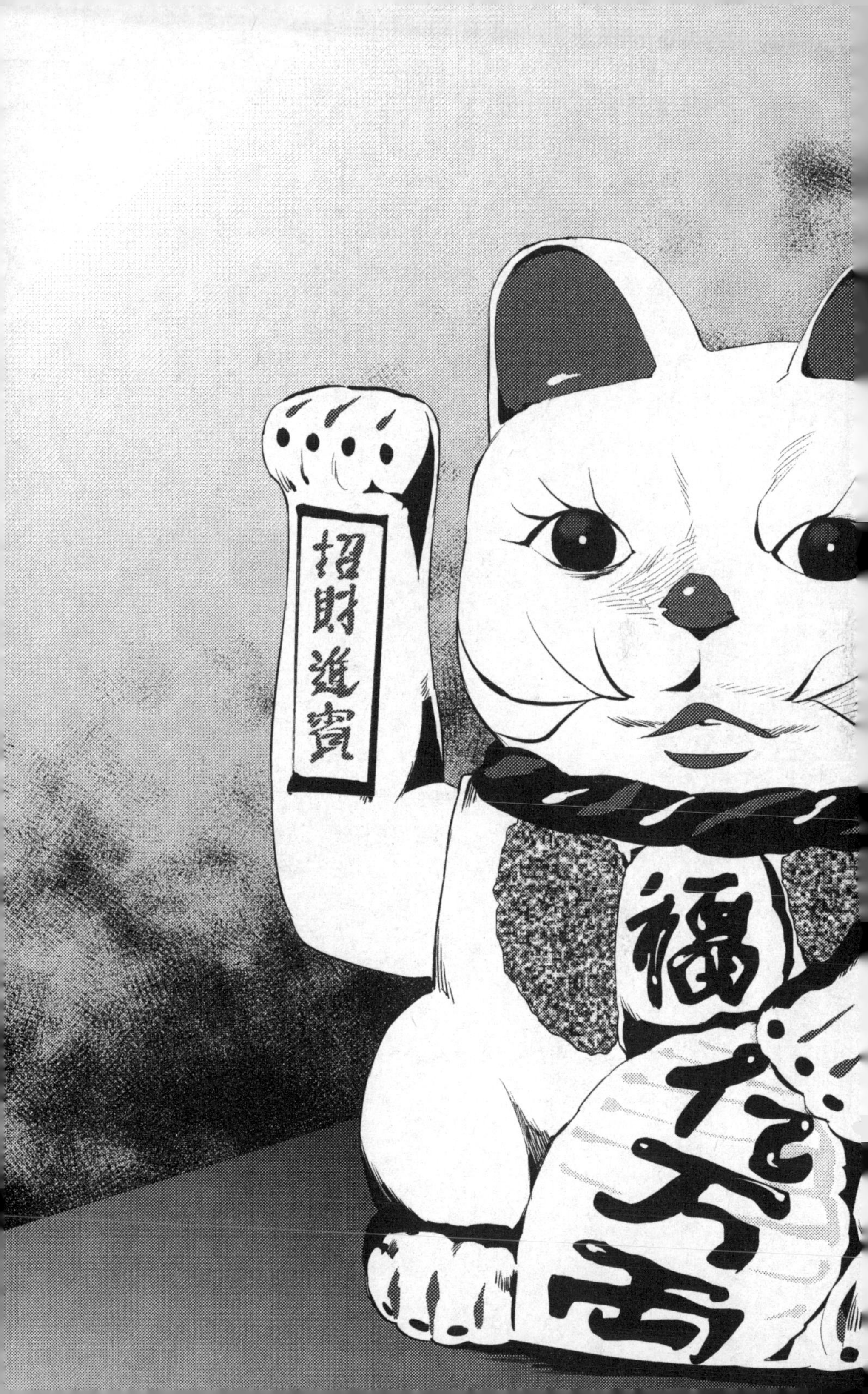
招財進寶
福

SHERLOCK

THE BLIND BANKER

Chapter 4

Illustration by:
Jay.

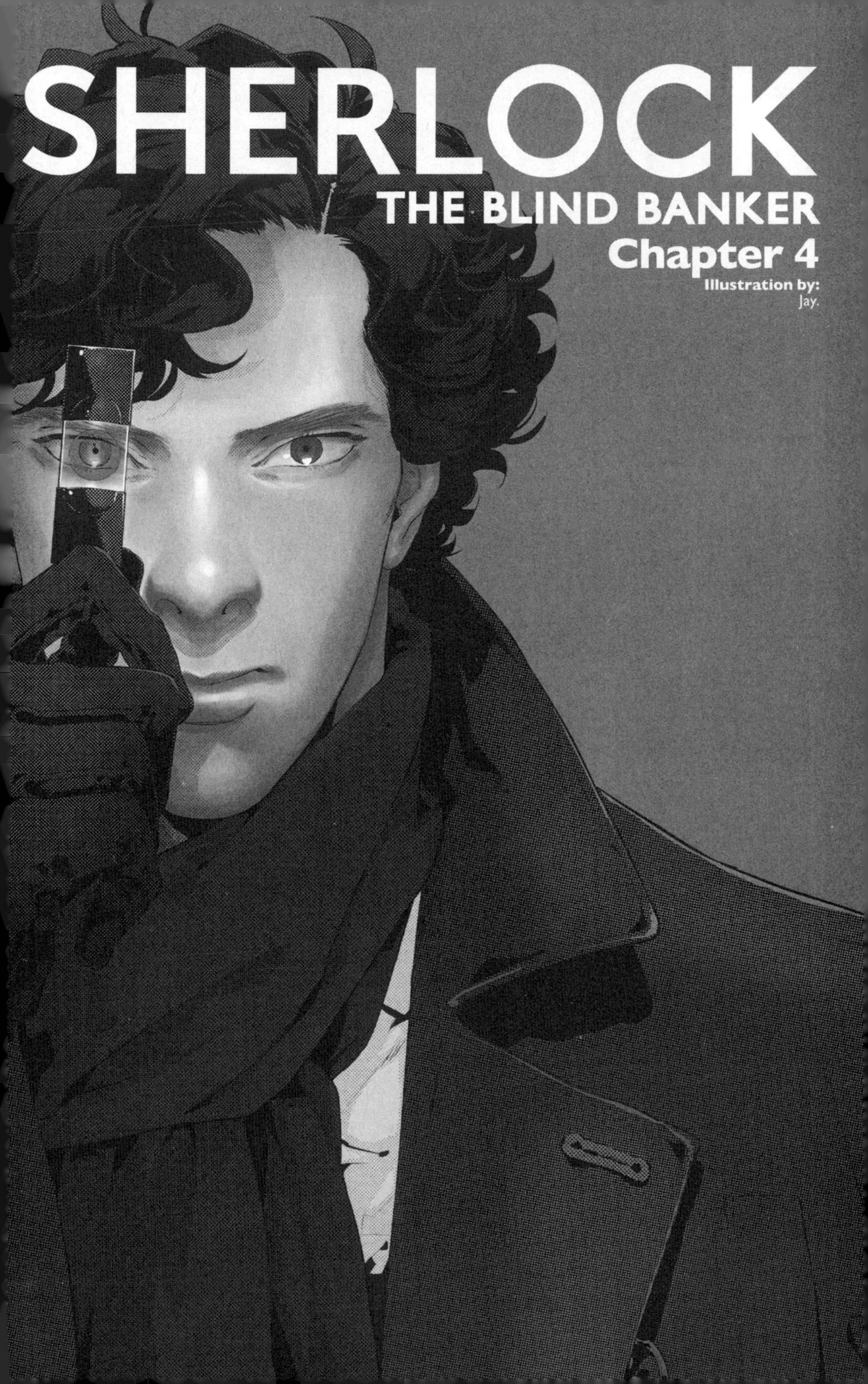

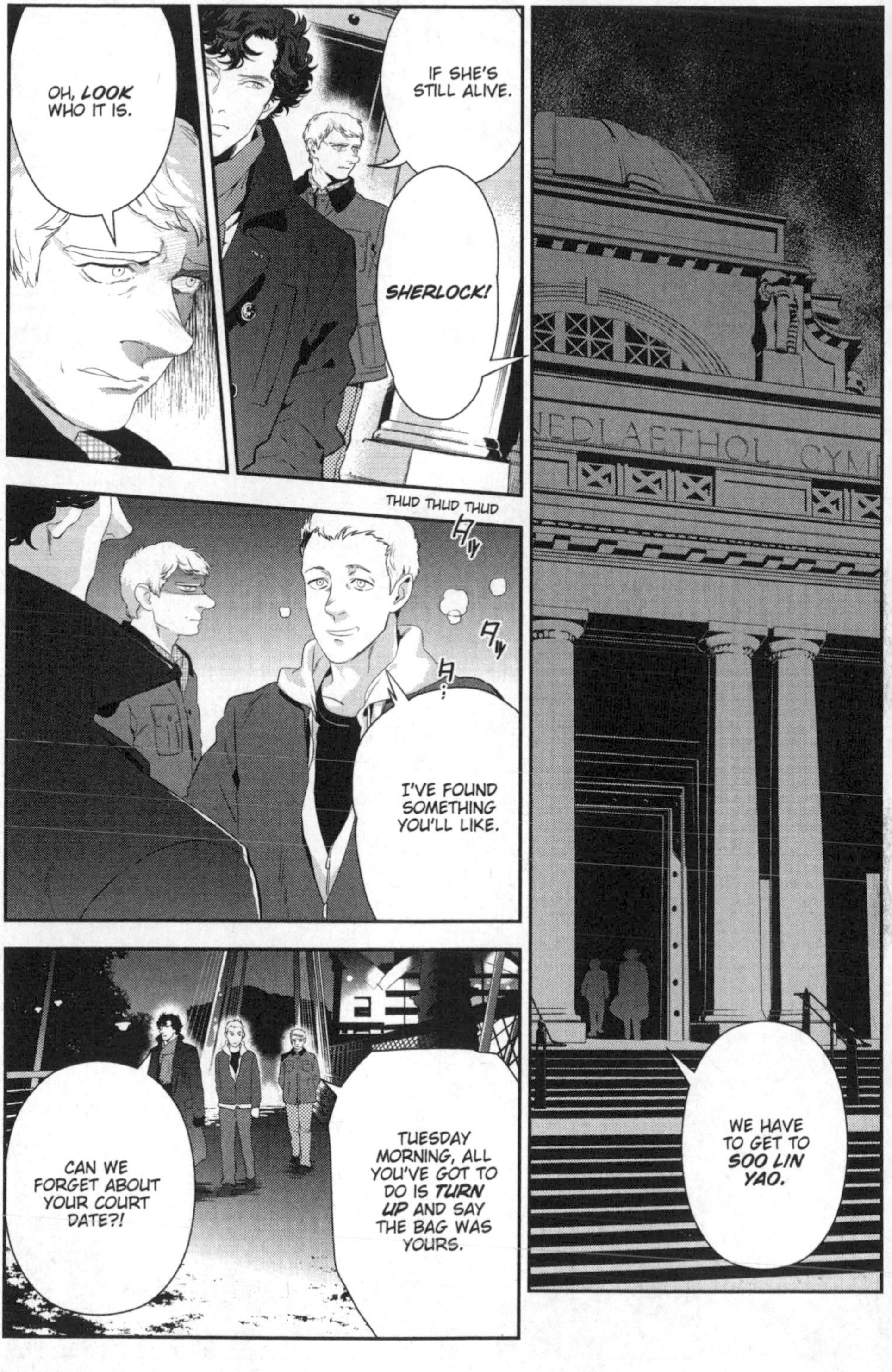
TUESDAY MORNING, ALL YOU'VE GOT TO DO IS TURN UP AND SAY THE BAG WAS YOURS.
CAN WE FORGET ABOUT YOUR COURT DATE?!
WE HAVE TO GET TO SOO LIN YAO.
IF SHE'S STILL ALIVE.
SHERLOCK!
OH, LOOK WHO IT IS.
THUD THUD THUD
I'VE FOUND SOMETHING YOU'LL LIKE.

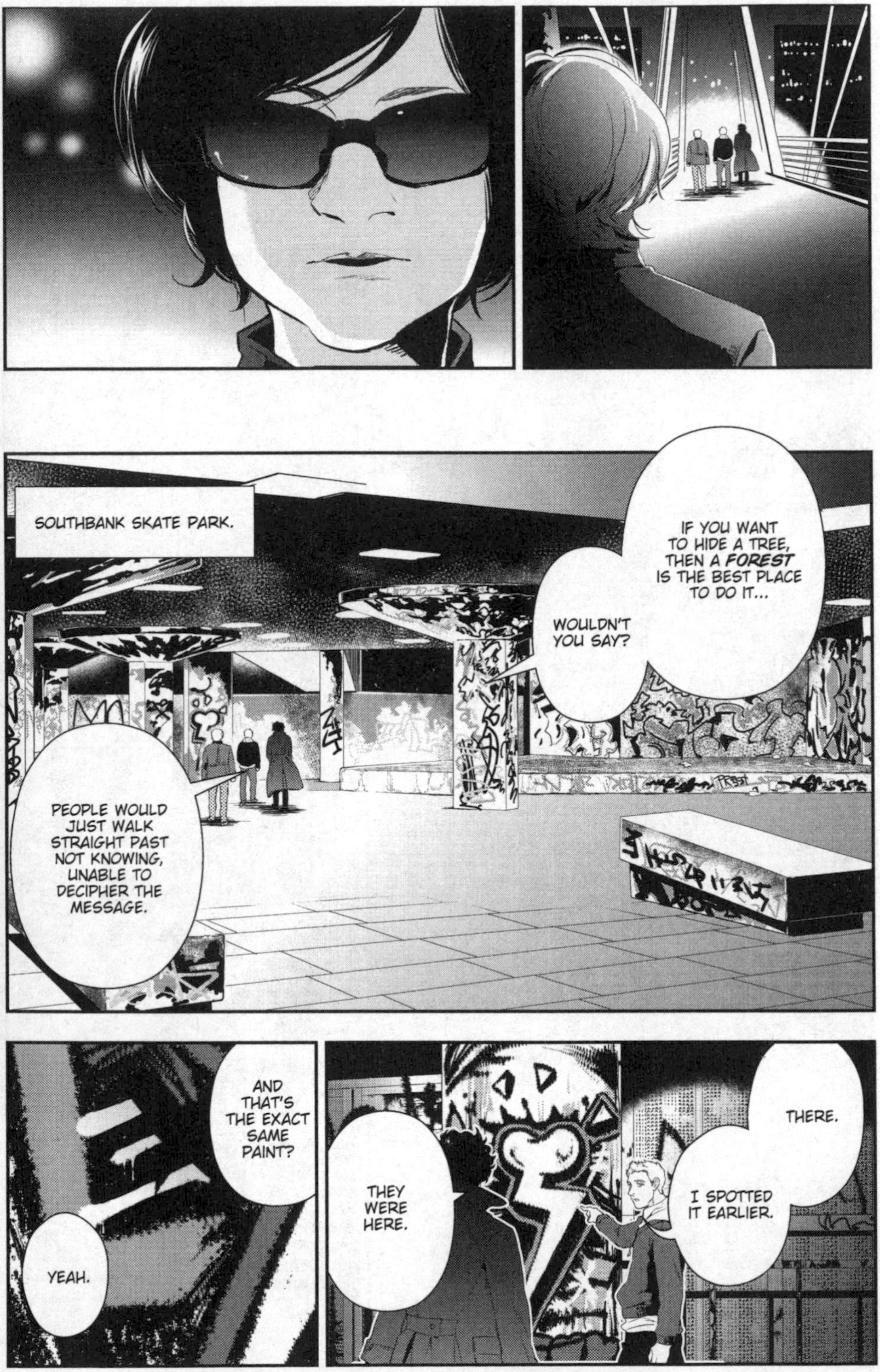
IF YOU WANT TO HIDE A TREE, THEN A ***FOREST*** IS THE BEST PLACE TO DO IT...
WOULDN'T YOU SAY?
SOUTHBANK SKATE PARK.
PEOPLE WOULD JUST WALK STRAIGHT PAST NOT KNOWING, UNABLE TO DECIPHER THE MESSAGE.
THERE.
I SPOTTED IT EARLIER.
THEY WERE HERE.
AND THAT'S THE EXACT SAME PAINT?
YEAH.

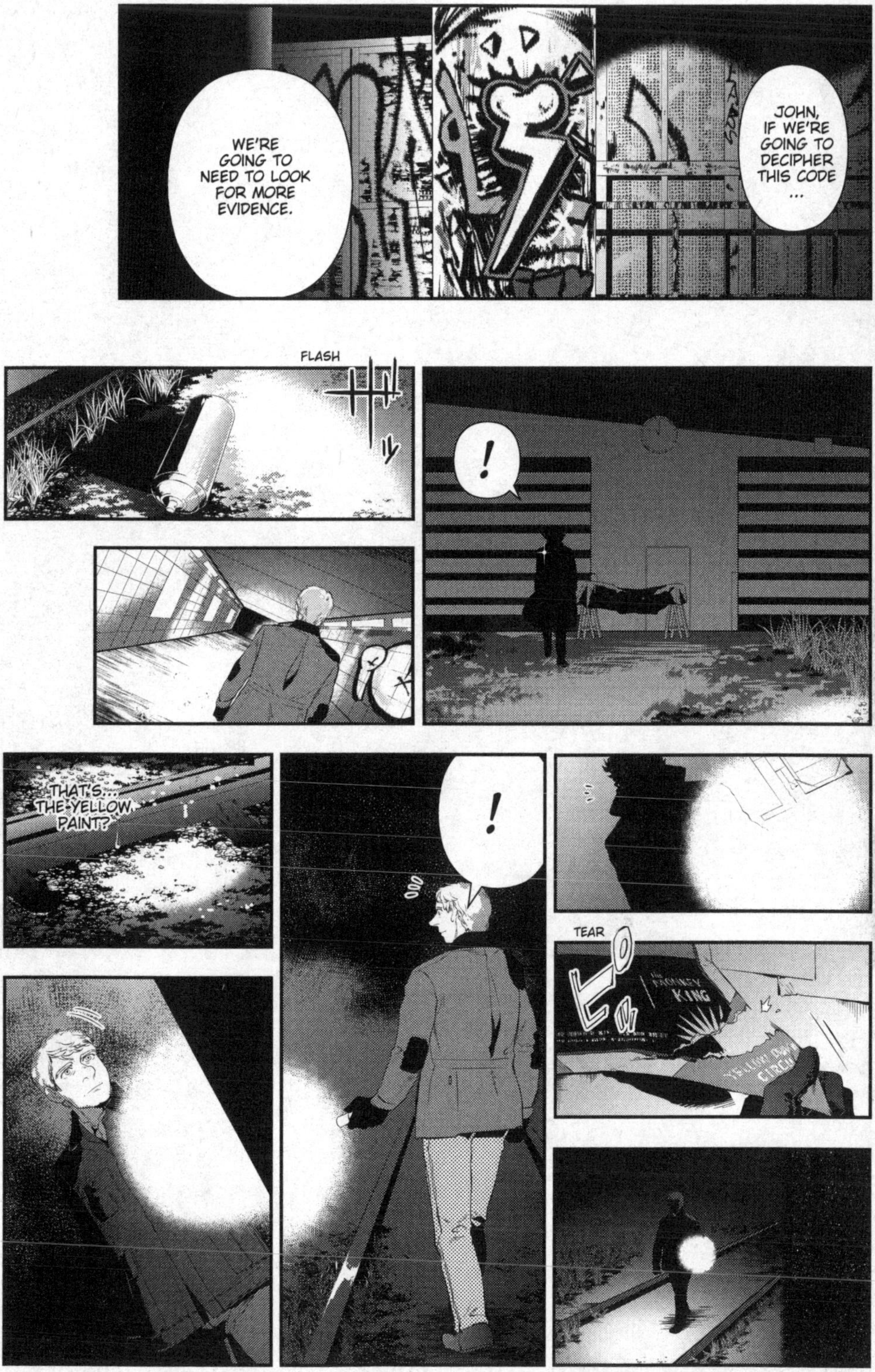
JOHN, IF WE'RE GOING TO DECIPHER THIS CODE ...
WE'RE GOING TO NEED TO LOOK FOR MORE EVIDENCE.
!
FLASH
TEAR
!
THAT'S... THE YELLOW PAINT?

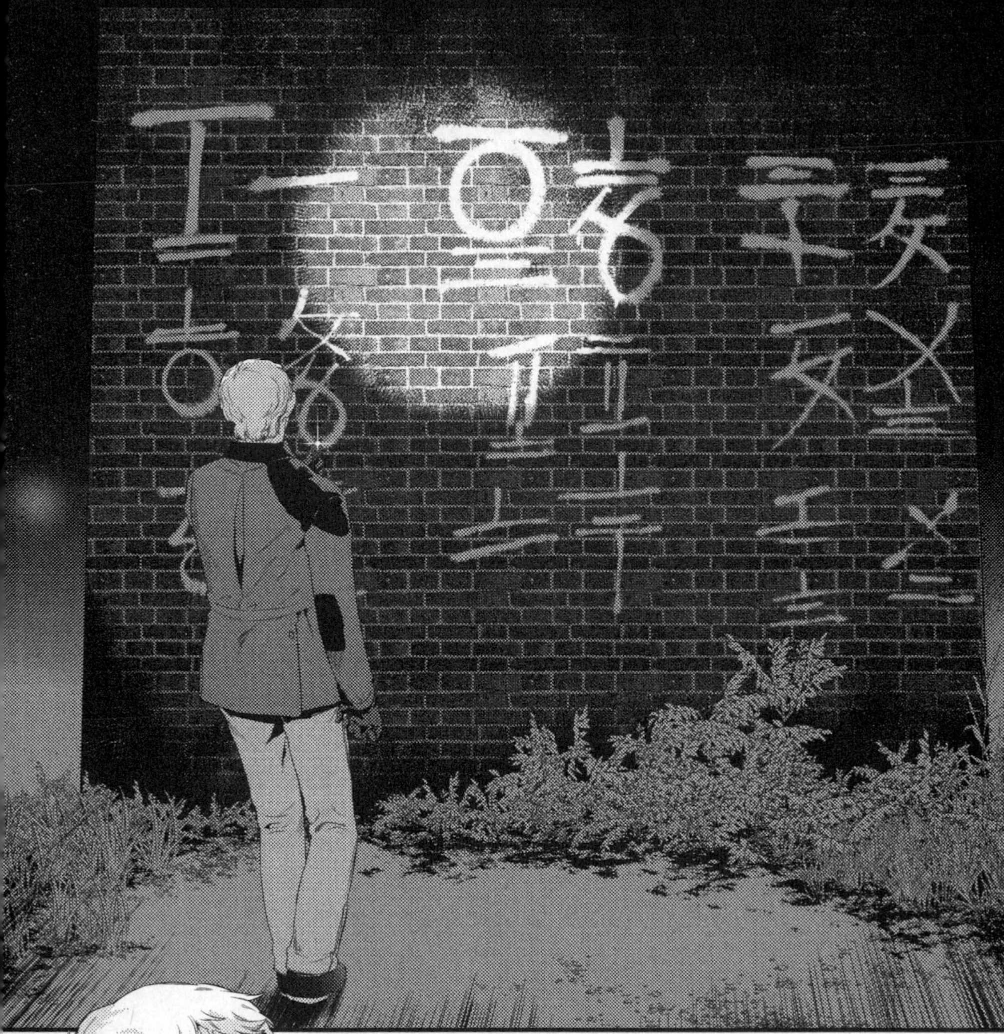

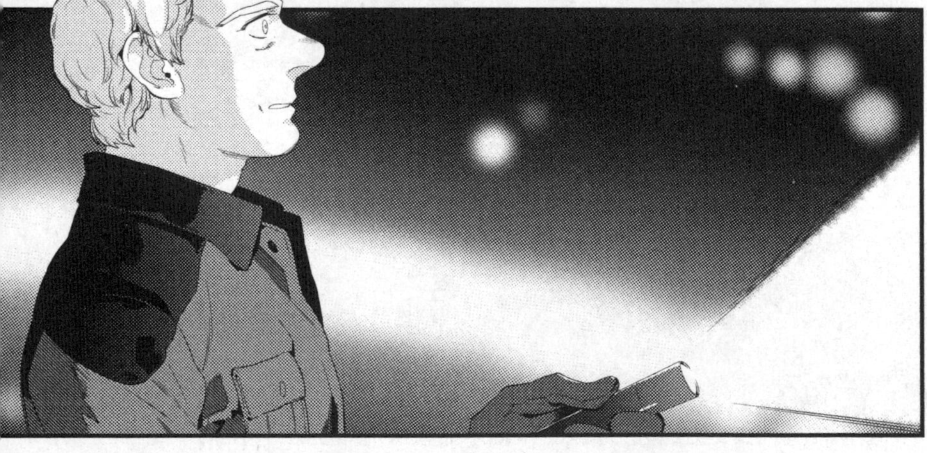

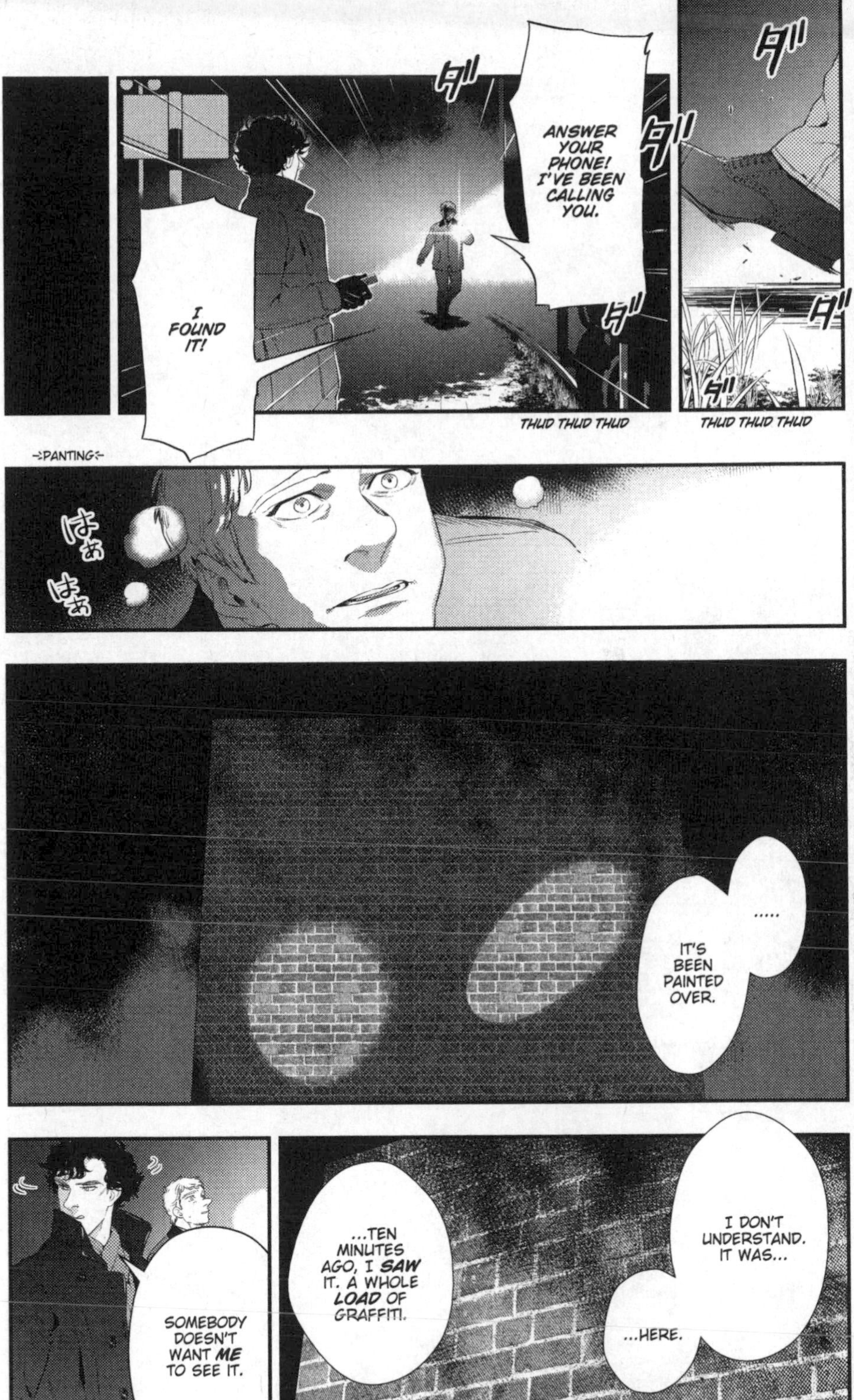
ダ
ダ
ダ
ダ
THUD THUD THUD
ダ
ANSWER YOUR PHONE! I'VE BEEN CALLING YOU.
ダ
I FOUND IT!
THUD THUD THUD
PANTING
はぁ
はぁ
.....
IT'S BEEN PAINTED OVER.
I DON'T UNDERSTAND. IT WAS...
...HERE.
...TEN MINUTES AGO, I SAW IT. A WHOLE LOAD OF GRAFFITI.
SOMEBODY DOESN'T WANT ME TO SEE IT.

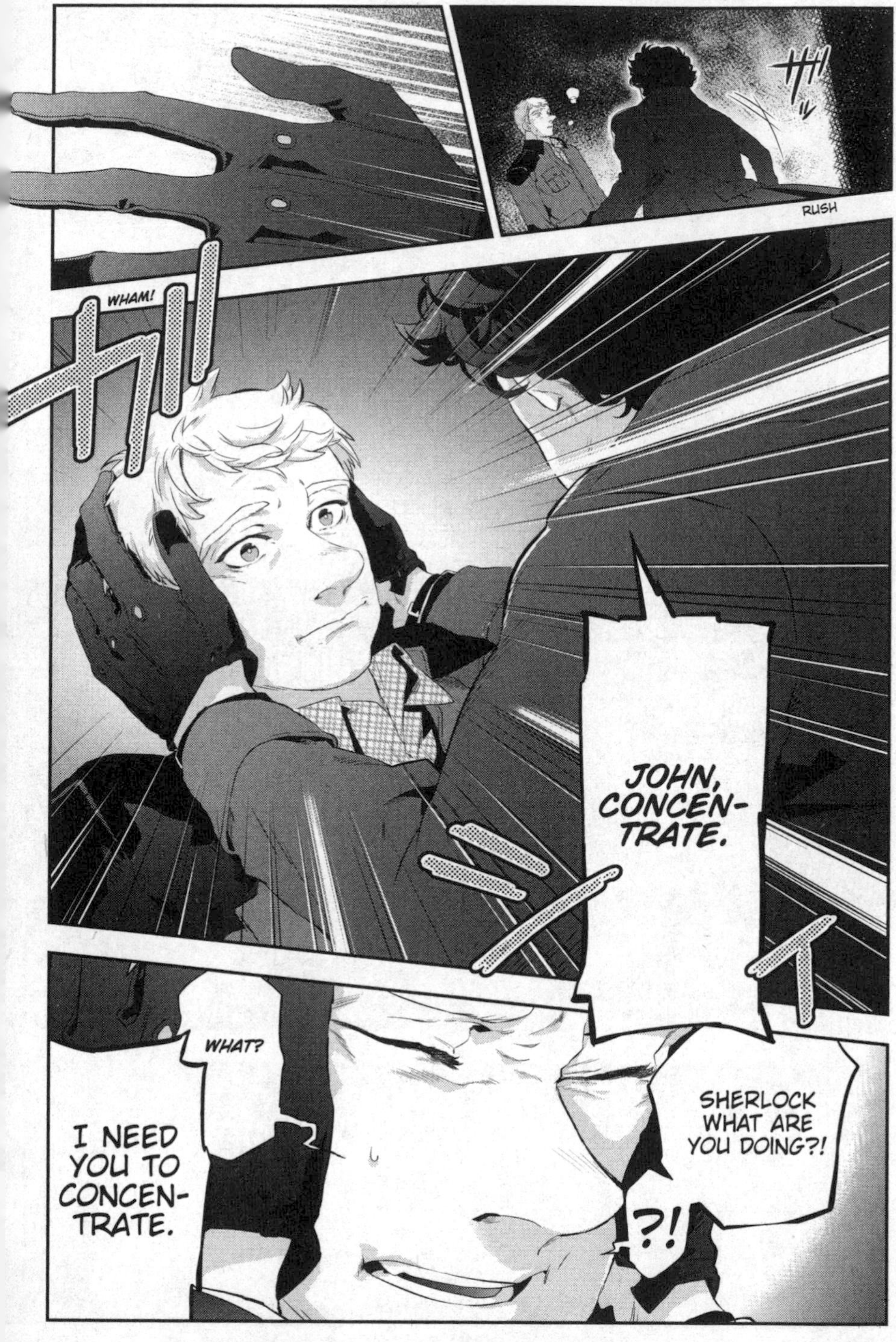
RUSH
WHAM!
JOHN, CONCENTRATE.
SHERLOCK WHAT ARE YOU DOING?!
?!
WHAT?
I NEED YOU TO CONCENTRATE.

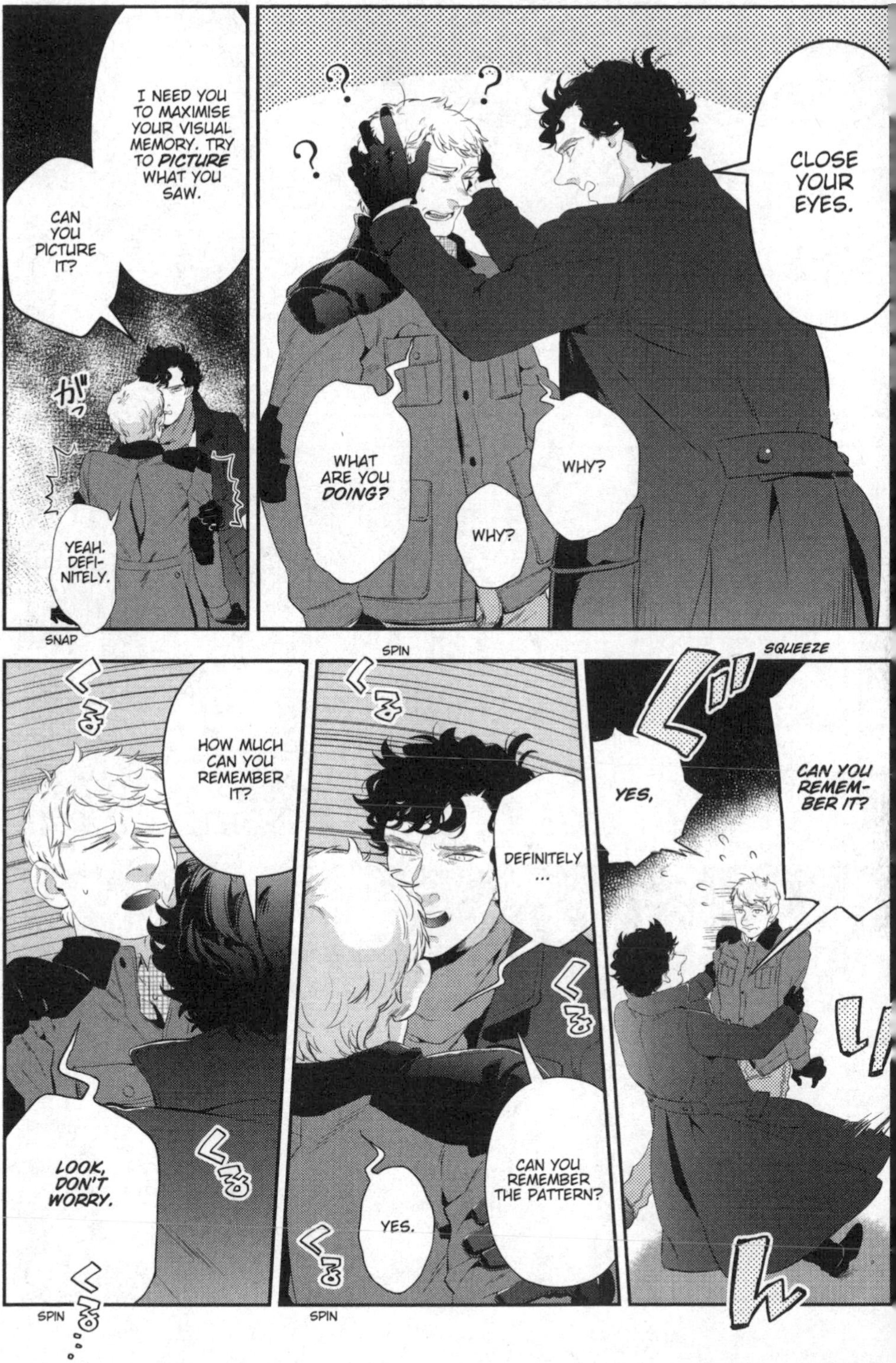
CLOSE YOUR EYES.
WHAT ARE YOU *DOING?*
WHY?
WHY?
I NEED YOU TO MAXIMISE YOUR VISUAL MEMORY. TRY TO *PICTURE* WHAT YOU SAW.
CAN YOU PICTURE IT?
がっ
SNAP
YEAH. DEFINITELY.
SQUEEZE
ぐいん
CAN YOU REMEMBER IT?
YES,
SPIN
くる
DEFINITELY ...
くる
CAN YOU REMEMBER THE PATTERN?
YES.
くる
SPIN
くる
HOW MUCH CAN YOU REMEMBER IT?
くる
LOOK, DON'T WORRY.
くる...
SPIN

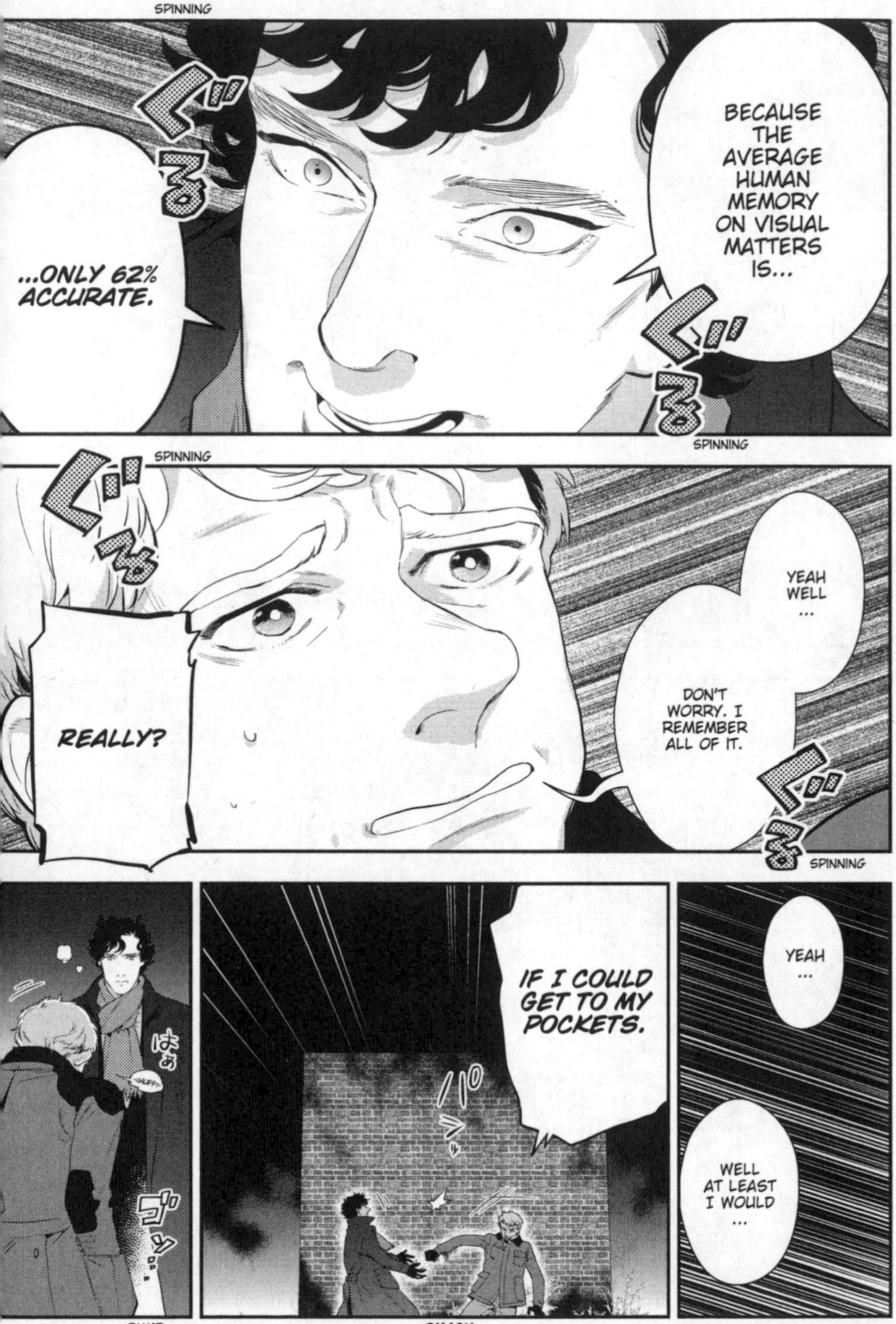
SPINNING
BECAUSE THE AVERAGE HUMAN MEMORY ON VISUAL MATTERS IS...
SPINNING
...ONLY 62% ACCURATE.
SPINNING
YEAH WELL ...
DON'T WORRY. I REMEMBER ALL OF IT.
SPINNING
REALLY?
YEAH ...
WELL AT LEAST I WOULD ...
IF I COULD GET TO MY POCKETS.
SMACK
-HUFF-
BUMP...

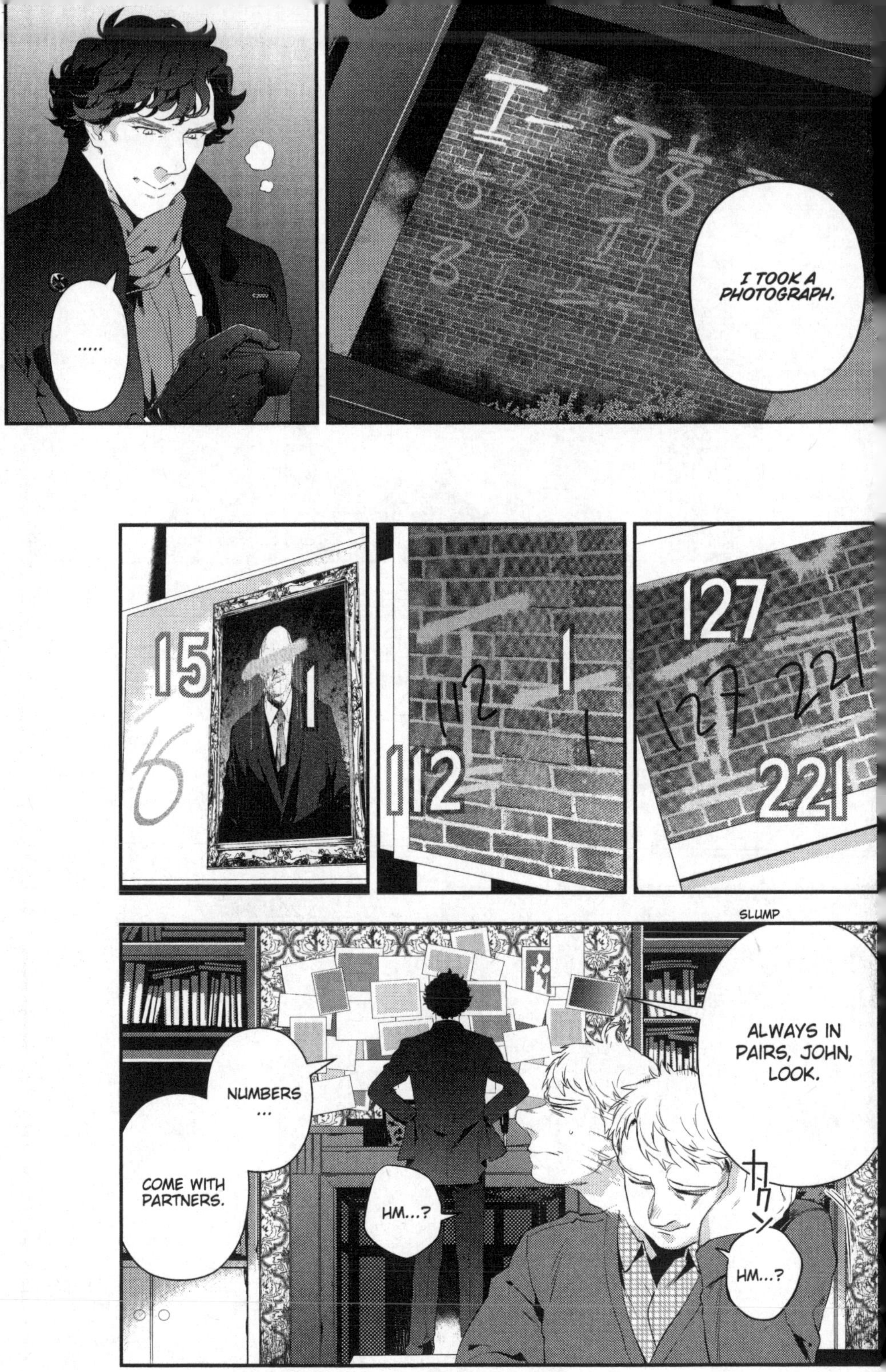
I TOOK A PHOTOGRAPH.
.....
127
221
1
112
15
1
SLUMP
ALWAYS IN PAIRS, JOHN, LOOK.
カクン
HM...?
NUMBERS ...
HM...?
COME WITH PARTNERS.

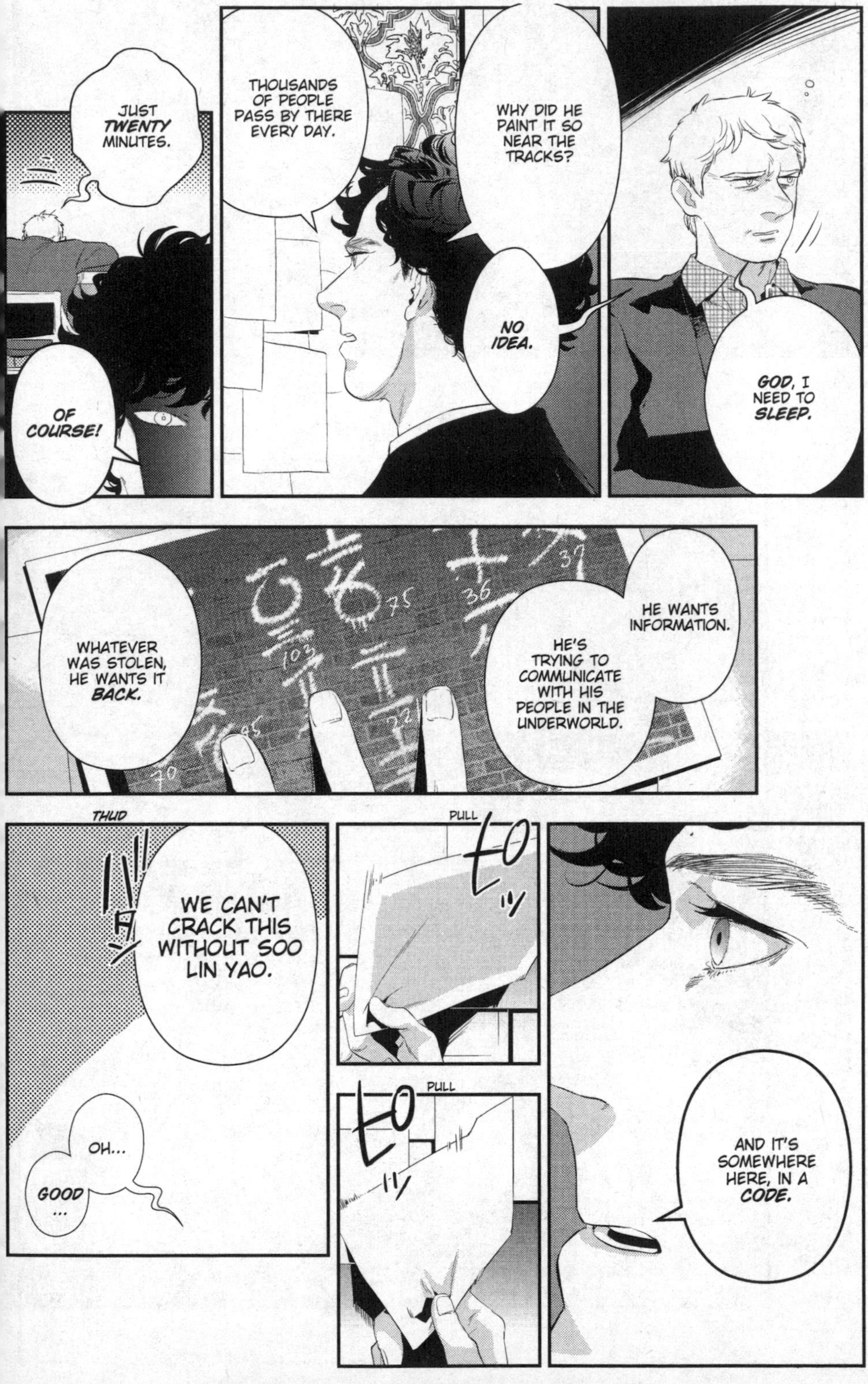
GOD, I NEED TO SLEEP.
WHY DID HE PAINT IT SO NEAR THE TRACKS?
NO IDEA.
THOUSANDS OF PEOPLE PASS BY THERE EVERY DAY.
JUST TWENTY MINUTES.
OF COURSE!
HE WANTS INFORMATION.
HE'S TRYING TO COMMUNICATE WITH HIS PEOPLE IN THE UNDERWORLD.
WHATEVER WAS STOLEN, HE WANTS IT BACK.
AND IT'S SOMEWHERE HERE, IN A CODE.
PULL
PULL
THUD
WE CAN'T CRACK THIS WITHOUT SOO LIN YAO.
OH... GOOD...

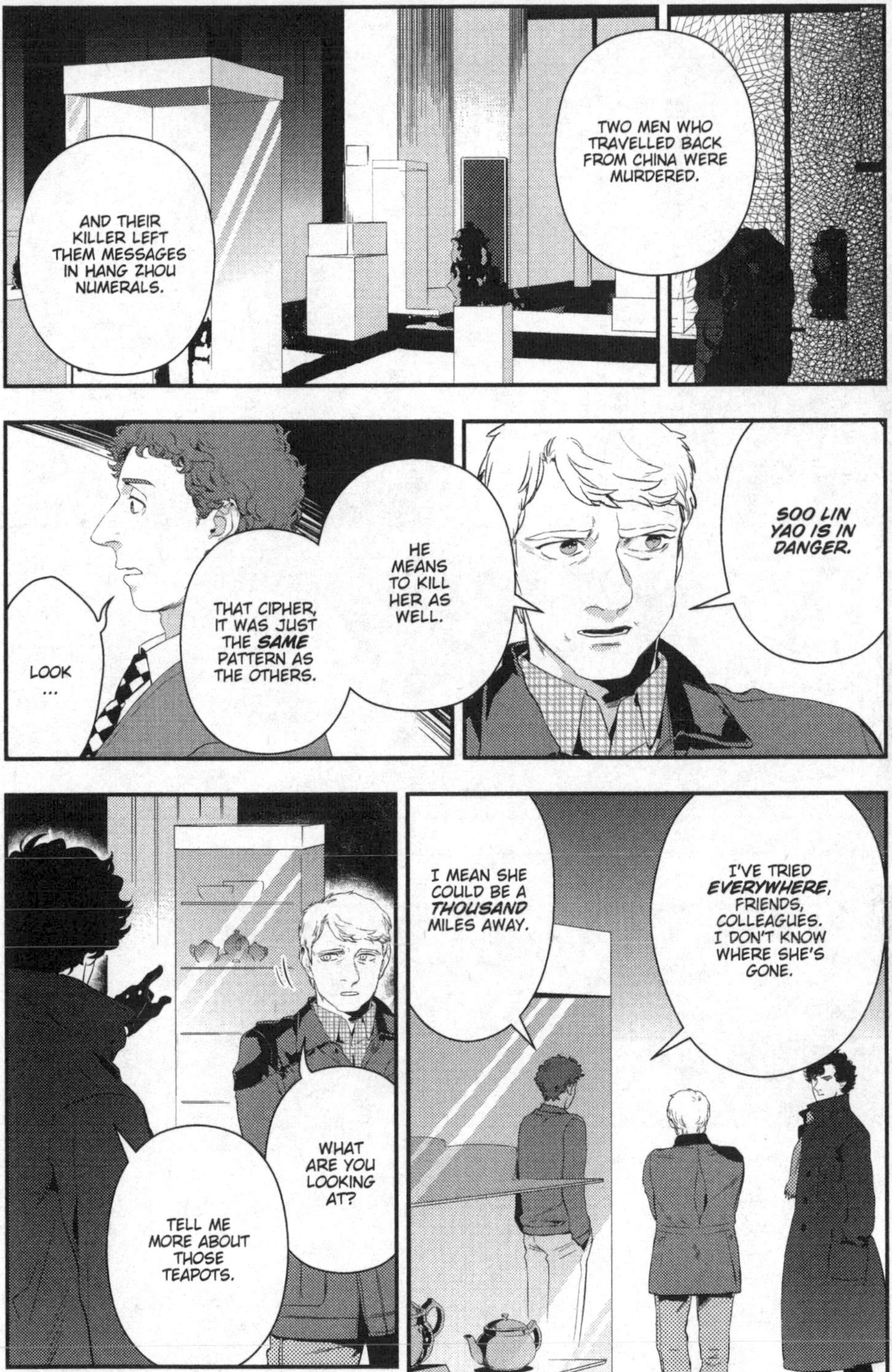
TWO MEN WHO TRAVELLED BACK FROM CHINA WERE MURDERED.
AND THEIR KILLER LEFT THEM MESSAGES IN HANG ZHOU NUMERALS.
SOO LIN YAO IS IN DANGER.
HE MEANS TO KILL HER AS WELL.
THAT CIPHER, IT WAS JUST THE SAME PATTERN AS THE OTHERS.
LOOK ...
I'VE TRIED EVERYWHERE, FRIENDS, COLLEAGUES. I DON'T KNOW WHERE SHE'S GONE.
I MEAN SHE COULD BE A THOUSAND MILES AWAY.
WHAT ARE YOU LOOKING AT?
TELL ME MORE ABOUT THOSE TEAPOTS.

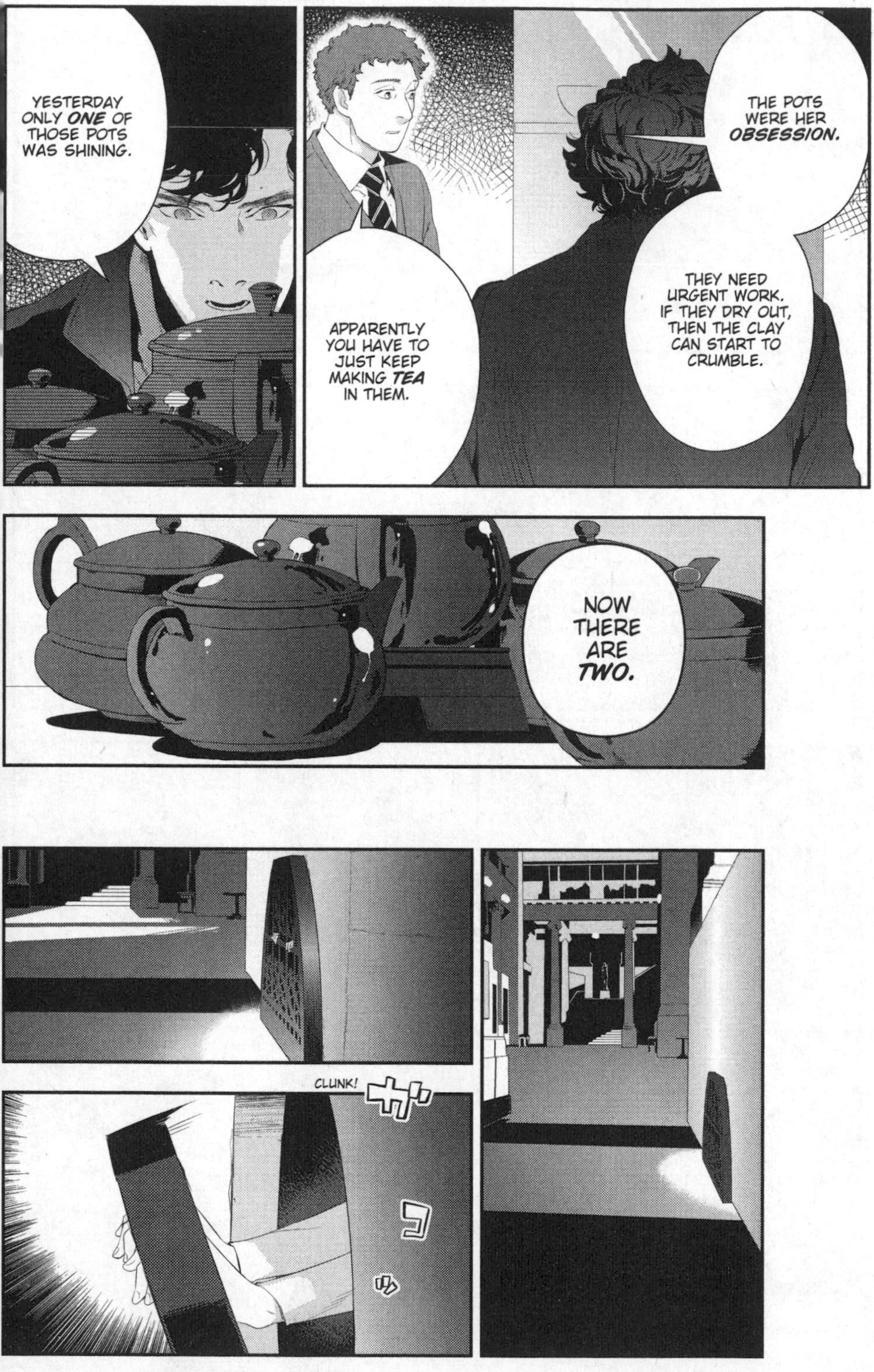
THE POTS WERE HER OBSESSION.
THEY NEED URGENT WORK. IF THEY DRY OUT, THEN THE CLAY CAN START TO CRUMBLE.
APPARENTLY YOU HAVE TO JUST KEEP MAKING TEA IN THEM.
YESTERDAY ONLY ONE OF THOSE POTS WAS SHINING.
NOW THERE ARE TWO.
CLUNK!

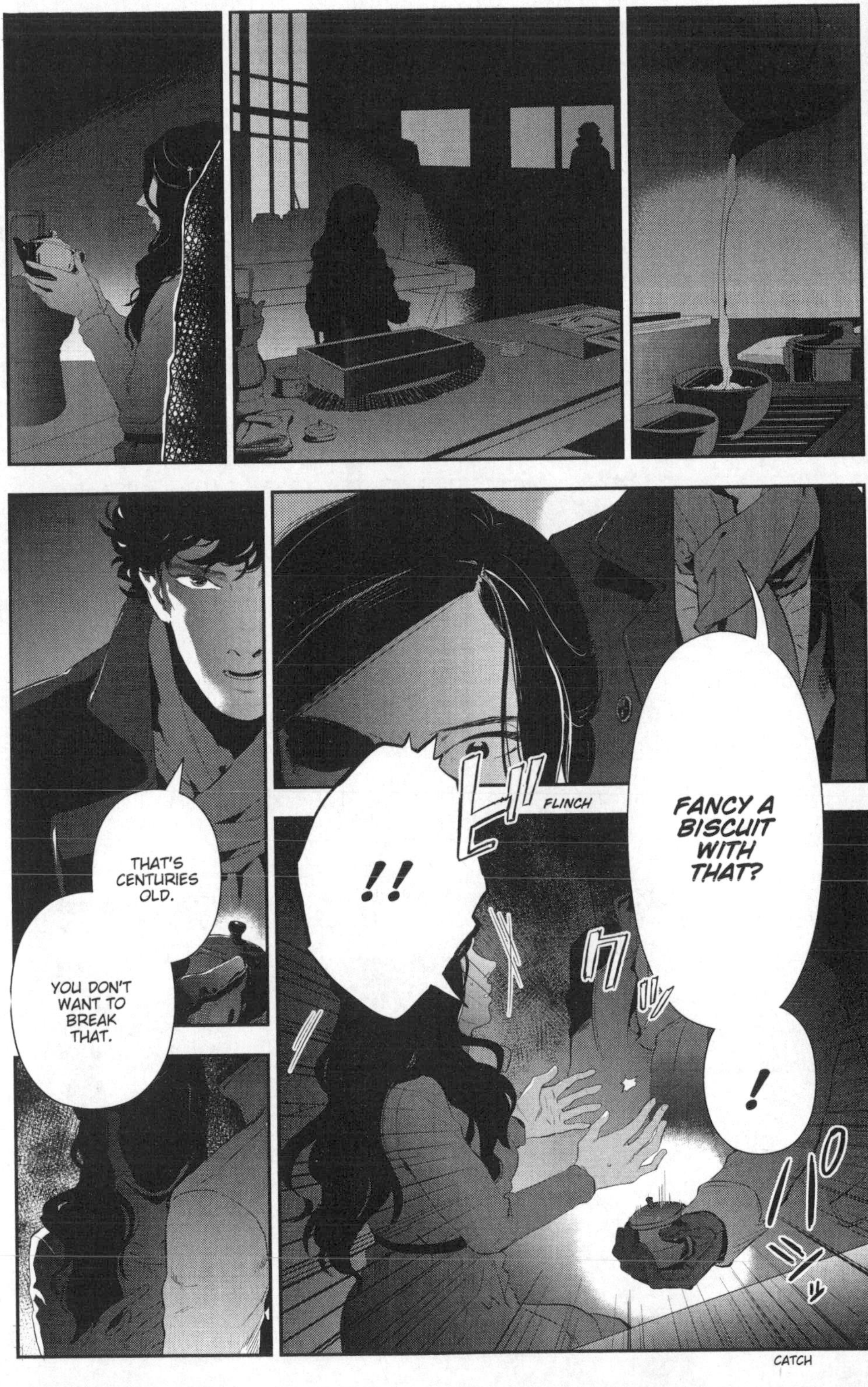
FANCY A BISCUIT WITH THAT?
FLINCH
!!
!
CATCH
THAT'S CENTURIES OLD.
YOU DON'T WANT TO BREAK THAT.

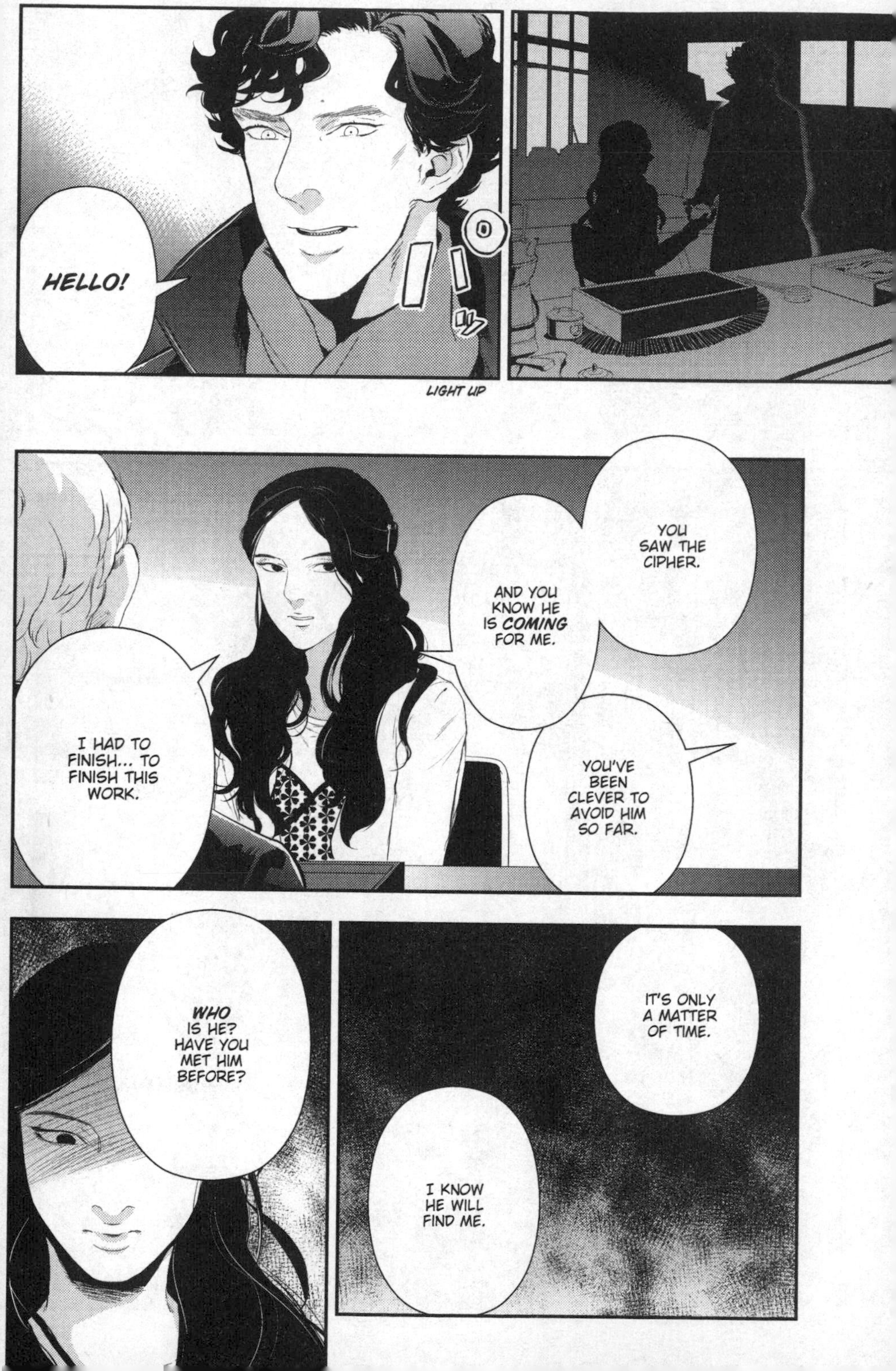
HELLO!
LIGHT UP
YOU SAW THE CIPHER.
AND YOU KNOW HE IS COMING FOR ME.
YOU'VE BEEN CLEVER TO AVOID HIM SO FAR.
I HAD TO FINISH... TO FINISH THIS WORK.
IT'S ONLY A MATTER OF TIME.
I KNOW HE WILL FIND ME.
WHO IS HE? HAVE YOU MET HIM BEFORE?

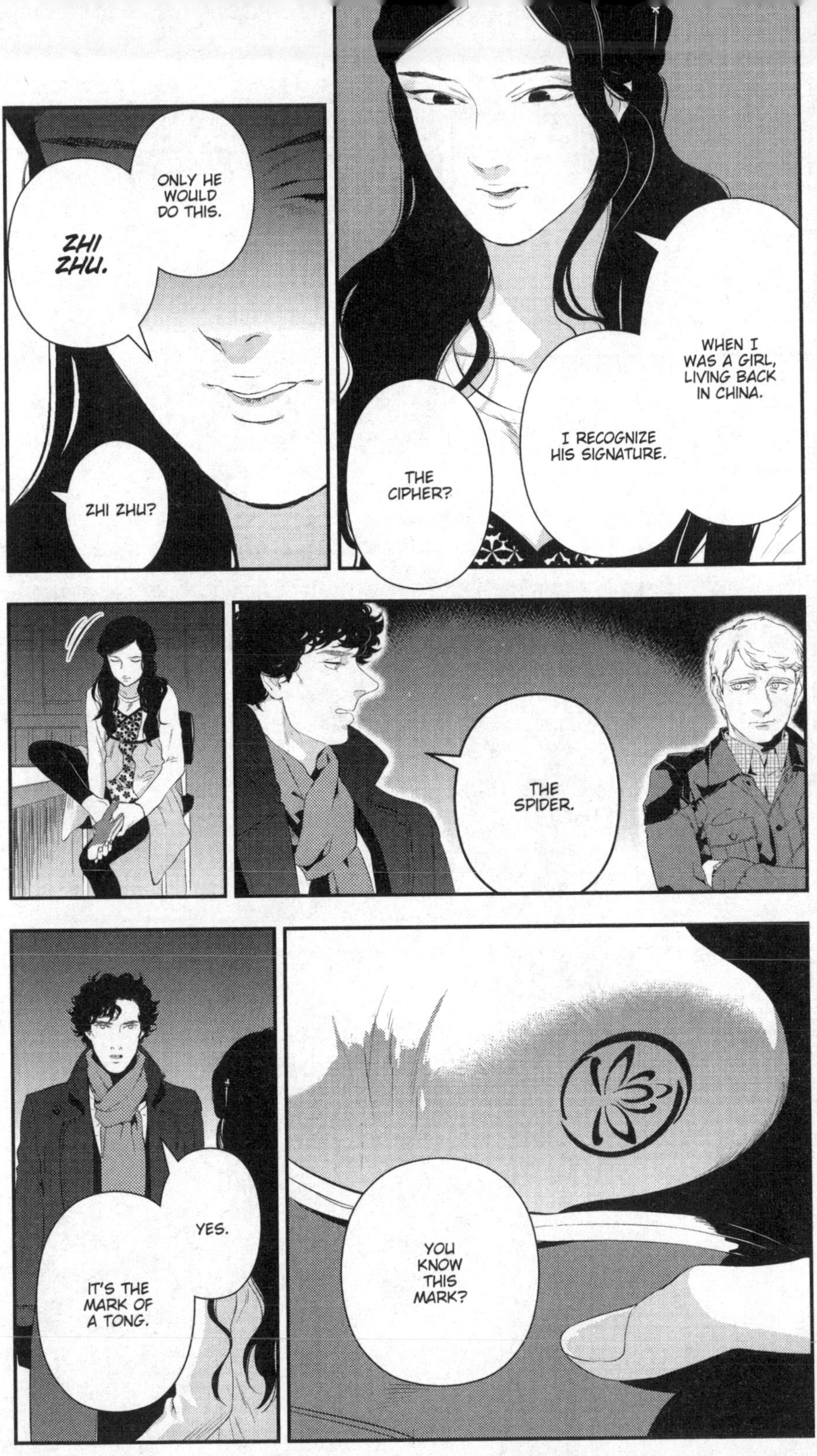
WHEN I WAS A GIRL, LIVING BACK IN CHINA.
I RECOGNIZE HIS SIGNATURE.
THE CIPHER?
ONLY HE WOULD DO THIS.
ZHI ZHU.
ZHI ZHU?
THE SPIDER.
YOU KNOW THIS MARK?
YES.
IT'S THE MARK OF A TONG.

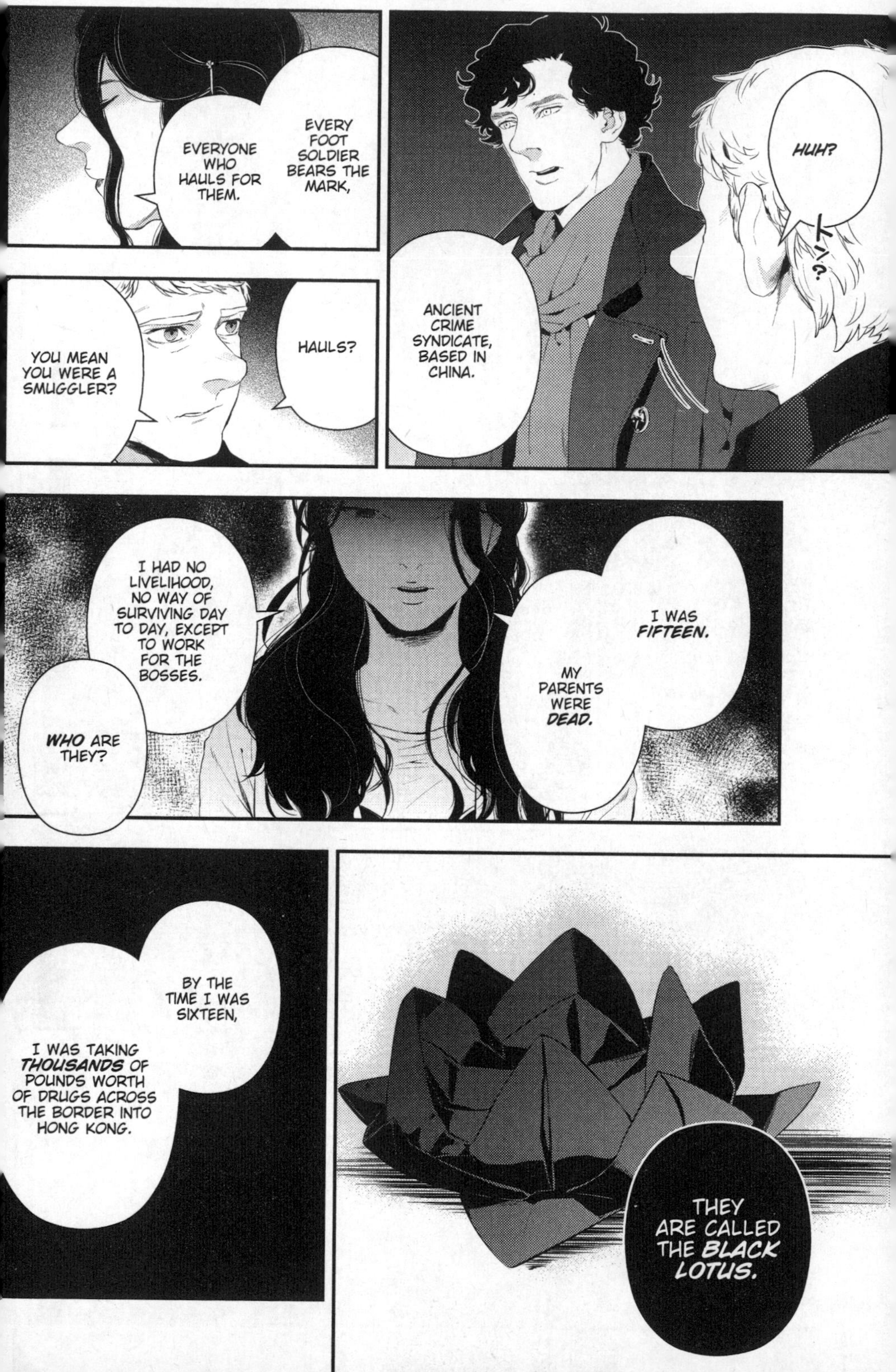
HUH?
ANCIENT CRIME SYNDICATE, BASED IN CHINA.
EVERY FOOT SOLDIER BEARS THE MARK,
EVERYONE WHO HAULS FOR THEM.
HAULS?
YOU MEAN YOU WERE A SMUGGLER?
I WAS *FIFTEEN.*
MY PARENTS WERE *DEAD.*
I HAD NO LIVELIHOOD, NO WAY OF SURVIVING DAY TO DAY, EXCEPT TO WORK FOR THE BOSSES.
WHO ARE THEY?
THEY ARE CALLED THE *BLACK LOTUS.*
BY THE TIME I WAS SIXTEEN,
I WAS TAKING *THOUSANDS* OF POUNDS WORTH OF DRUGS ACROSS THE BORDER INTO HONG KONG.

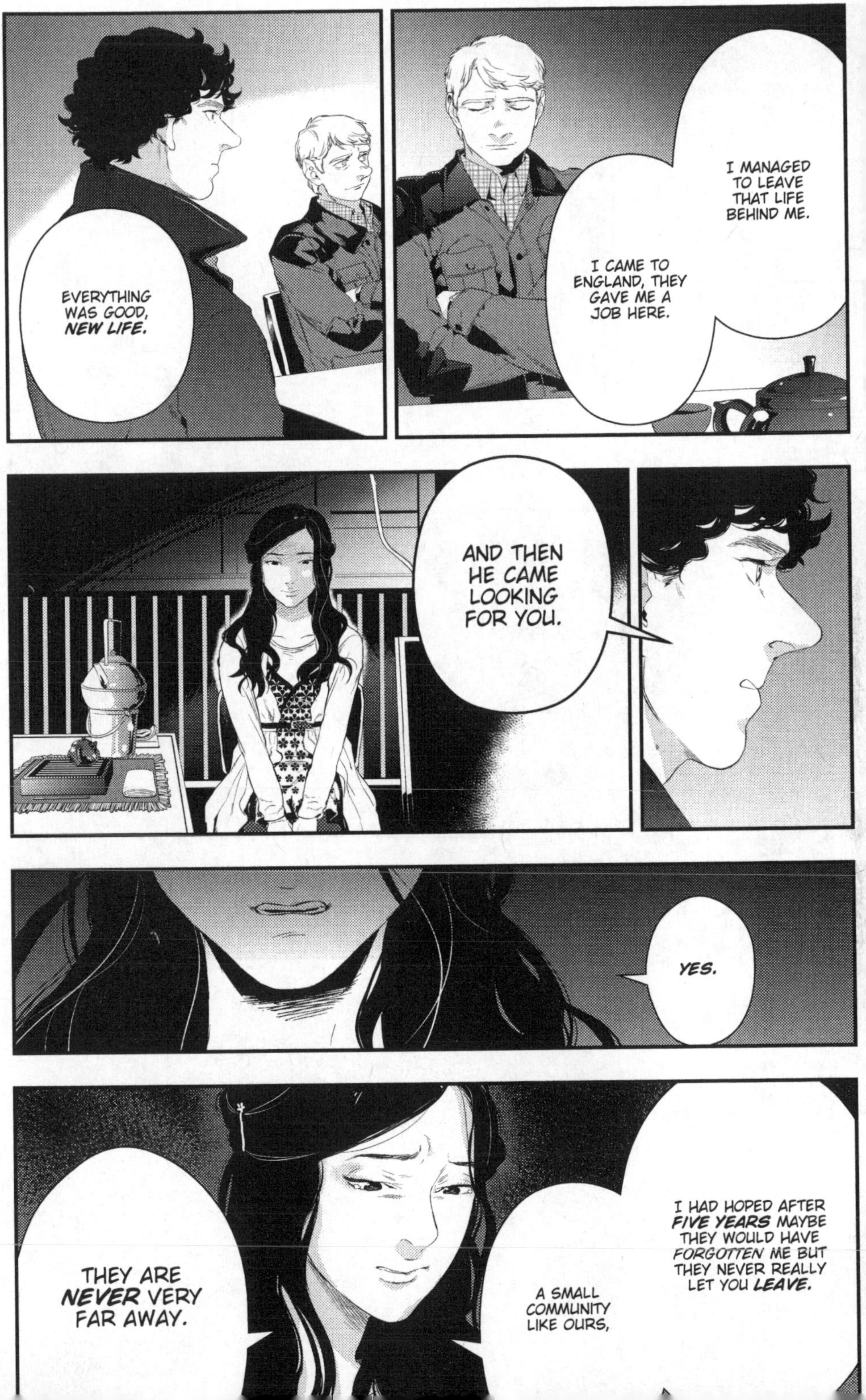
I MANAGED TO LEAVE THAT LIFE BEHIND ME.
I CAME TO ENGLAND, THEY GAVE ME A JOB HERE.
EVERYTHING WAS GOOD, *NEW LIFE.*
AND THEN HE CAME LOOKING FOR YOU.
YES.
I HAD HOPED AFTER *FIVE YEARS* MAYBE THEY WOULD HAVE *FORGOTTEN* ME BUT THEY NEVER REALLY LET YOU *LEAVE.*
A SMALL COMMUNITY LIKE OURS,
THEY ARE *NEVER* VERY FAR AWAY.

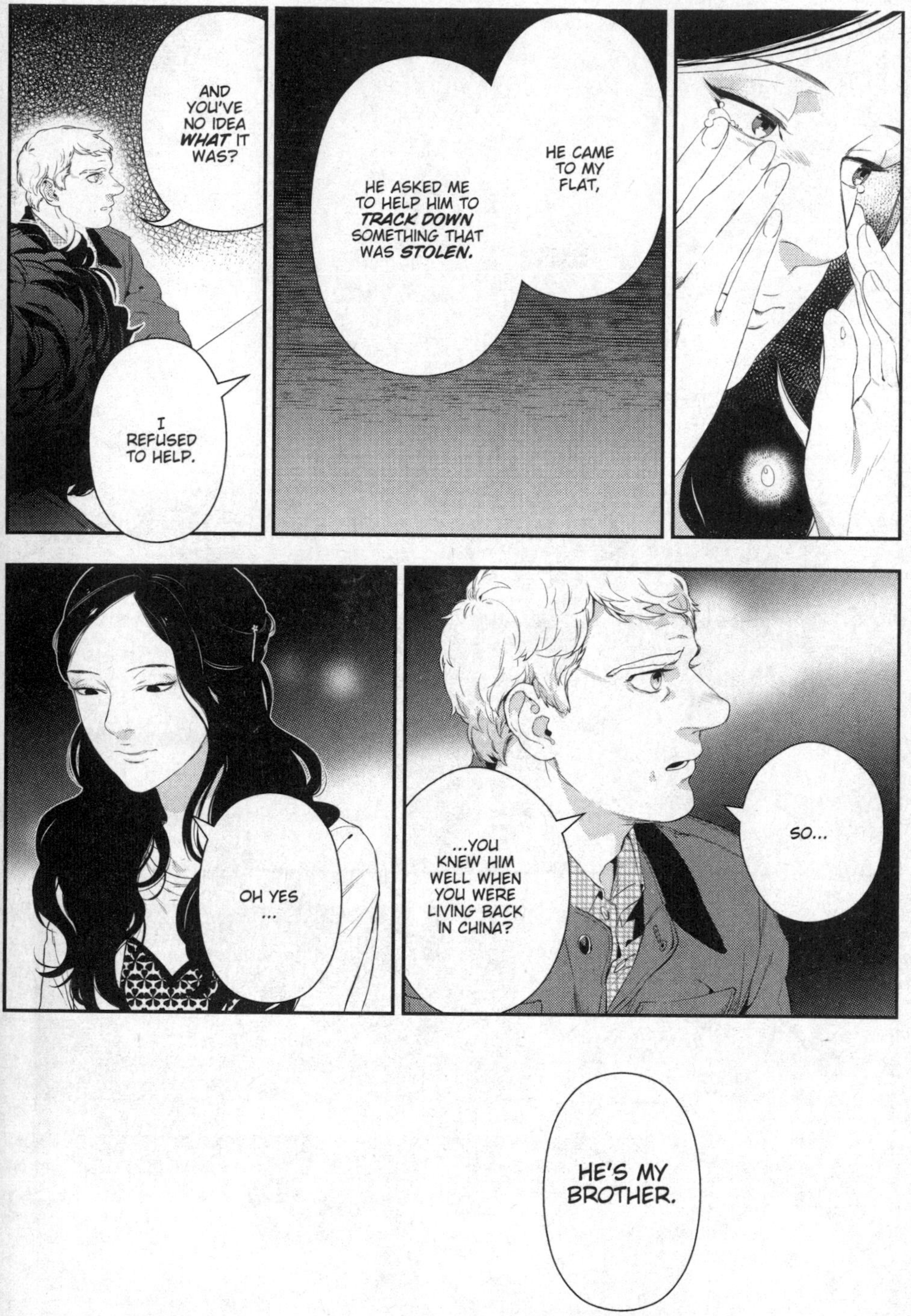
HE CAME TO MY FLAT,
HE ASKED ME TO HELP HIM TO TRACK DOWN SOMETHING THAT WAS STOLEN.
AND YOU'VE NO IDEA WHAT IT WAS?
I REFUSED TO HELP.
SO...
...YOU KNEW HIM WELL WHEN YOU WERE LIVING BACK IN CHINA?
OH YES ...
HE'S MY BROTHER.

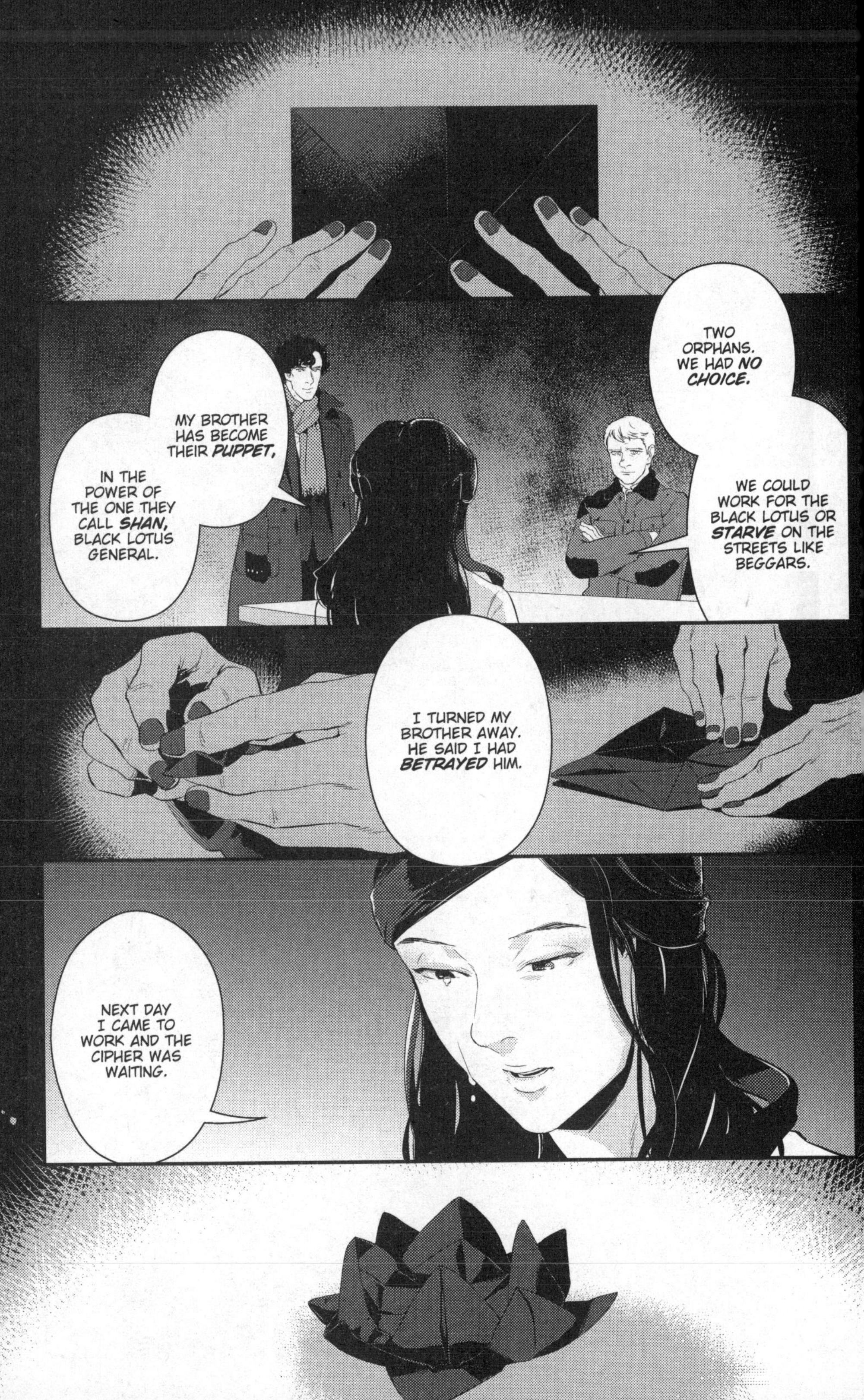
TWO ORPHANS. WE HAD **NO CHOICE.**
WE COULD WORK FOR THE BLACK LOTUS OR **STARVE** ON THE STREETS LIKE BEGGARS.
MY BROTHER HAS BECOME THEIR **PUPPET,**
IN THE POWER OF THE ONE THEY CALL **SHAN,** BLACK LOTUS GENERAL.
I TURNED MY BROTHER AWAY. HE SAID I HAD **BETRAYED** HIM.
NEXT DAY I CAME TO WORK AND THE CIPHER WAS WAITING.

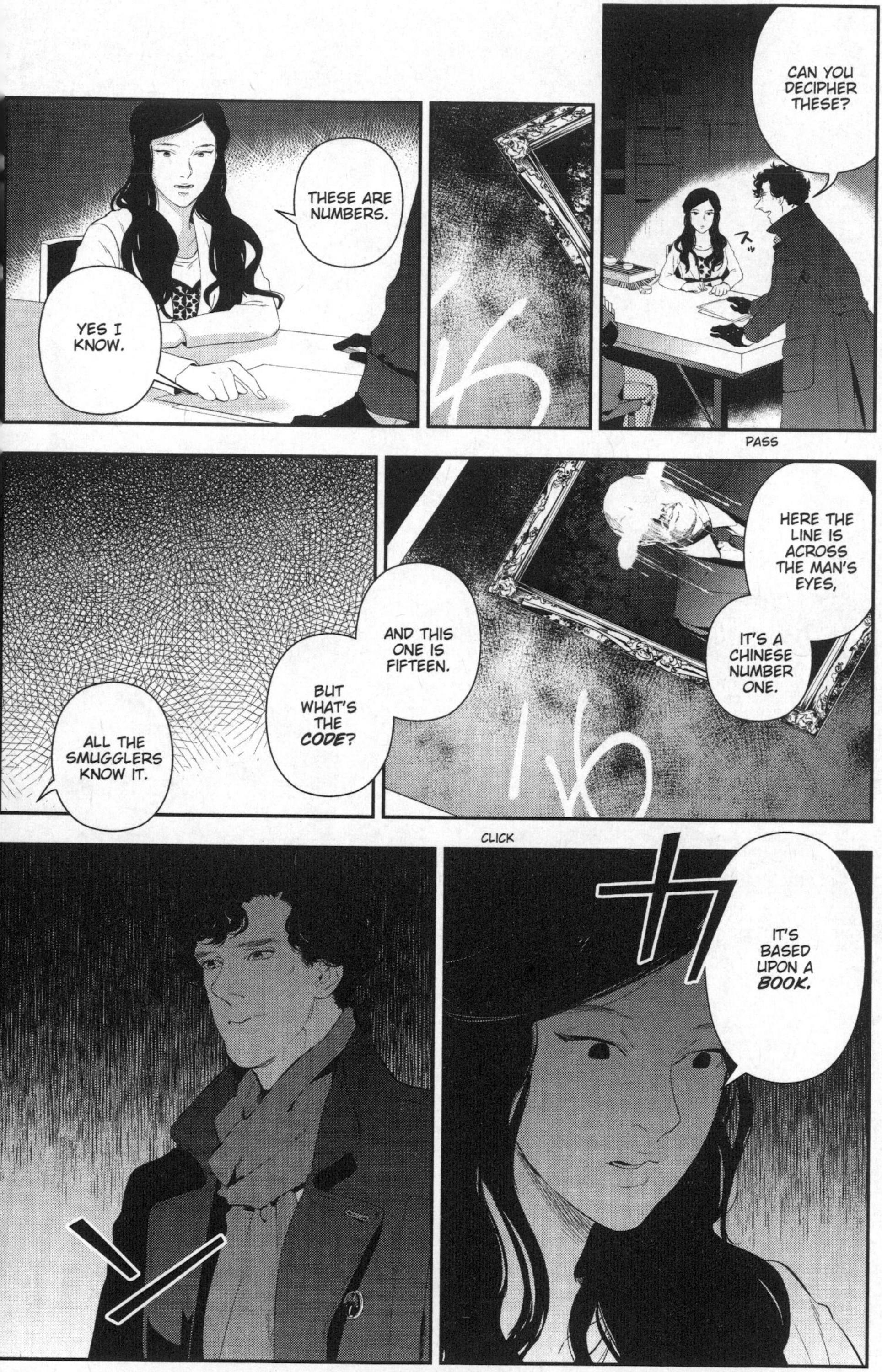
CAN YOU DECIPHER THESE?
スッ
PASS
THESE ARE NUMBERS.
YES I KNOW.
HERE THE LINE IS ACROSS THE MAN'S EYES,
IT'S A CHINESE NUMBER ONE.
AND THIS ONE IS FIFTEEN.
BUT WHAT'S THE *CODE*?
ALL THE SMUGGLERS KNOW IT.
CLICK
IT'S BASED UPON A *BOOK.*

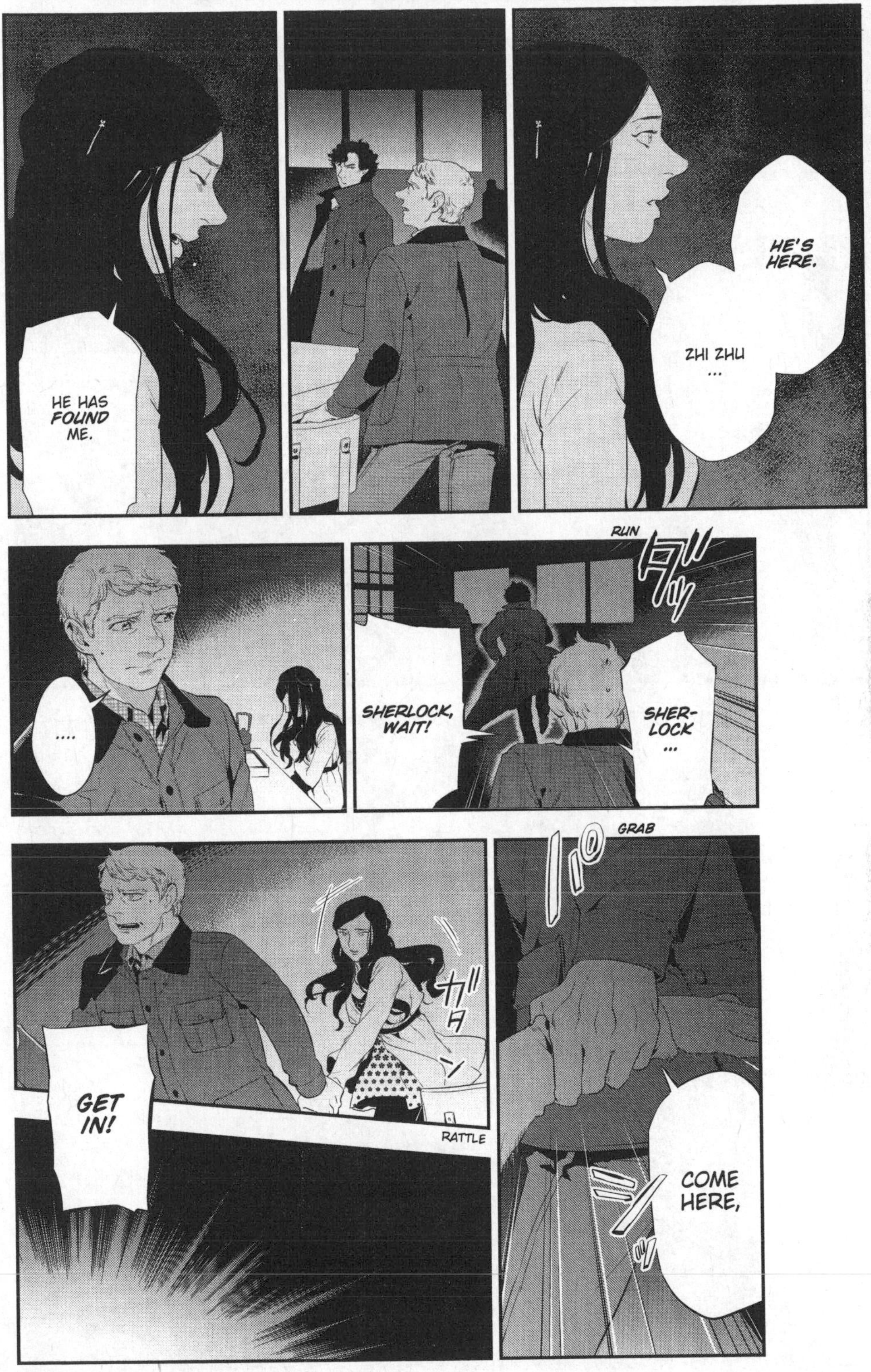
HE'S HERE.
ZHI ZHU ...
HE HAS FOUND ME.
RUN
SHER-LOCK ...
SHERLOCK, WAIT!
....
GRAB
COME HERE,
GET IN!
RATTLE

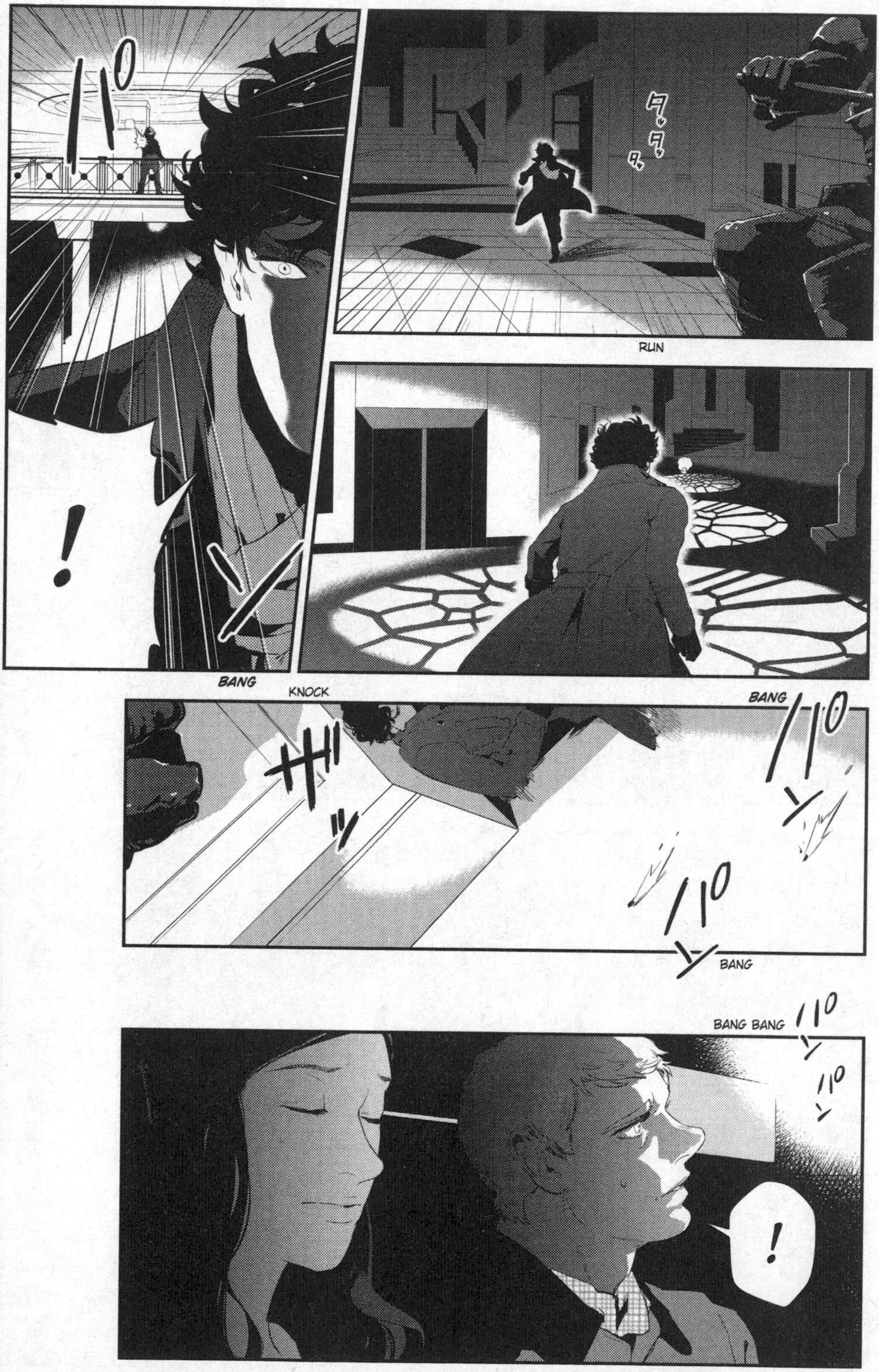

RUN
!
BANG
BANG
BANG
KNOCK
BANG BANG
!

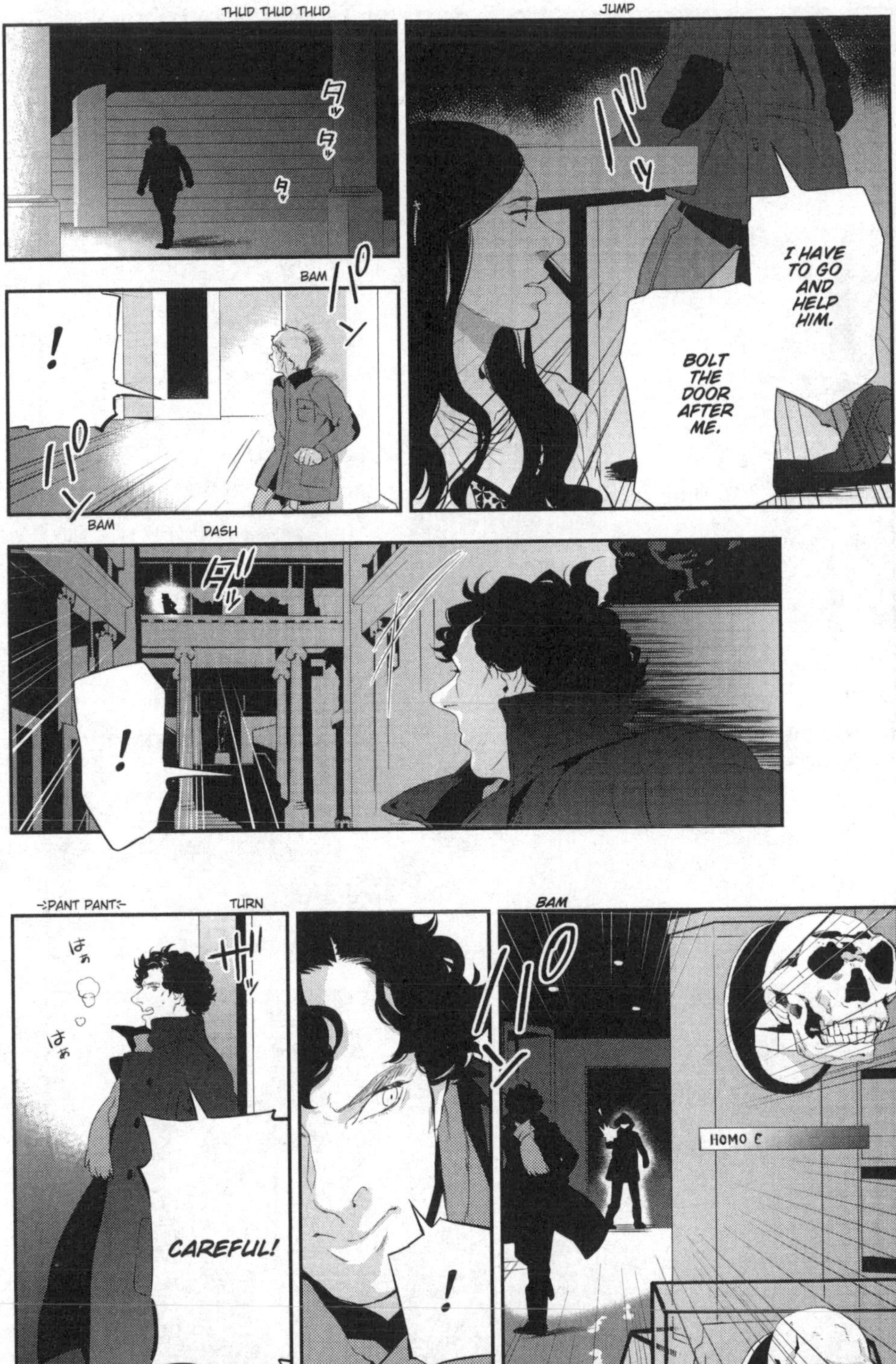
JUMP
I HAVE TO GO AND HELP HIM.
BOLT THE DOOR AFTER ME.
THUD THUD THUD
BAM
!
BAM
DASH
!
BAM
HOMO E
!
PANT PANT
TURN
CAREFUL!

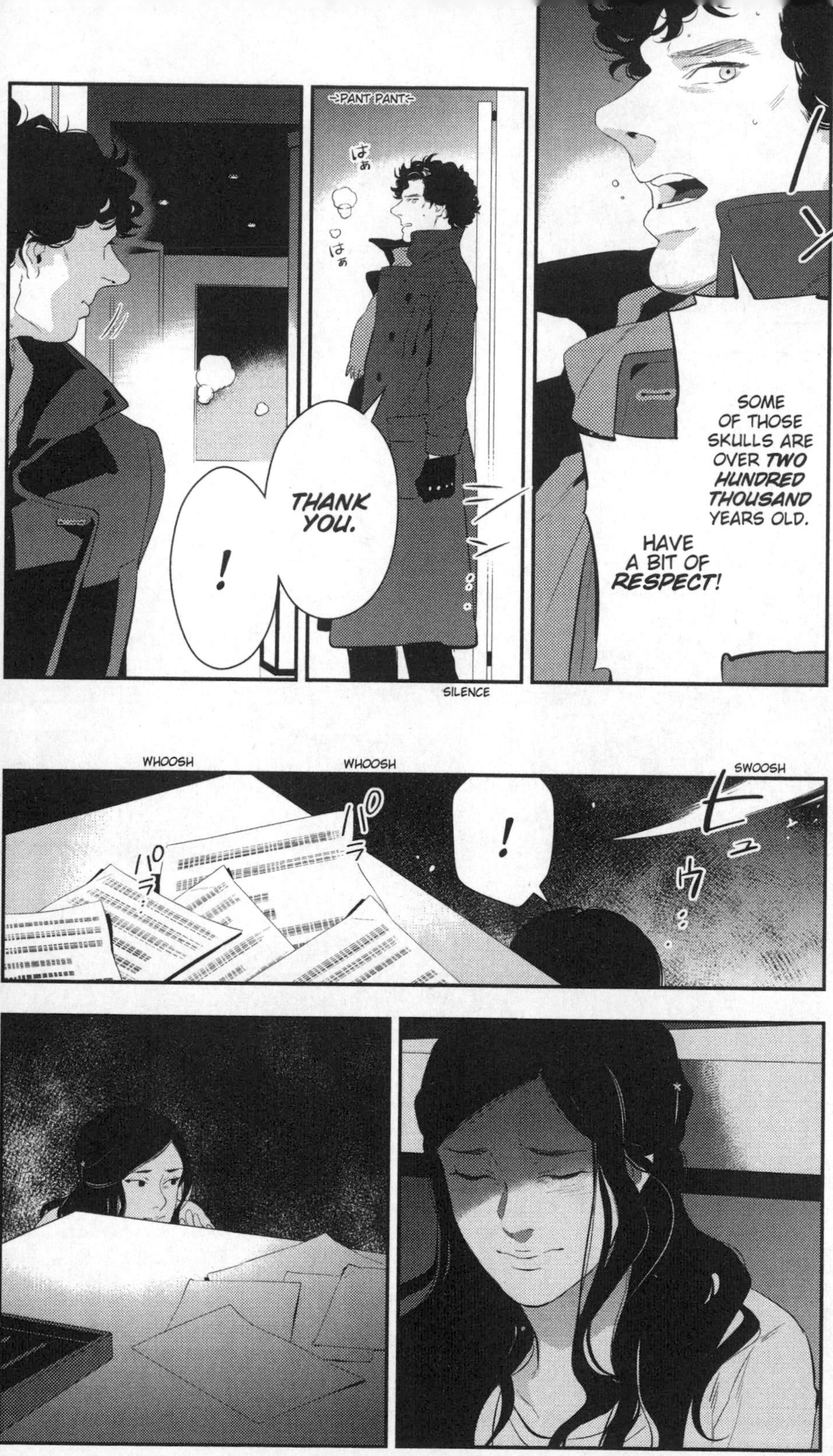
パン
BAM!
SOME OF THOSE SKULLS ARE OVER TWO HUNDRED THOUSAND YEARS OLD.
HAVE A BIT OF RESPECT!
PANT PANT
はぁ
はぁ
THANK YOU.
SILENCE
!
SWOOSH
ヒュウ
!
WHOOSH
パラ
WHOOSH
パラ

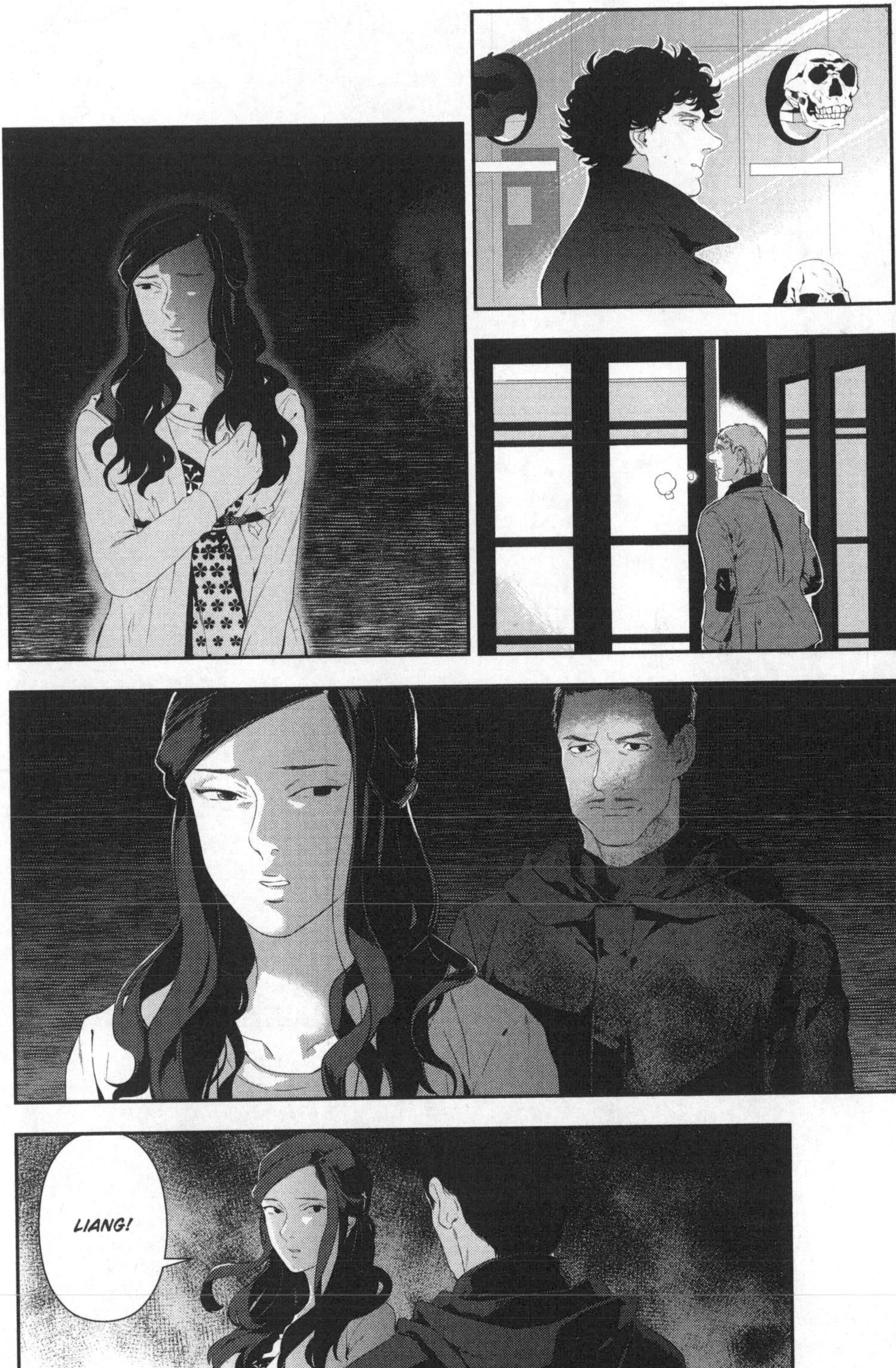
LIANG!

大哥

是你…

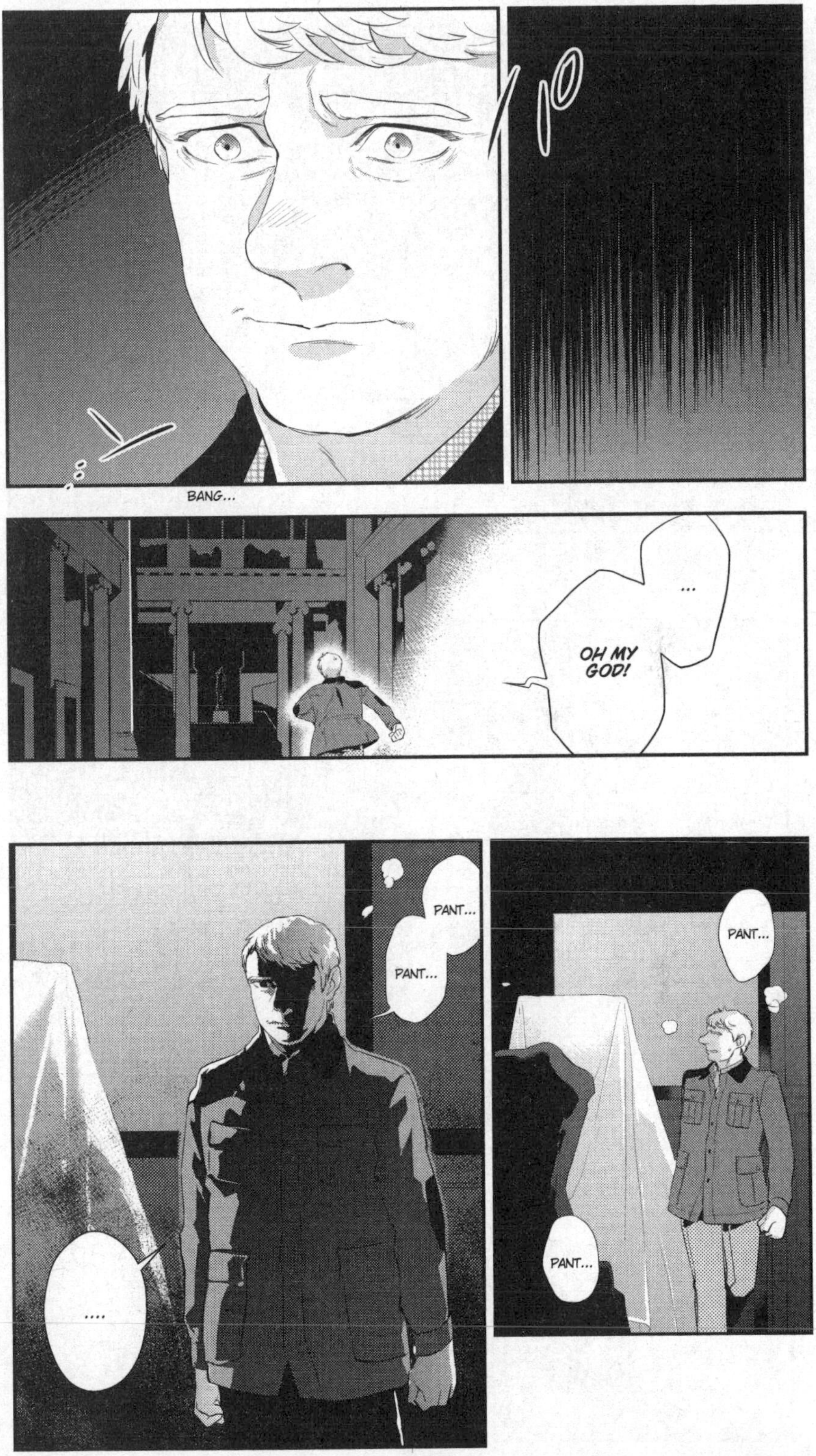
BANG...
...
OH MY GOD!
PANT...
PANT...
PANT...
PANT...
....

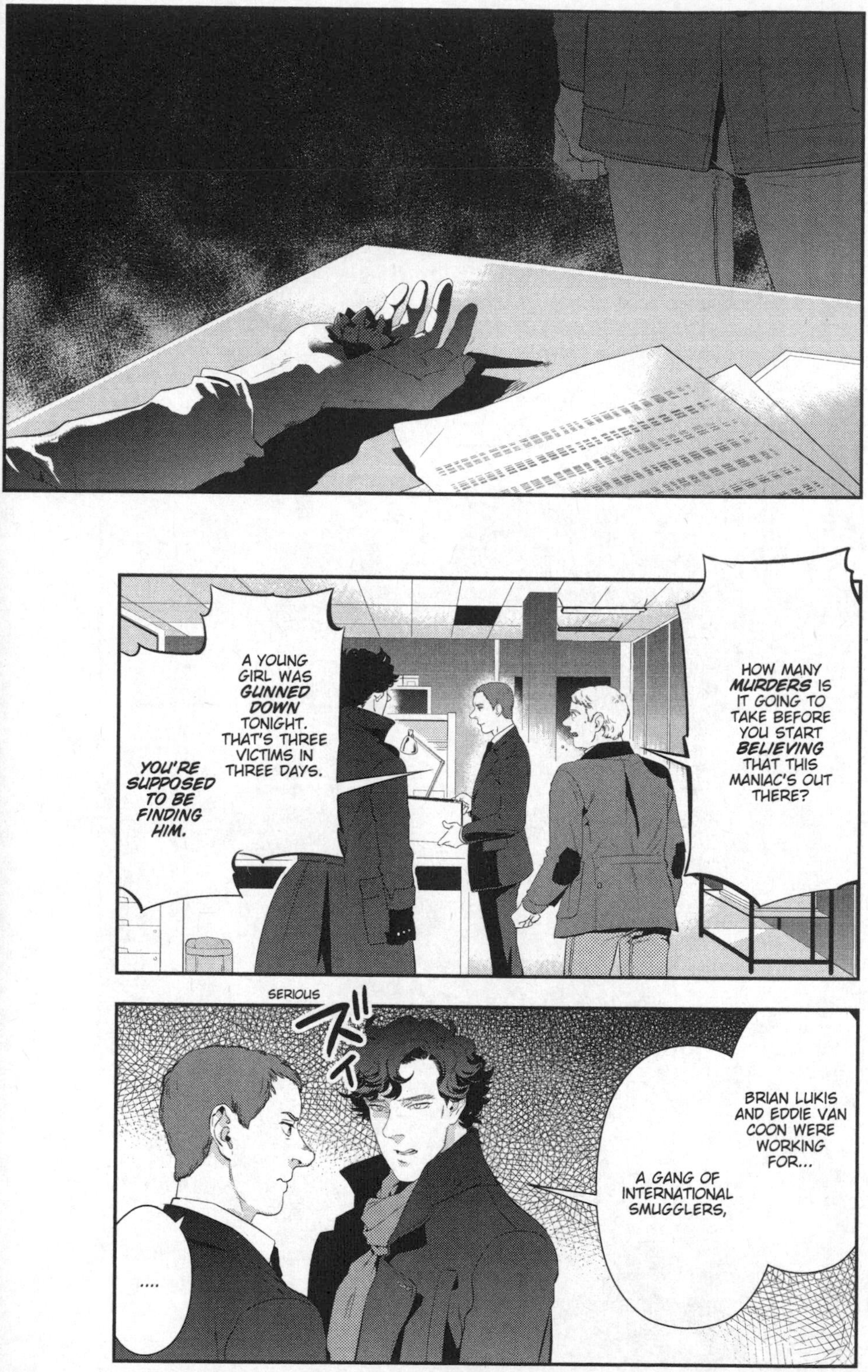
HOW MANY MURDERS IS IT GOING TO TAKE BEFORE YOU START BELIEVING THAT THIS MANIAC'S OUT THERE?
A YOUNG GIRL WAS GUNNED DOWN TONIGHT. THAT'S THREE VICTIMS IN THREE DAYS.
YOU'RE SUPPOSED TO BE FINDING HIM.
ズィ
SERIOUS
BRIAN LUKIS AND EDDIE VAN COON WERE WORKING FOR...
A GANG OF INTERNATIONAL SMUGGLERS,
....

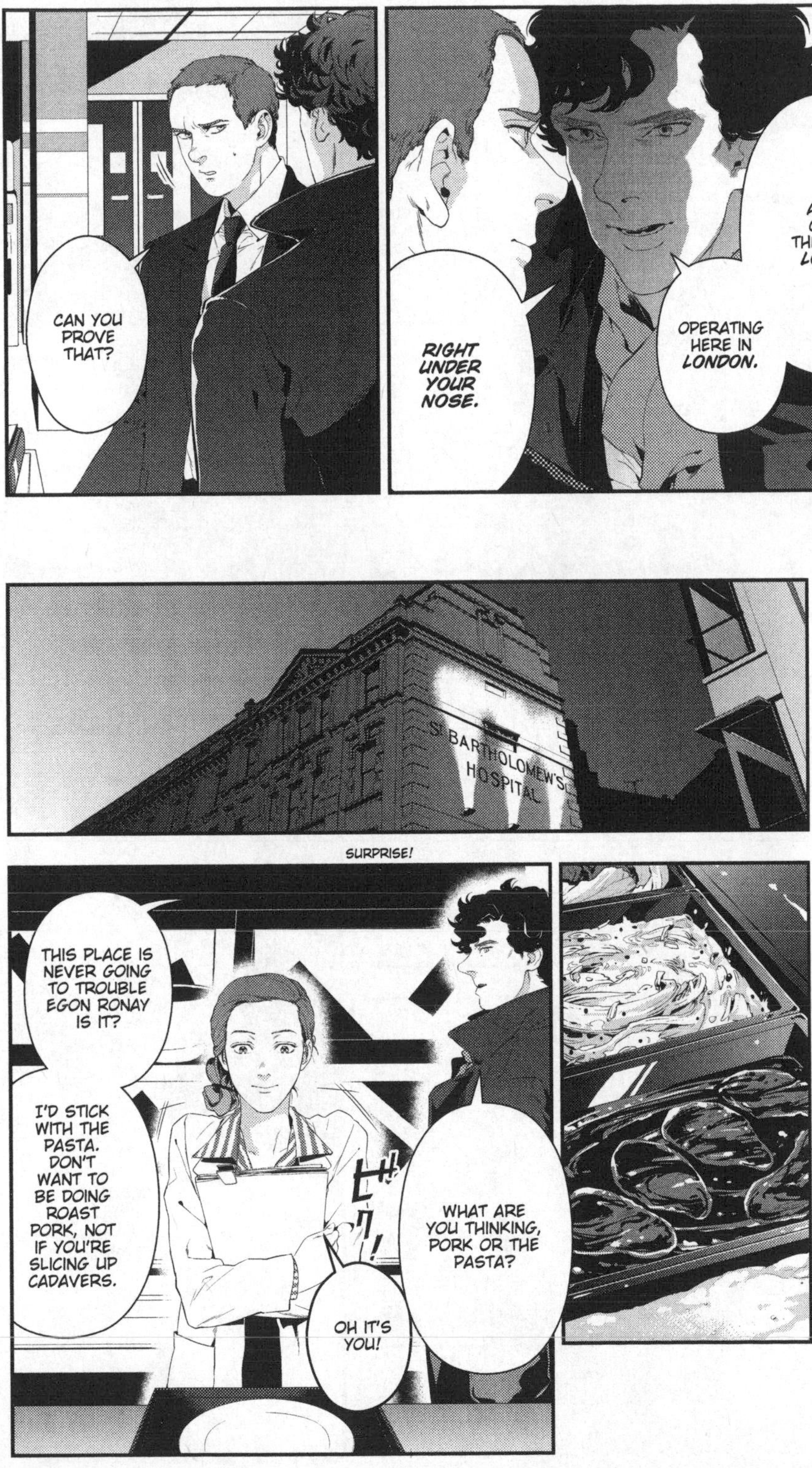
A GANG CALLED THE BLACK LOTUS...
OPERATING HERE IN LONDON.
RIGHT UNDER YOUR NOSE.
CAN YOU PROVE THAT?
ST BARTHOLOMEW'S HOSPITAL
SURPRISE!
WHAT ARE YOU THINKING, PORK OR THE PASTA?
ビクッ!
OH IT'S YOU!
THIS PLACE IS NEVER GOING TO TROUBLE EGON RONAY IS IT?
I'D STICK WITH THE PASTA. DON'T WANT TO BE DOING ROAST PORK, NOT IF YOU'RE SLICING UP CADAVERS.

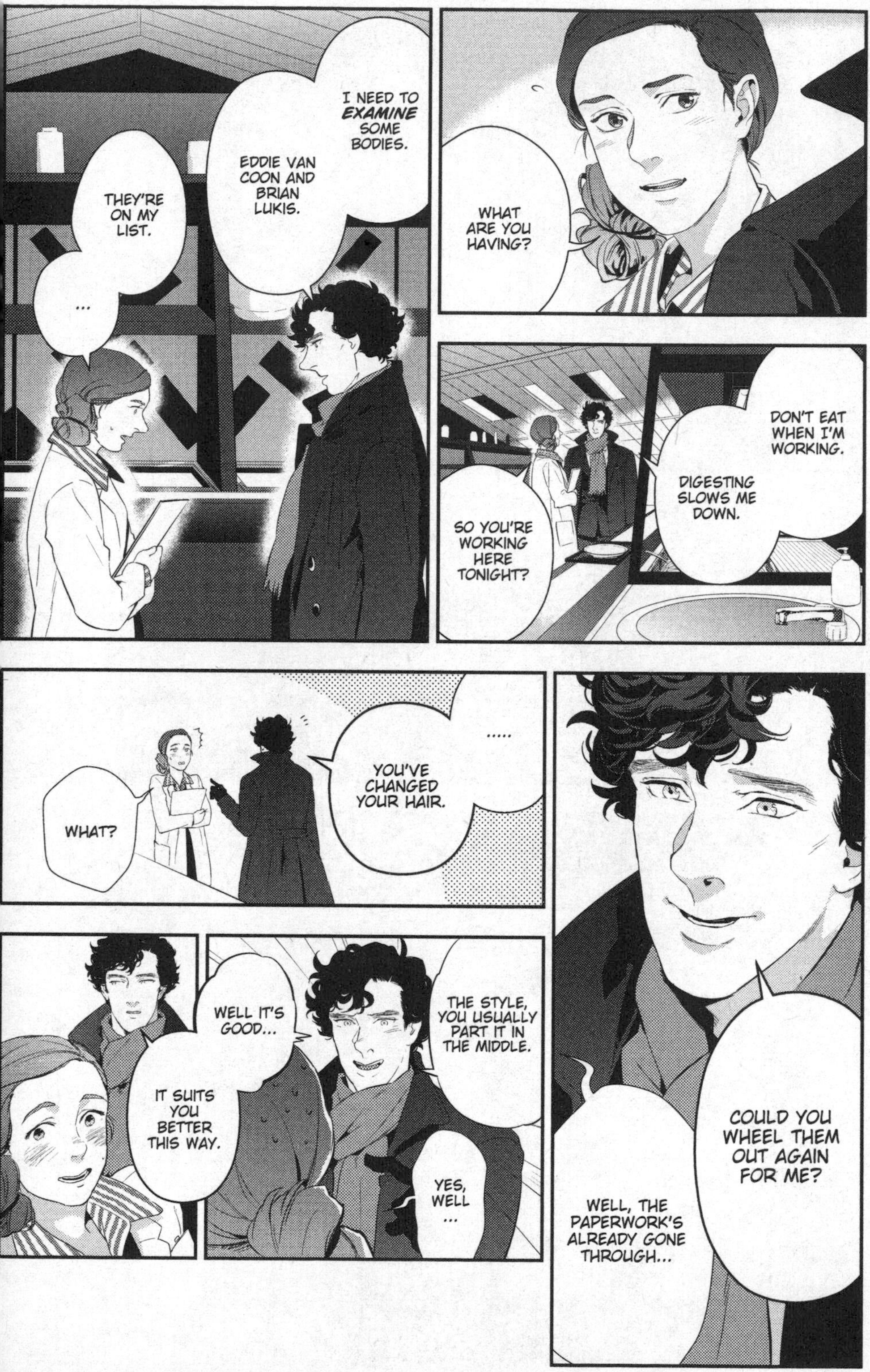
WHAT ARE YOU HAVING?
DON'T EAT WHEN I'M WORKING.
DIGESTING SLOWS ME DOWN.
SO YOU'RE WORKING HERE TONIGHT?
I NEED TO **EXAMINE** SOME BODIES.
EDDIE VAN COON AND BRIAN LUKIS.
THEY'RE ON MY LIST.
...
COULD YOU WHEEL THEM OUT AGAIN FOR ME?
WELL, THE PAPERWORK'S ALREADY GONE THROUGH...
.....
YOU'VE CHANGED YOUR HAIR.
WHAT?
THE STYLE, YOU USUALLY PART IT IN THE MIDDLE.
WELL IT'S GOOD...
YES, WELL ...
IT SUITS YOU BETTER THIS WAY.

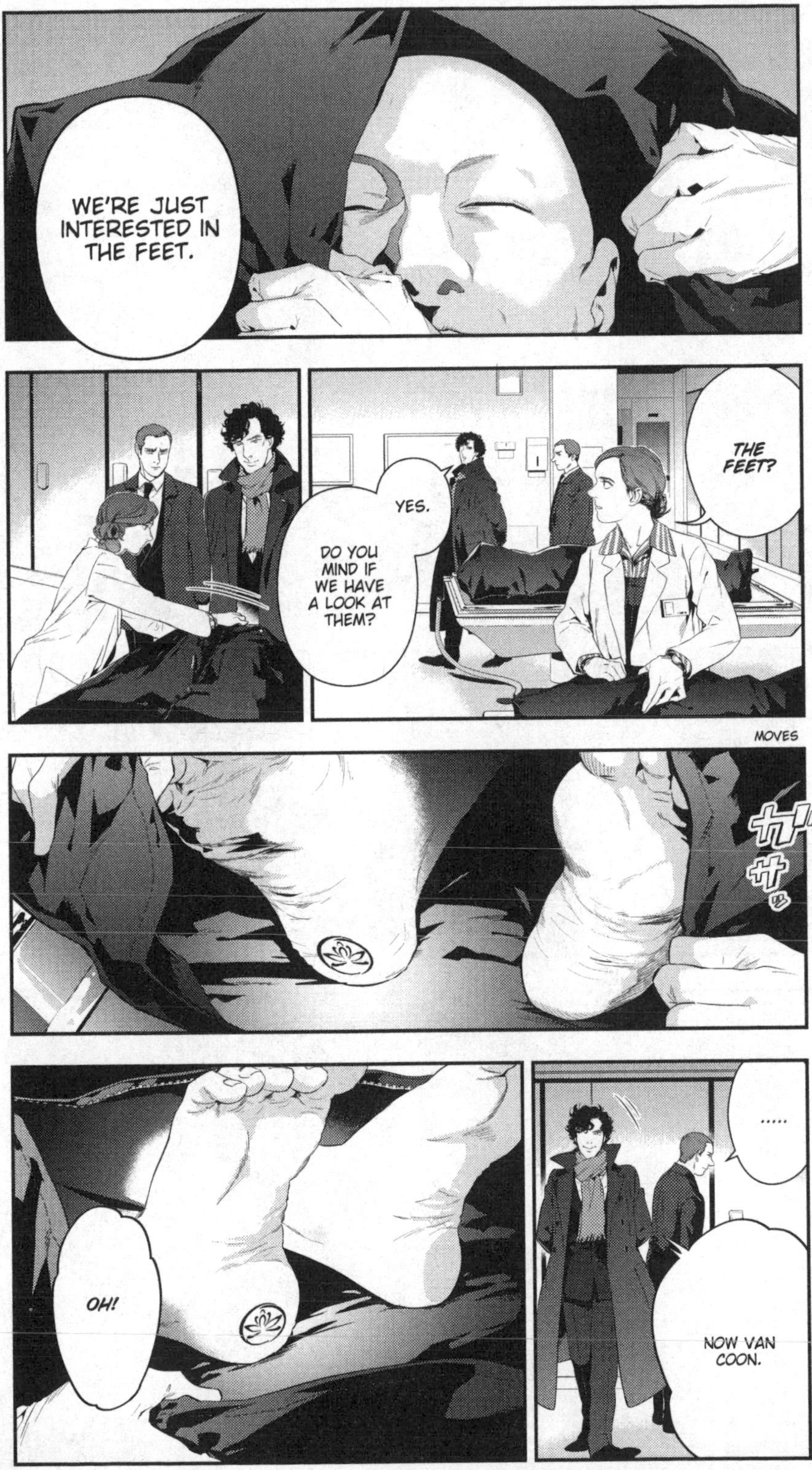
WE'RE JUST INTERESTED IN THE FEET.
THE FEET?
YES.
DO YOU MIND IF WE HAVE A LOOK AT THEM?
MOVES
.....
NOW VAN COON.
OH!

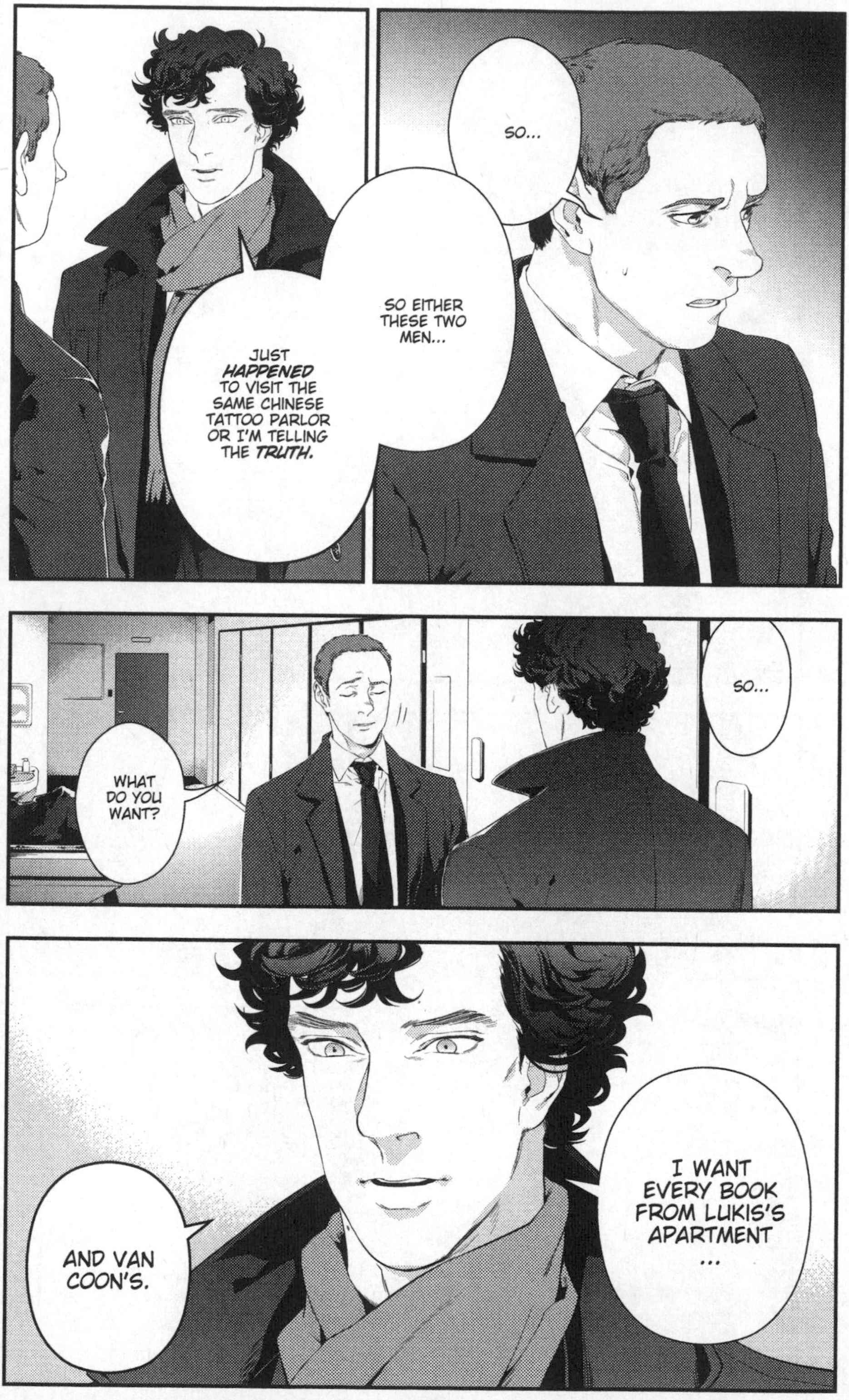
SO...
SO EITHER THESE TWO MEN...
JUST ***HAPPENED*** TO VISIT THE SAME CHINESE TATTOO PARLOR OR I'M TELLING THE ***TRUTH.***
SO...
WHAT DO YOU WANT?
I WANT EVERY BOOK FROM LUKIS'S APARTMENT ...
AND VAN COON'S.

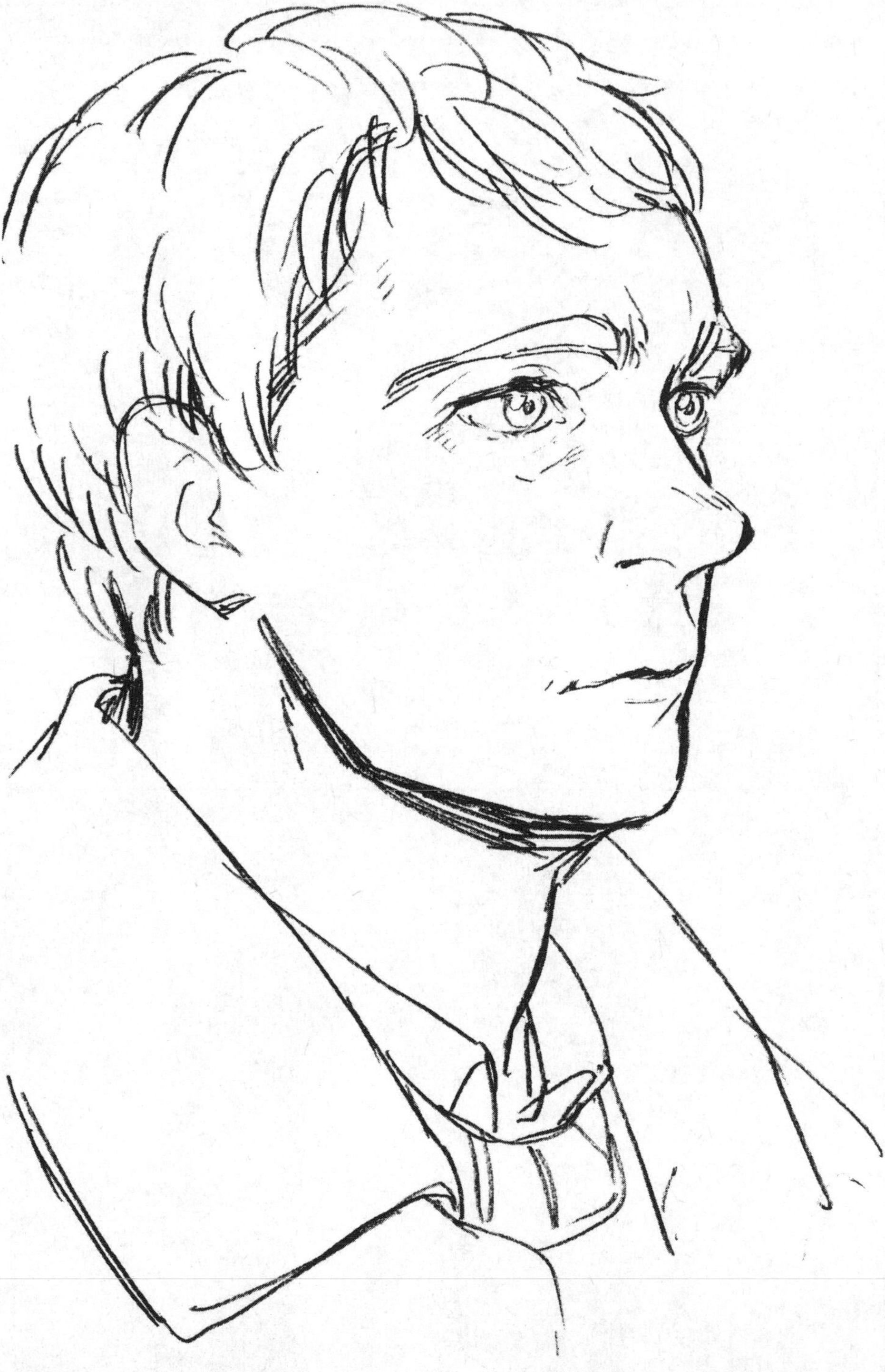

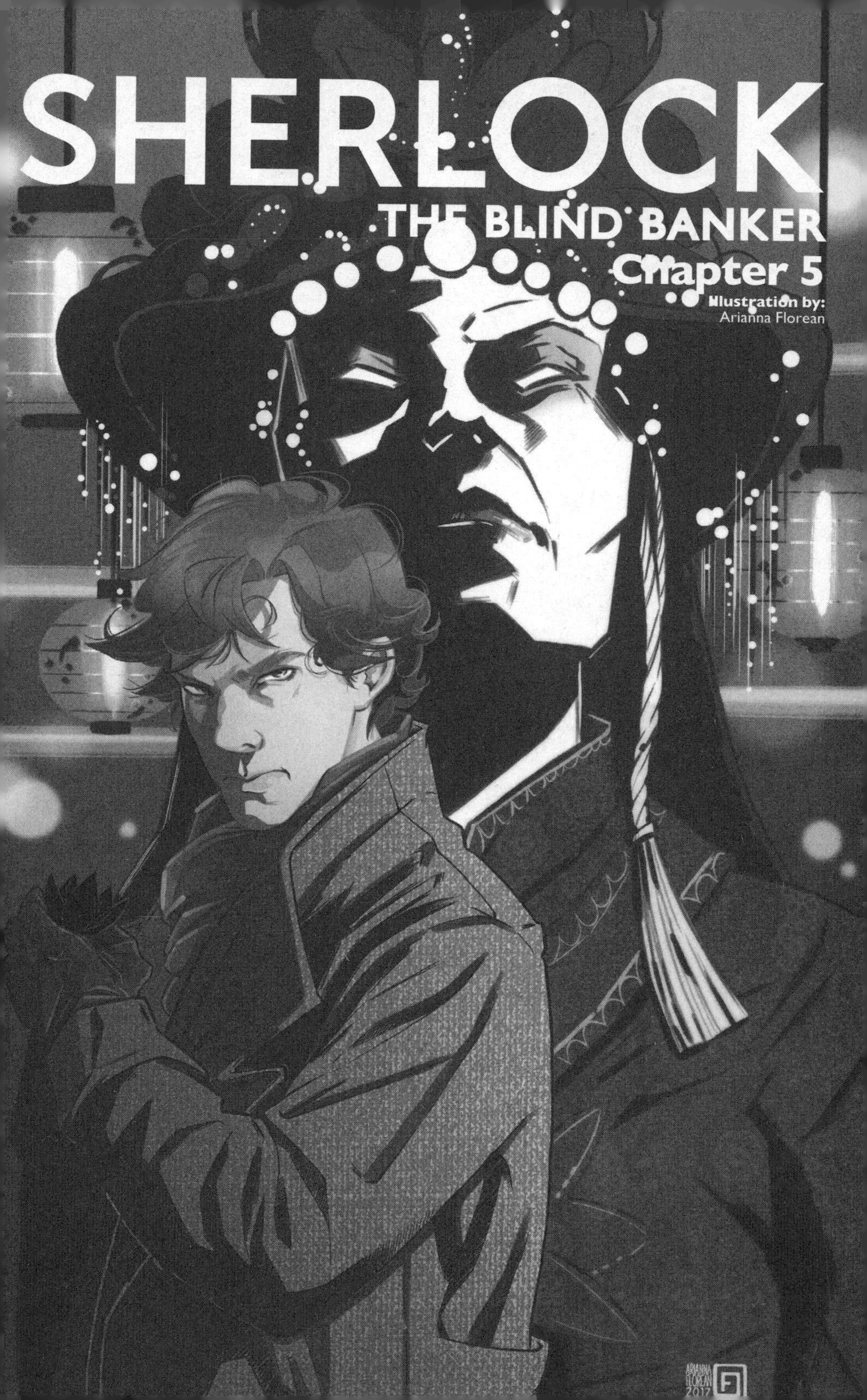
SHERLOCK
THE BLIND BANKER
Chapter 5
Illustration by:
Arianna Florean

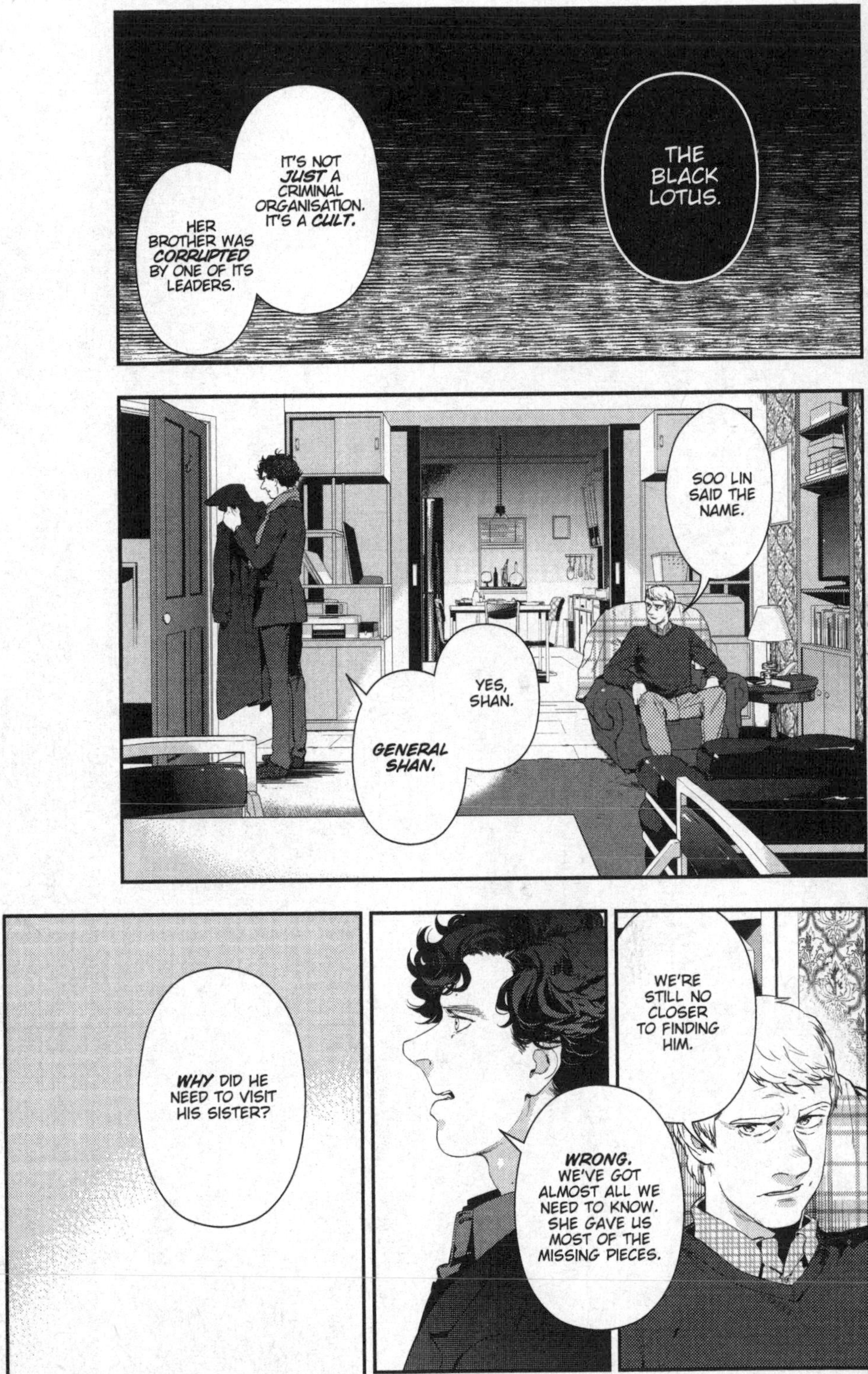
THE BLACK LOTUS.
IT'S NOT *JUST* A CRIMINAL ORGANISATION. IT'S A *CULT*.
HER BROTHER WAS *CORRUPTED* BY ONE OF ITS LEADERS.
SOO LIN SAID THE NAME.
YES, SHAN.
GENERAL SHAN.
WE'RE STILL NO CLOSER TO FINDING HIM.
WRONG. WE'VE GOT ALMOST ALL WE NEED TO KNOW. SHE GAVE US MOST OF THE MISSING PIECES.
WHY DID HE NEED TO VISIT HIS SISTER?

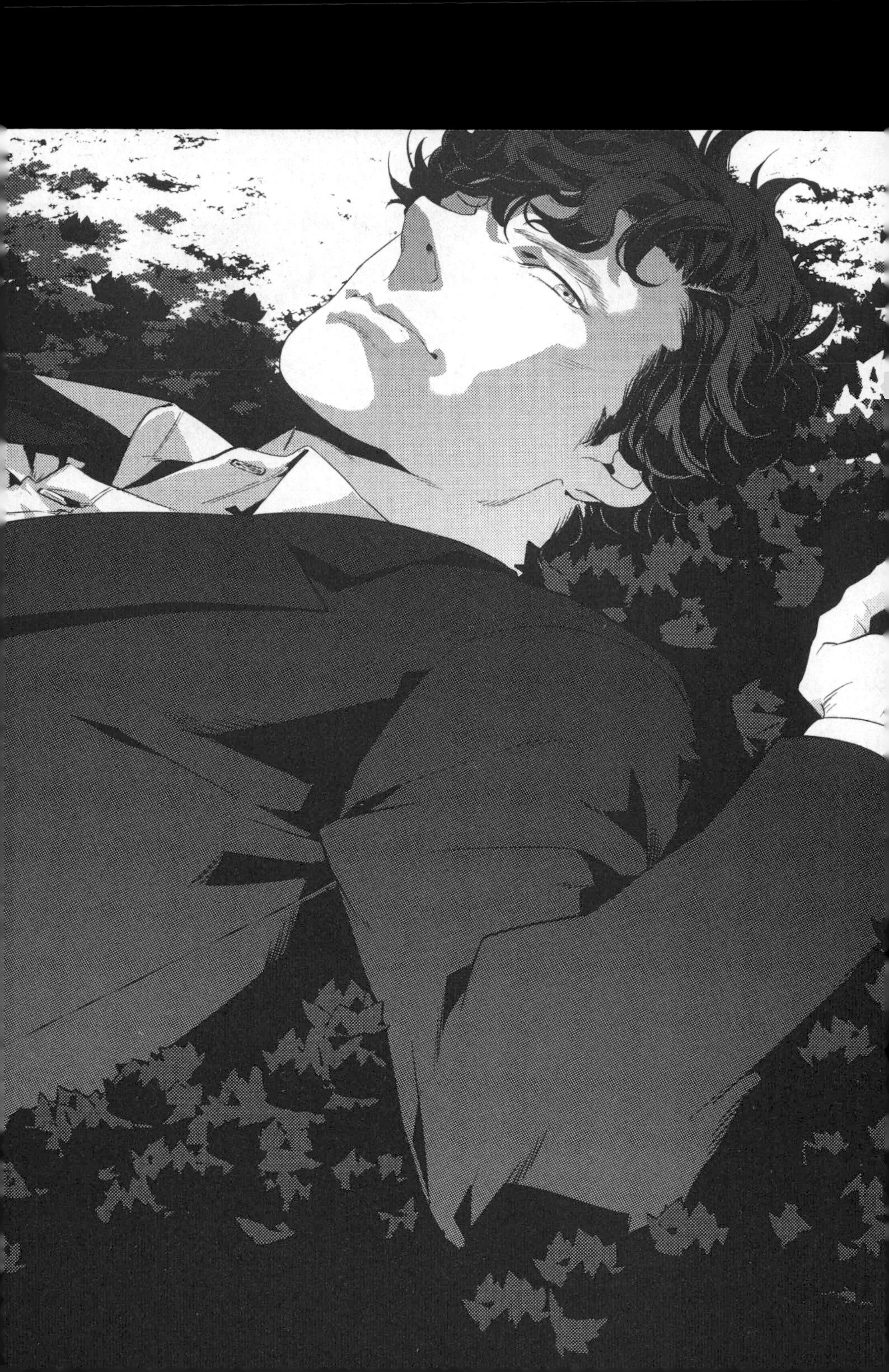

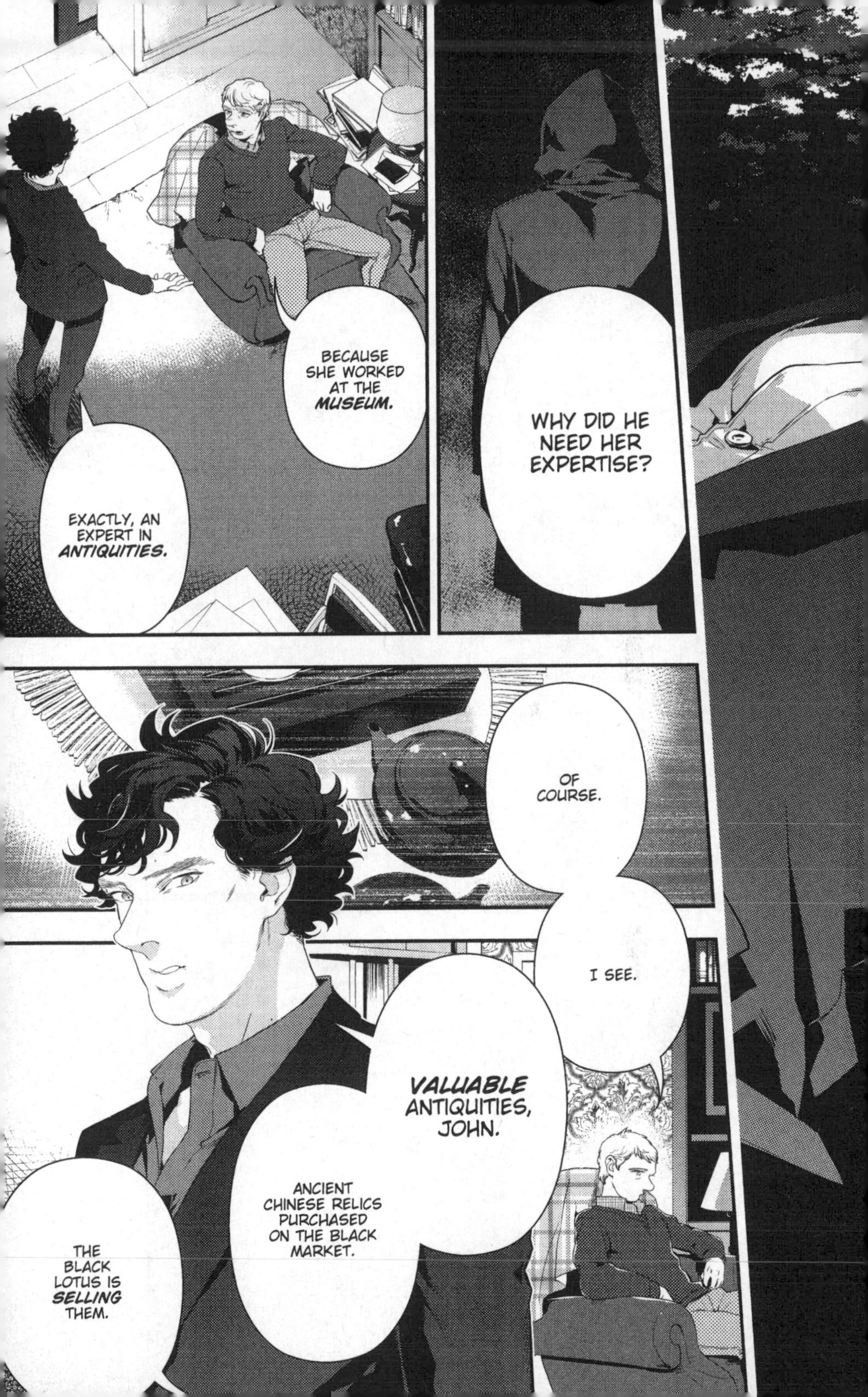
WHY DID HE NEED HER EXPERTISE?
BECAUSE SHE WORKED AT THE MUSEUM.
EXACTLY, AN EXPERT IN ANTIQUITIES.
OF COURSE.
I SEE.
VALUABLE ANTIQUITIES, JOHN.
ANCIENT CHINESE RELICS PURCHASED ON THE BLACK MARKET.
THE BLACK LOTUS IS SELLING THEM.

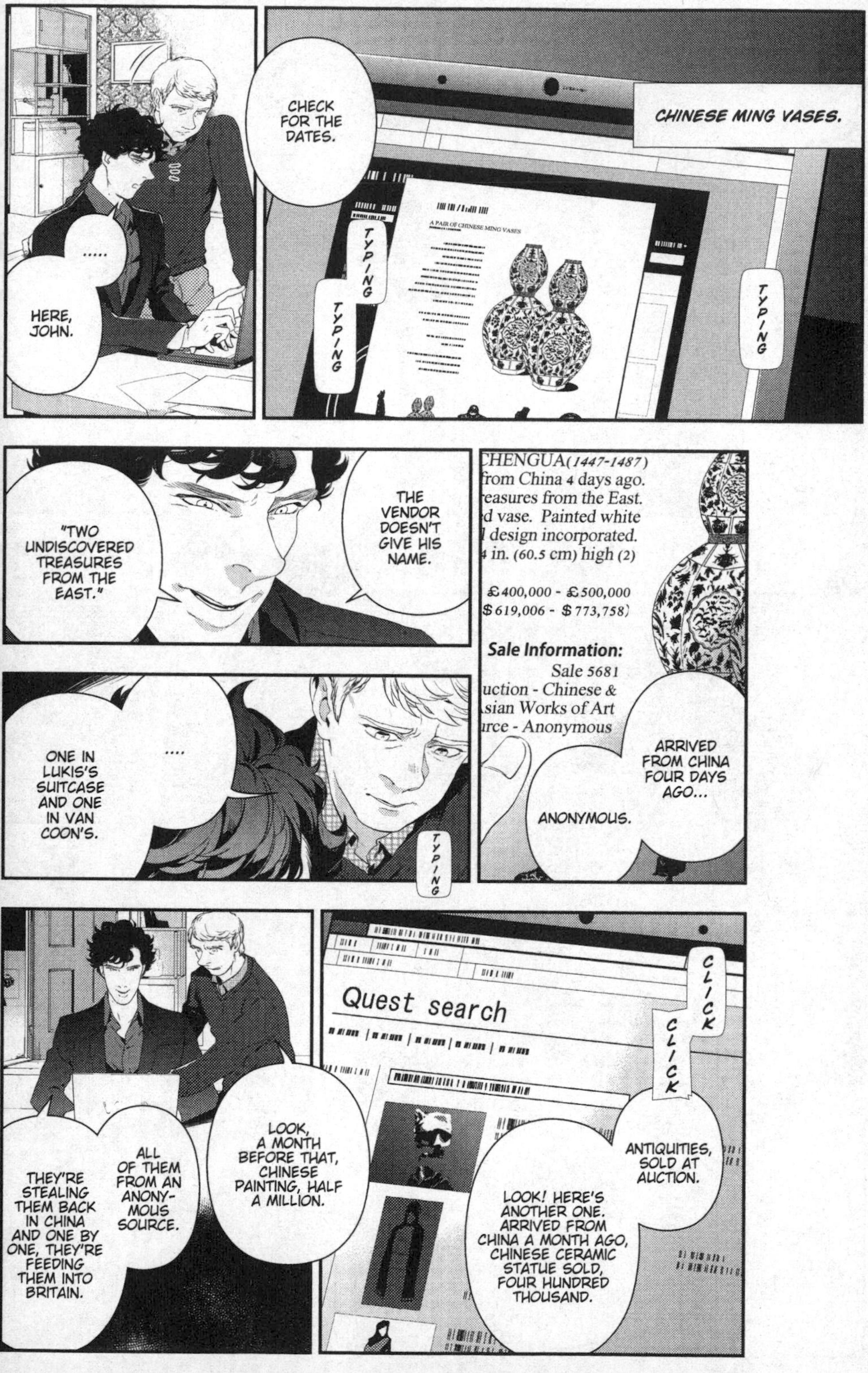
CHINESE MING VASES.
TYPING
A PAIR OF CHINESE MING VASES
TYPING
TYPING
CHECK FOR THE DATES.
.....
HERE, JOHN.
CHENGUA(1447-1487)
from China 4 days ago.
reasures from the East.
d vase. Painted white
l design incorporated.
4 in. (60.5 cm) high (2)
£400,000 - £500,000
($619,006 - $773,758)
Sale Information:
Sale 5681
uction - Chinese &
Asian Works of Art
urce - Anonymous
ARRIVED FROM CHINA FOUR DAYS AGO...
ANONYMOUS.
THE VENDOR DOESN'T GIVE HIS NAME.
"TWO UNDISCOVERED TREASURES FROM THE EAST."
....
ONE IN LUKIS'S SUITCASE AND ONE IN VAN COON'S.
TYPING
CLICK
CLICK
Quest search
ANTIQUITIES, SOLD AT AUCTION.
LOOK! HERE'S ANOTHER ONE. ARRIVED FROM CHINA A MONTH AGO, CHINESE CERAMIC STATUE SOLD, FOUR HUNDRED THOUSAND.
LOOK, A MONTH BEFORE THAT, CHINESE PAINTING, HALF A MILLION.
ALL OF THEM FROM AN ANONY-MOUS SOURCE.
THEY'RE STEALING THEM BACK IN CHINA AND ONE BY ONE, THEY'RE FEEDING THEM INTO BRITAIN.

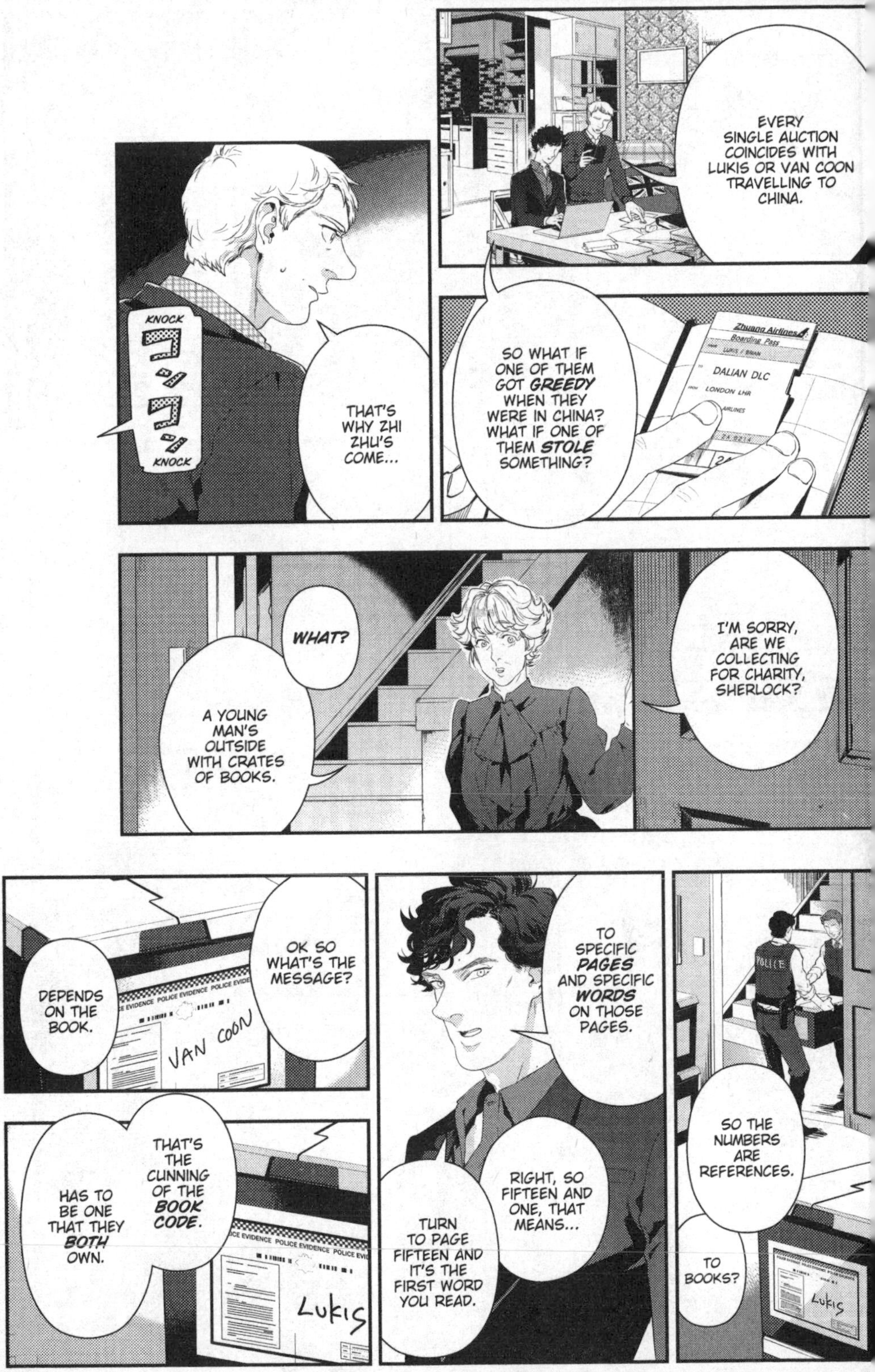
EVERY SINGLE AUCTION COINCIDES WITH LUKIS OR VAN COON TRAVELLING TO CHINA.
Zhuang Airlines
Boarding Pass
DALIAN DLC
LONDON LHR
SO WHAT IF ONE OF THEM GOT ***GREEDY*** WHEN THEY WERE IN CHINA? WHAT IF ONE OF THEM ***STOLE*** SOMETHING?
THAT'S WHY ZHI ZHU'S COME...
KNOCK
コッコッ
KNOCK
I'M SORRY, ARE WE COLLECTING FOR CHARITY, SHERLOCK?
WHAT?
A YOUNG MAN'S OUTSIDE WITH CRATES OF BOOKS.
POLICE
SO THE NUMBERS ARE REFERENCES.
TO BOOKS?
LUKIS
TO SPECIFIC ***PAGES*** AND SPECIFIC ***WORDS*** ON THOSE PAGES.
RIGHT, SO FIFTEEN AND ONE, THAT MEANS...
TURN TO PAGE FIFTEEN AND IT'S THE FIRST WORD YOU READ.
OK SO WHAT'S THE MESSAGE?
DEPENDS ON THE BOOK.
POLICE EVIDENCE POLICE EVIDENCE POLICE EVIDE
VAN COON
THAT'S THE CUNNING OF THE ***BOOK CODE***.
HAS TO BE ONE THAT THEY ***BOTH*** OWN.
POLICE EVIDENCE POLICE EVIDENCE POLICE EVID
LUKIS

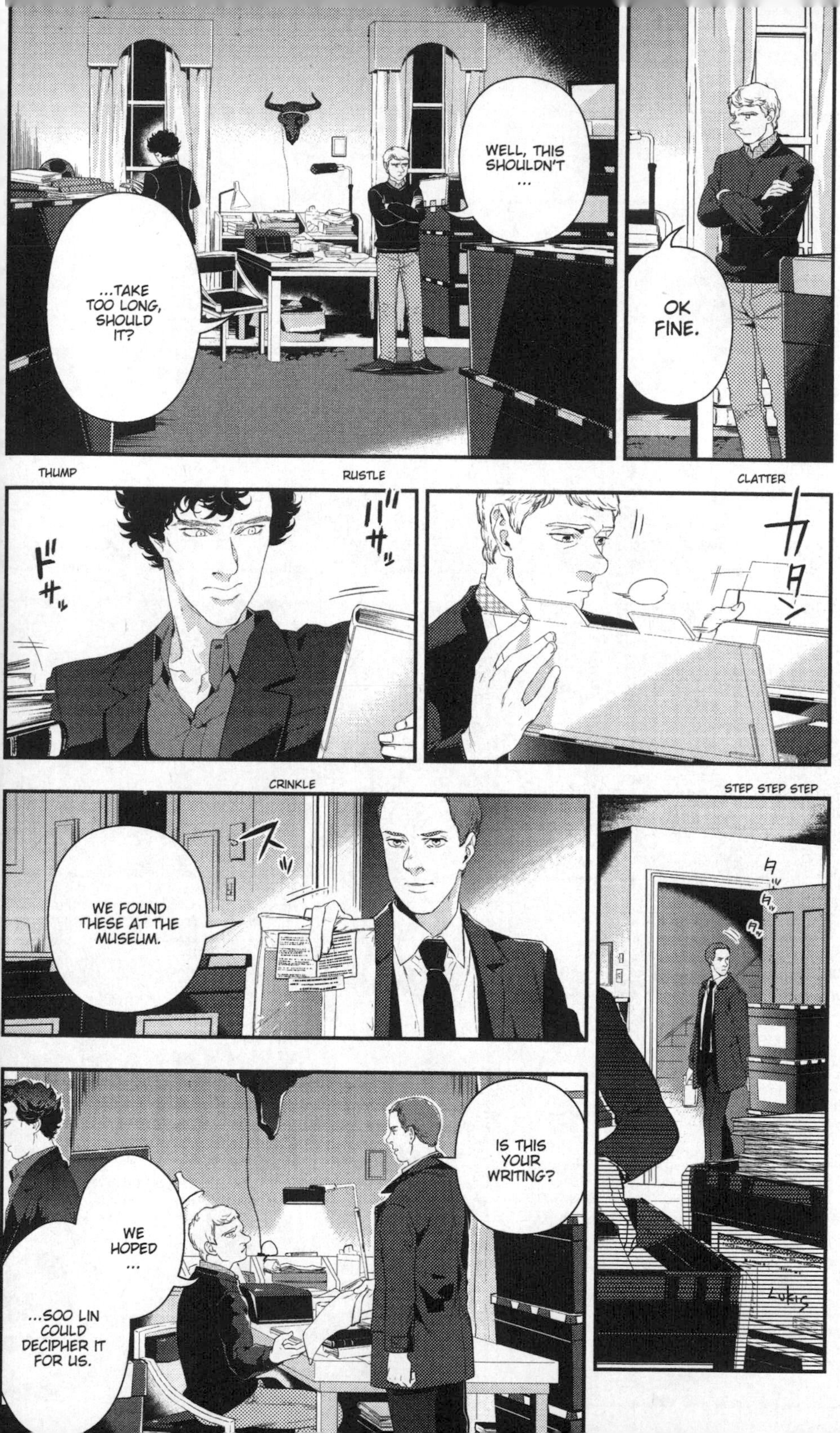
OK FINE.
WELL, THIS SHOULDN'T ...
...TAKE TOO LONG, SHOULD IT?
CLATTER
RUSTLE
THUMP
STEP STEP STEP
CRINKLE
WE FOUND THESE AT THE MUSEUM.
IS THIS YOUR WRITING?
WE HOPED ...
...SOO LIN COULD DECIPHER IT FOR US.

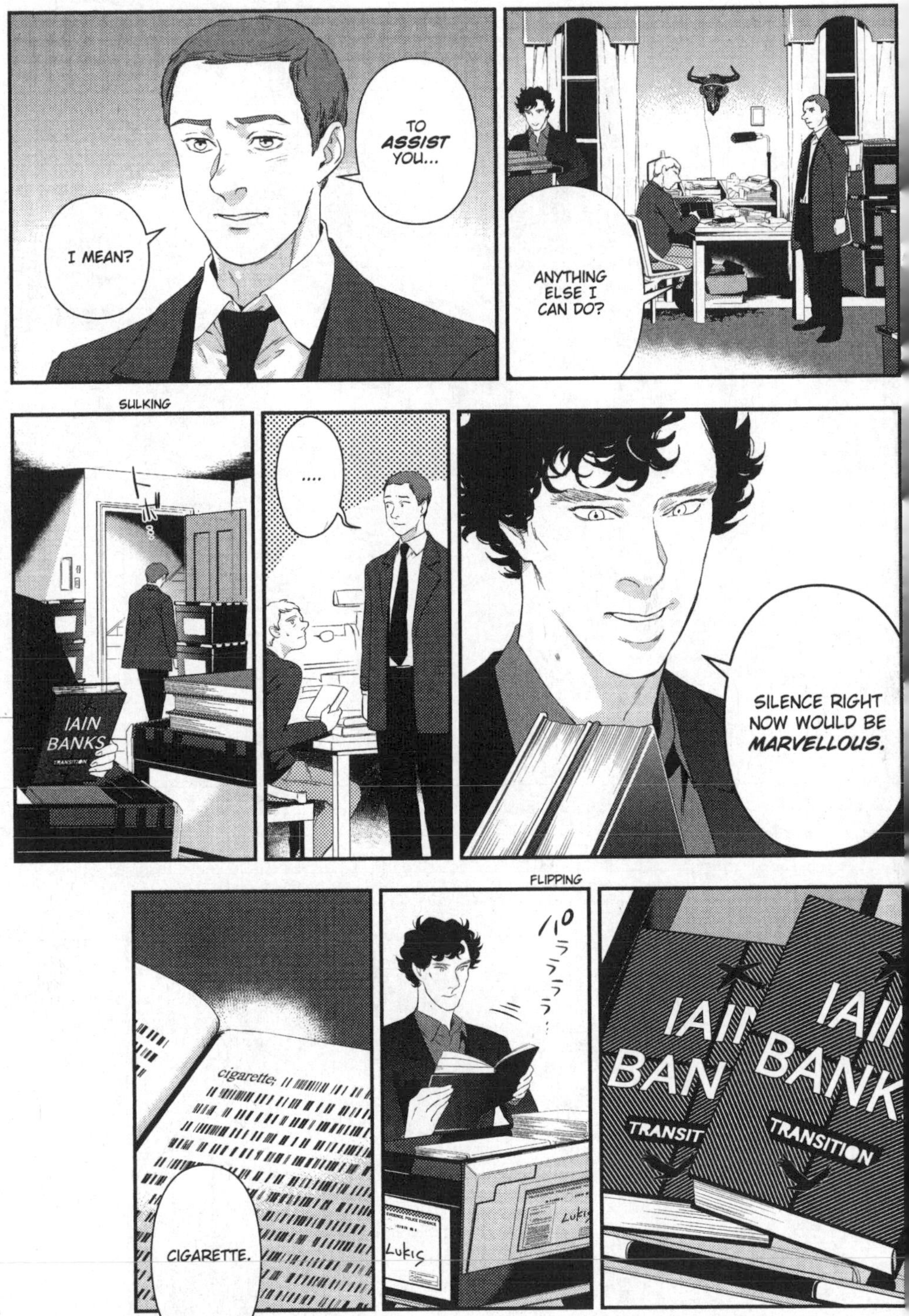
ANYTHING ELSE I CAN DO?
TO ASSIST YOU...
I MEAN?
SILENCE RIGHT NOW WOULD BE MARVELLOUS.
....
SULKING
IAIN BANKS
TRANSITION
IAIN BANK
TRANSITION
FLIPPING
LUKIS
cigarette;
CIGARETTE.

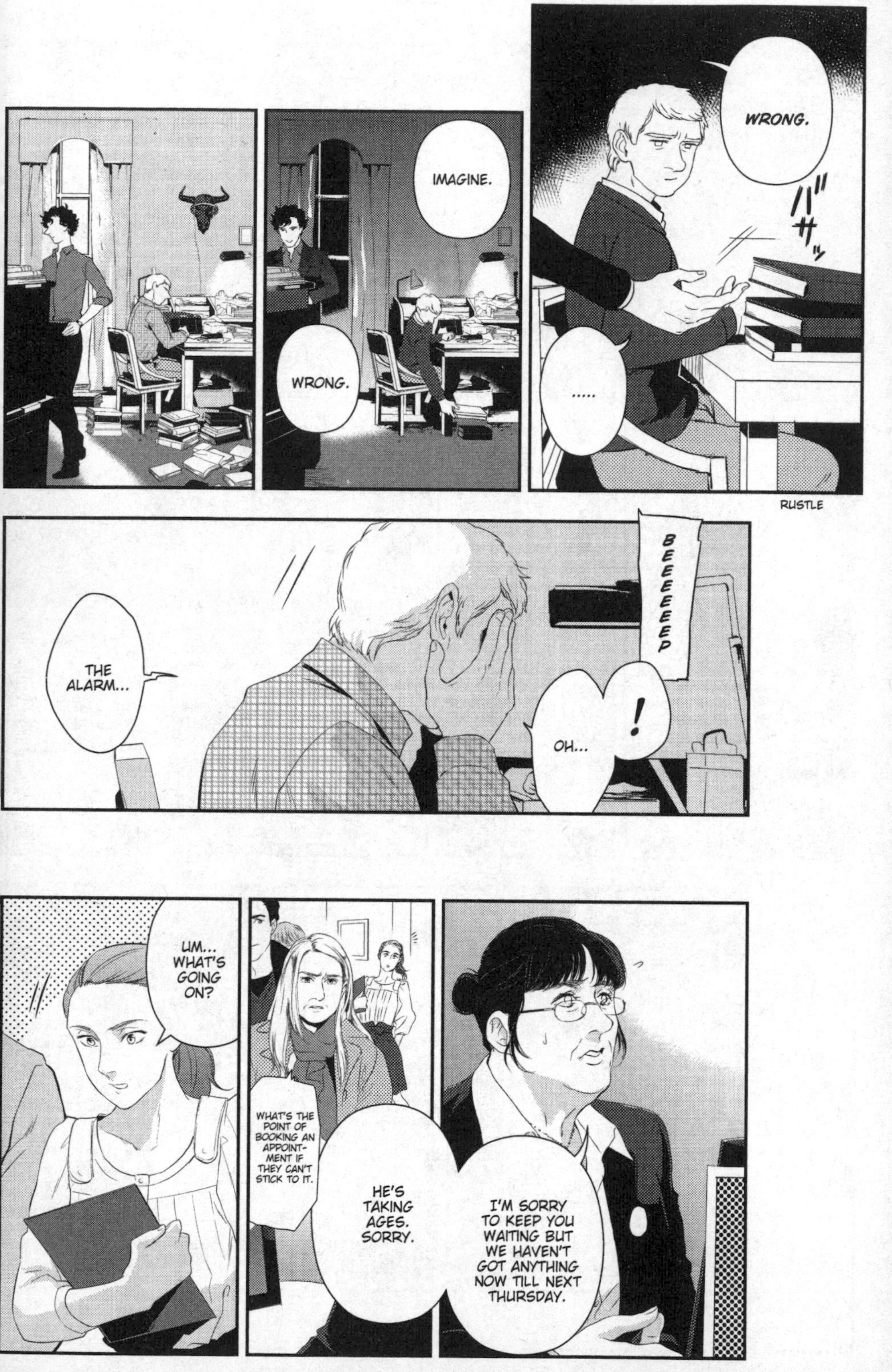
WRONG.
バサッ
.....
RUSTLE
IMAGINE.
WRONG.
BEEEEEEP
!
OH...
THE ALARM...
I'M SORRY TO KEEP YOU WAITING BUT WE HAVEN'T GOT ANYTHING NOW TILL NEXT THURSDAY.
HE'S TAKING AGES. SORRY.
WHAT'S THE POINT OF BOOKING AN APPOINT-MENT IF THEY CAN'T STICK TO IT.
UM... WHAT'S GOING ON?

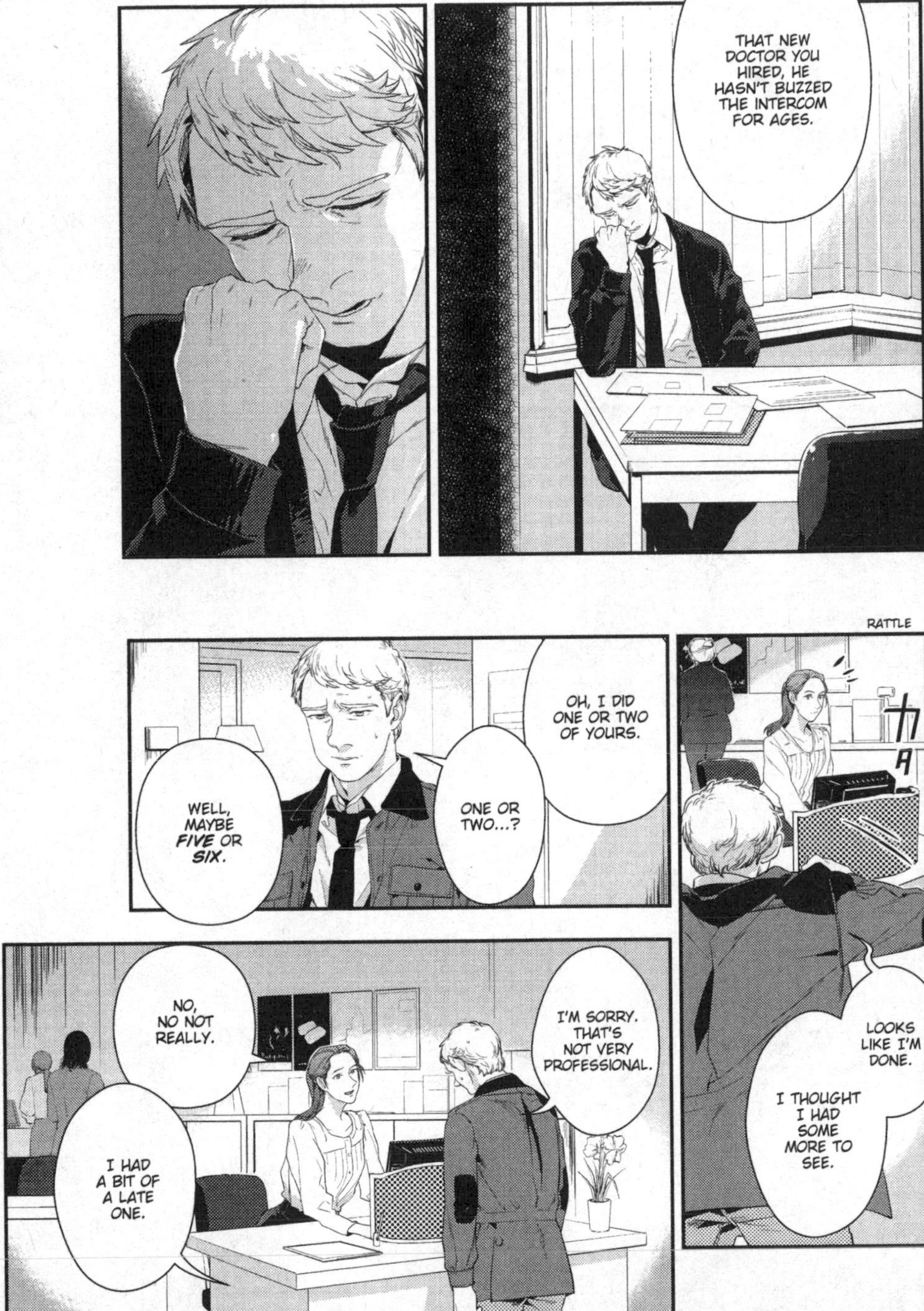
THAT NEW DOCTOR YOU HIRED, HE HASN'T BUZZED THE INTERCOM FOR AGES.
RATTLE
カタ
LOOKS LIKE I'M DONE.
I THOUGHT I HAD SOME MORE TO SEE.
OH, I DID ONE OR TWO OF YOURS.
ONE OR TWO...?
WELL, MAYBE *FIVE* OR *SIX*.
I'M SORRY. THAT'S NOT VERY PROFESSIONAL.
NO, NO NOT REALLY.
I HAD A BIT OF A LATE ONE.

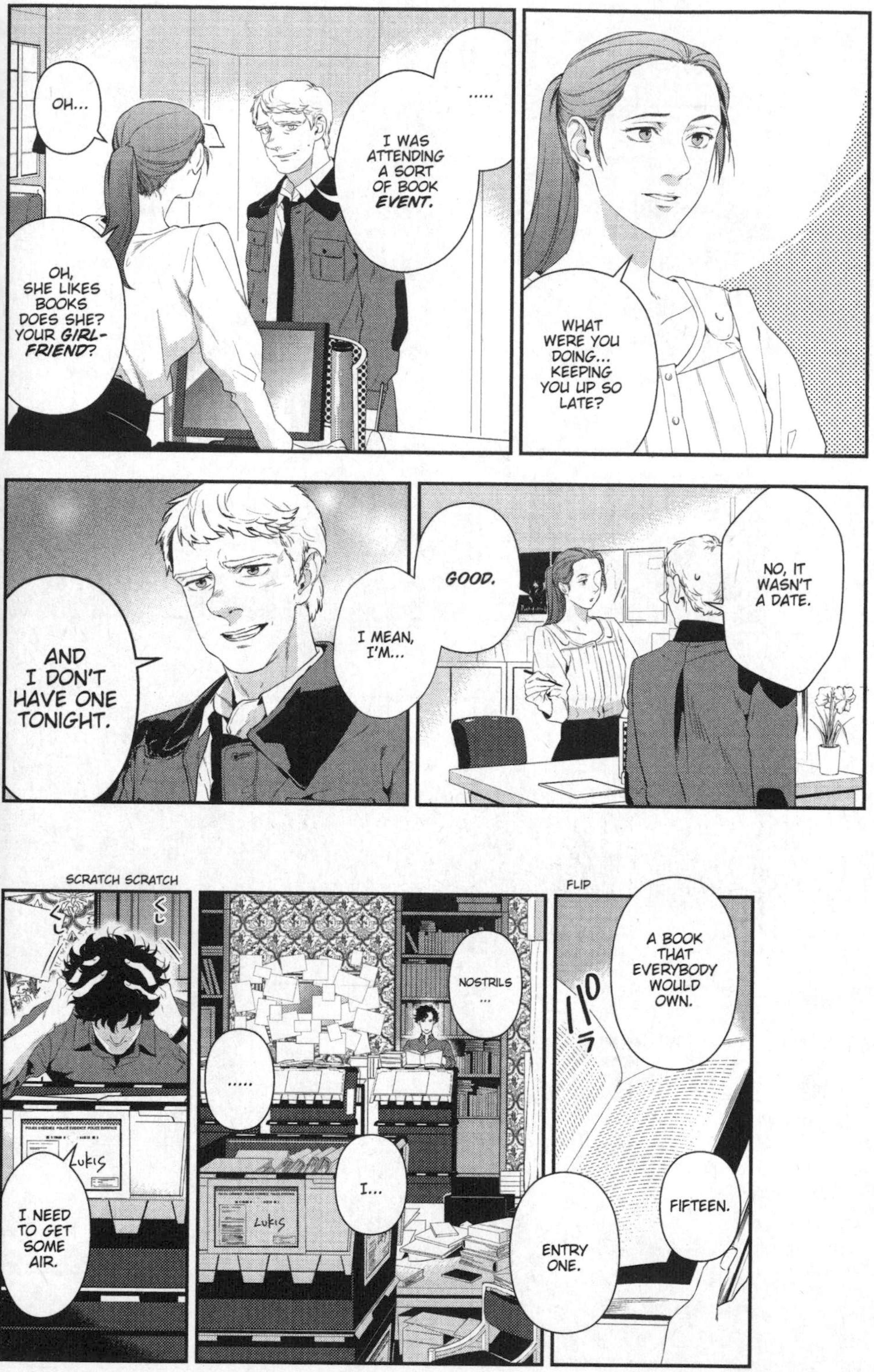
WHAT WERE YOU DOING... KEEPING YOU UP SO LATE?
.....
I WAS ATTENDING A SORT OF BOOK EVENT.
OH...
OH, SHE LIKES BOOKS DOES SHE? YOUR GIRLFRIEND?
NO, IT WASN'T A DATE.
GOOD.
I MEAN, I'M...
AND I DON'T HAVE ONE TONIGHT.
FLIP
A BOOK THAT EVERYBODY WOULD OWN.
FIFTEEN.
ENTRY ONE.
NOSTRILS ...
.....
I...
SCRATCH SCRATCH
I NEED TO GET SOME AIR.

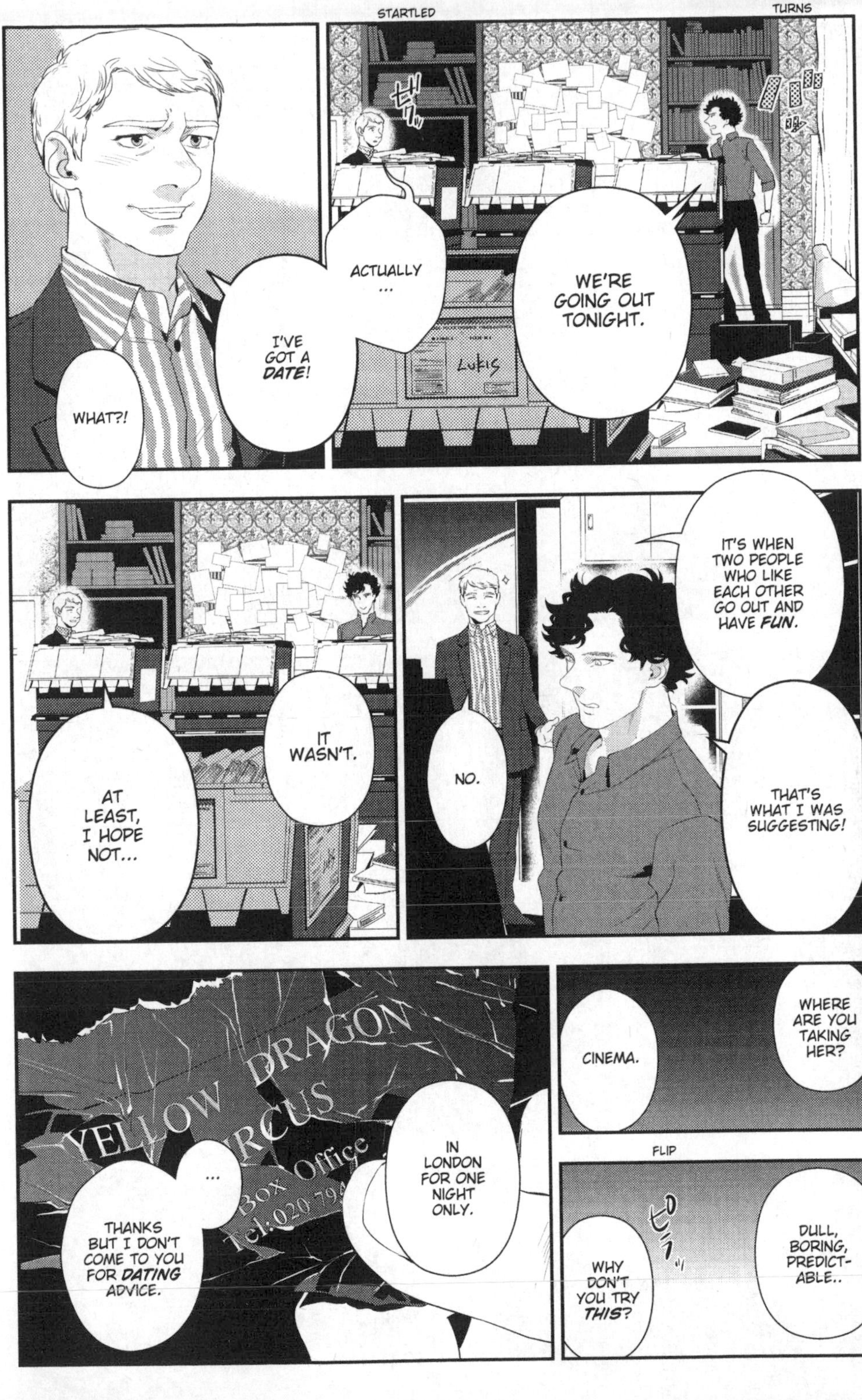
TURNS
WE'RE GOING OUT TONIGHT.
STARTLED
ACTUALLY ... I'VE GOT A *DATE*!
WHAT?!
IT'S WHEN TWO PEOPLE WHO LIKE EACH OTHER GO OUT AND HAVE *FUN*.
THAT'S WHAT I WAS SUGGESTING!
NO.
IT WASN'T.
AT LEAST, I HOPE NOT...
WHERE ARE YOU TAKING HER?
CINEMA.
FLIP
DULL, BORING, PREDICT-ABLE..
WHY DON'T YOU TRY *THIS*?
YELLOW DRAGON
Box Office
IN LONDON FOR ONE NIGHT ONLY.
...
THANKS BUT I DON'T COME TO YOU FOR *DATING* ADVICE.

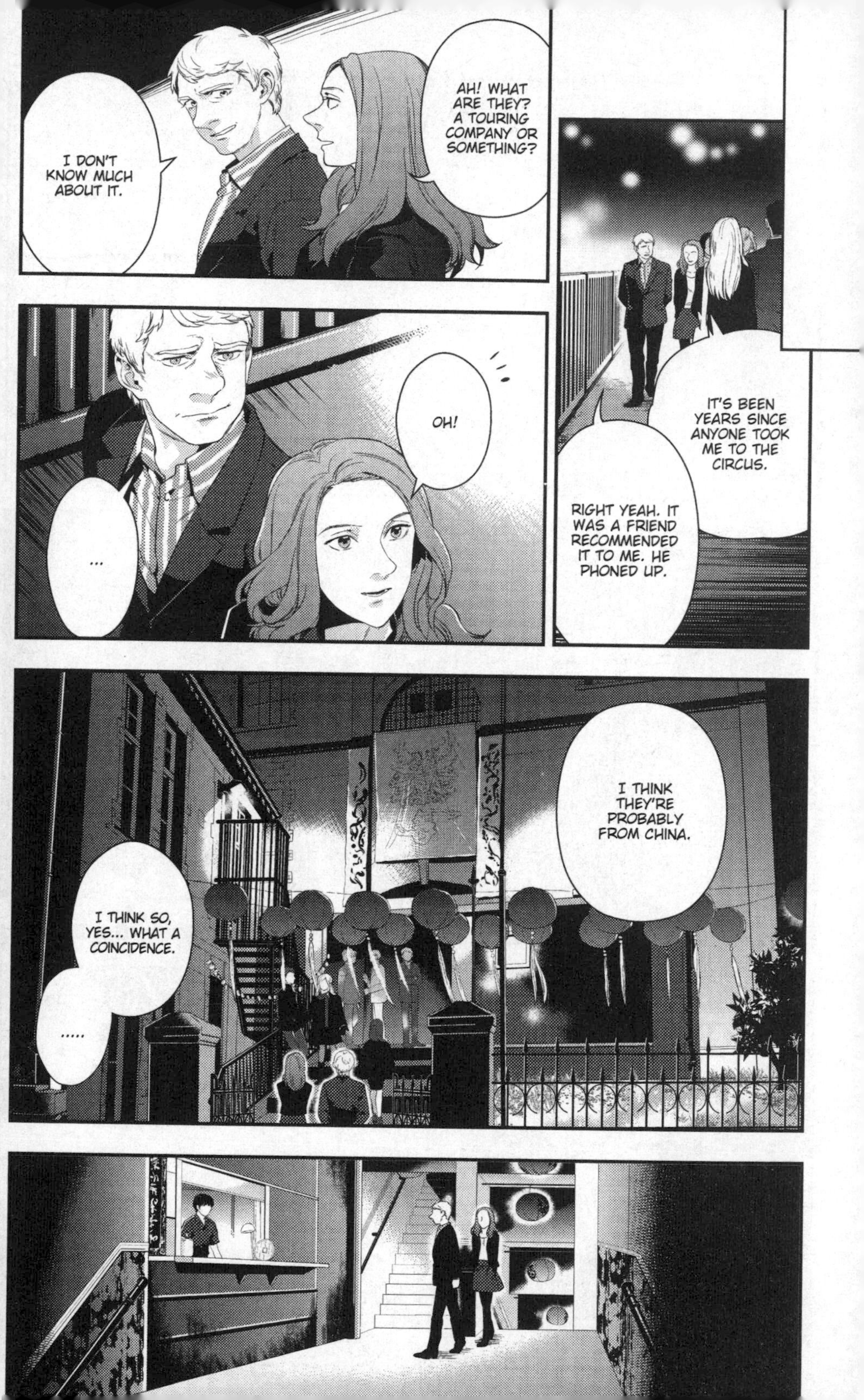
IT'S BEEN YEARS SINCE ANYONE TOOK ME TO THE CIRCUS.
RIGHT YEAH. IT WAS A FRIEND RECOMMENDED IT TO ME. HE PHONED UP.
AH! WHAT ARE THEY? A TOURING COMPANY OR SOMETHING?
I DON'T KNOW MUCH ABOUT IT.
OH!
...
I THINK THEY'RE PROBABLY FROM CHINA.
I THINK SO, YES... WHAT A COINCIDENCE.
.....

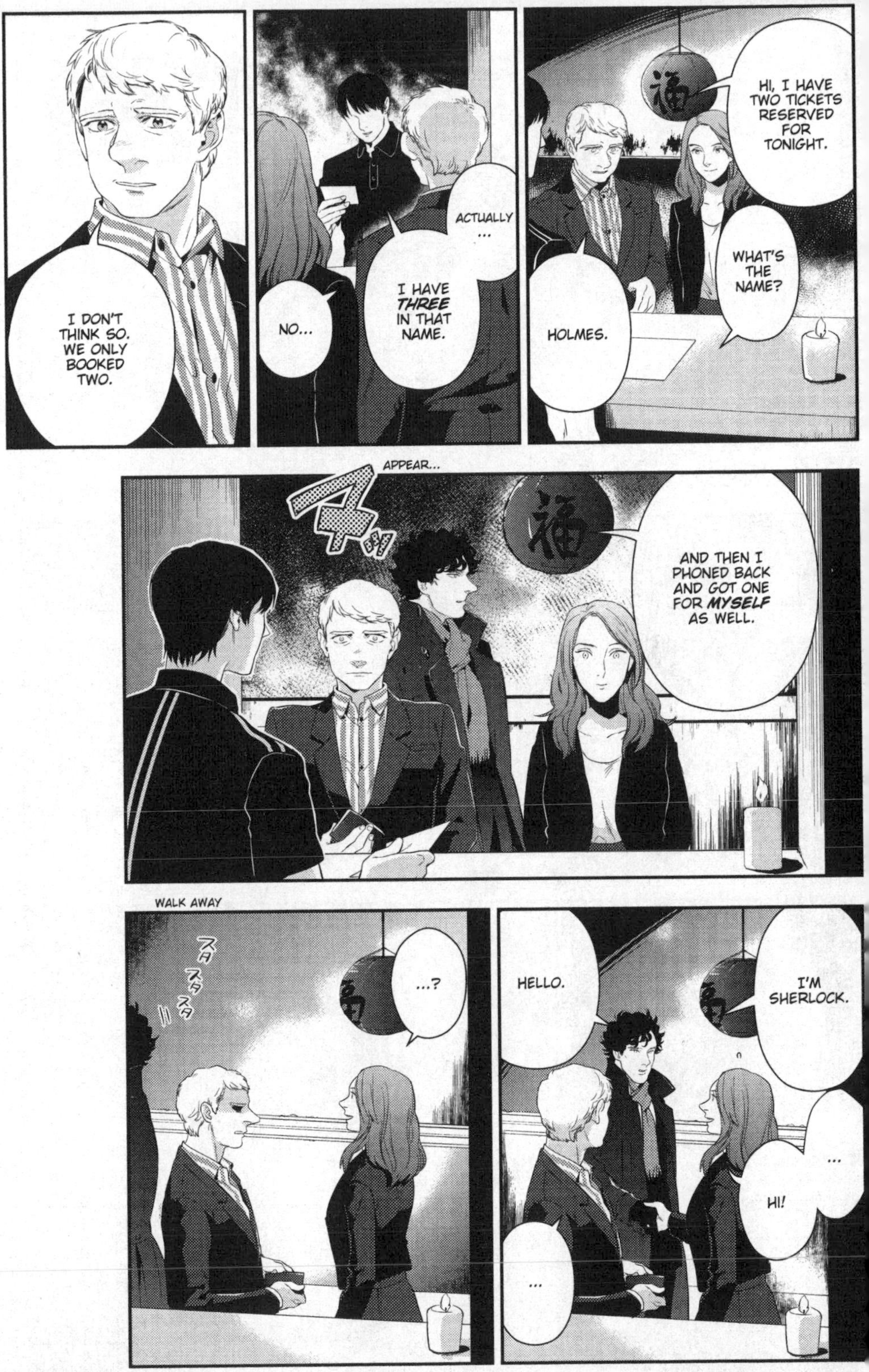
HI, I HAVE TWO TICKETS RESERVED FOR TONIGHT.
WHAT'S THE NAME?
HOLMES.
ACTUALLY ...
I HAVE *THREE* IN THAT NAME.
NO...
I DON'T THINK SO. WE ONLY BOOKED TWO.
APPEAR...
AND THEN I PHONED BACK AND GOT ONE FOR *MYSELF* AS WELL.
I'M SHERLOCK.
HELLO.
...
HI!
...
WALK AWAY
スタスタスタ
...?

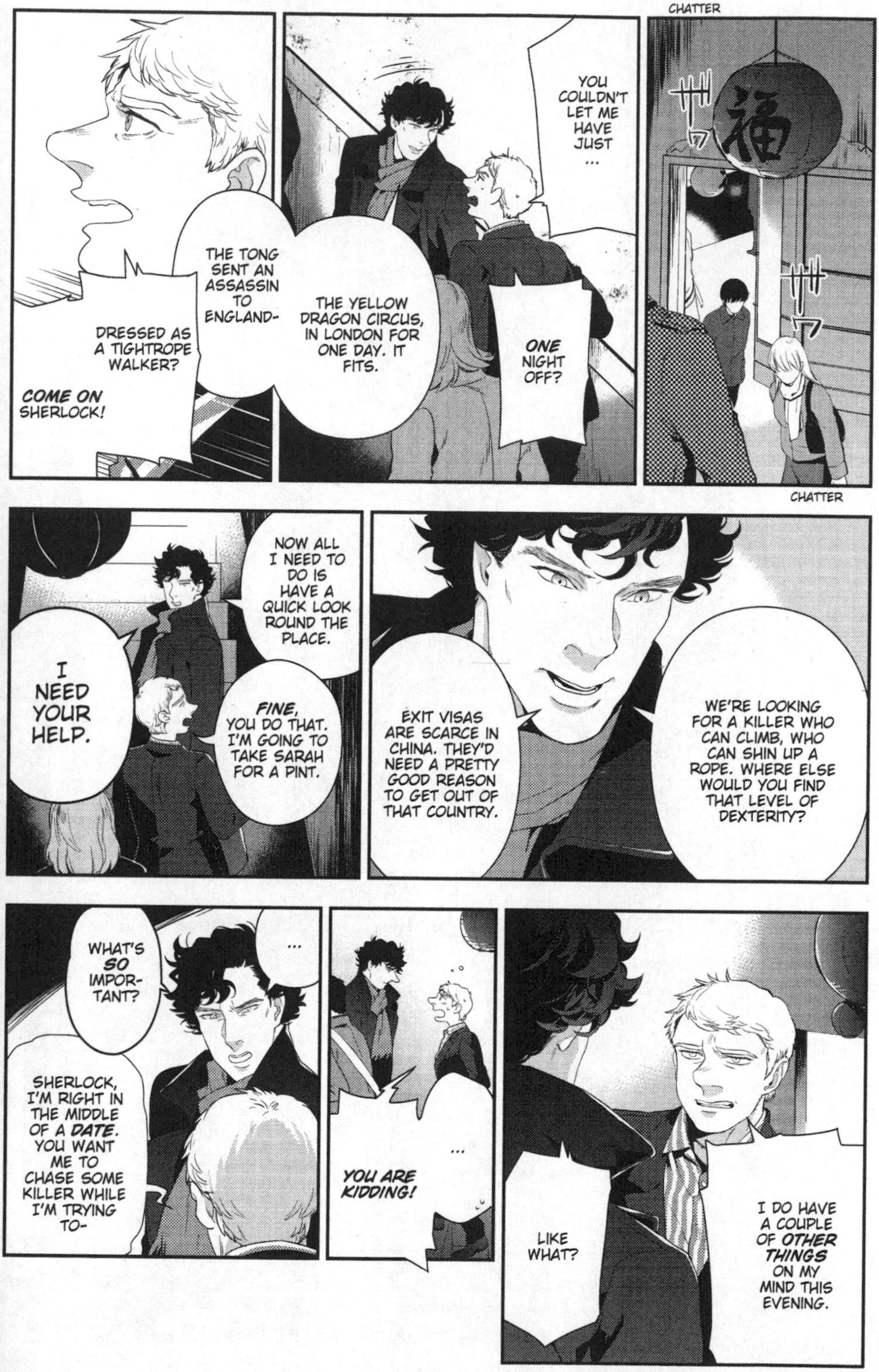
CHATTER
ザワ
ザワ
CHATTER
YOU COULDN'T LET ME HAVE JUST ...
ONE NIGHT OFF?
THE TONG SENT AN ASSASSIN TO ENGLAND-
THE YELLOW DRAGON CIRCUS, IN LONDON FOR ONE DAY. IT FITS.
DRESSED AS A TIGHTROPE WALKER?
COME ON SHERLOCK!
WE'RE LOOKING FOR A KILLER WHO CAN CLIMB, WHO CAN SHIN UP A ROPE. WHERE ELSE WOULD YOU FIND THAT LEVEL OF DEXTERITY?
EXIT VISAS ARE SCARCE IN CHINA. THEY'D NEED A PRETTY GOOD REASON TO GET OUT OF THAT COUNTRY.
NOW ALL I NEED TO DO IS HAVE A QUICK LOOK ROUND THE PLACE.
FINE, YOU DO THAT. I'M GOING TO TAKE SARAH FOR A PINT.
I NEED YOUR HELP.
I DO HAVE A COUPLE OF OTHER THINGS ON MY MIND THIS EVENING.
LIKE WHAT?
...
YOU ARE KIDDING!
...
WHAT'S SO IMPORTANT?
SHERLOCK, I'M RIGHT IN THE MIDDLE OF A DATE. YOU WANT ME TO CHASE SOME KILLER WHILE I'M TRYING TO-

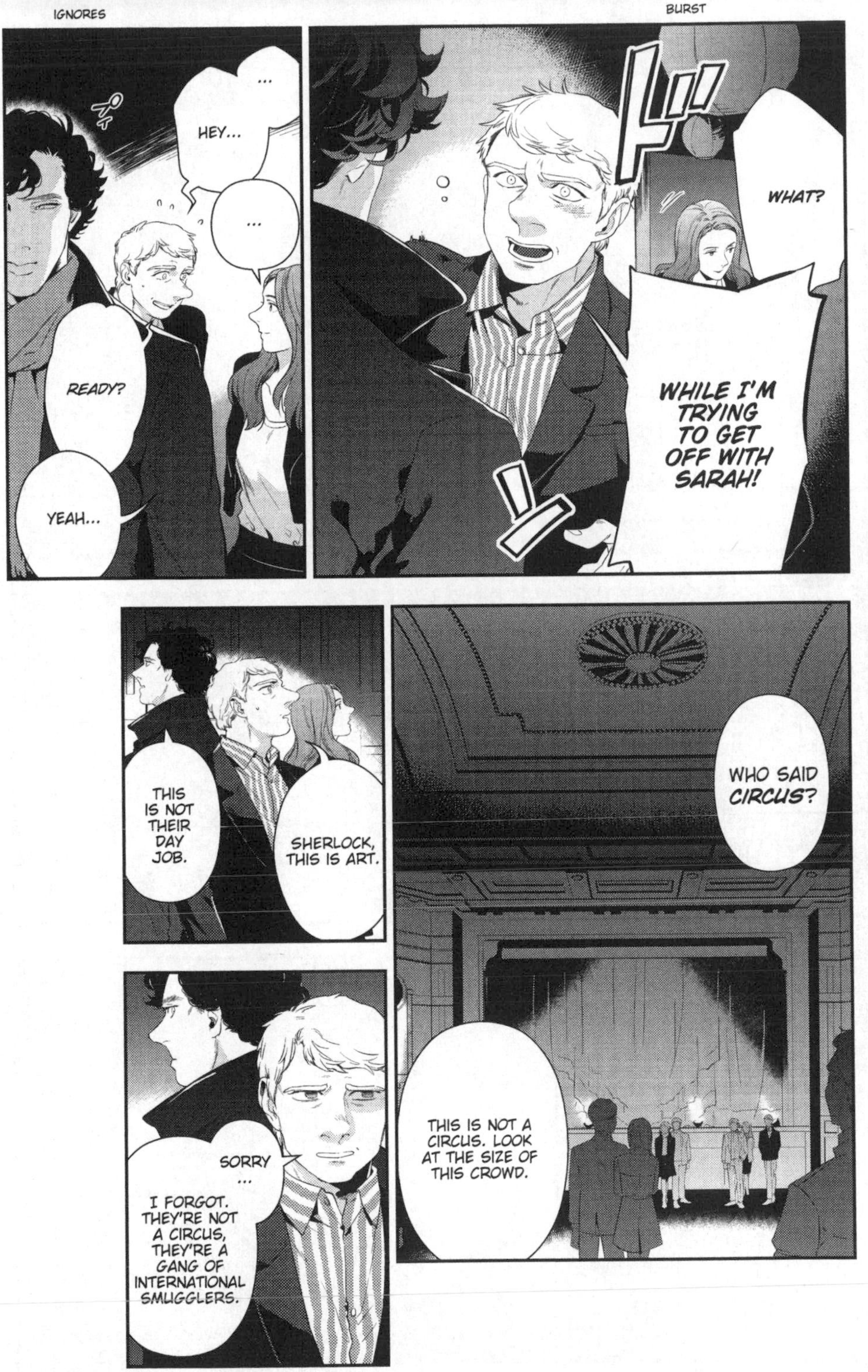
BURST
WHAT?
WHILE I'M TRYING TO GET OFF WITH SARAH!
IGNORES
...
HEY...
...
READY?
YEAH...
WHO SAID CIRCUS?
THIS IS NOT A CIRCUS. LOOK AT THE SIZE OF THIS CROWD.
SHERLOCK, THIS IS ART.
THIS IS NOT THEIR DAY JOB.
SORRY ...
I FORGOT. THEY'RE NOT A CIRCUS, THEY'RE A GANG OF INTERNATIONAL SMUGGLERS.

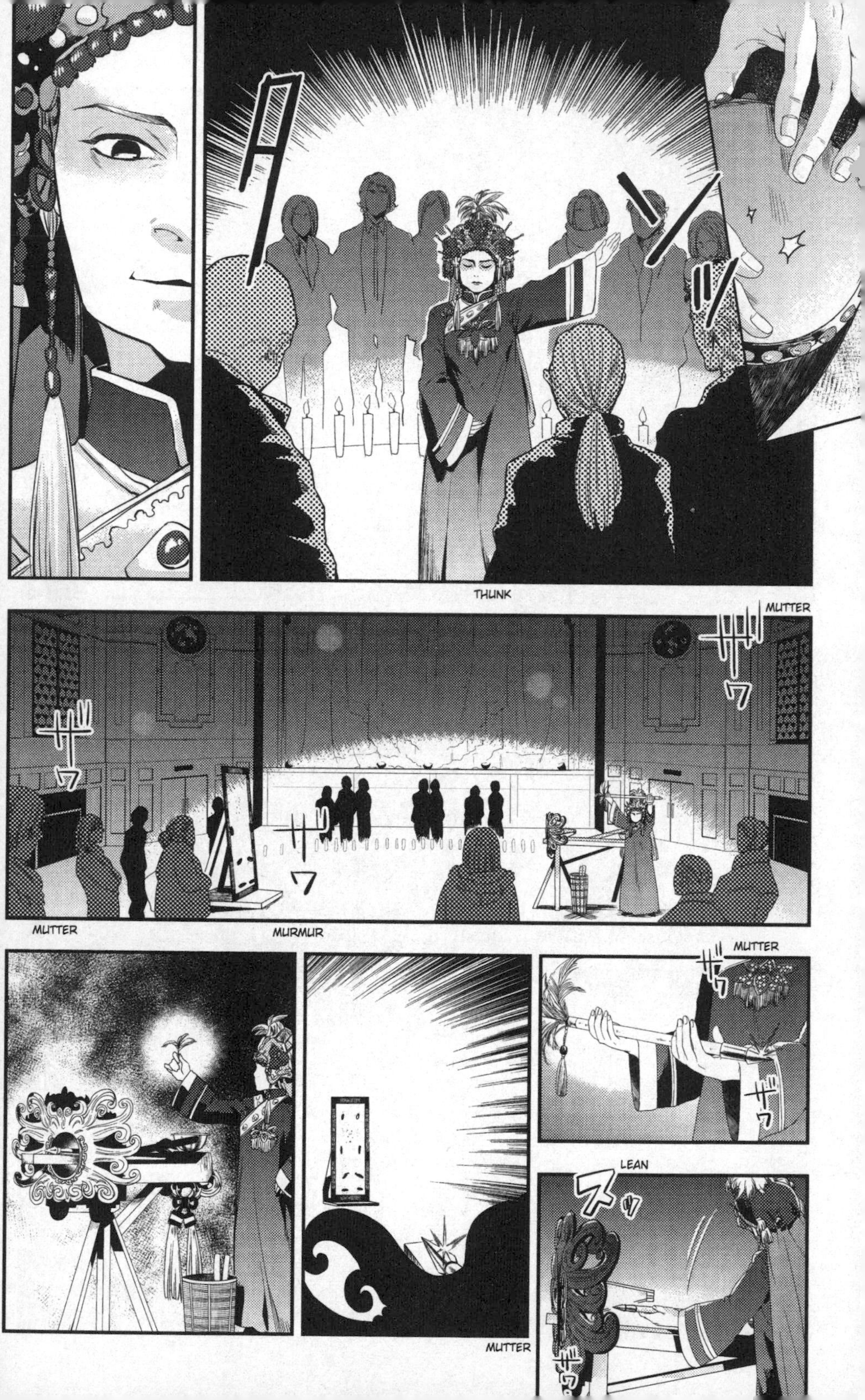

THUNK
MUTTER
MURMUR
MUTTER
MUTTER
LEAN
MUTTER

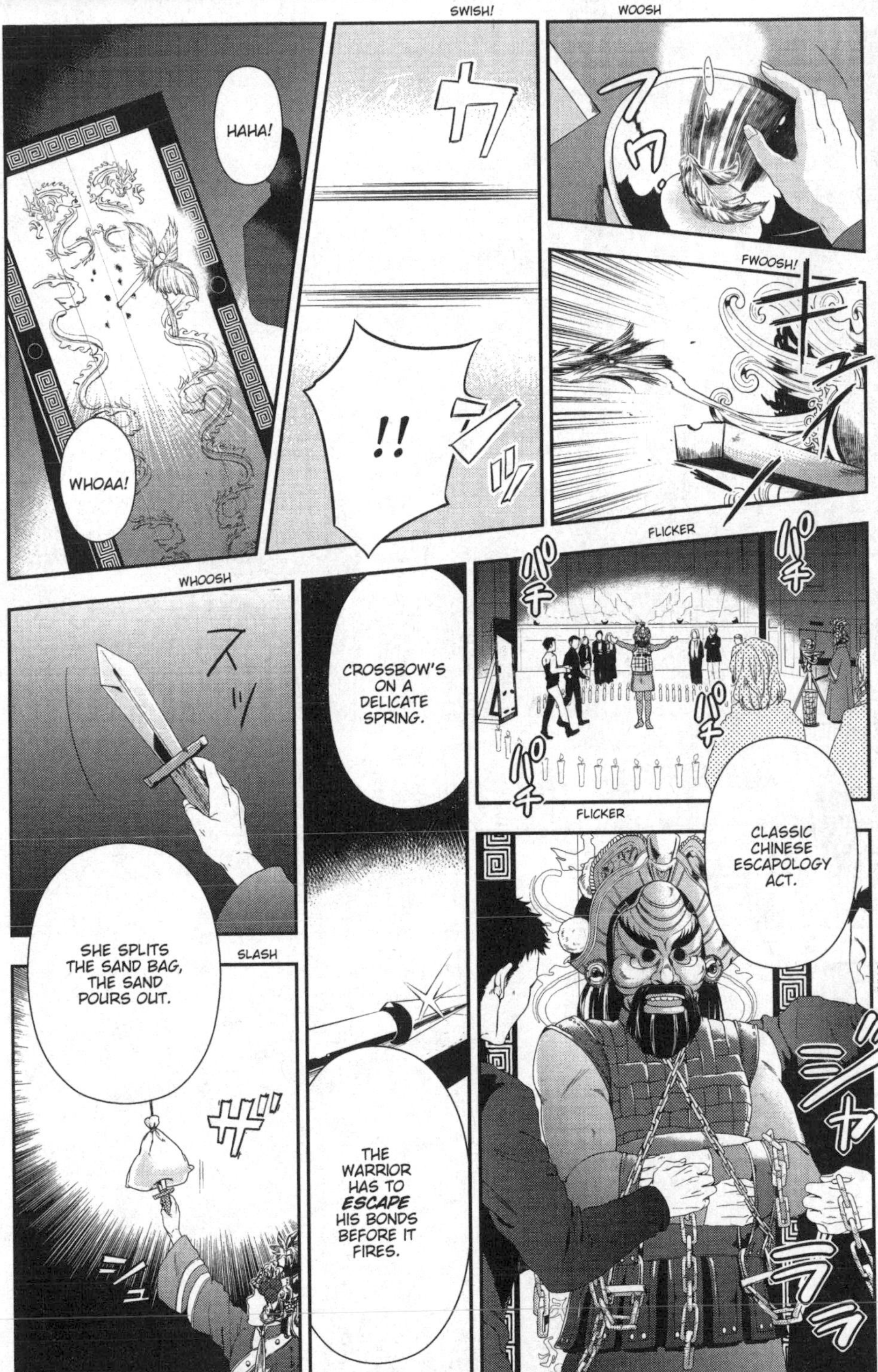
WOOSH
FWOOSH!
SWISH!
!!
HAHA!
WHOAA!
FLICKER
FLICKER
CLASSIC CHINESE ESCAPOLOGY ACT.
CLINK
CLINK
CROSSBOW'S ON A DELICATE SPRING.
THE WARRIOR HAS TO *ESCAPE* HIS BONDS BEFORE IT FIRES.
WHOOSH
SLASH
SHE SPLITS THE SAND BAG, THE SAND POURS OUT.

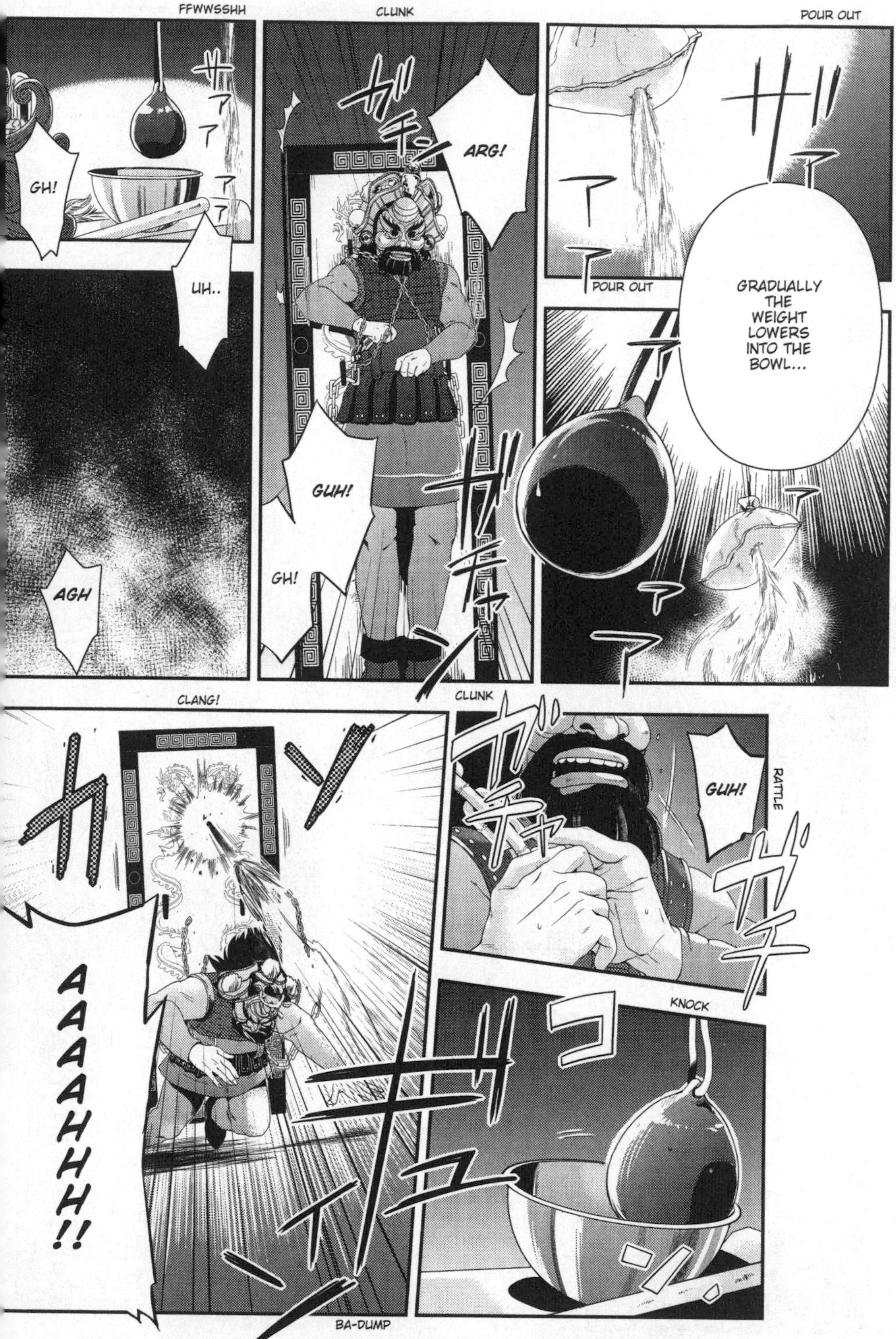
POUR OUT
POUR OUT
GRADUALLY THE WEIGHT LOWERS INTO THE BOWL...
CLUNK
ARG!
GUH!
GH!
FFWWSSHH
GH!
UH..
AGH
CLUNK
GUH!
RATTLE
KNOCK
BA-DUMP
CLANG!
AAAAAHHHH!!

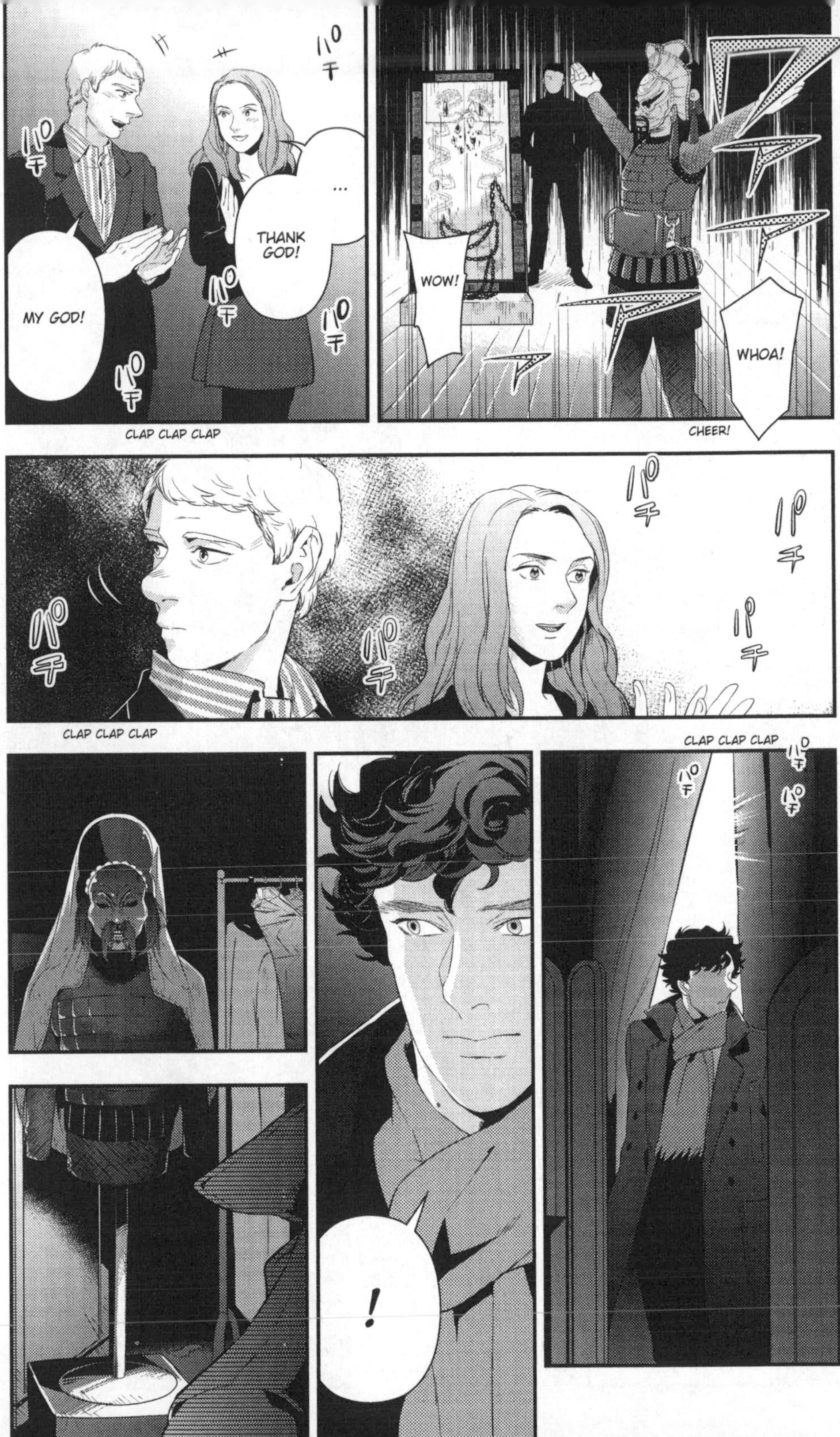
WOW!
WHOA!
CHEER!
...
THANK GOD!
MY GOD!
CLAP CLAP CLAP
CLAP CLAP CLAP
CLAP CLAP CLAP
!

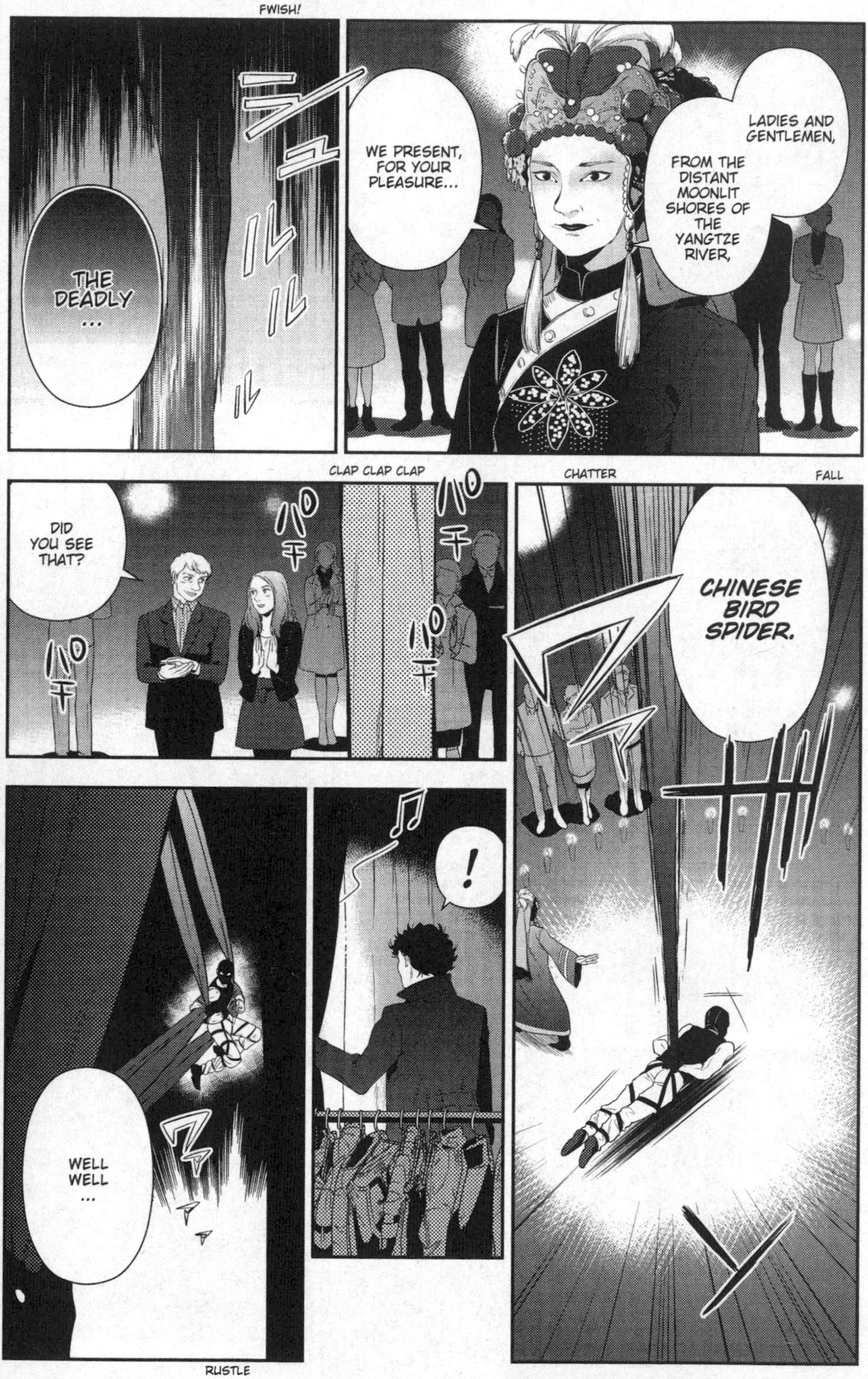
LADIES AND GENTLEMEN,
FROM THE DISTANT MOONLIT SHORES OF THE YANGTZE RIVER,
WE PRESENT, FOR YOUR PLEASURE...
FWISH!
THE DEADLY...
CHATTER
FALL
CHINESE BIRD SPIDER.
CLAP CLAP CLAP
DID YOU SEE THAT?
!
WELL WELL ...
RUSTLE

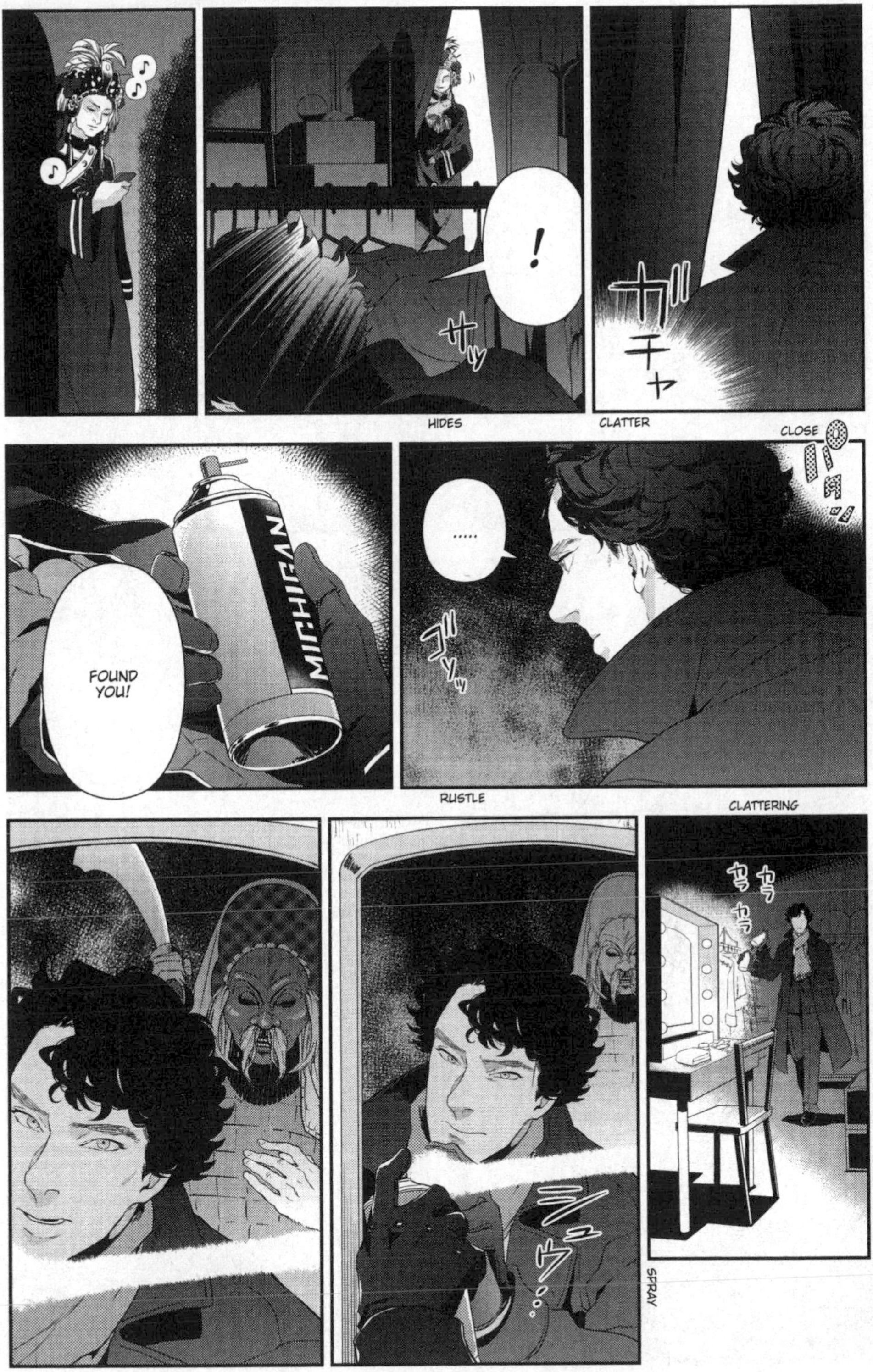
ガチャ
CLATTER
!
サッ
HIDES
パタッ
CLOSE
……
ゴソッ
RUSTLE
MICHIGAN
FOUND YOU!
カラカラ
CLATTERING
シュウ…
SPRAY

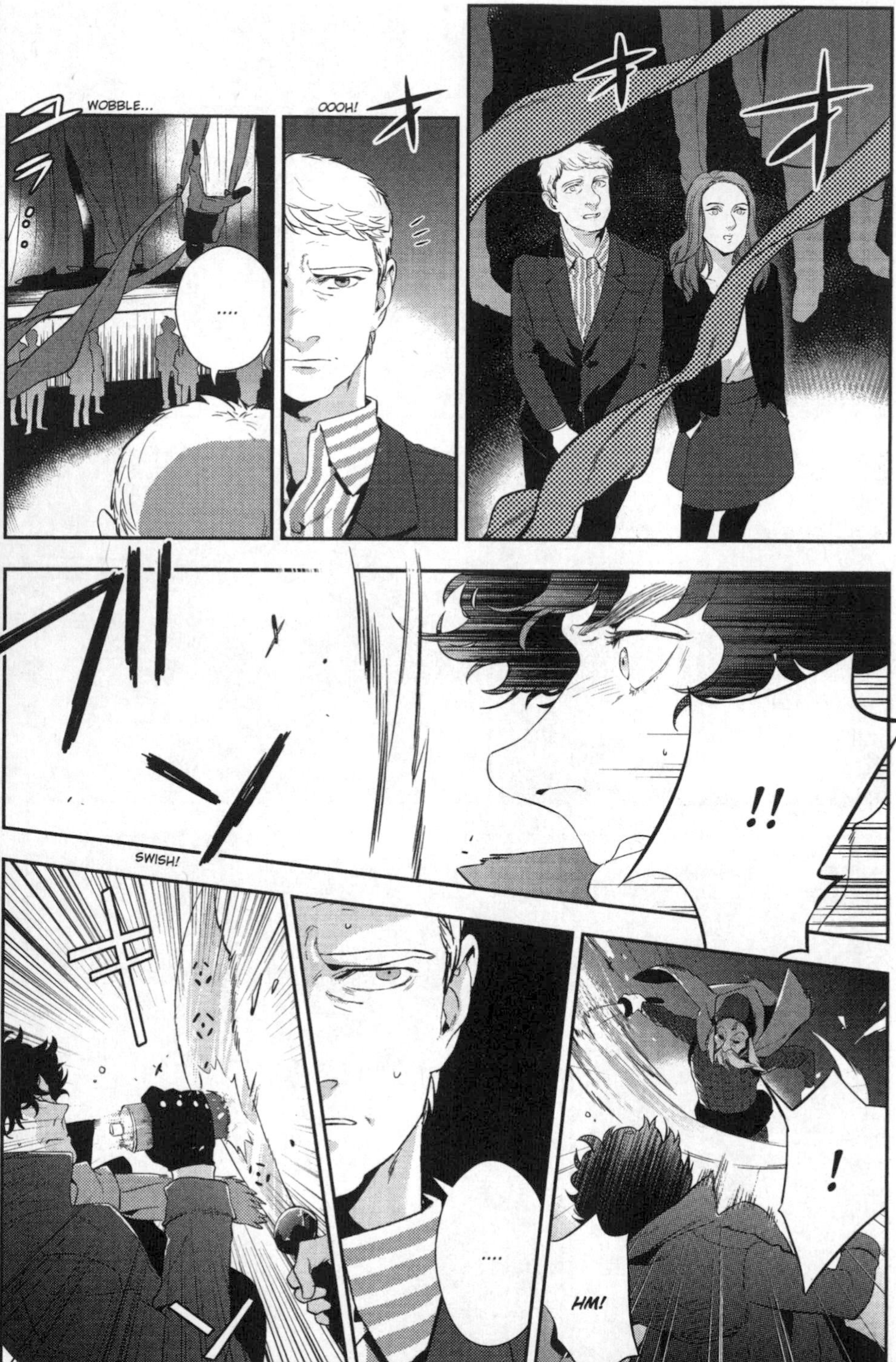
OOOH!
WOBBLE...
....
!!
SWISH!
!
HM!
....
PLINK

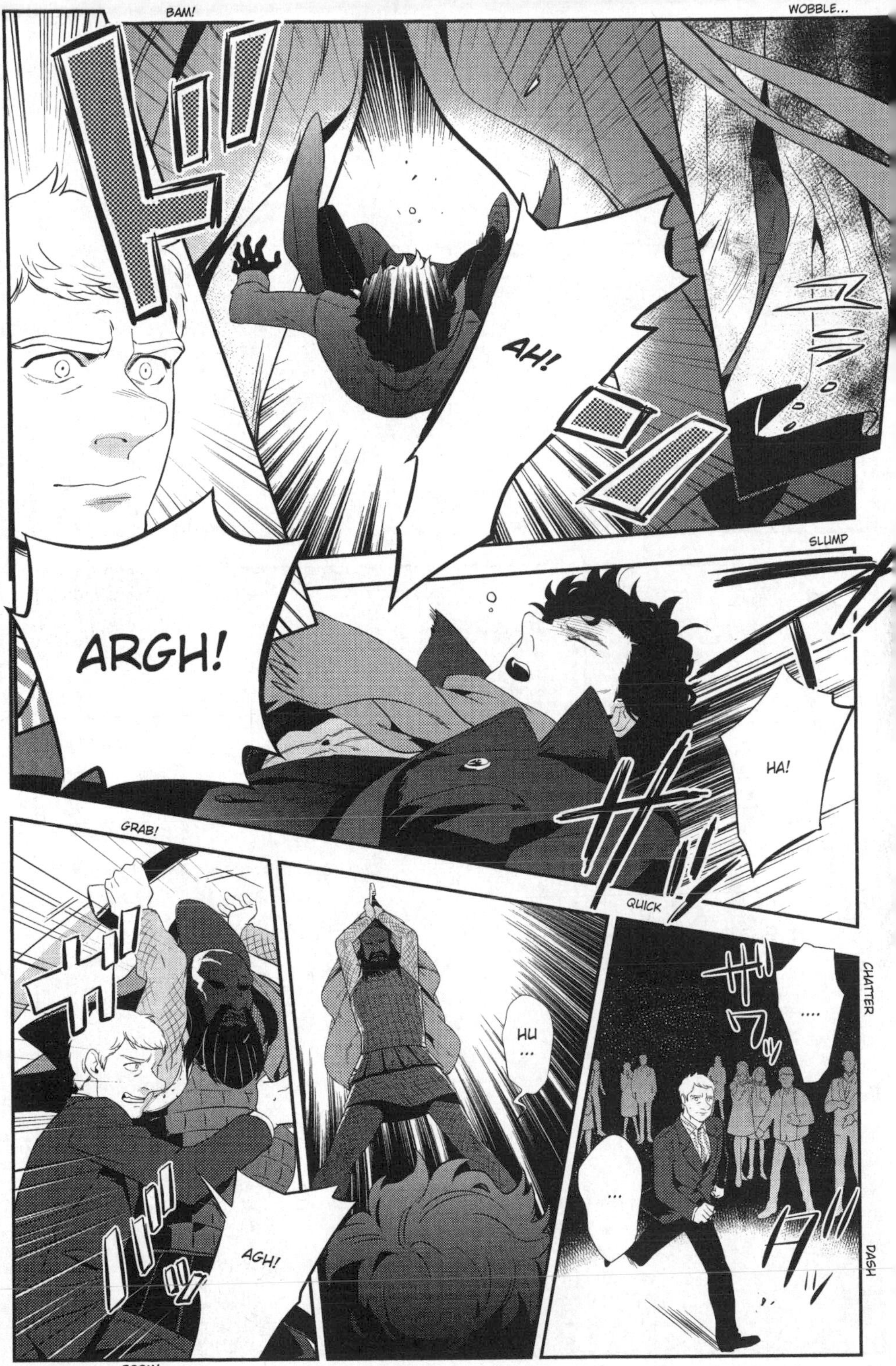
WOBBLE...
BAM!
AH!
ARGH!
SLUMP
HA!
QUICK
CHATTER
....
...
DASH
HU
...
GRAB!
AGH!
ZOOM!

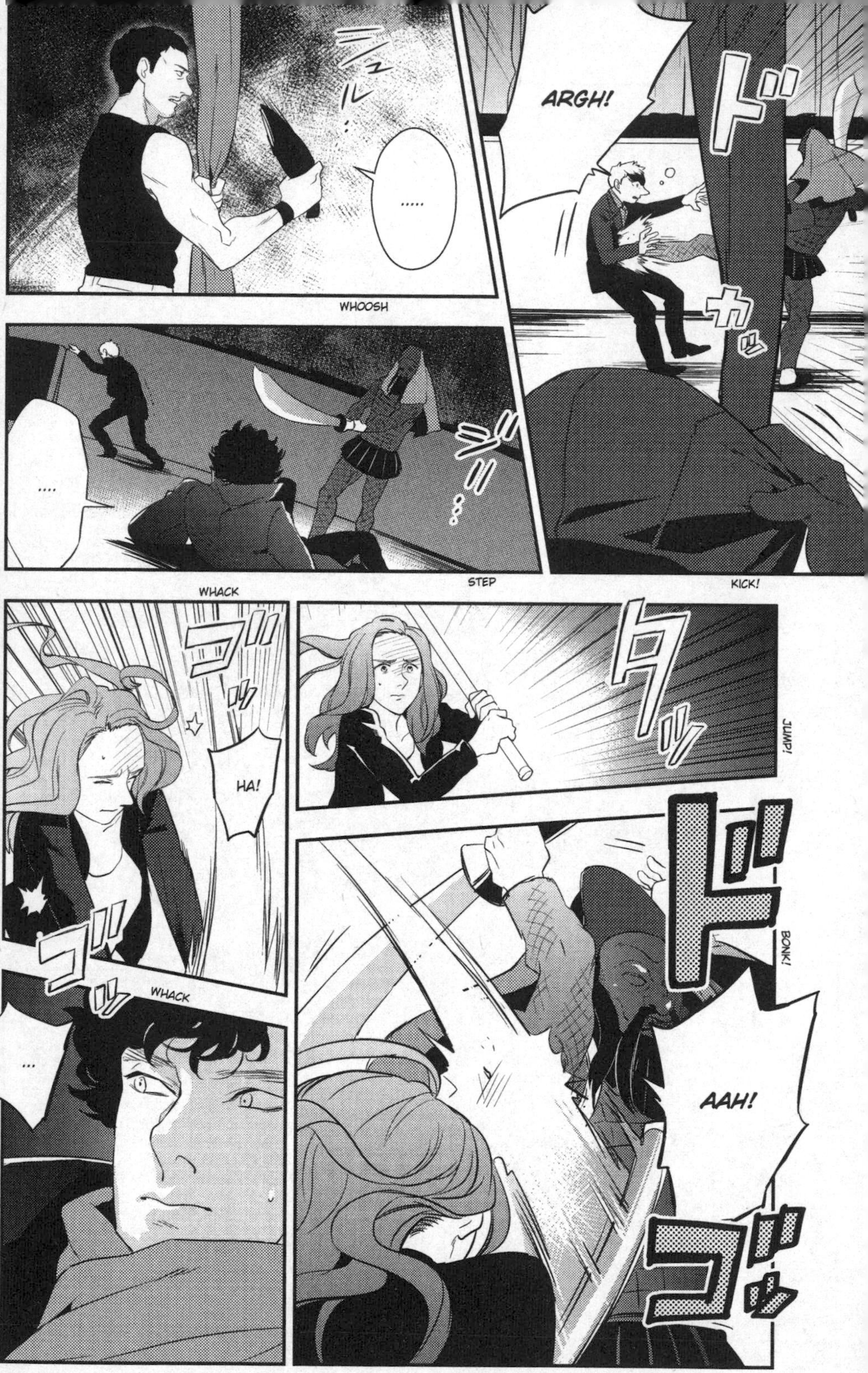
ARGH!
KICK!
.....
WHOOSH
....
STEP
JUMP!
WHACK
HA!
BONK!
AAH!
WHACK
...

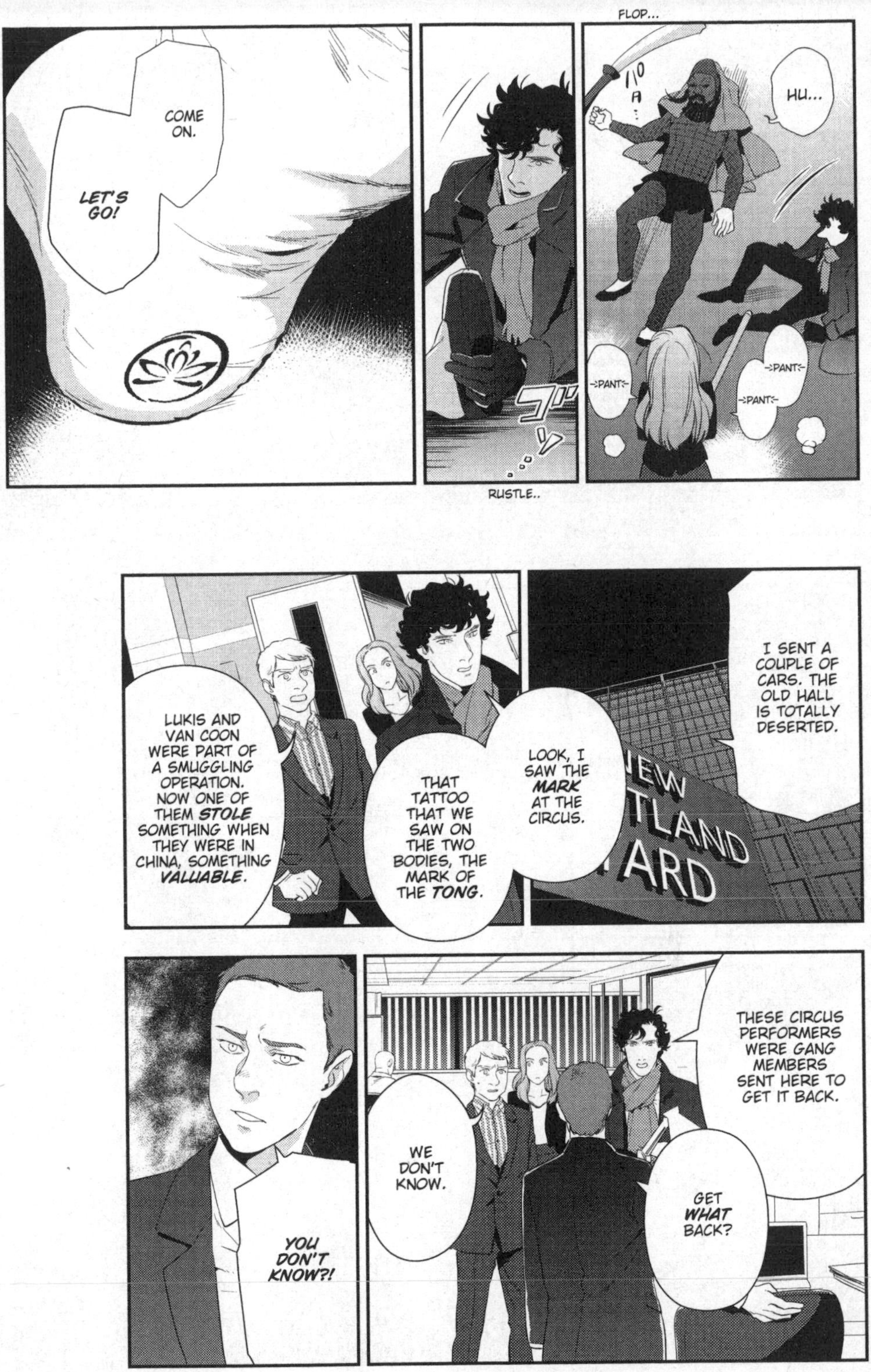
FLOP...
HU...
PANT
PANT
PANT
RUSTLE..
COME ON.
LET'S GO!
I SENT A COUPLE OF CARS. THE OLD HALL IS TOTALLY DESERTED.
LOOK, I SAW THE MARK AT THE CIRCUS.
THAT TATTOO THAT WE SAW ON THE TWO BODIES, THE MARK OF THE TONG.
LUKIS AND VAN COON WERE PART OF A SMUGGLING OPERATION. NOW ONE OF THEM STOLE SOMETHING WHEN THEY WERE IN CHINA, SOMETHING VALUABLE.
THESE CIRCUS PERFORMERS WERE GANG MEMBERS SENT HERE TO GET IT BACK.
GET WHAT BACK?
WE DON'T KNOW.
YOU DON'T KNOW?!

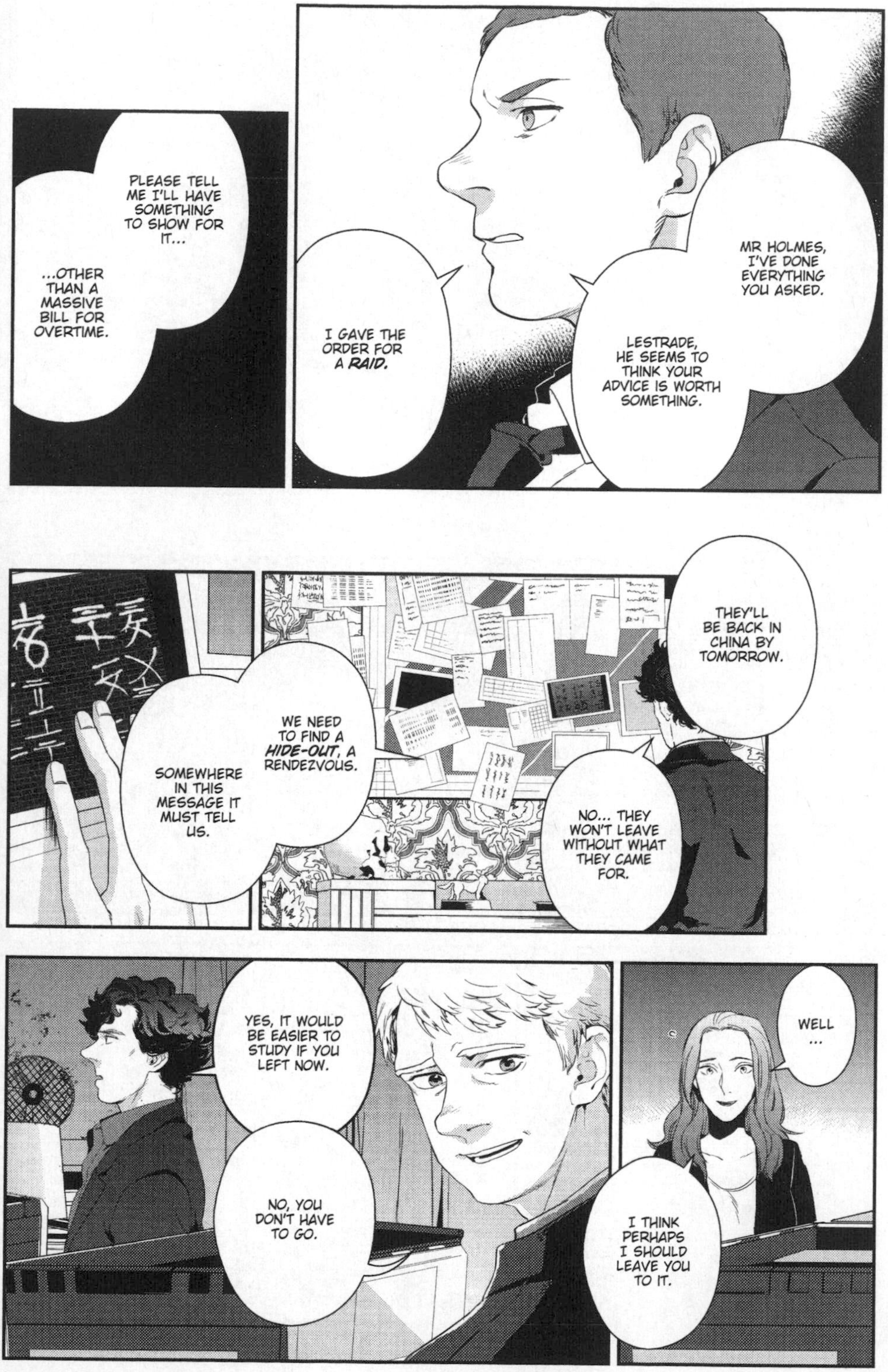
MR HOLMES, I'VE DONE EVERYTHING YOU ASKED.
LESTRADE, HE SEEMS TO THINK YOUR ADVICE IS WORTH SOMETHING.
I GAVE THE ORDER FOR A *RAID.*
PLEASE TELL ME I'LL HAVE SOMETHING TO SHOW FOR IT...
...OTHER THAN A MASSIVE BILL FOR OVERTIME.
THEY'LL BE BACK IN CHINA BY TOMORROW.
WE NEED TO FIND A *HIDE-OUT*, A RENDEZVOUS.
NO... THEY WON'T LEAVE WITHOUT WHAT THEY CAME FOR.
SOMEWHERE IN THIS MESSAGE IT MUST TELL US.
WELL ...
I THINK PERHAPS I SHOULD LEAVE YOU TO IT.
YES, IT WOULD BE EASIER TO STUDY IF YOU LEFT NOW.
NO, YOU DON'T HAVE TO GO.

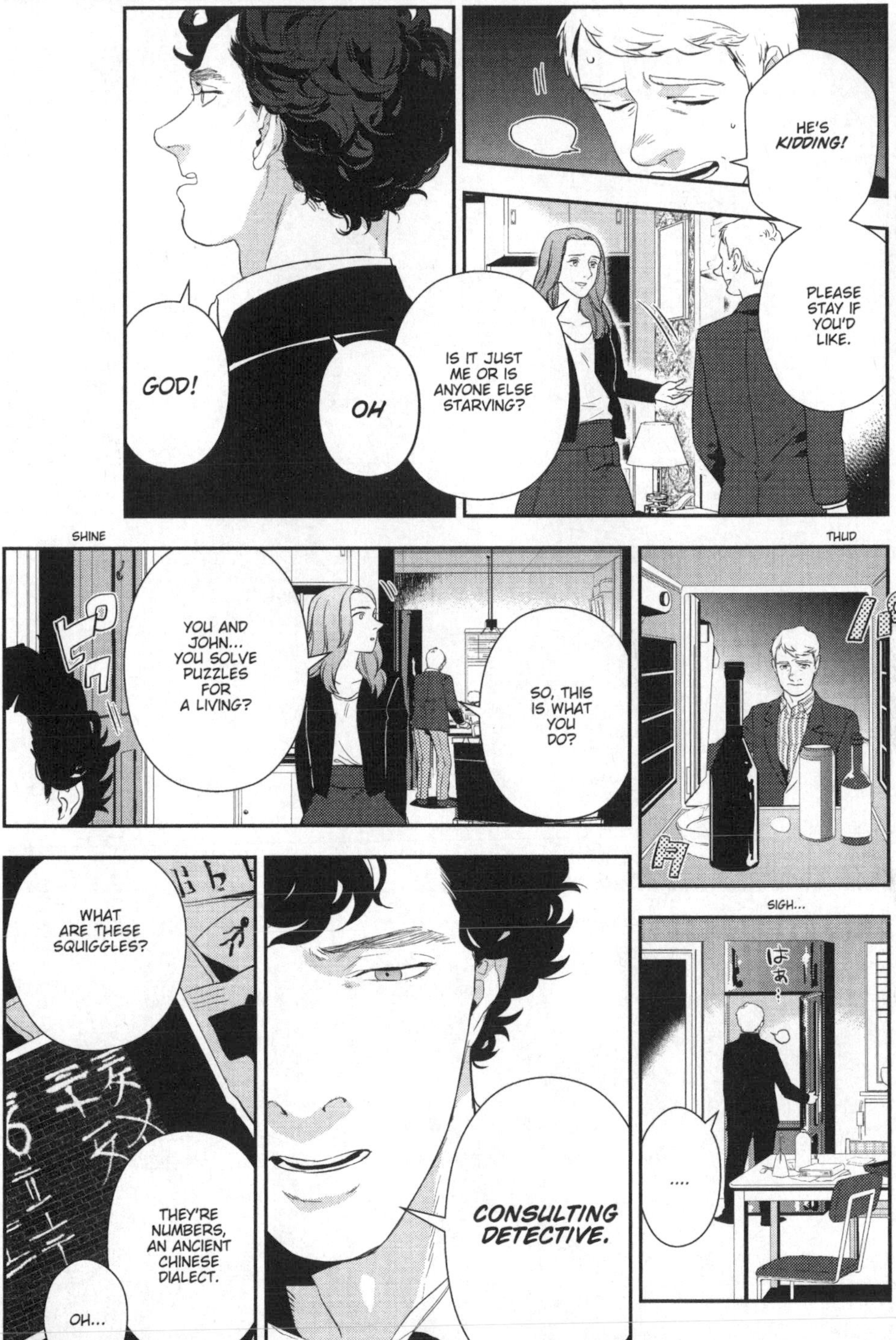
HE'S KIDDING!
PLEASE STAY IF YOU'D LIKE.
IS IT JUST ME OR IS ANYONE ELSE STARVING?
OH
GOD!
THUD
SHINE
SO, THIS IS WHAT YOU DO?
YOU AND JOHN... YOU SOLVE PUZZLES FOR A LIVING?
SIGH...
はぁ…
....
CONSULTING DETECTIVE.
WHAT ARE THESE SQUIGGLES?
THEY'RE NUMBERS, AN ANCIENT CHINESE DIALECT.
OH...

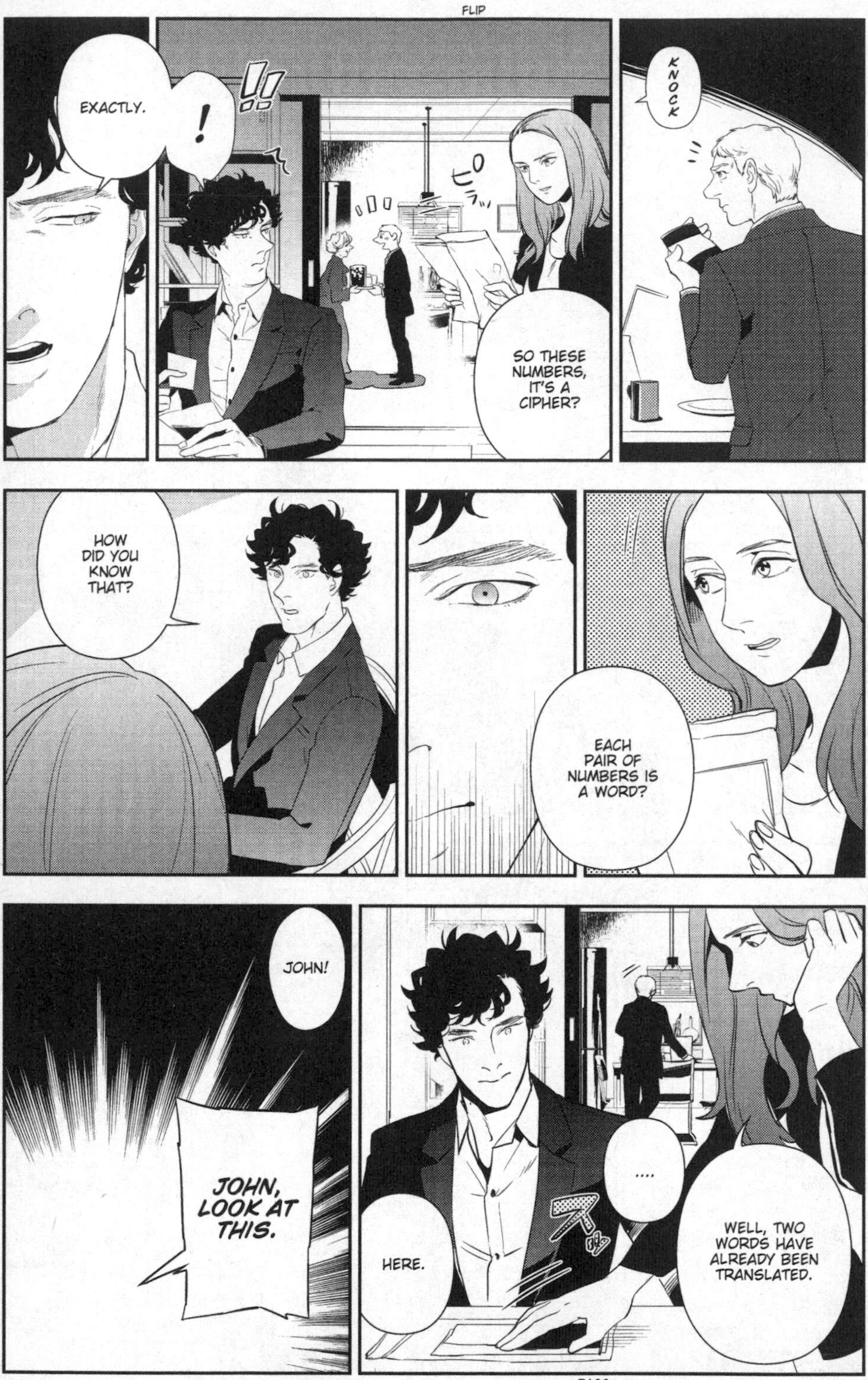
KNOCK
FLIP
SO THESE NUMBERS, IT'S A CIPHER?
!!
!
EXACTLY.
EACH PAIR OF NUMBERS IS A WORD?
HOW DID YOU KNOW THAT?
WELL, TWO WORDS HAVE ALREADY BEEN TRANSLATED.
....
HERE.
PASS
JOHN!
JOHN, LOOK AT THIS.

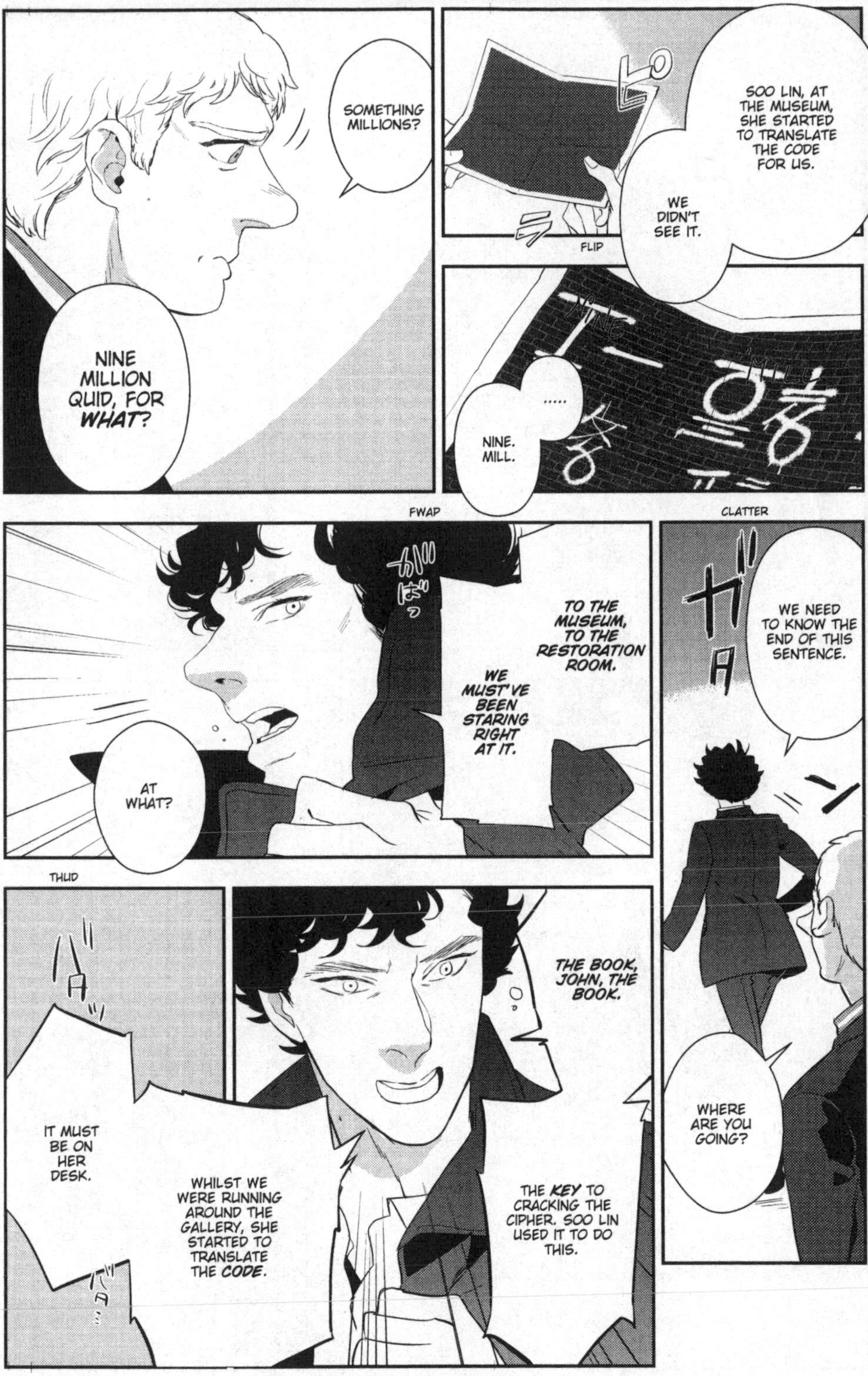
SOO LIN, AT THE MUSEUM, SHE STARTED TO TRANSLATE THE CODE FOR US.
WE DIDN'T SEE IT.
FLIP
NINE
MILL
.....
NINE. MILL.
SOMETHING MILLIONS?
NINE MILLION QUID, FOR WHAT?
CLATTER
WE NEED TO KNOW THE END OF THIS SENTENCE.
WHERE ARE YOU GOING?
FWAP
TO THE MUSEUM, TO THE RESTORATION ROOM.
WE MUST'VE BEEN STARING RIGHT AT IT.
AT WHAT?
THUD
THE BOOK, JOHN, THE BOOK.
THE KEY TO CRACKING THE CIPHER. SOO LIN USED IT TO DO THIS.
WHILST WE WERE RUNNING AROUND THE GALLERY, SHE STARTED TO TRANSLATE THE CODE.
IT MUST BE ON HER DESK.

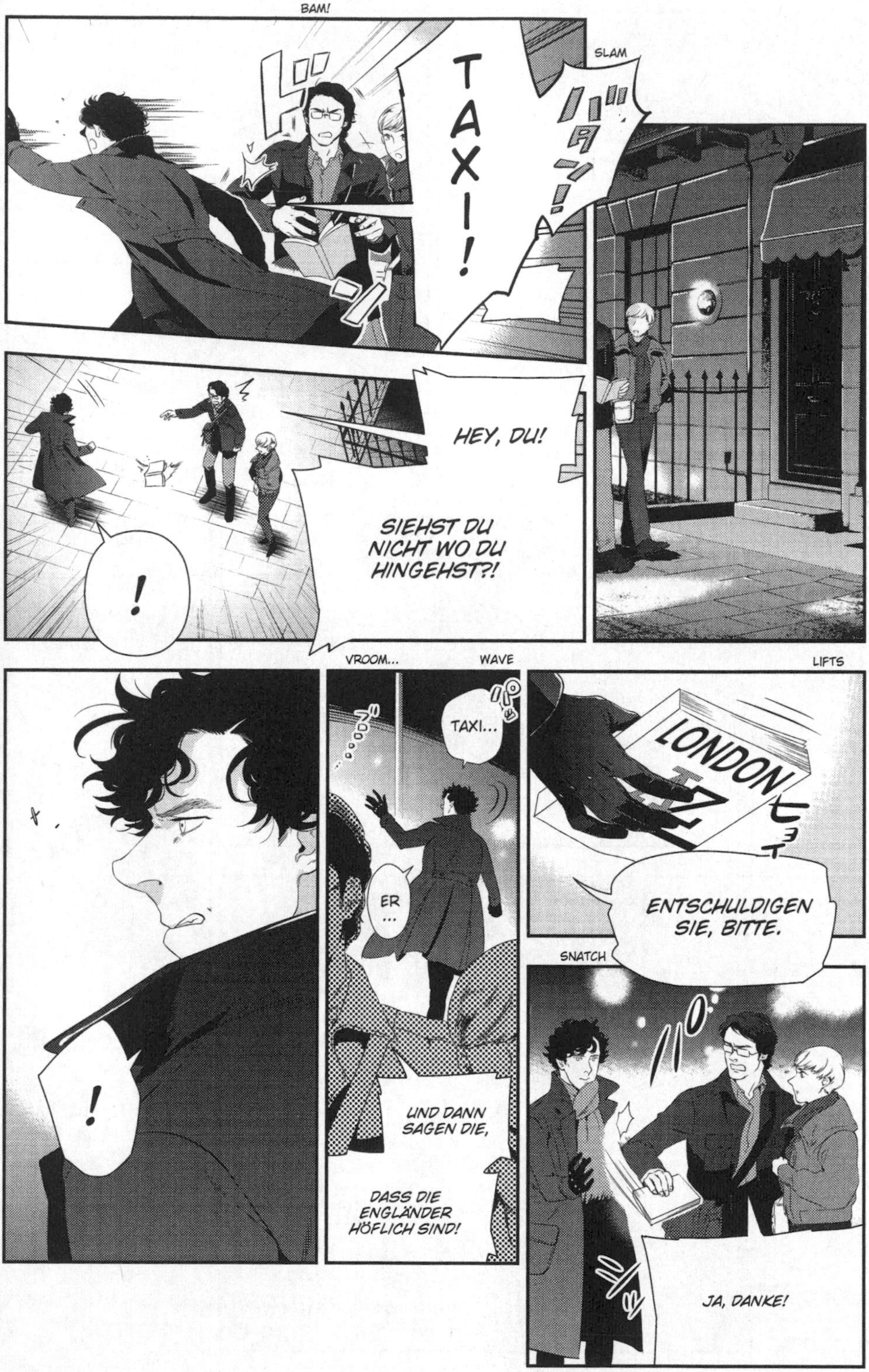
SLAM
BAM!
TAXI!
HEY, DU!
SIEHST DU NICHT WO DU HINGEHST?!
!
LIFTS
LONDON
ENTSCHULDIGEN SIE, BITTE.
SNATCH
JA, DANKE!
VROOM...
WAVE
TAXI...
ER ...
UND DANN SAGEN DIE,
DASS DIE ENGLÄNDER HÖFLICH SIND!
!

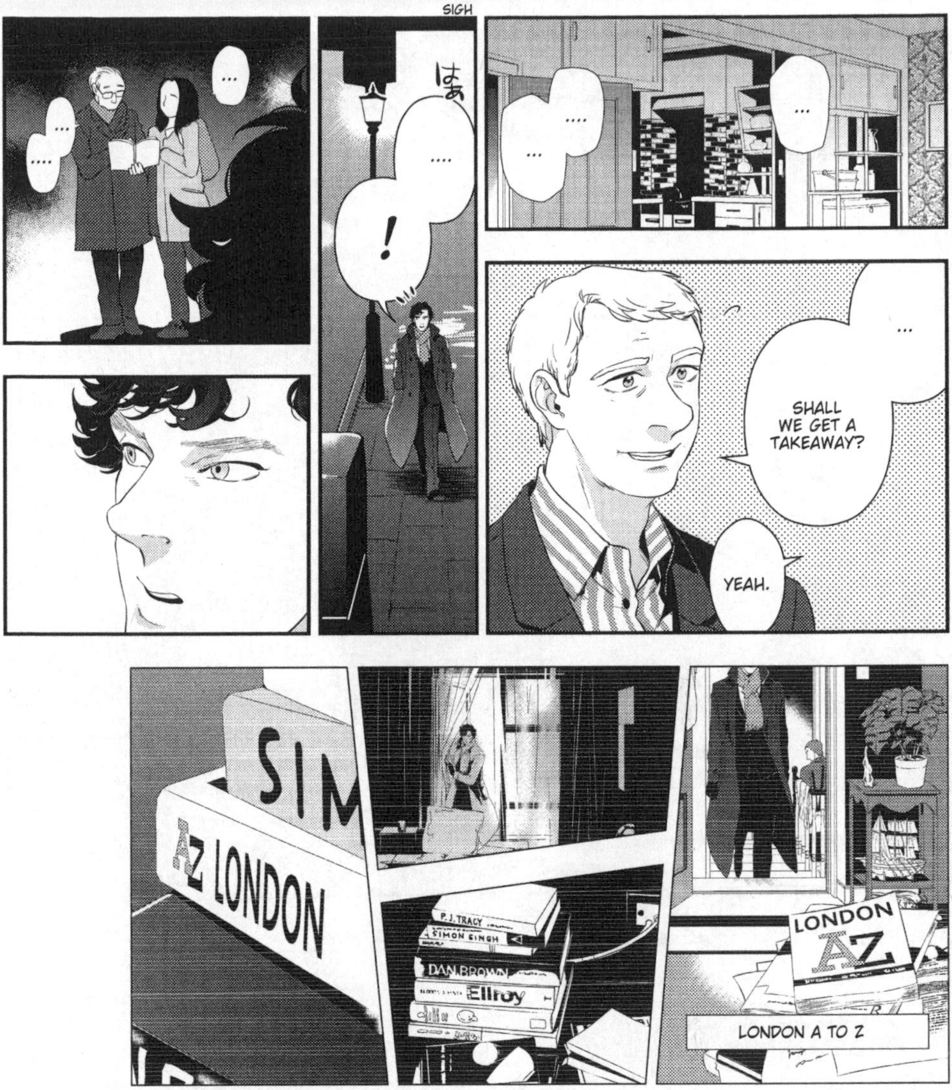
...
....
...
...
SHALL WE GET A TAKEAWAY?
YEAH.
SIGH
はあ
....
!
....
...
....
LONDON A Z
LONDON A TO Z
P.J. TRACY
SIMON SINGH
DAN BROWN
Ellroy
SIM
AZ LONDON

A BOOK EVERYBODY WOULD OWN.

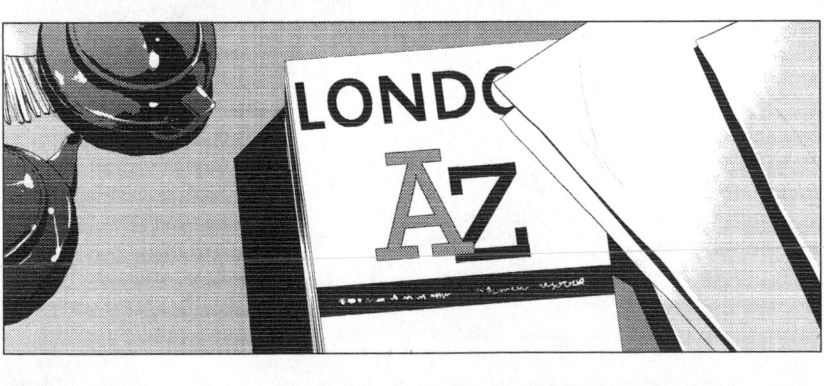
LONDO
AZ

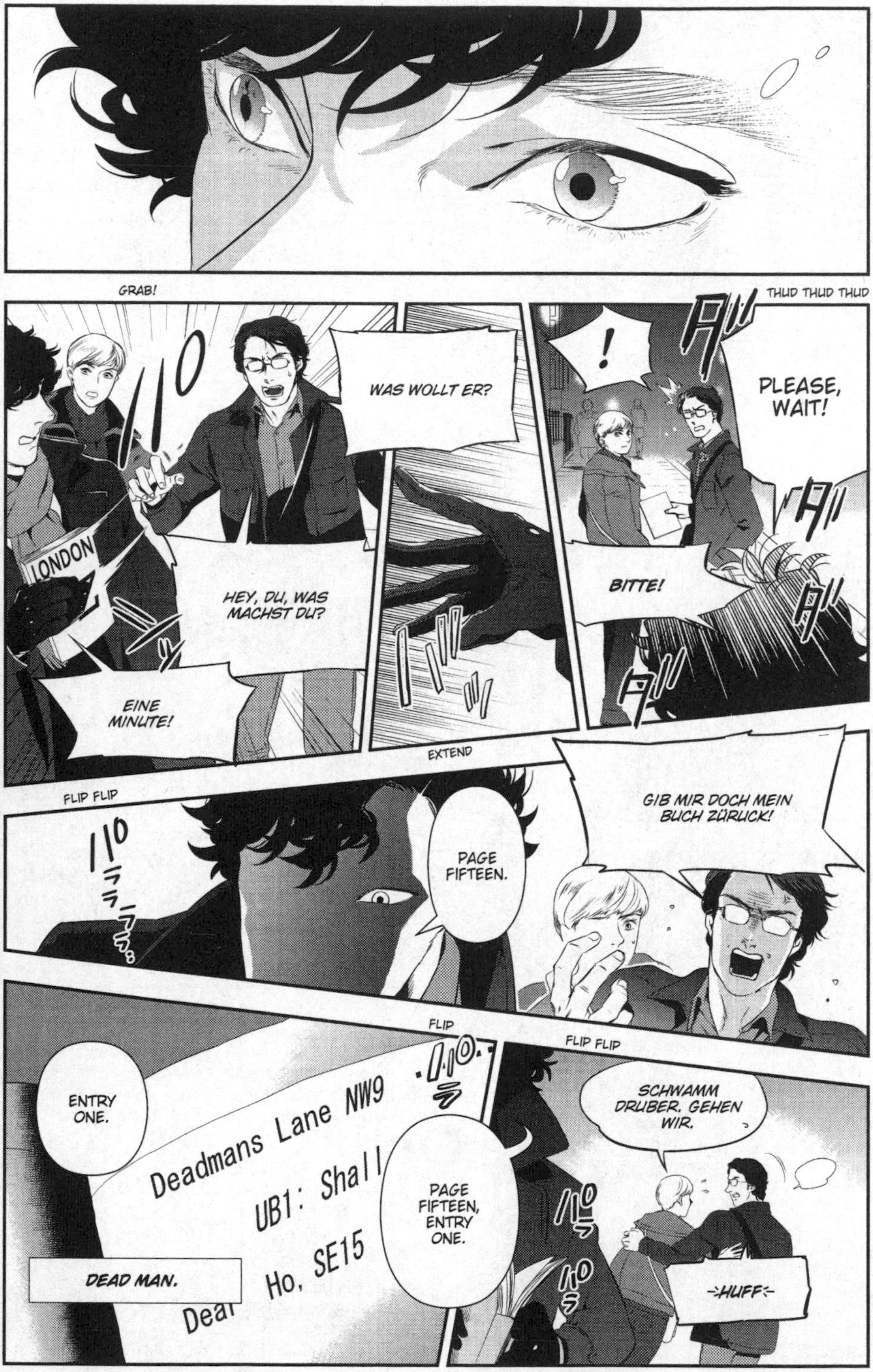
THUD THUD THUD
!
PLEASE, WAIT!
BITTE!
WAS WOLLT ER?
EXTEND
GRAB!
HEY, DU, WAS MACHST DU?
EINE MINUTE!
LONDON
GIB MIR DOCH MEIN BUCH ZURÜCK!
PAGE FIFTEEN.
FLIP FLIP
FLIP FLIP
SCHWAMM DRUBER. GEHEN WIR.
HUFF
FLIP
ENTRY ONE.
Deadmans Lane NW9
PAGE FIFTEEN, ENTRY ONE.
DEAD MAN.

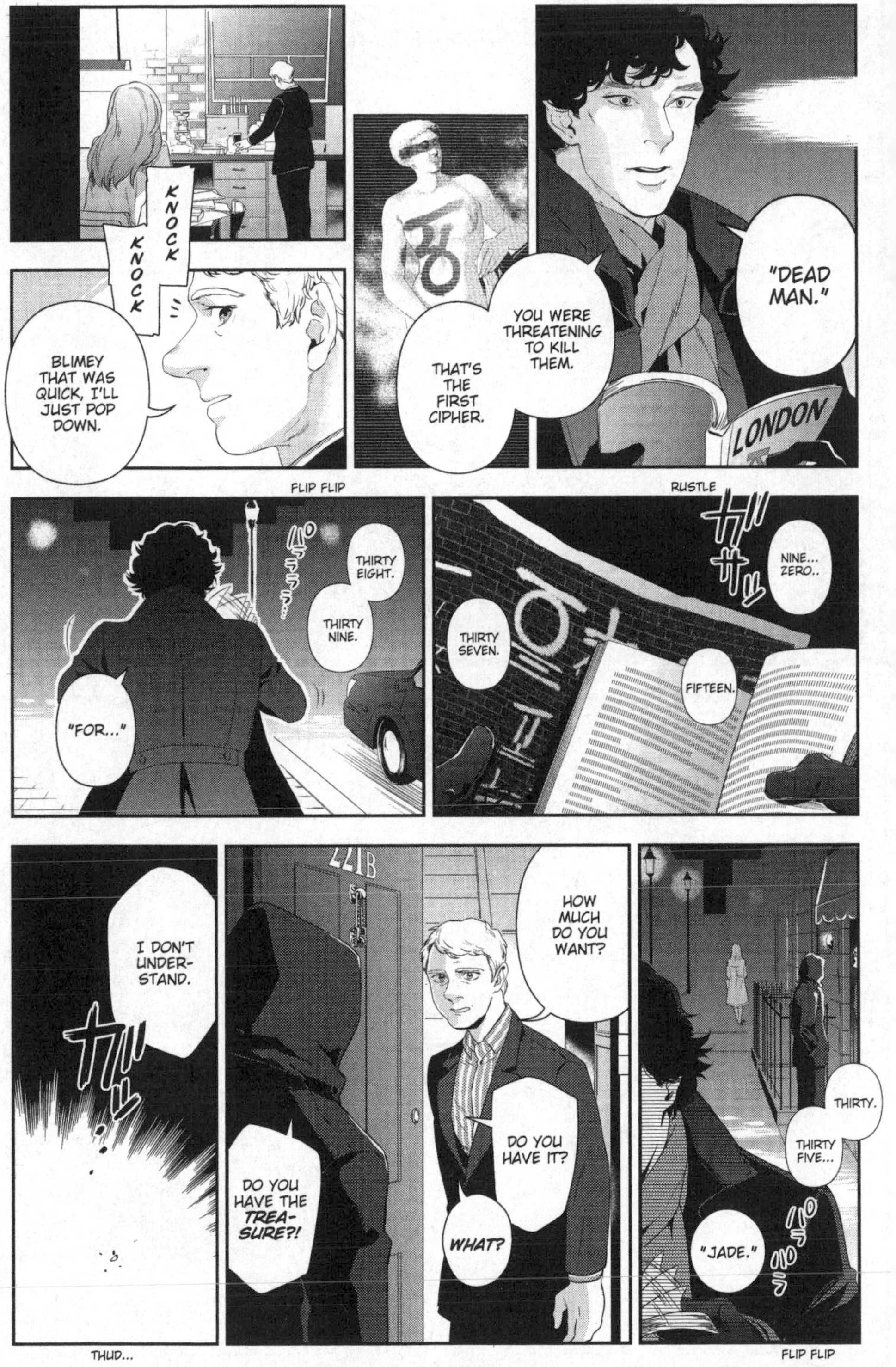
"DEAD MAN."
YOU WERE THREATENING TO KILL THEM.
THAT'S THE FIRST CIPHER.
KNOCK KNOCK
BLIMEY THAT WAS QUICK, I'LL JUST POP DOWN.
RUSTLE
NINE... ZERO..
THIRTY SEVEN.
FIFTEEN.
FLIP FLIP
THIRTY EIGHT.
THIRTY NINE.
"FOR..."
FLIP FLIP
THIRTY.
THIRTY FIVE...
"JADE."
221B
HOW MUCH DO YOU WANT?
DO YOU HAVE IT?
WHAT?
DO YOU HAVE THE TREASURE?!
I DON'T UNDERSTAND.
THUD...

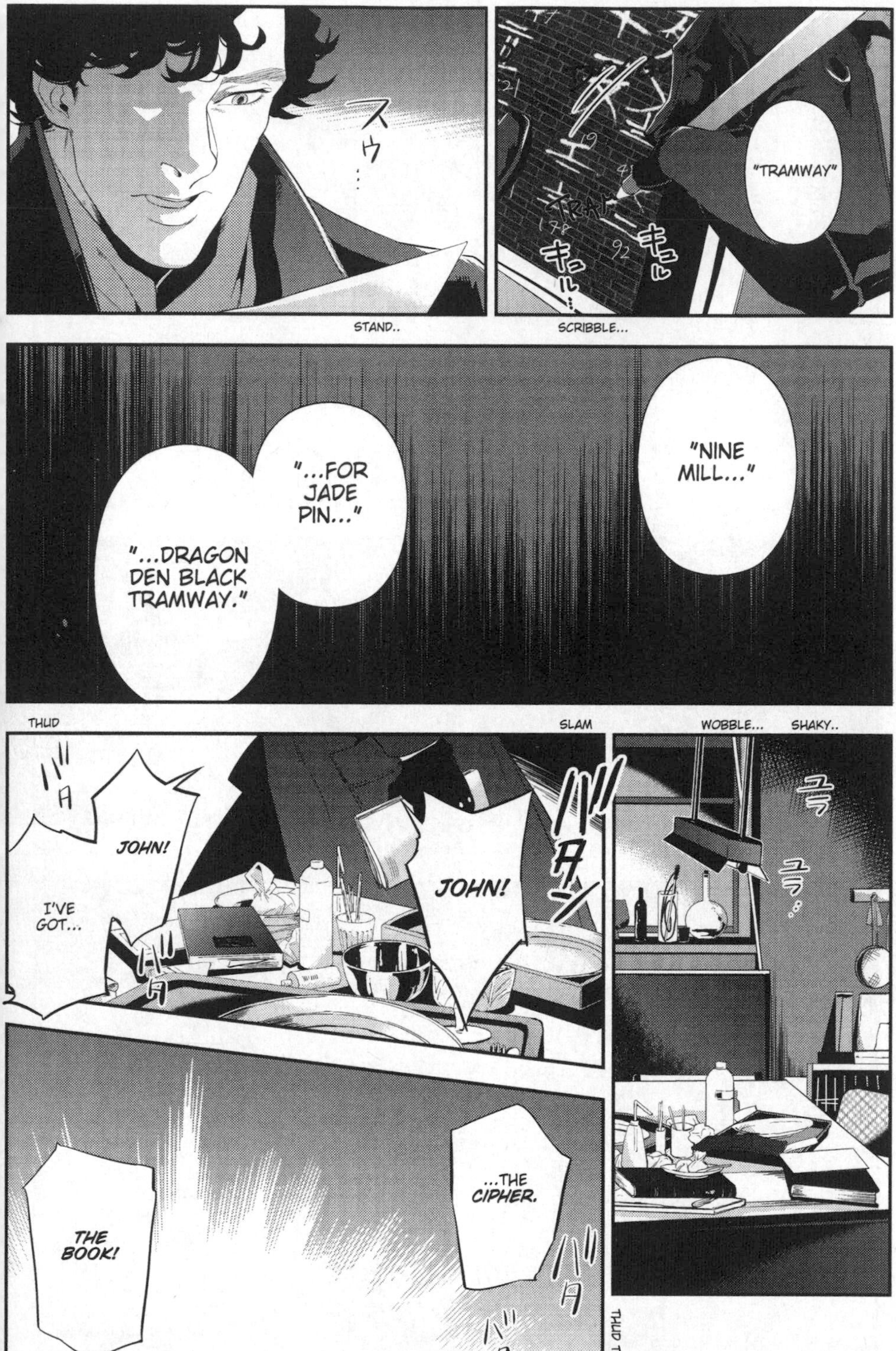

"TRAMWAY"
キュキュル…
SCRIBBLE...
スゥ…
STAND..
"NINE MILL..."
"...FOR JADE PIN..."
"...DRAGON DEN BLACK TRAMWAY."
ユラユラ
WOBBLE...
SHAKY..
JOHN!
バタン
SLAM
バタ
THUD
JOHN!
I'VE GOT...
バタバタ
THUD THUD
...THE CIPHER.
THE BOOK!

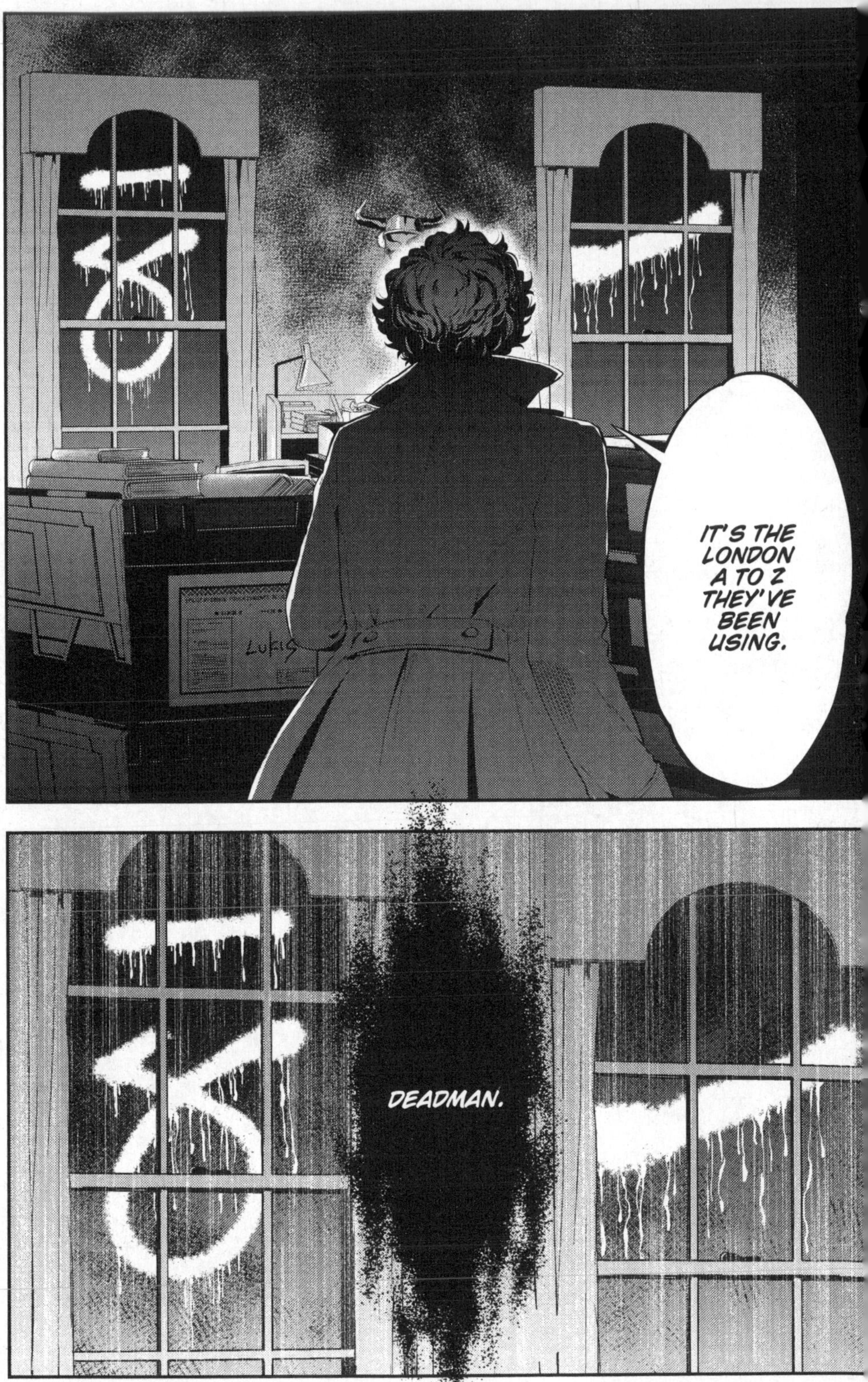
IT'S THE LONDON A TO Z THEY'VE BEEN USING.
DEADMAN.

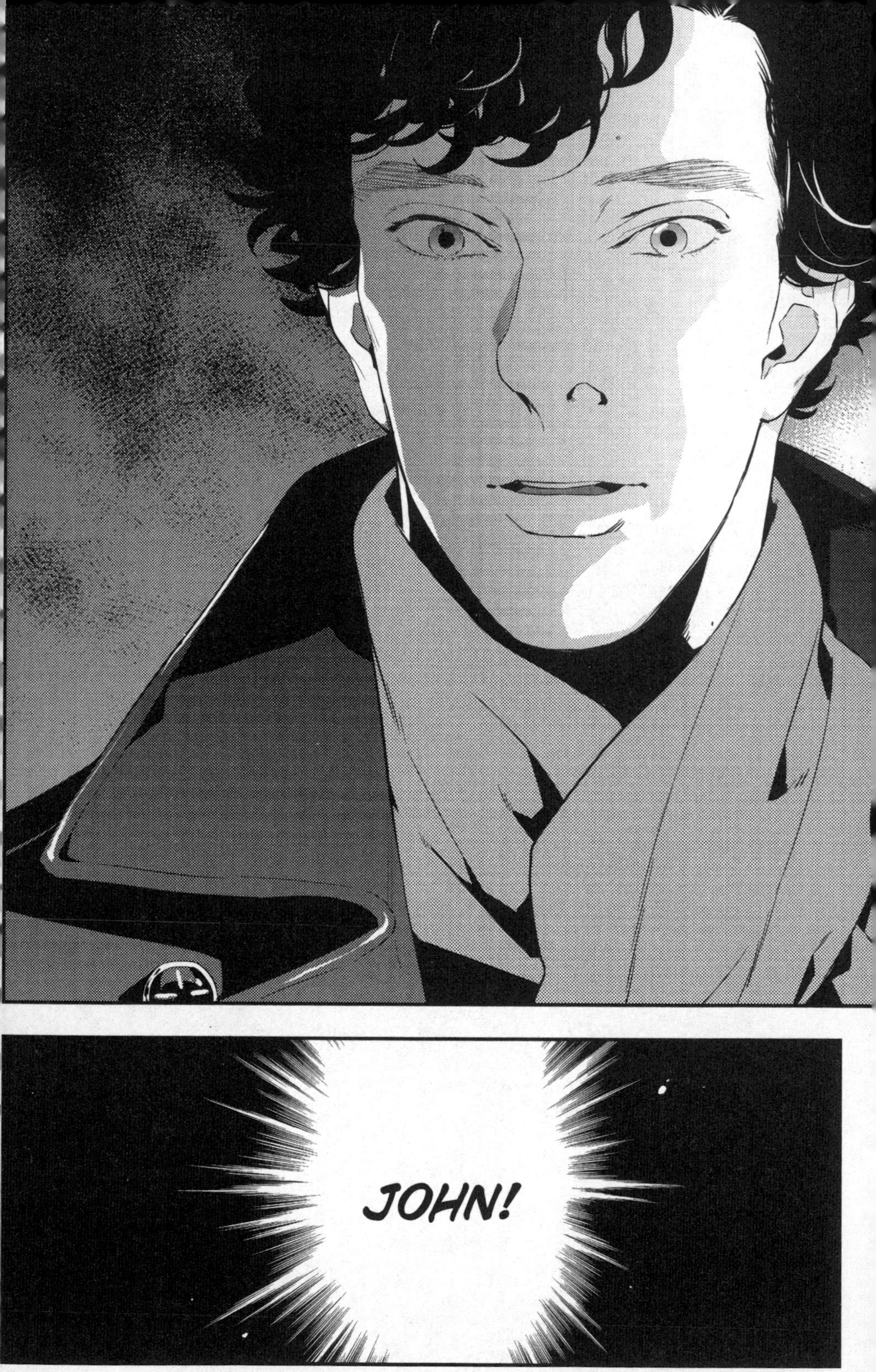
JOHN!

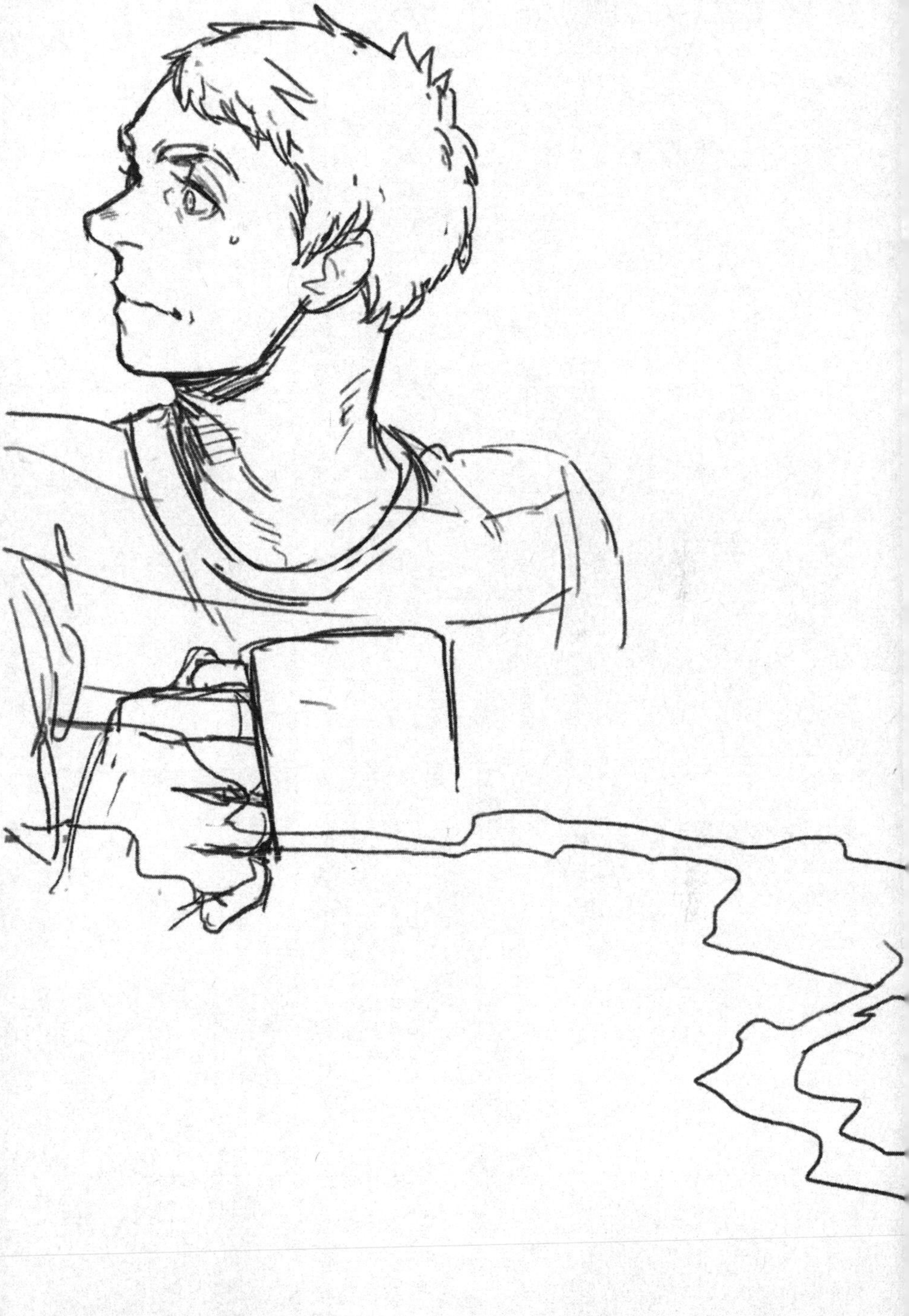

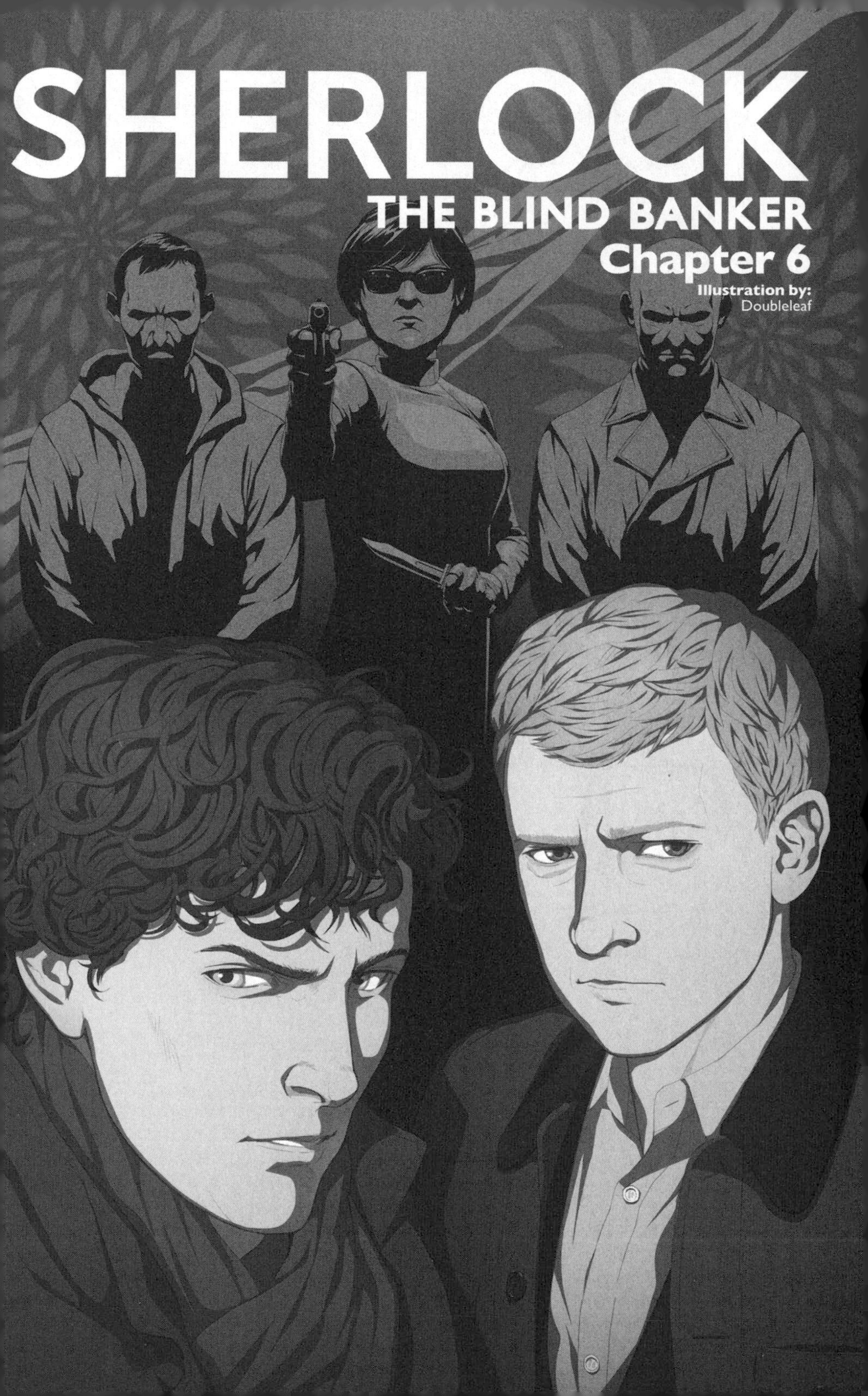
SHERLOCK
THE BLIND BANKER
Chapter 6
Illustration by:
Doubleleaf

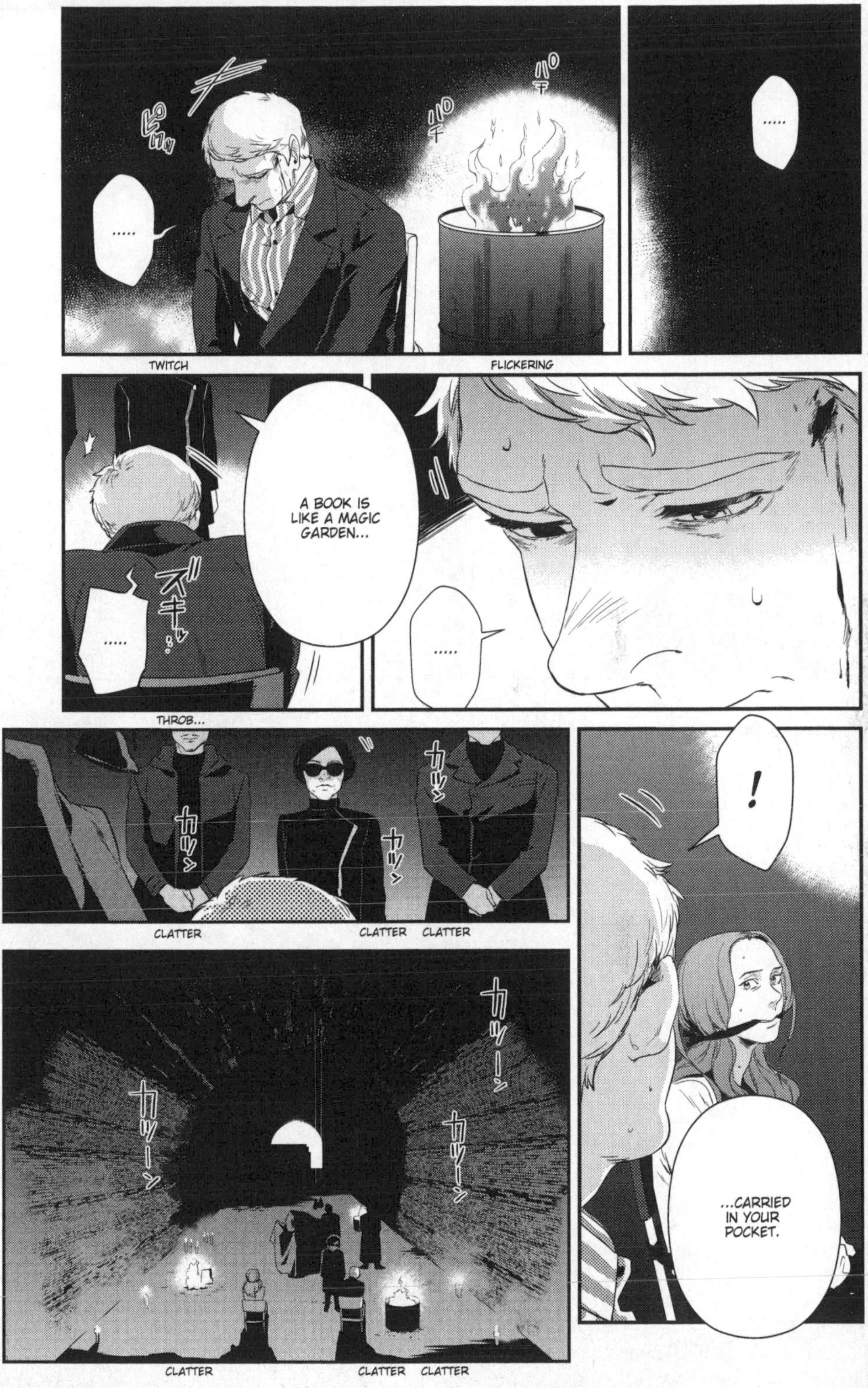
......
......
TWITCH
FLICKERING
......
A BOOK IS LIKE A MAGIC GARDEN...
......
THROB...
!
...CARRIED IN YOUR POCKET.
CLATTER
CLATTER
CLATTER
CLATTER
CLATTER
CLATTER

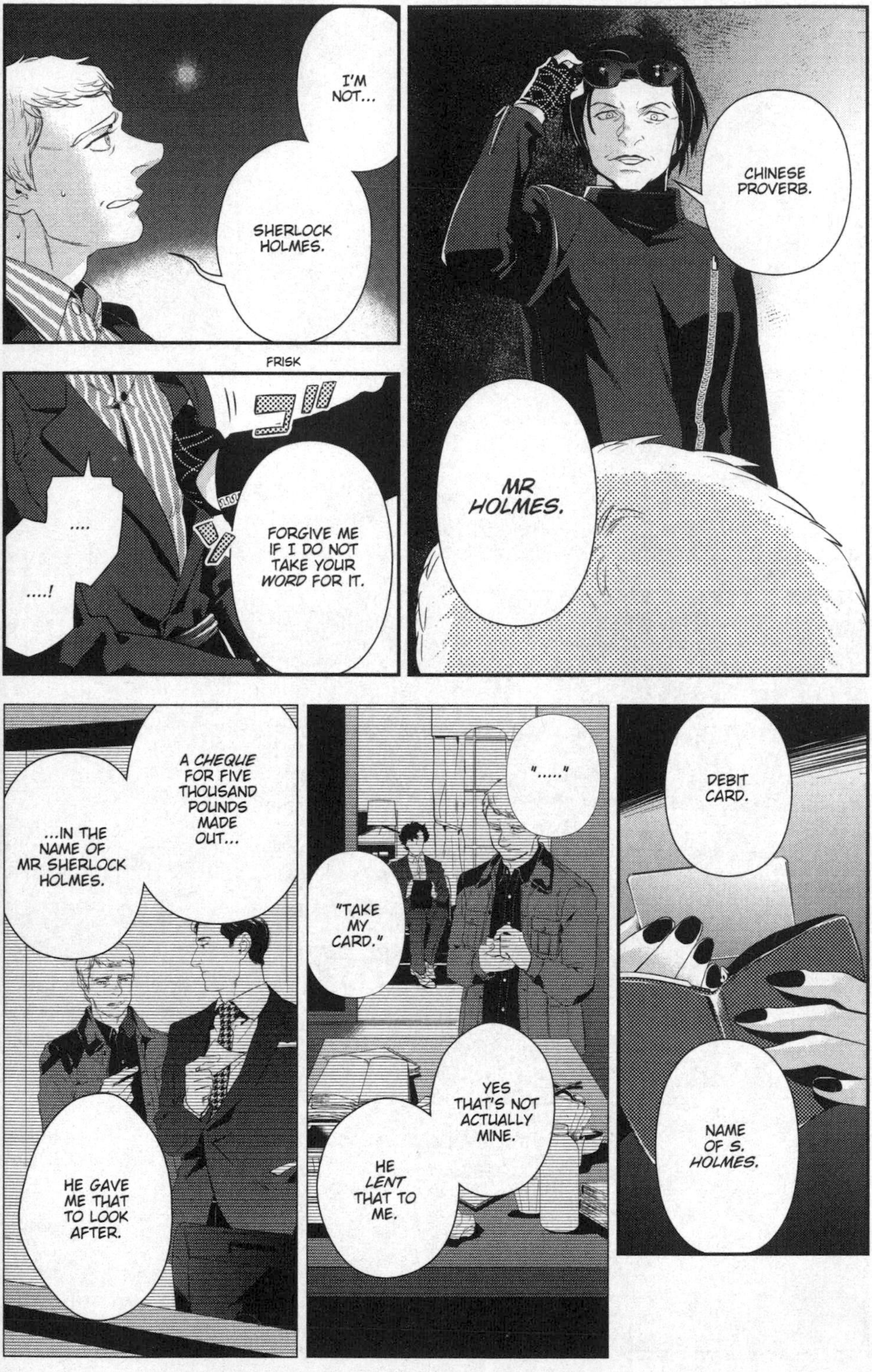
CHINESE PROVERB.
MR HOLMES.
I'M NOT...
SHERLOCK HOLMES.
FRISK
FORGIVE ME IF I DO NOT TAKE YOUR WORD FOR IT.
....
....!
DEBIT CARD.
NAME OF S. HOLMES.
"....."
"TAKE MY CARD."
YES THAT'S NOT ACTUALLY MINE.
HE LENT THAT TO ME.
A CHEQUE FOR FIVE THOUSAND POUNDS MADE OUT...
...IN THE NAME OF MR SHERLOCK HOLMES.
HE GAVE ME THAT TO LOOK AFTER.

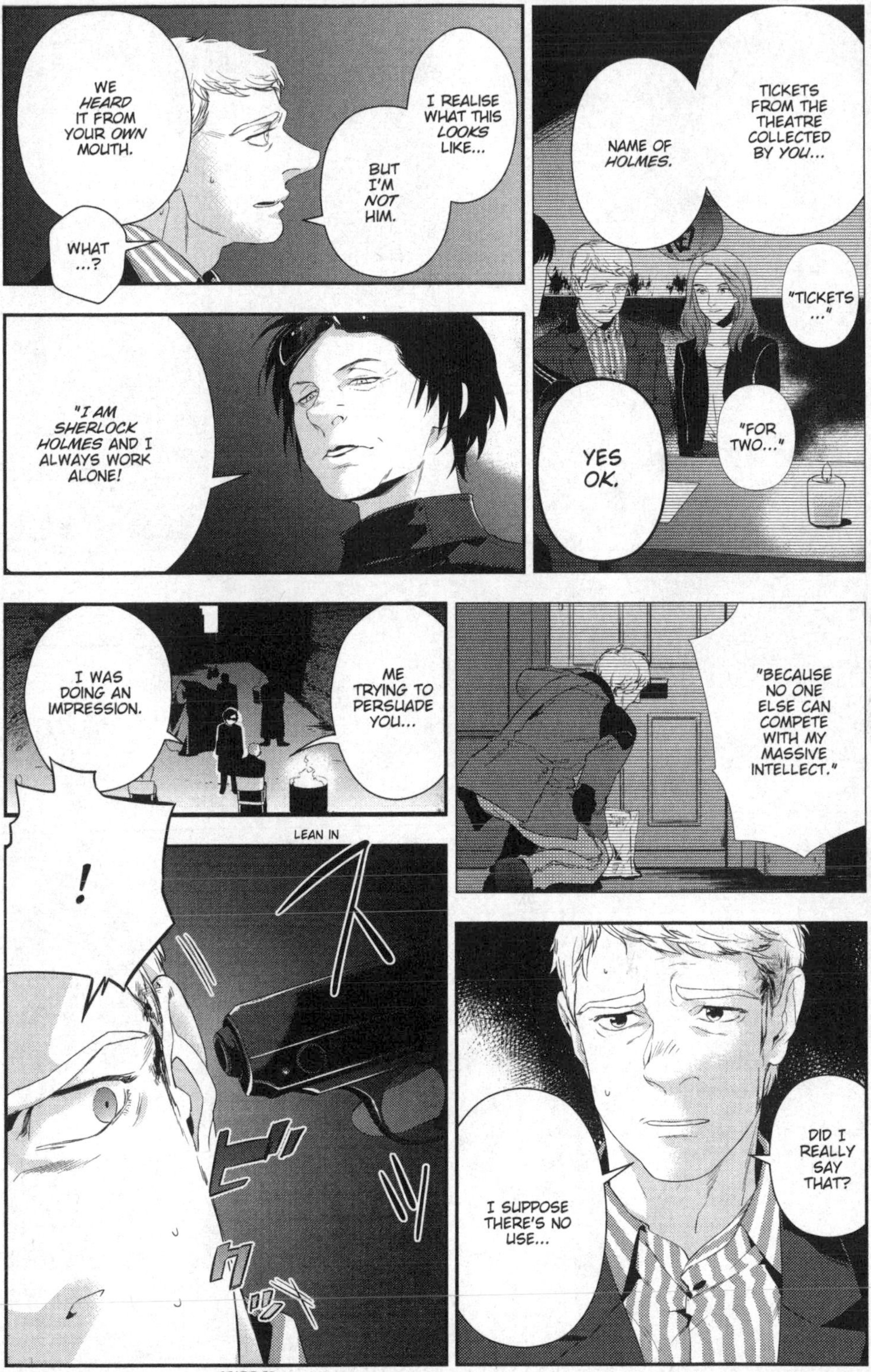
TICKETS FROM THE THEATRE COLLECTED BY YOU...
NAME OF HOLMES.
"TICKETS..."
"FOR TWO..."
YES OK.
I REALISE WHAT THIS LOOKS LIKE...
BUT I'M NOT HIM.
WE HEARD IT FROM YOUR OWN MOUTH.
WHAT...?
"I AM SHERLOCK HOLMES AND I ALWAYS WORK ALONE!
"BECAUSE NO ONE ELSE CAN COMPETE WITH MY MASSIVE INTELLECT."
ME TRYING TO PERSUADE YOU...
I WAS DOING AN IMPRESSION.
DID I REALLY SAY THAT?
I SUPPOSE THERE'S NO USE...
LEAN IN
!
STARTLED

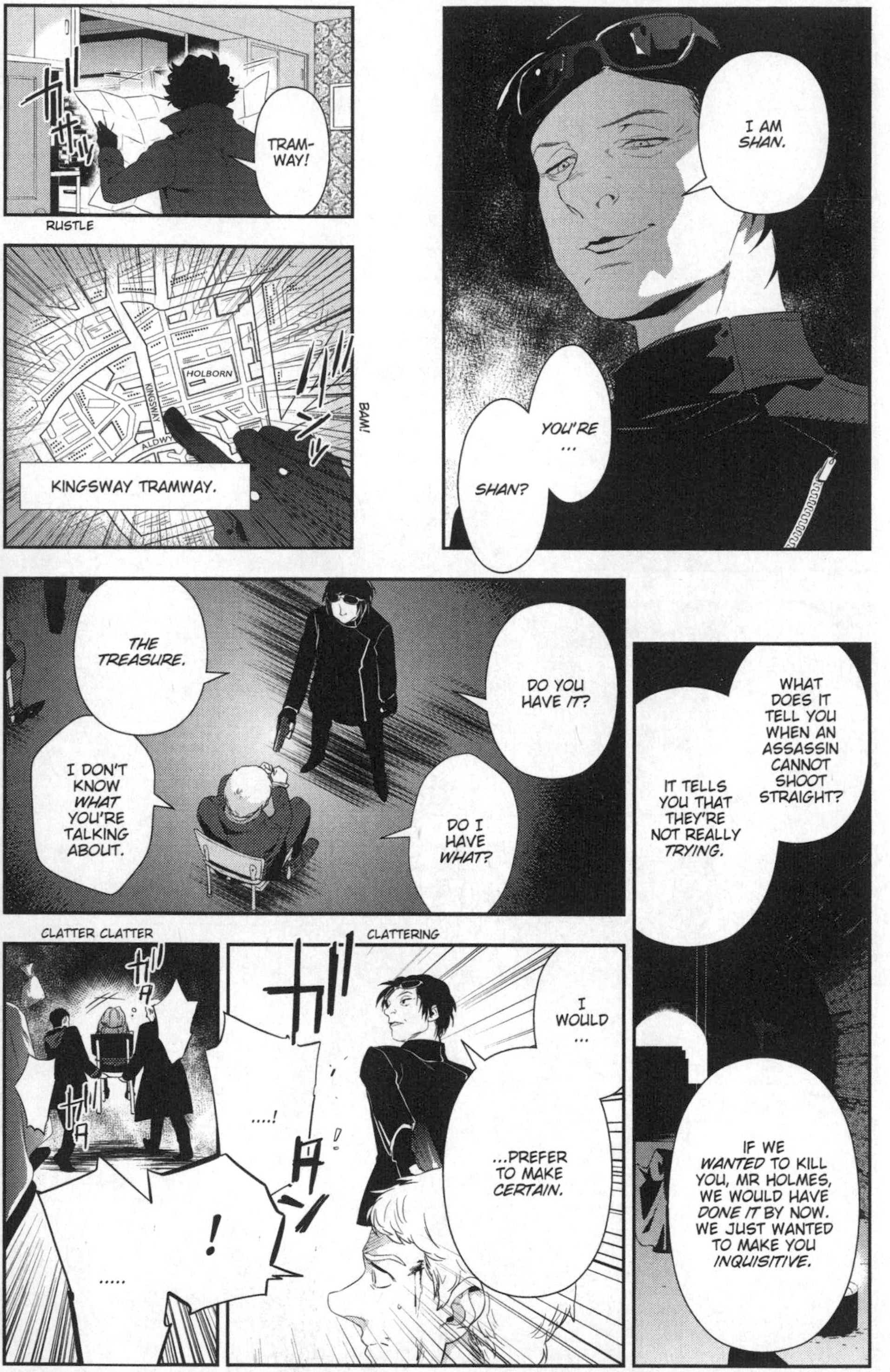
I AM SHAN.
YOU'RE ... SHAN?
TRAM-WAY!
RUSTLE
BAM!
HOLBORN
KINGSWAY
KINGSWAY TRAMWAY.
WHAT DOES IT TELL YOU WHEN AN ASSASSIN CANNOT SHOOT STRAIGHT?
IT TELLS YOU THAT THEY'RE NOT REALLY TRYING.
IF WE WANTED TO KILL YOU, MR HOLMES, WE WOULD HAVE DONE IT BY NOW. WE JUST WANTED TO MAKE YOU INQUISITIVE.
DO YOU HAVE IT?
THE TREASURE.
DO I HAVE WHAT?
I DON'T KNOW WHAT YOU'RE TALKING ABOUT.
CLATTERING
I WOULD ...
...PREFER TO MAKE CERTAIN.
....!
!
.....
CLATTER CLATTER

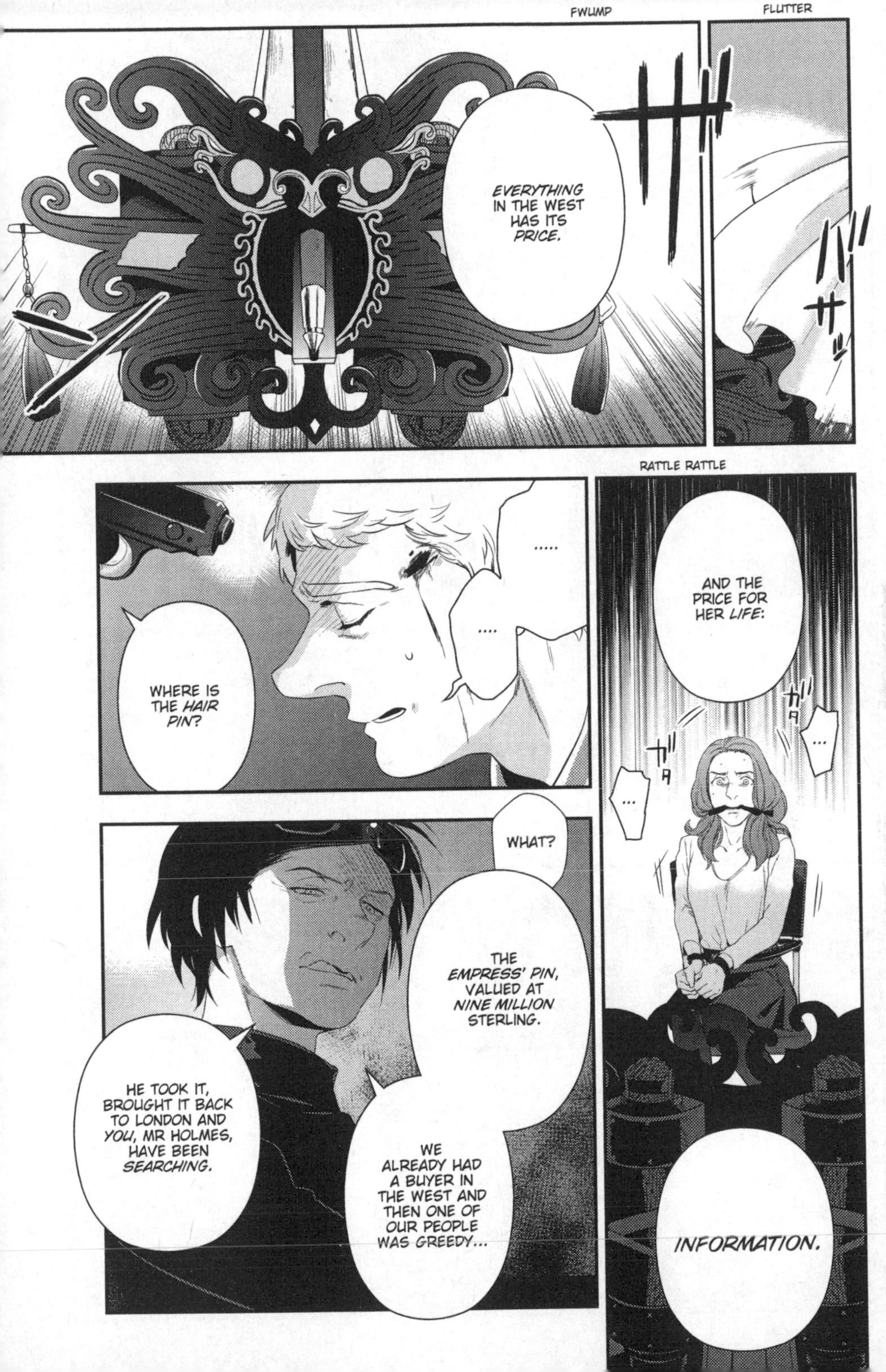
FLUTTER
FWUMP
EVERYTHING IN THE WEST HAS ITS PRICE.
RATTLE RATTLE
AND THE PRICE FOR HER LIFE:
...
...
INFORMATION.
.....
....
WHERE IS THE HAIR PIN?
WHAT?
THE EMPRESS' PIN, VALUED AT NINE MILLION STERLING.
WE ALREADY HAD A BUYER IN THE WEST AND THEN ONE OF OUR PEOPLE WAS GREEDY...
HE TOOK IT, BROUGHT IT BACK TO LONDON AND YOU, MR HOLMES, HAVE BEEN SEARCHING.

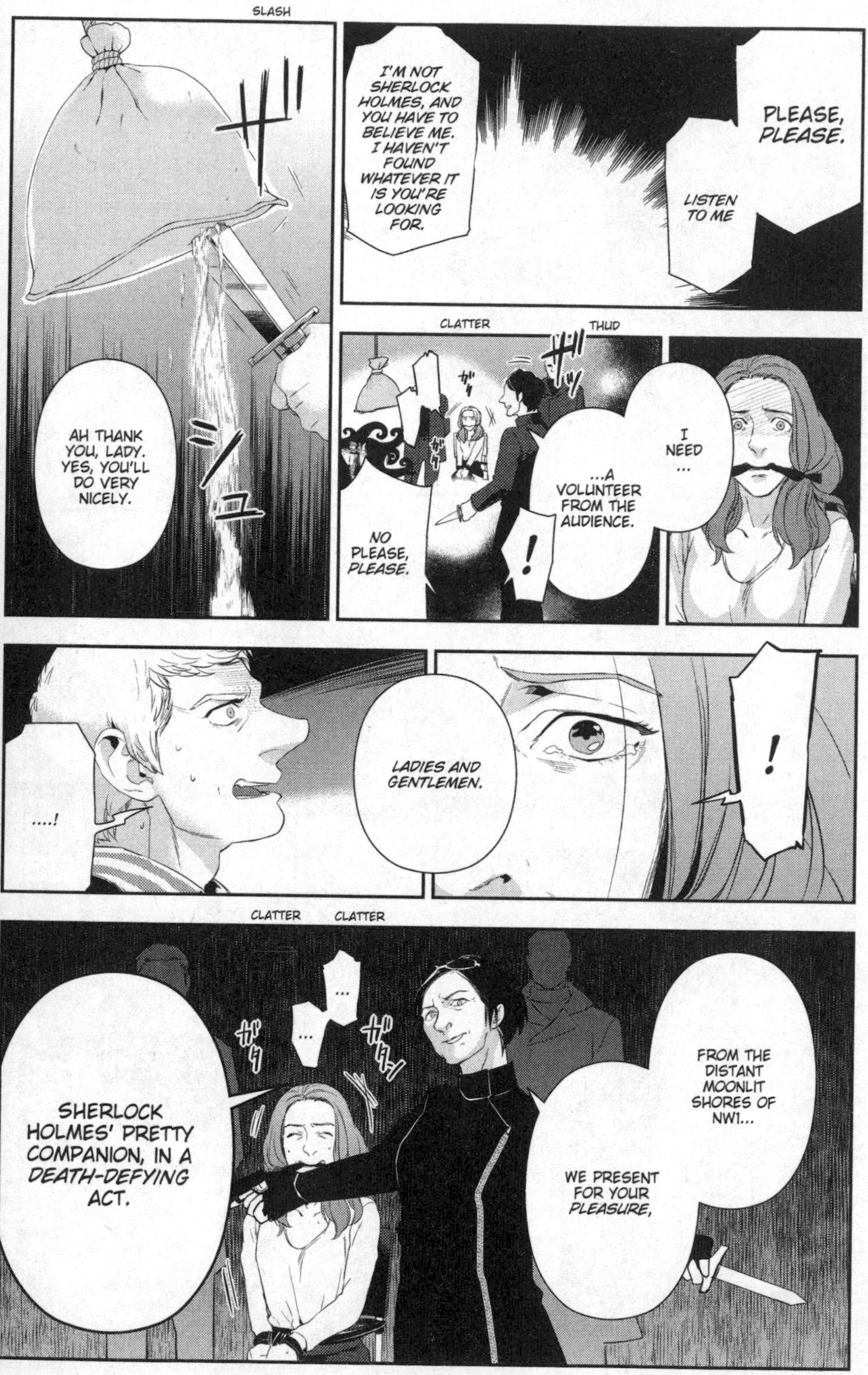
PLEASE, PLEASE.
LISTEN TO ME
I'M NOT SHERLOCK HOLMES, AND YOU HAVE TO BELIEVE ME. I HAVEN'T FOUND WHATEVER IT IS YOU'RE LOOKING FOR.
THUD
CLATTER
I NEED ...
...A VOLUNTEER FROM THE AUDIENCE.
!
NO PLEASE, PLEASE.
SLASH
AH THANK YOU, LADY. YES, YOU'LL DO VERY NICELY.
!
LADIES AND GENTLEMEN.
....!
CLATTER CLATTER
FROM THE DISTANT MOONLIT SHORES OF NW1...
WE PRESENT FOR YOUR *PLEASURE*,
...
...
SHERLOCK HOLMES' PRETTY COMPANION, IN A *DEATH-DEFYING* ACT.

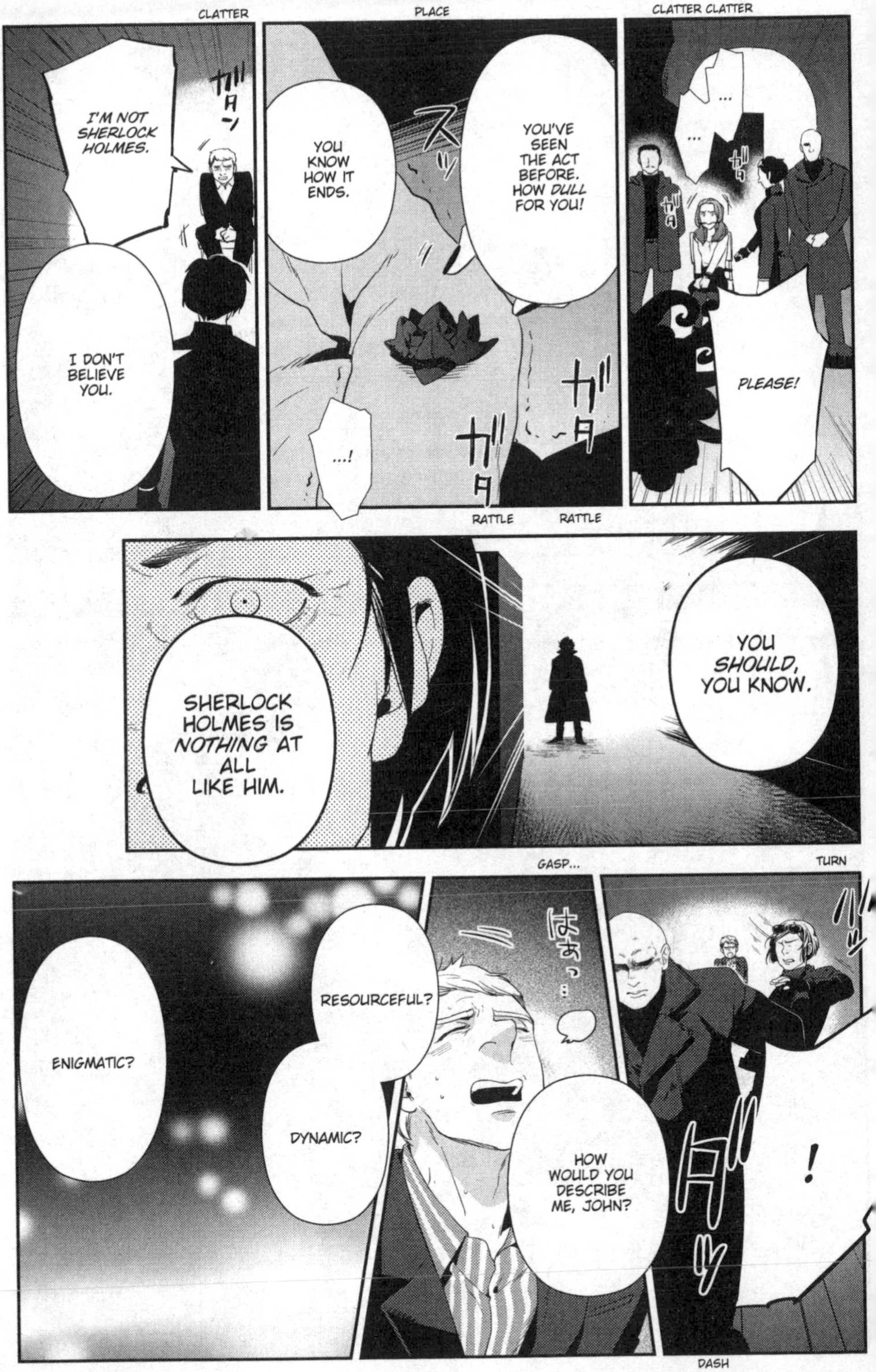
CLATTER CLATTER
...
...
PLEASE!
PLACE
YOU'VE SEEN THE ACT BEFORE. HOW DULL FOR YOU!
YOU KNOW HOW IT ENDS.
...!
RATTLE
RATTLE
CLATTER
I'M NOT SHERLOCK HOLMES.
I DON'T BELIEVE YOU.
YOU SHOULD, YOU KNOW.
SHERLOCK HOLMES IS NOTHING AT ALL LIKE HIM.
TURN
!
DASH
GASP...
HOW WOULD YOU DESCRIBE ME, JOHN?
RESOURCEFUL?
DYNAMIC?
ENIGMATIC?

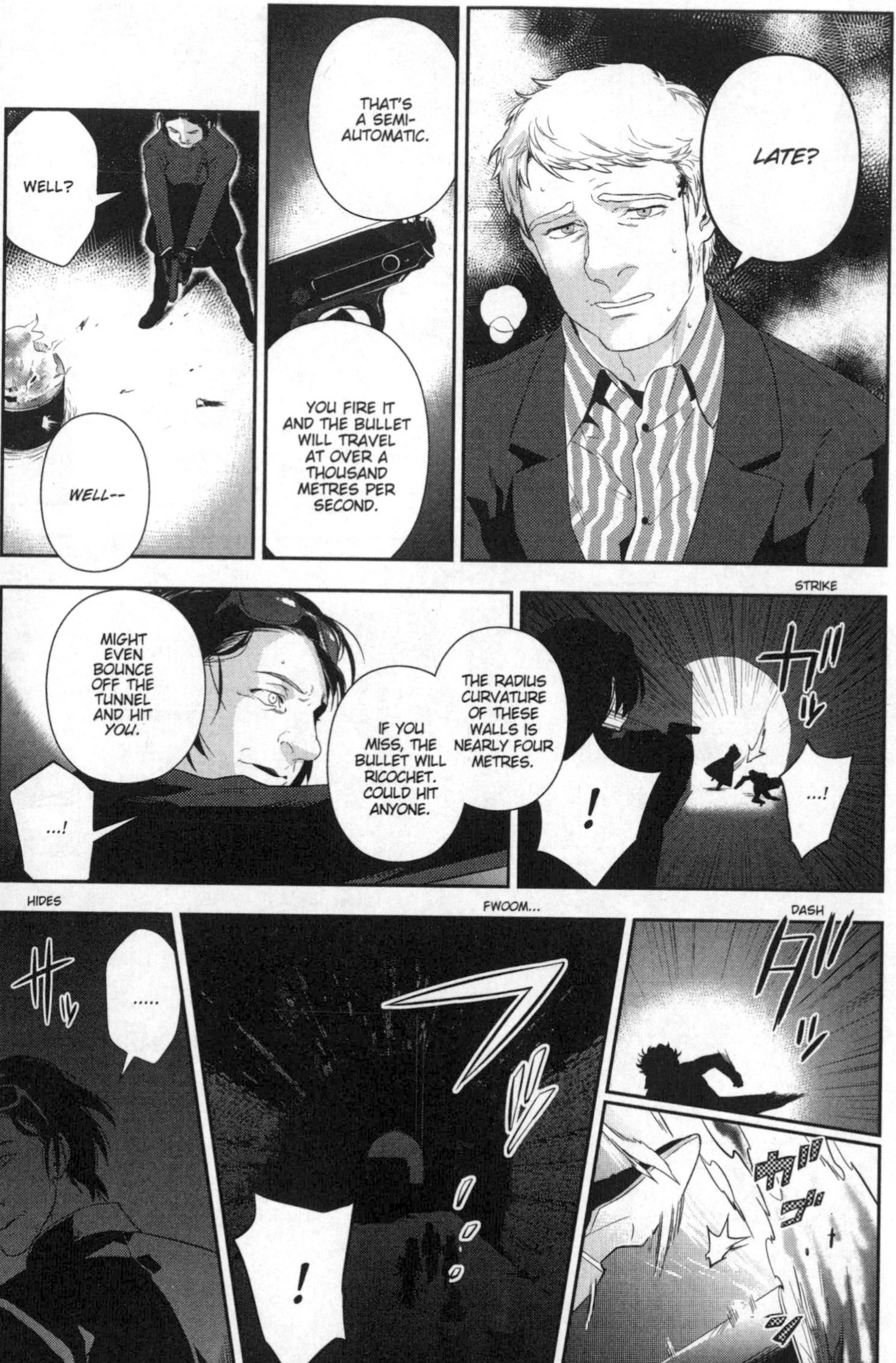
LATE?
THAT'S A SEMI-AUTOMATIC.
YOU FIRE IT AND THE BULLET WILL TRAVEL AT OVER A THOUSAND METRES PER SECOND.
WELL?
WELL--
STRIKE
!
...!
THE RADIUS CURVATURE OF THESE WALLS IS NEARLY FOUR METRES.
IF YOU MISS, THE BULLET WILL RICOCHET. COULD HIT ANYONE.
MIGHT EVEN BOUNCE OFF THE TUNNEL AND HIT *YOU*.
...!
DASH
CLOMP
FWOOM...
!
HIDES
.....

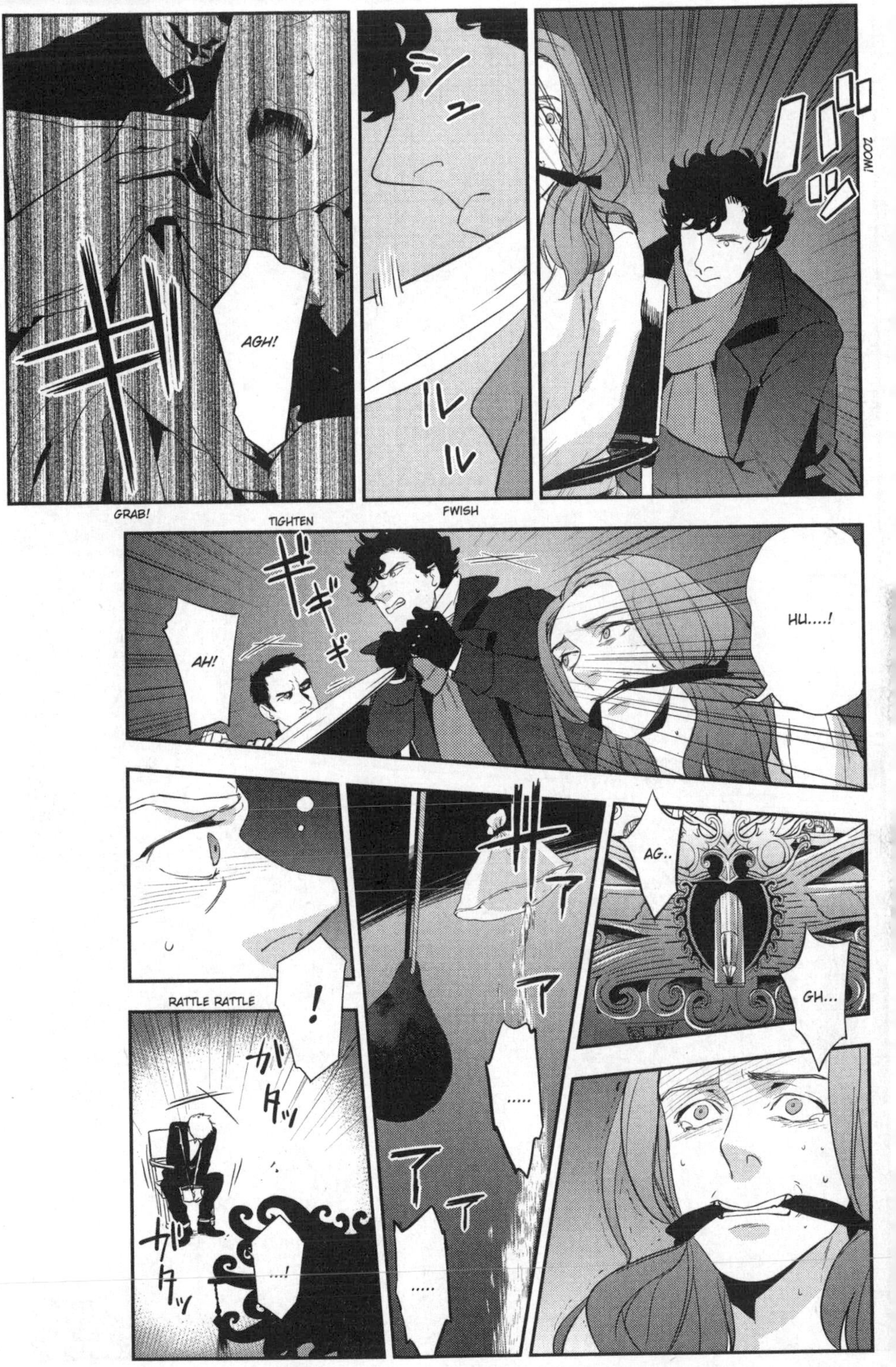

ZOOM!
FWISH
AGH!
GRAB!
HU....!
TIGHTEN
AH!
AG..
GH...
.....
.....
RATTLE RATTLE
!
...!

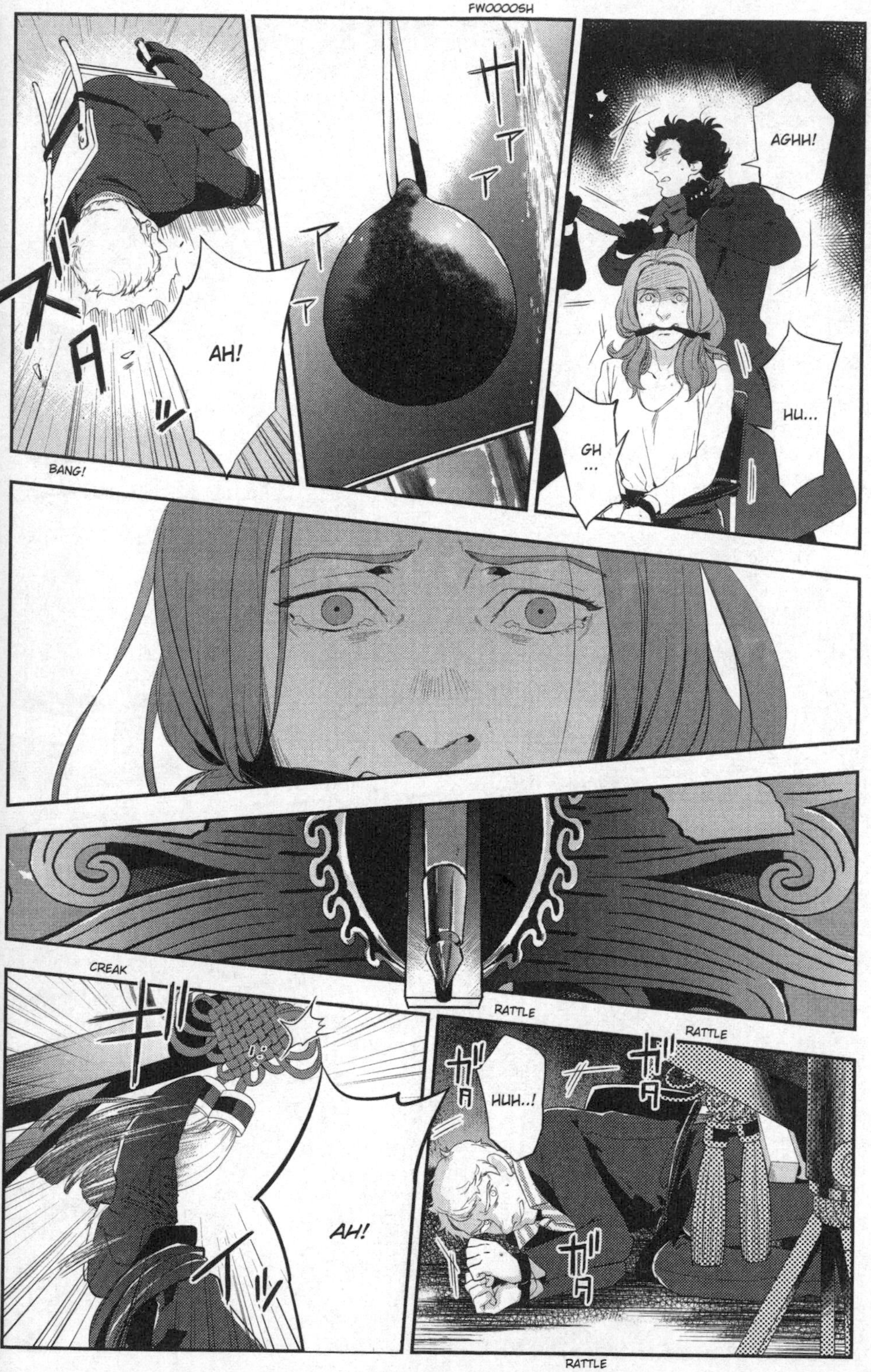
AGHH!
HU...
GH ...
FWOOOOSH
AH!
BANG!
RATTLE
RATTLE
HUH..!
RATTLE
CREAK
AH!

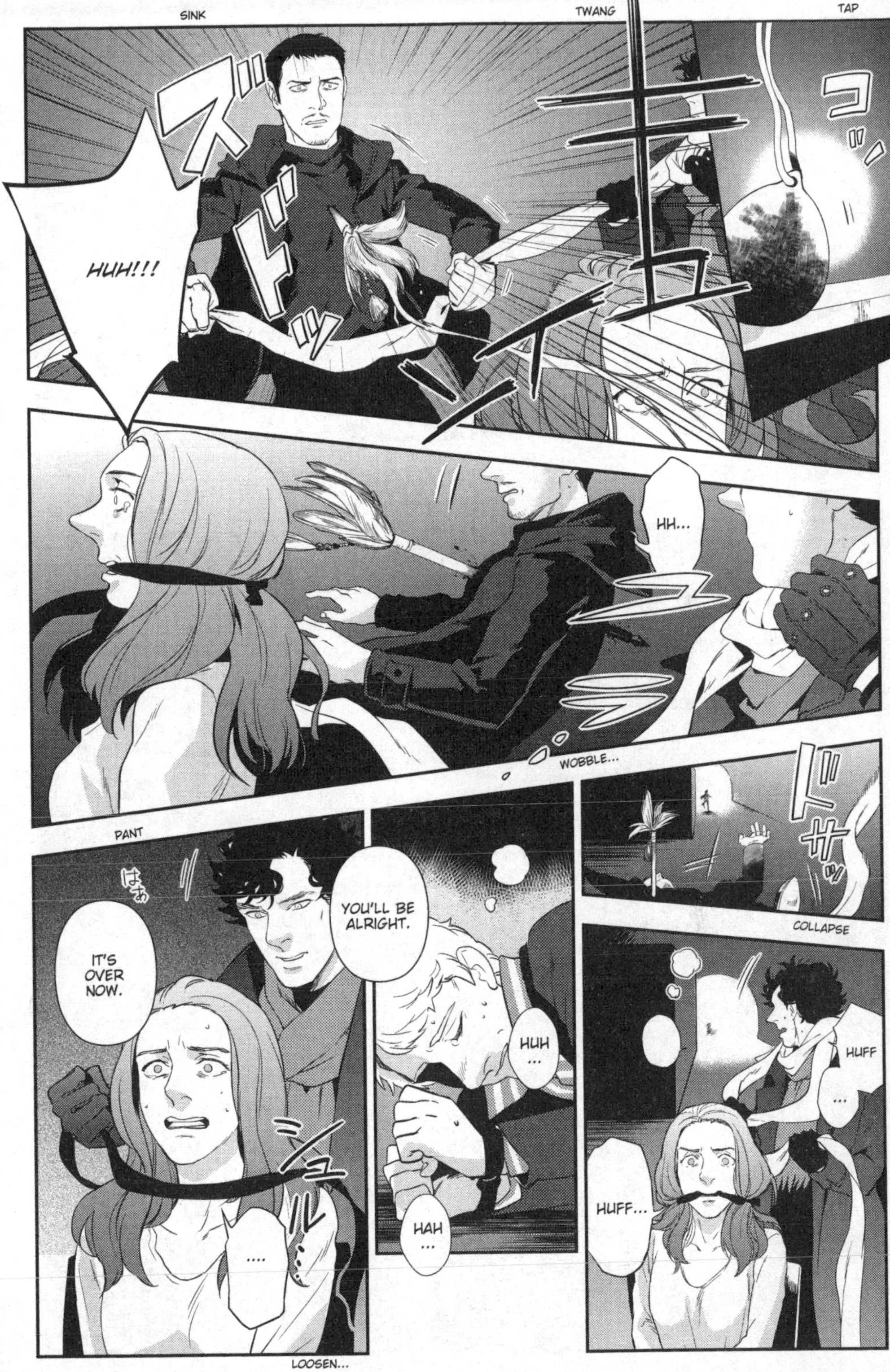
TAP
TWANG
SINK
HUH!!!
HH...
WOBBLE...
COLLAPSE
HUFF
...
HUFF...
YOU'LL BE ALRIGHT.
HUH
...
HAH
...
PANT
はぁ
IT'S OVER NOW.
....
LOOSEN...

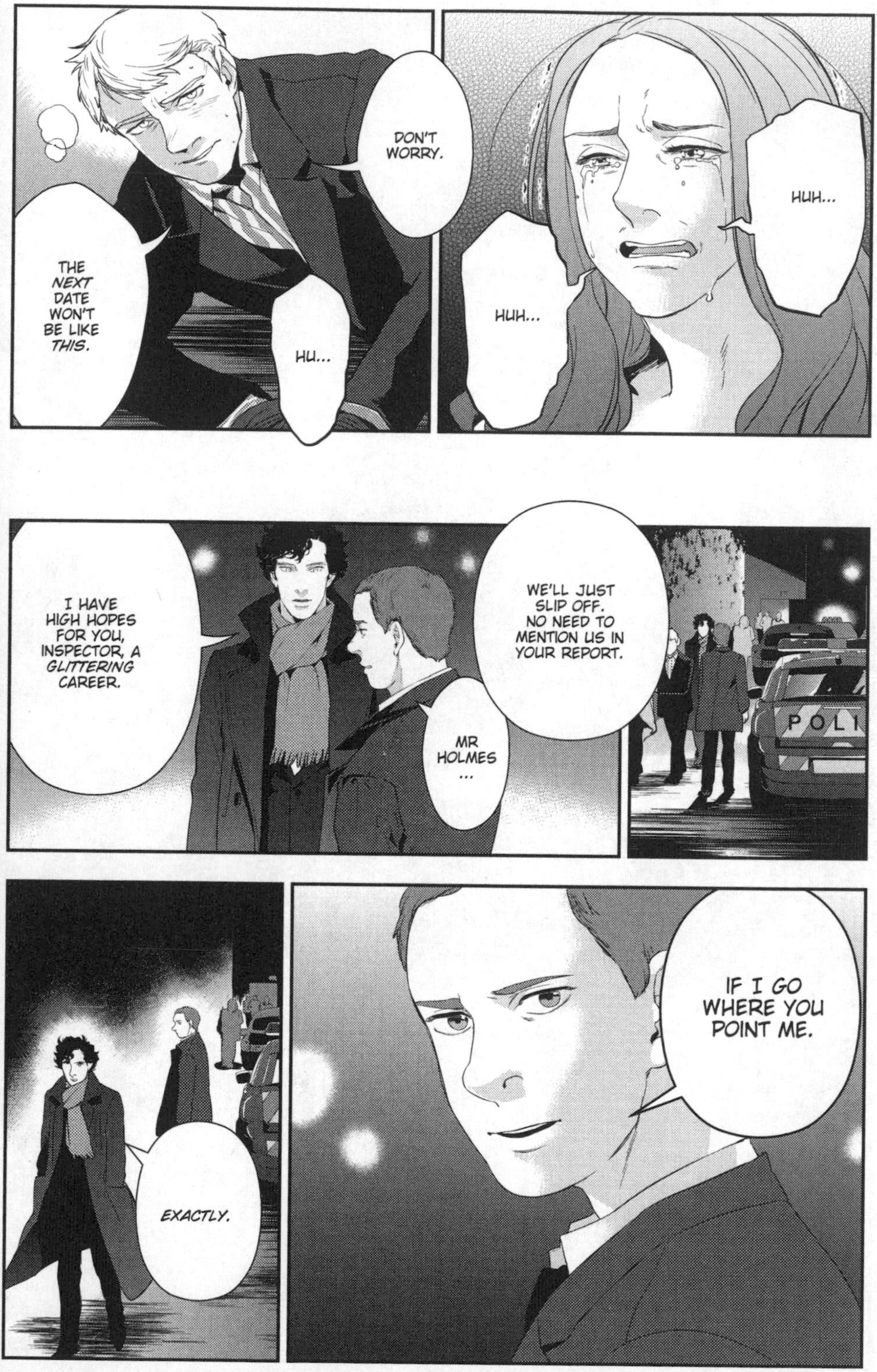
HUH...
HUH...
DON'T WORRY.
THE *NEXT* DATE WON'T BE LIKE *THIS*.
HU...
POLI
WE'LL JUST SLIP OFF. NO NEED TO MENTION US IN YOUR REPORT.
MR HOLMES ...
I HAVE HIGH HOPES FOR YOU, INSPECTOR, A *GLITTERING* CAREER.
IF I GO WHERE YOU POINT ME.
EXACTLY.

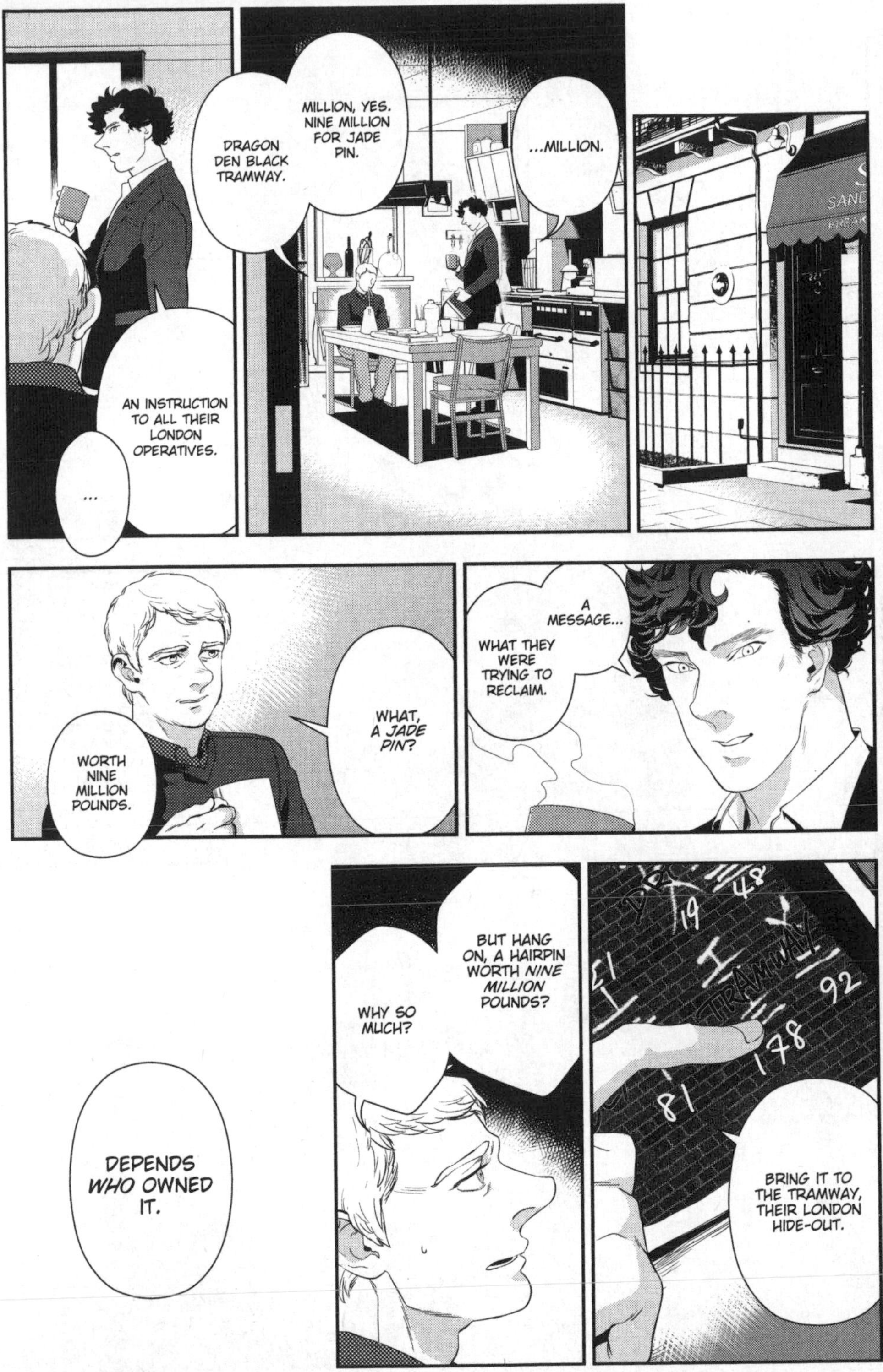
...MILLION.
MILLION, YES. NINE MILLION FOR JADE PIN.
DRAGON DEN BLACK TRAMWAY.
AN INSTRUCTION TO ALL THEIR LONDON OPERATIVES.
...
A MESSAGE...
WHAT THEY WERE TRYING TO RECLAIM.
WHAT, A *JADE* PIN?
WORTH NINE MILLION POUNDS.
TRAMWAY
BRING IT TO THE TRAMWAY, THEIR LONDON HIDE-OUT.
BUT HANG ON, A HAIRPIN WORTH *NINE MILLION* POUNDS?
WHY SO MUCH?
DEPENDS *WHO* OWNED IT.

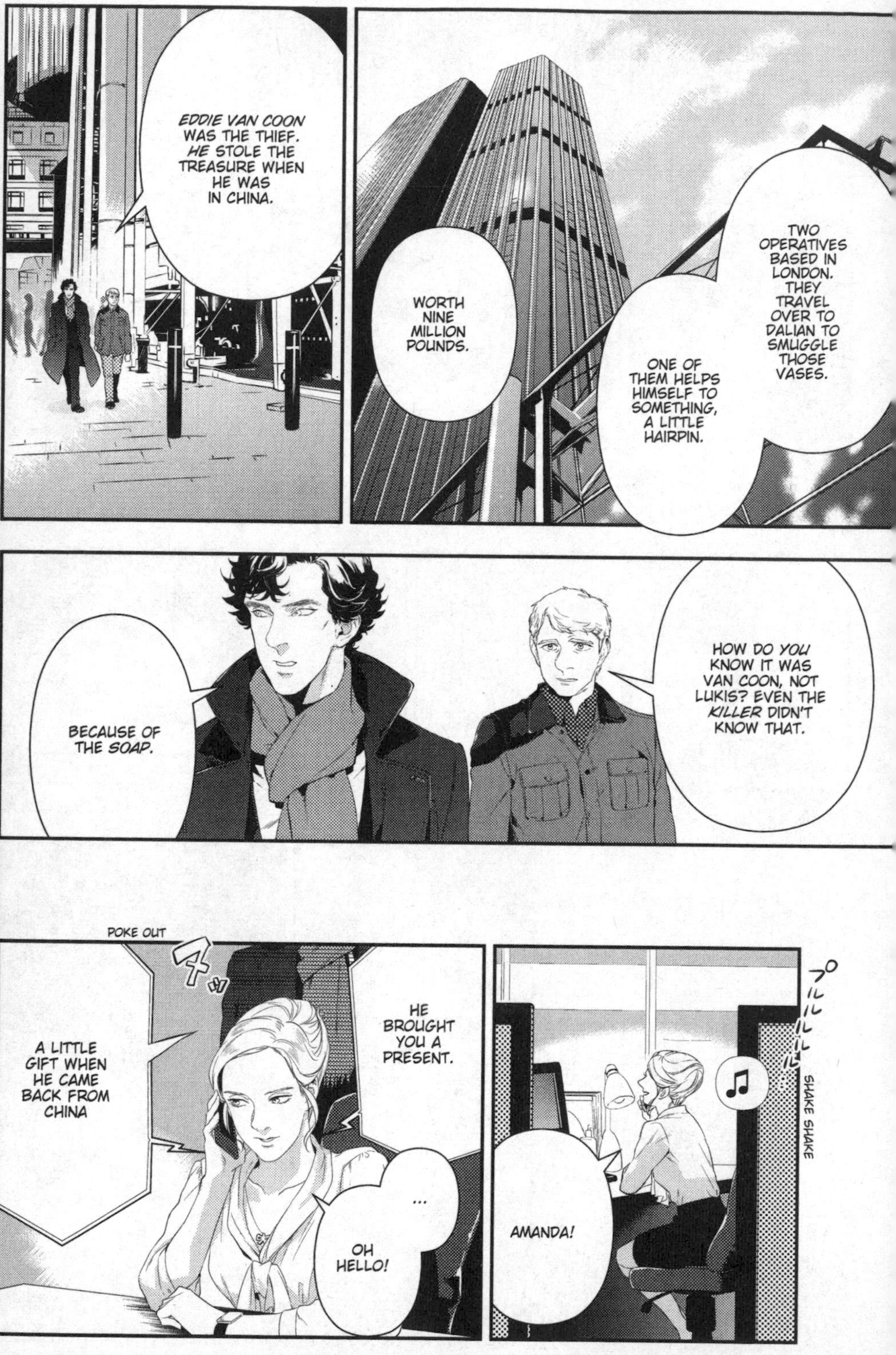
TWO OPERATIVES BASED IN LONDON. THEY TRAVEL OVER TO DALIAN TO SMUGGLE THOSE VASES.
ONE OF THEM HELPS HIMSELF TO SOMETHING, A LITTLE HAIRPIN.
WORTH NINE MILLION POUNDS.
EDDIE VAN COON WAS THE THIEF. *HE* STOLE THE TREASURE WHEN HE WAS IN CHINA.
HOW DO *YOU* KNOW IT WAS VAN COON, NOT LUKIS? EVEN THE *KILLER* DIDN'T KNOW THAT.
BECAUSE OF THE *SOAP*.
SHAKE SHAKE
AMANDA!
OH HELLO!
...
HE BROUGHT YOU A PRESENT.
POKE OUT
A LITTLE GIFT WHEN HE CAME BACK FROM CHINA

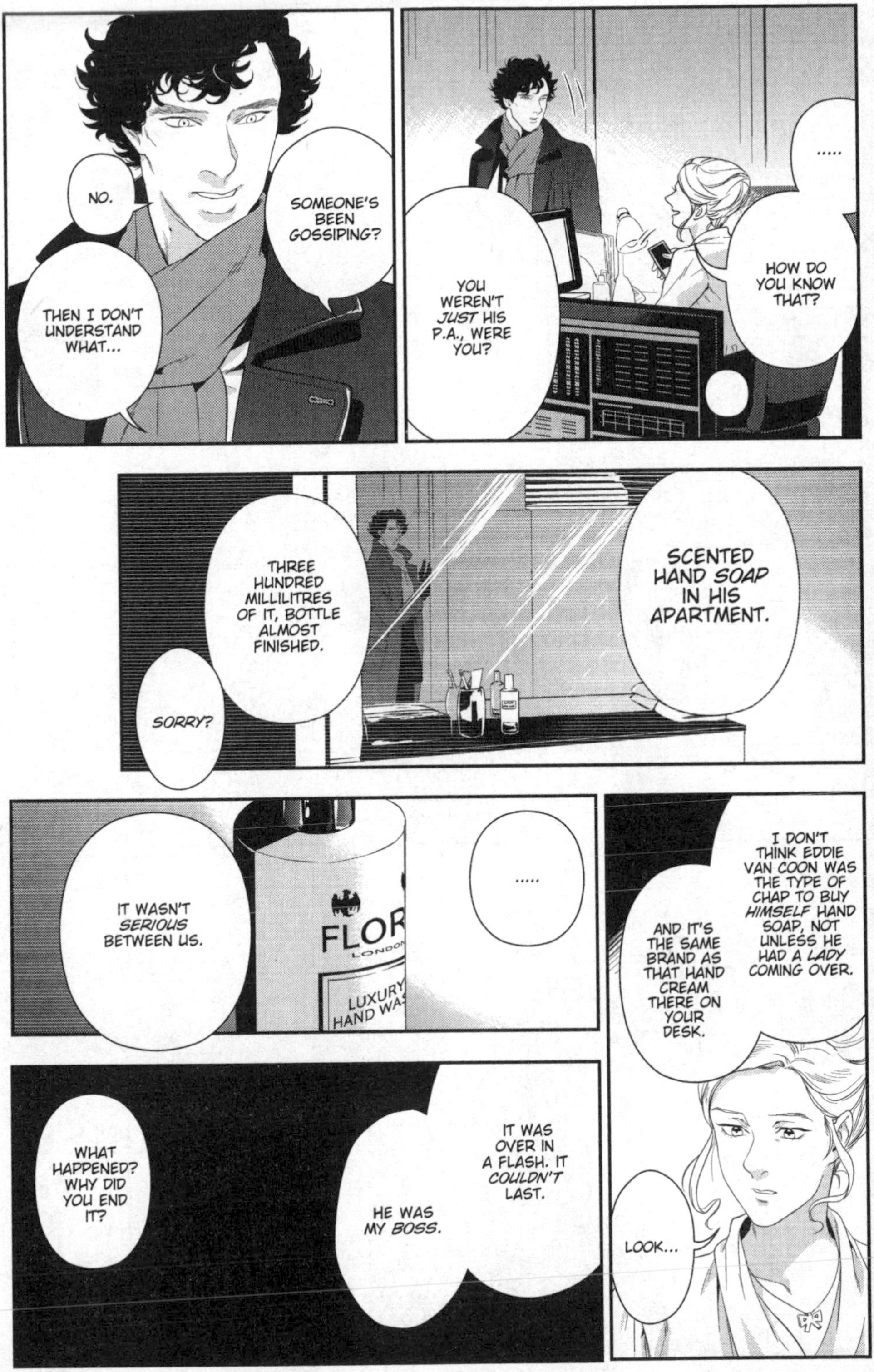
.....
HOW DO YOU KNOW THAT?
YOU WEREN'T *JUST* HIS P.A., WERE YOU?
SOMEONE'S BEEN GOSSIPING?
NO.
THEN I DON'T UNDERSTAND WHAT...
SCENTED HAND *SOAP* IN HIS APARTMENT.
THREE HUNDRED MILLILITRES OF IT, BOTTLE ALMOST FINISHED.
SORRY?
I DON'T THINK EDDIE VAN COON WAS THE TYPE OF CHAP TO BUY *HIMSELF* HAND SOAP, NOT UNLESS HE HAD A *LADY* COMING OVER.
AND IT'S THE SAME BRAND AS THAT HAND CREAM THERE ON YOUR DESK.
LOOK...
.....
FLOR
LONDON
LUXURY
HAND WAS
IT WASN'T *SERIOUS* BETWEEN US.
IT WAS OVER IN A FLASH. IT *COULDN'T* LAST.
HE WAS MY *BOSS*.
WHAT HAPPENED? WHY DID YOU END IT?

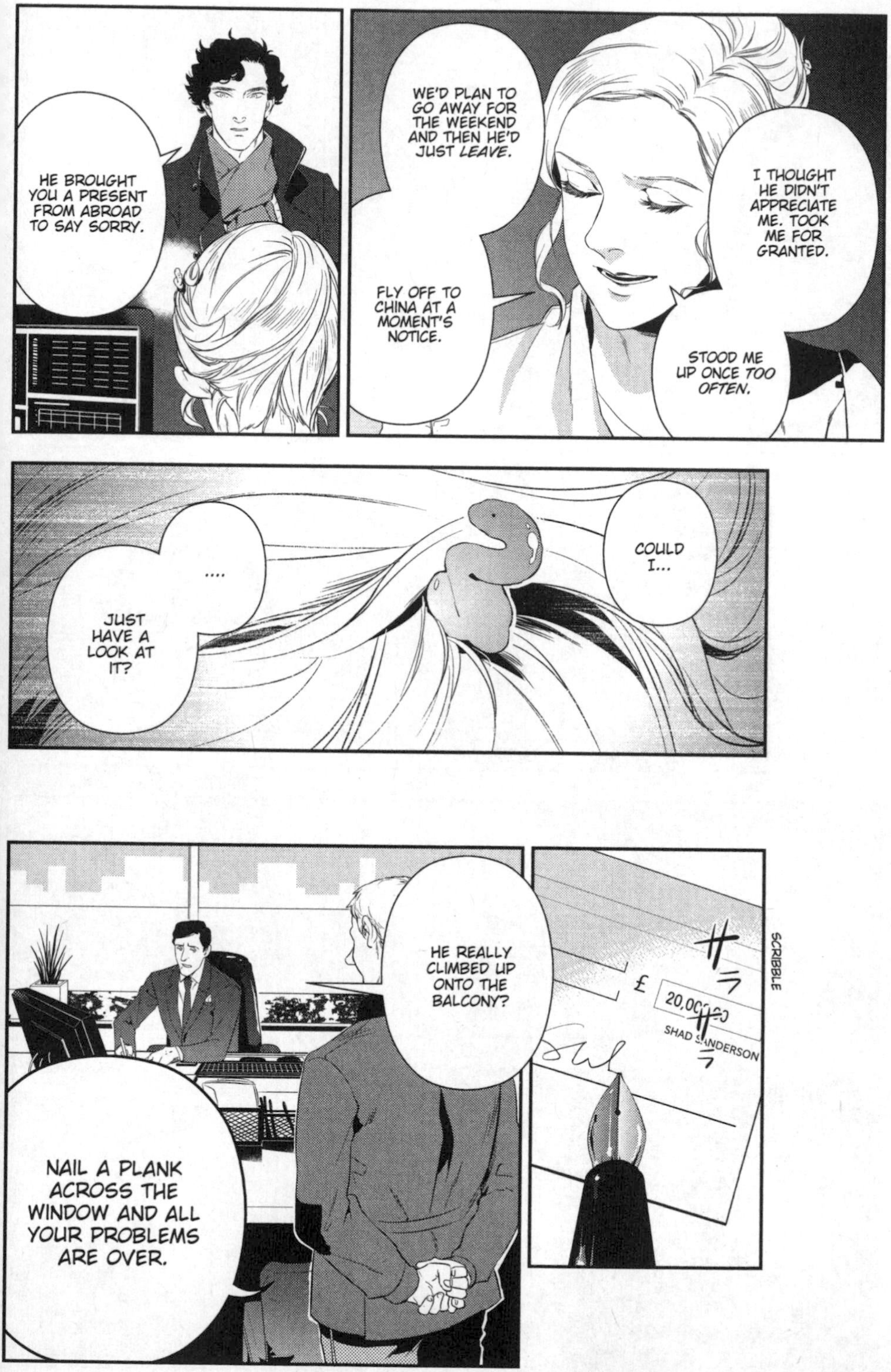
I THOUGHT HE DIDN'T APPRECIATE ME. TOOK ME FOR GRANTED.
STOOD ME UP ONCE *TOO* OFTEN.
WE'D PLAN TO GO AWAY FOR THE WEEKEND AND THEN HE'D JUST *LEAVE*.
FLY OFF TO CHINA AT A MOMENT'S NOTICE.
HE BROUGHT YOU A PRESENT FROM ABROAD TO SAY SORRY.
COULD I...
....
JUST HAVE A LOOK AT IT?
SCRIBBLE
HE REALLY CLIMBED UP ONTO THE BALCONY?
NAIL A PLANK ACROSS THE WINDOW AND ALL YOUR PROBLEMS ARE OVER.

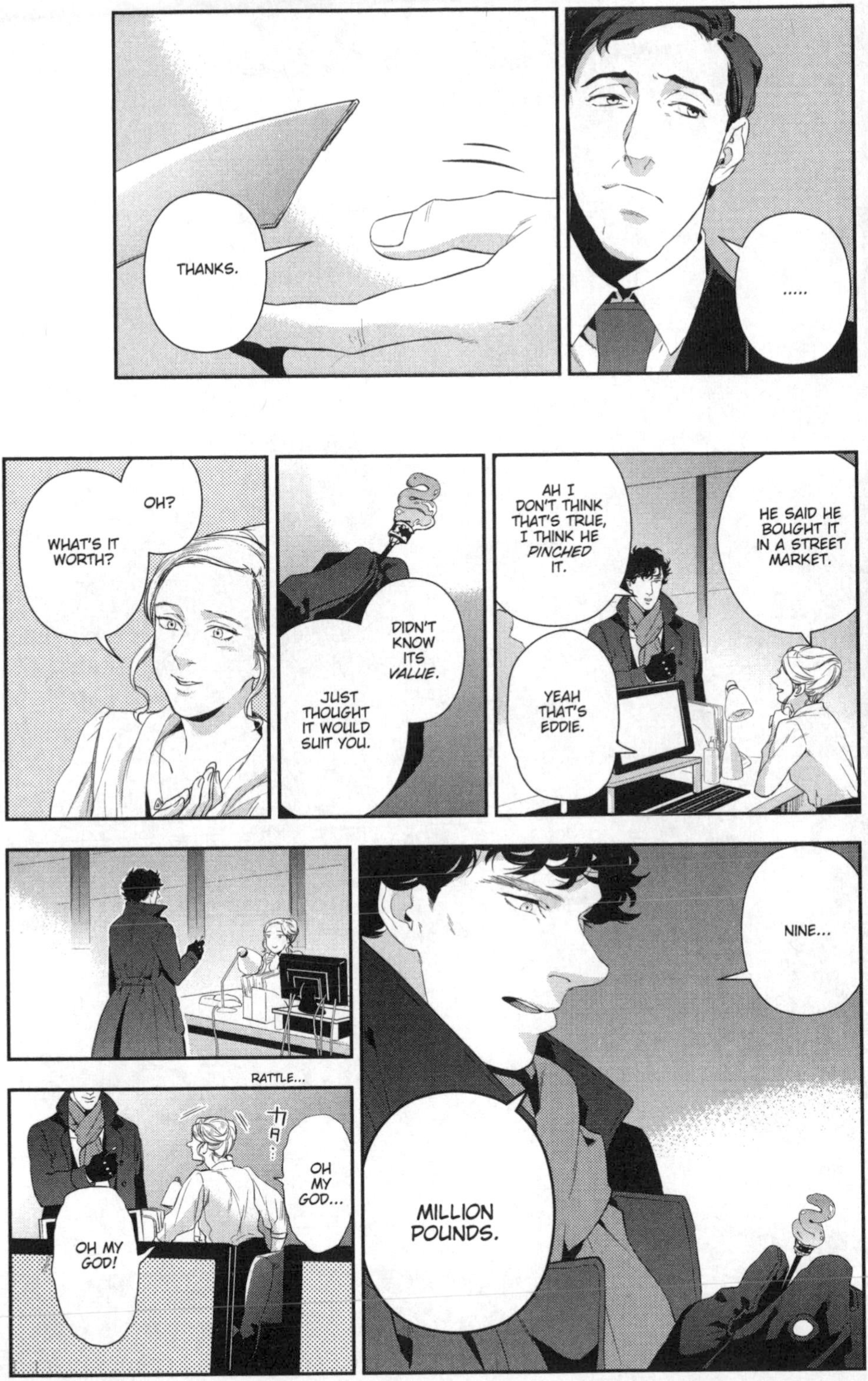
.....
THANKS.
HE SAID HE BOUGHT IT IN A STREET MARKET.
AH I DON'T THINK THAT'S TRUE, I THINK HE *PINCHED* IT.
YEAH THAT'S EDDIE.
DIDN'T KNOW ITS *VALUE*.
JUST THOUGHT IT WOULD SUIT YOU.
OH?
WHAT'S IT WORTH?
NINE...
MILLION POUNDS.
RATTLE...
カタ...
OH MY GOD...
OH MY GOD!

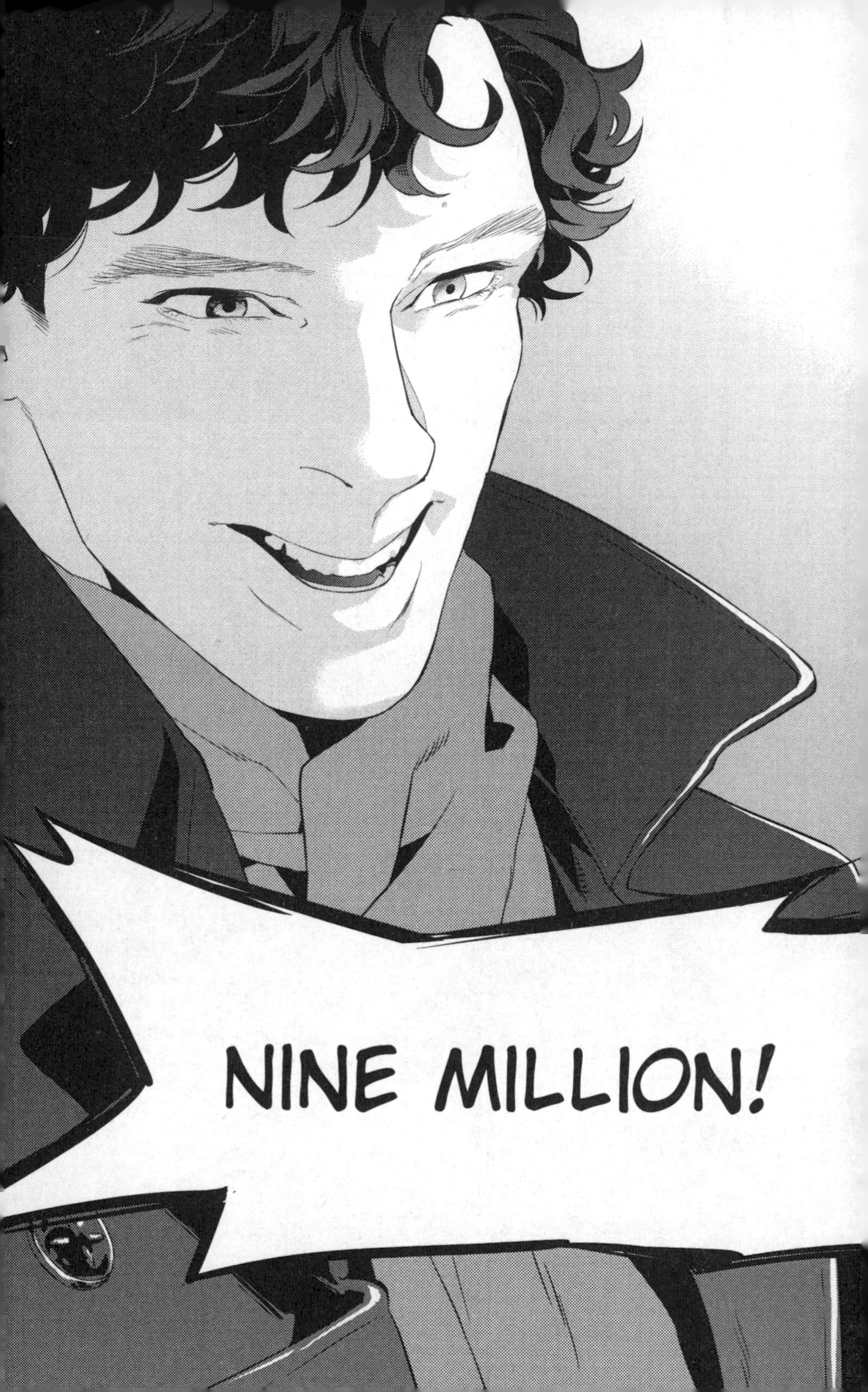
NINE MILLION!

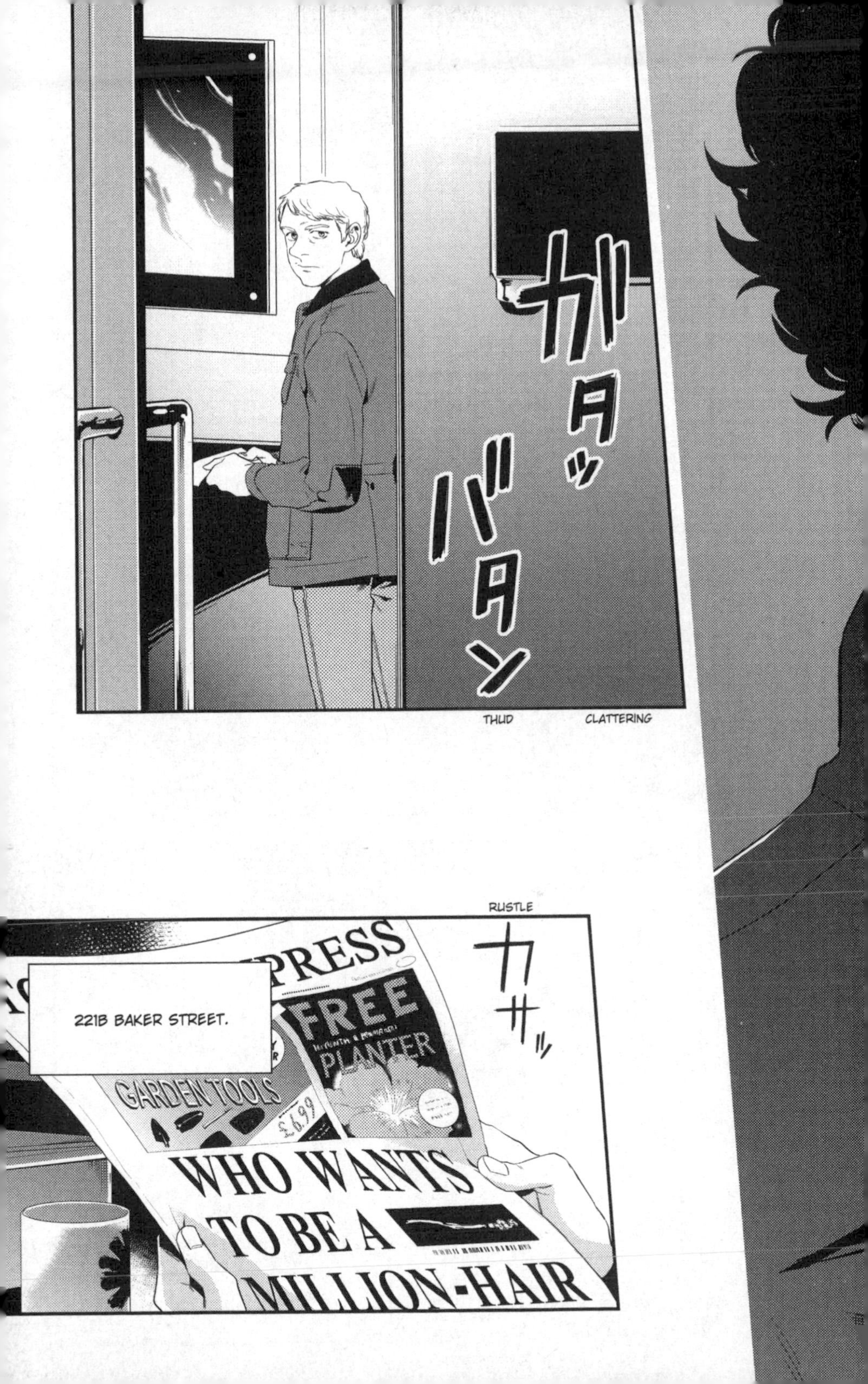

ガタッ
バタン
CLATTERING
THUD
RUSTLE
カサッ
221B BAKER STREET.
PRESS
FREE
PLANTER
GARDEN TOOLS
£6.99
WHO WANTS TO BE A MILLION-HAIR

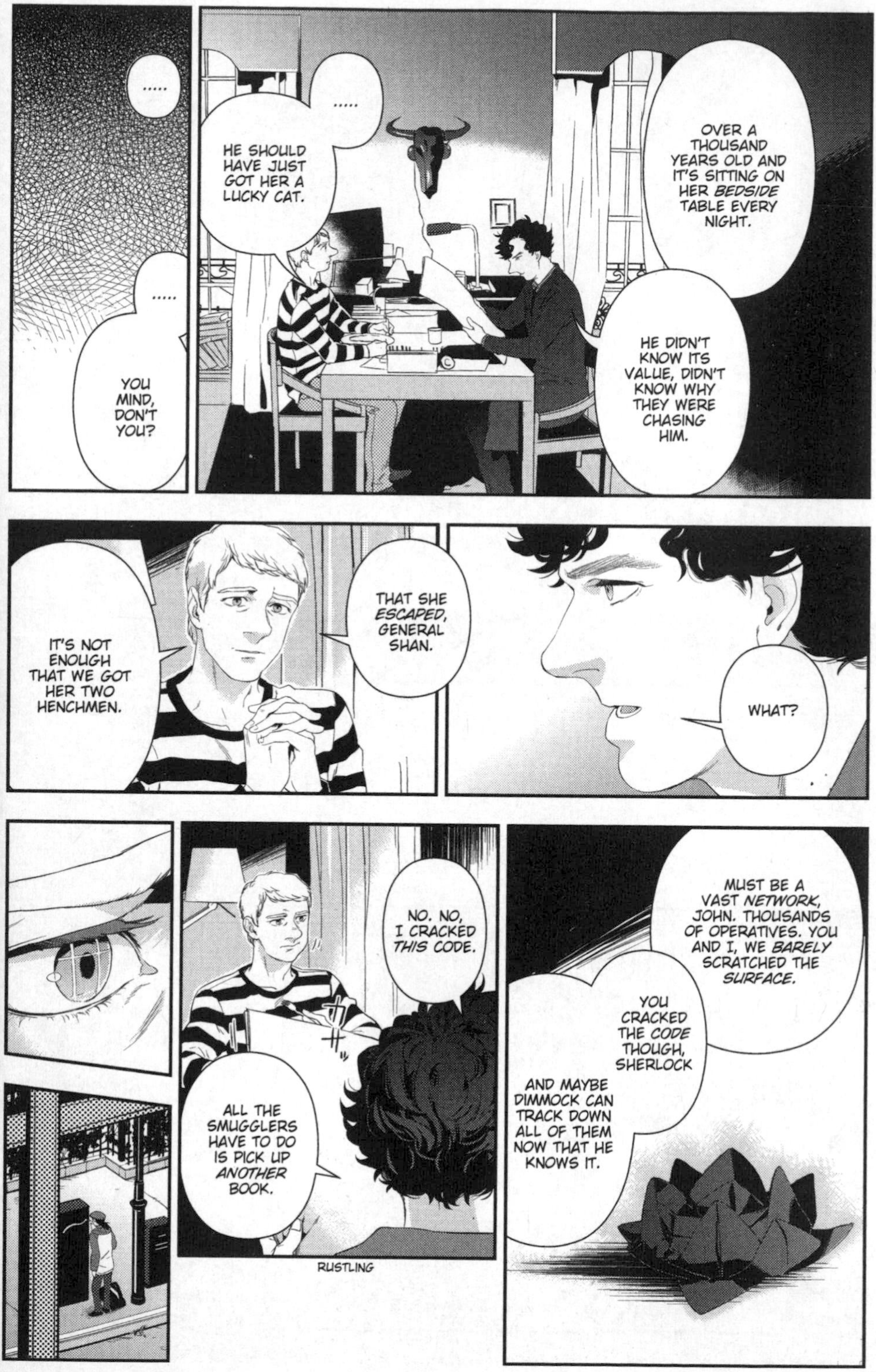
OVER A THOUSAND YEARS OLD AND IT'S SITTING ON HER *BEDSIDE* TABLE EVERY NIGHT.
HE DIDN'T KNOW ITS VALUE, DIDN'T KNOW WHY THEY WERE CHASING HIM.
......
HE SHOULD HAVE JUST GOT HER A LUCKY CAT.
......
......
YOU MIND, DON'T YOU?
WHAT?
THAT SHE *ESCAPED*, GENERAL SHAN.
IT'S NOT ENOUGH THAT WE GOT HER TWO HENCHMEN.
MUST BE A VAST *NETWORK*, JOHN. THOUSANDS OF OPERATIVES. YOU AND I, WE *BARELY* SCRATCHED THE *SURFACE*.
YOU CRACKED THE *CODE* THOUGH, SHERLOCK
AND MAYBE DIMMOCK CAN TRACK DOWN ALL OF THEM NOW THAT HE KNOWS IT.
NO. NO, I CRACKED *THIS* CODE.
ALL THE SMUGGLERS HAVE TO DO IS PICK UP *ANOTHER* BOOK.
RUSTLING

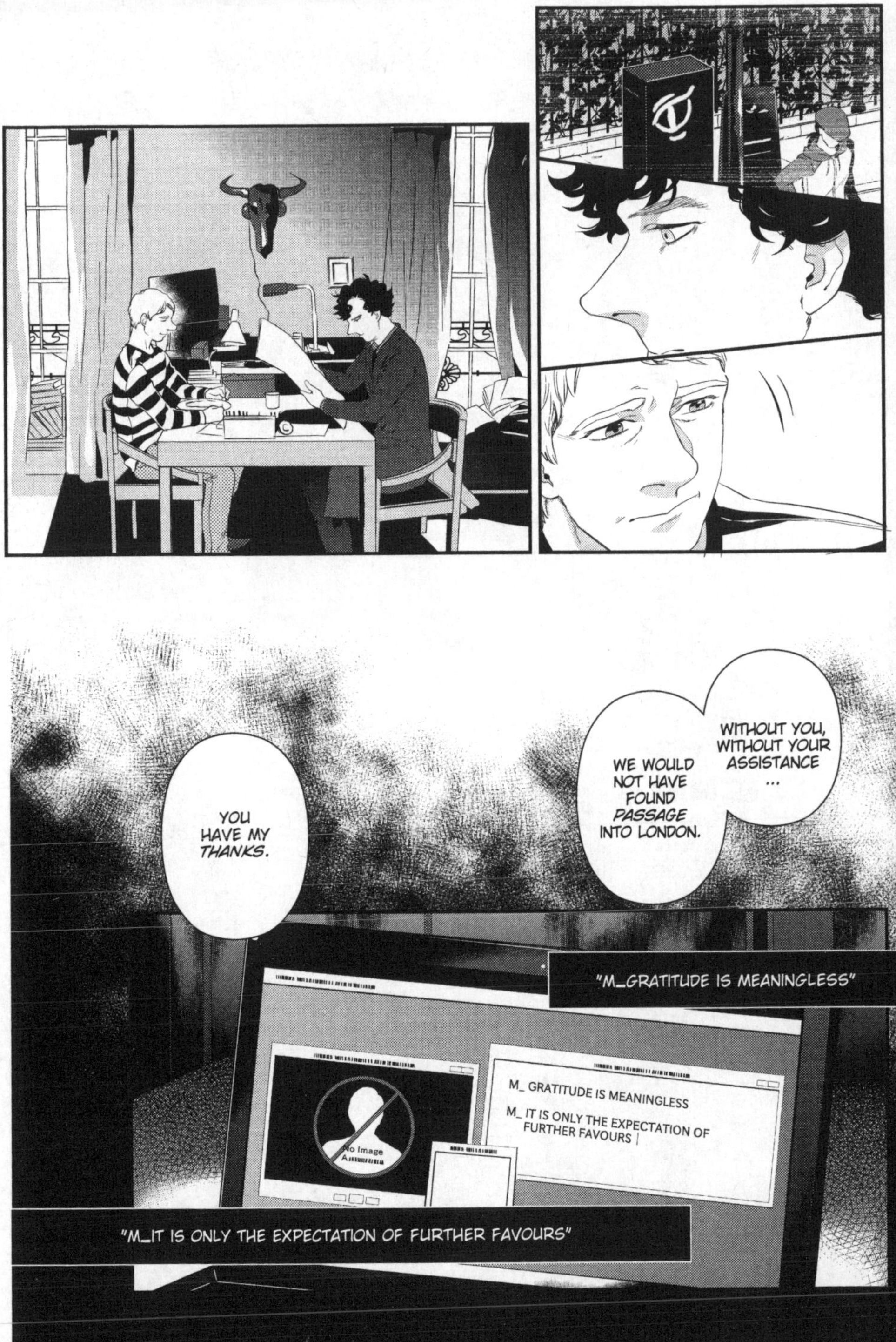
WITHOUT YOU, WITHOUT YOUR ASSISTANCE ...
WE WOULD NOT HAVE FOUND *PASSAGE* INTO LONDON.
YOU HAVE MY *THANKS*.
"M_GRATITUDE IS MEANINGLESS"
No Image
M_ GRATITUDE IS MEANINGLESS
M_ IT IS ONLY THE EXPECTATION OF FURTHER FAVOURS |
"M_IT IS ONLY THE EXPECTATION OF FURTHER FAVOURS"

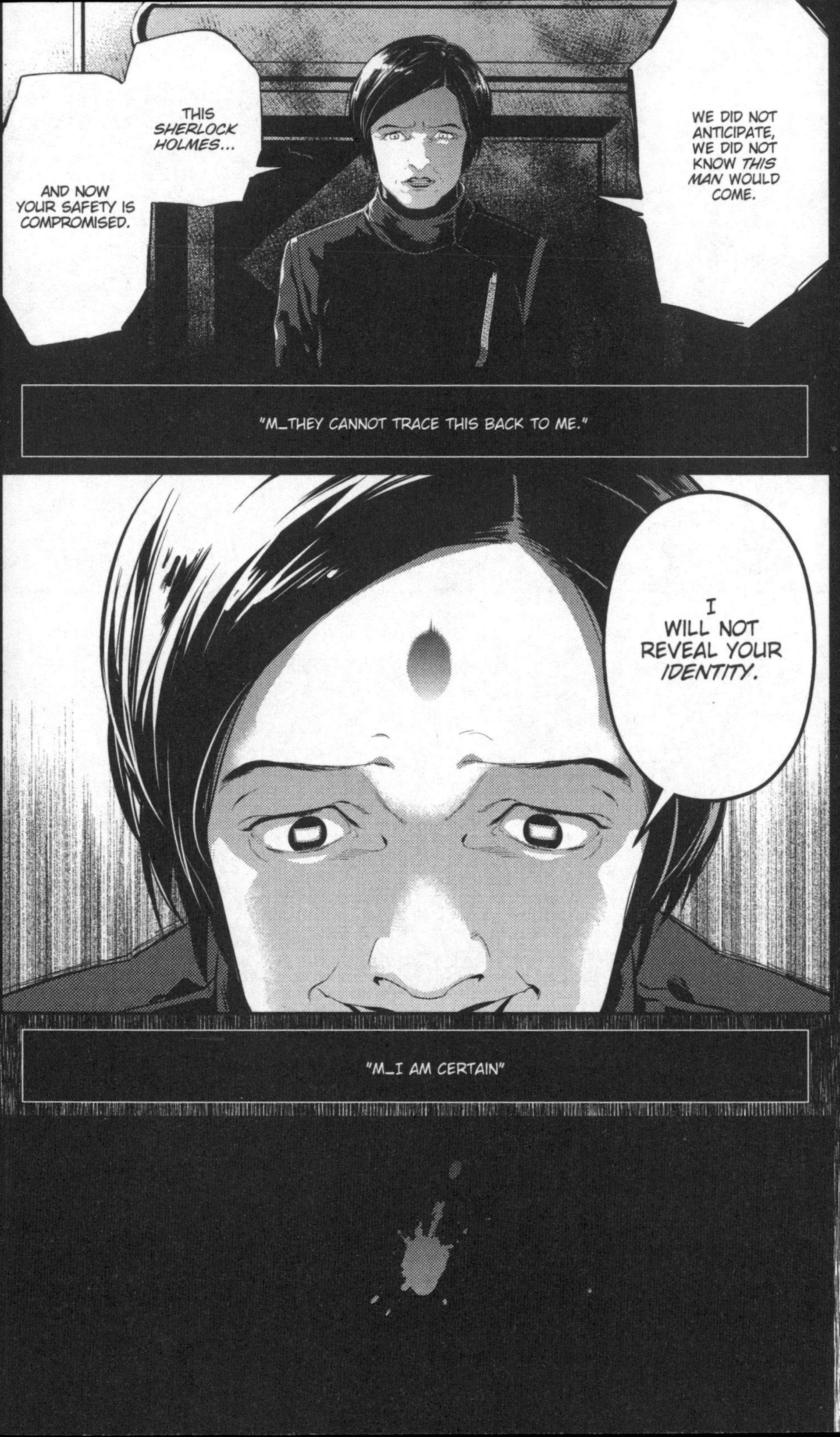
WE DID NOT ANTICIPATE, WE DID NOT KNOW *THIS MAN* WOULD COME.
THIS *SHERLOCK HOLMES*...
AND NOW YOUR SAFETY IS COMPROMISED.
"M_THEY CANNOT TRACE THIS BACK TO ME."
I WILL NOT REVEAL YOUR *IDENTITY*.
"M_I AM CERTAIN"

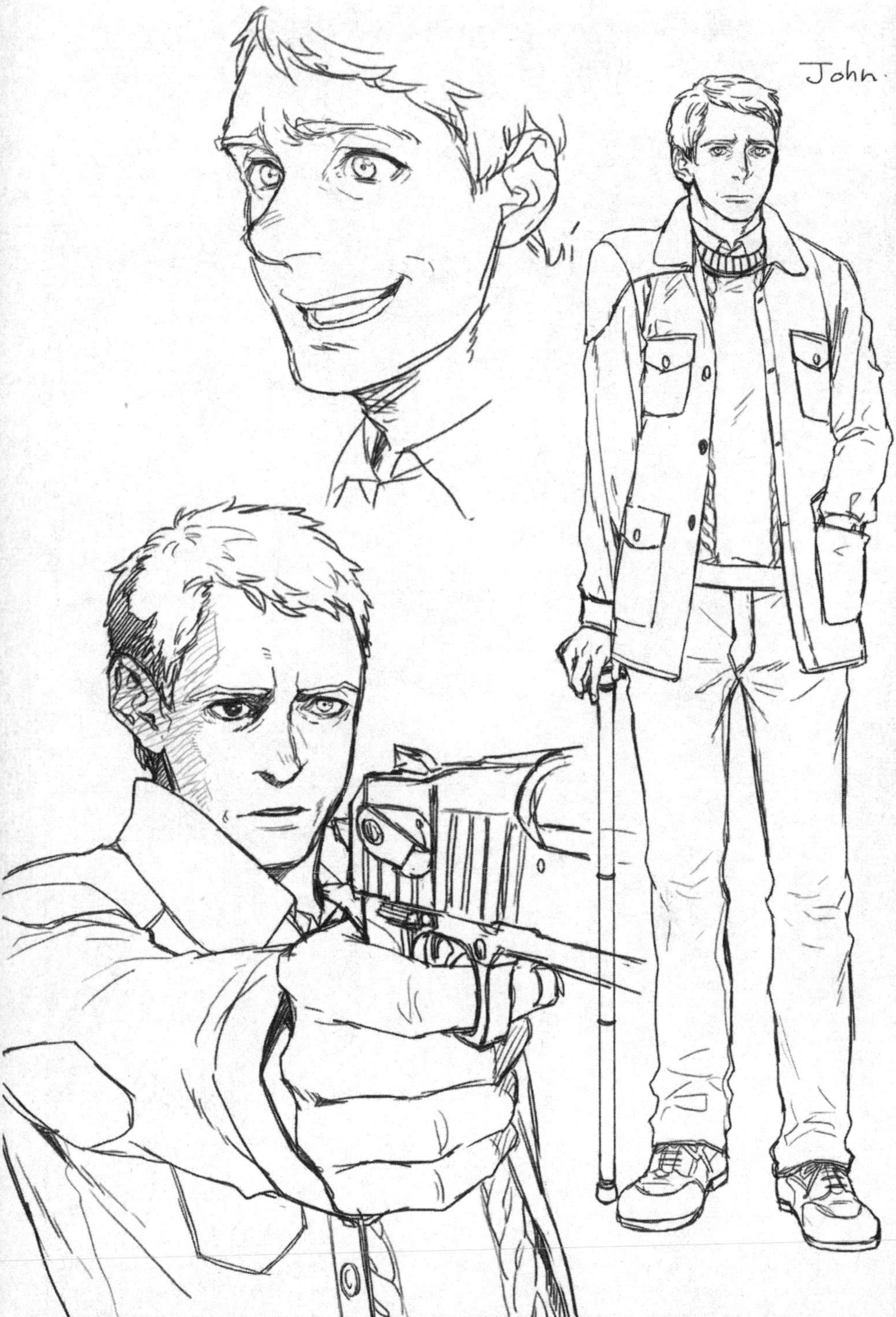
John.

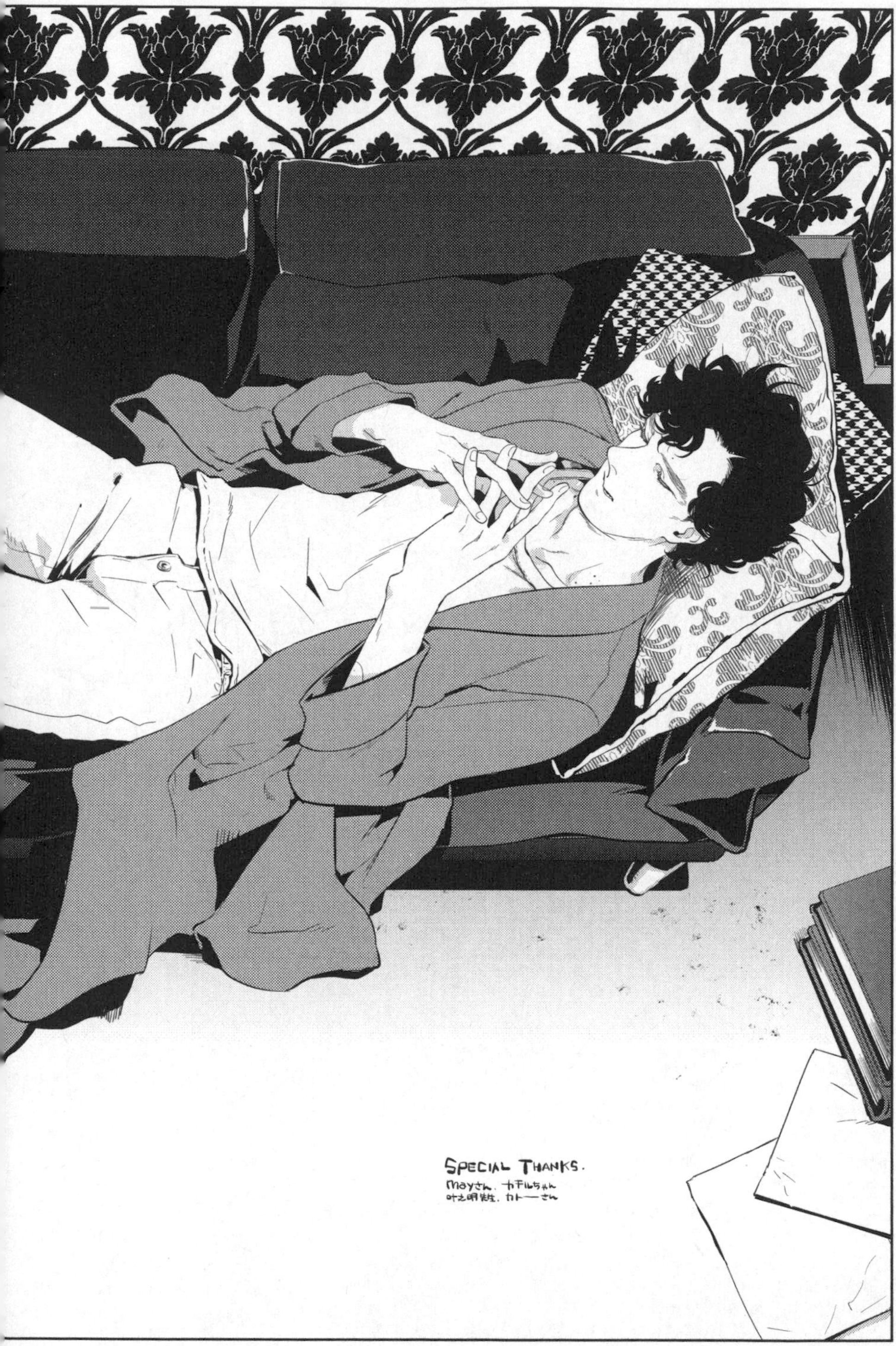
SPECIAL THANKS.
mayさん. カモルちゃん
叶之明先生. カトーさん

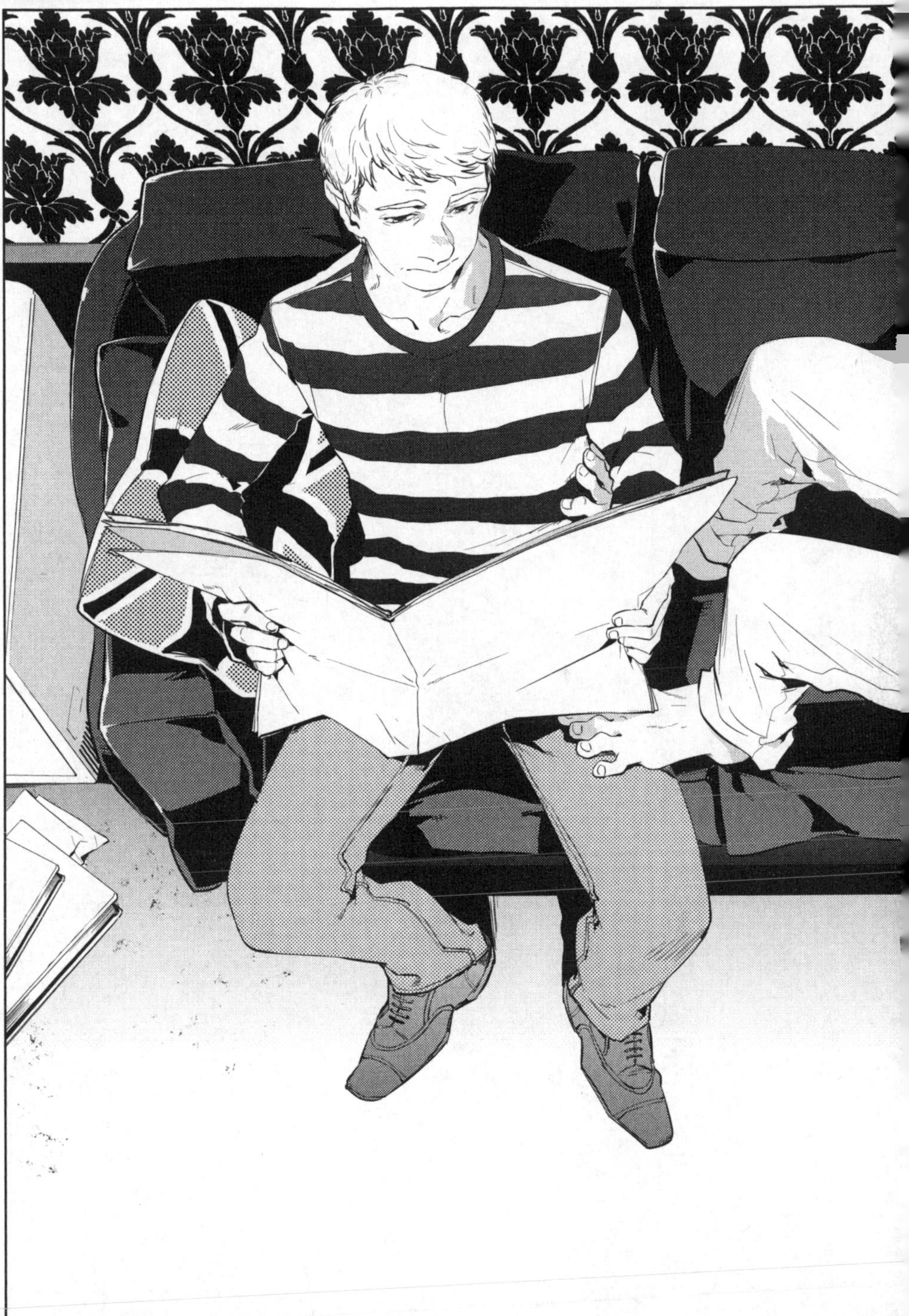

COVER GALLERY

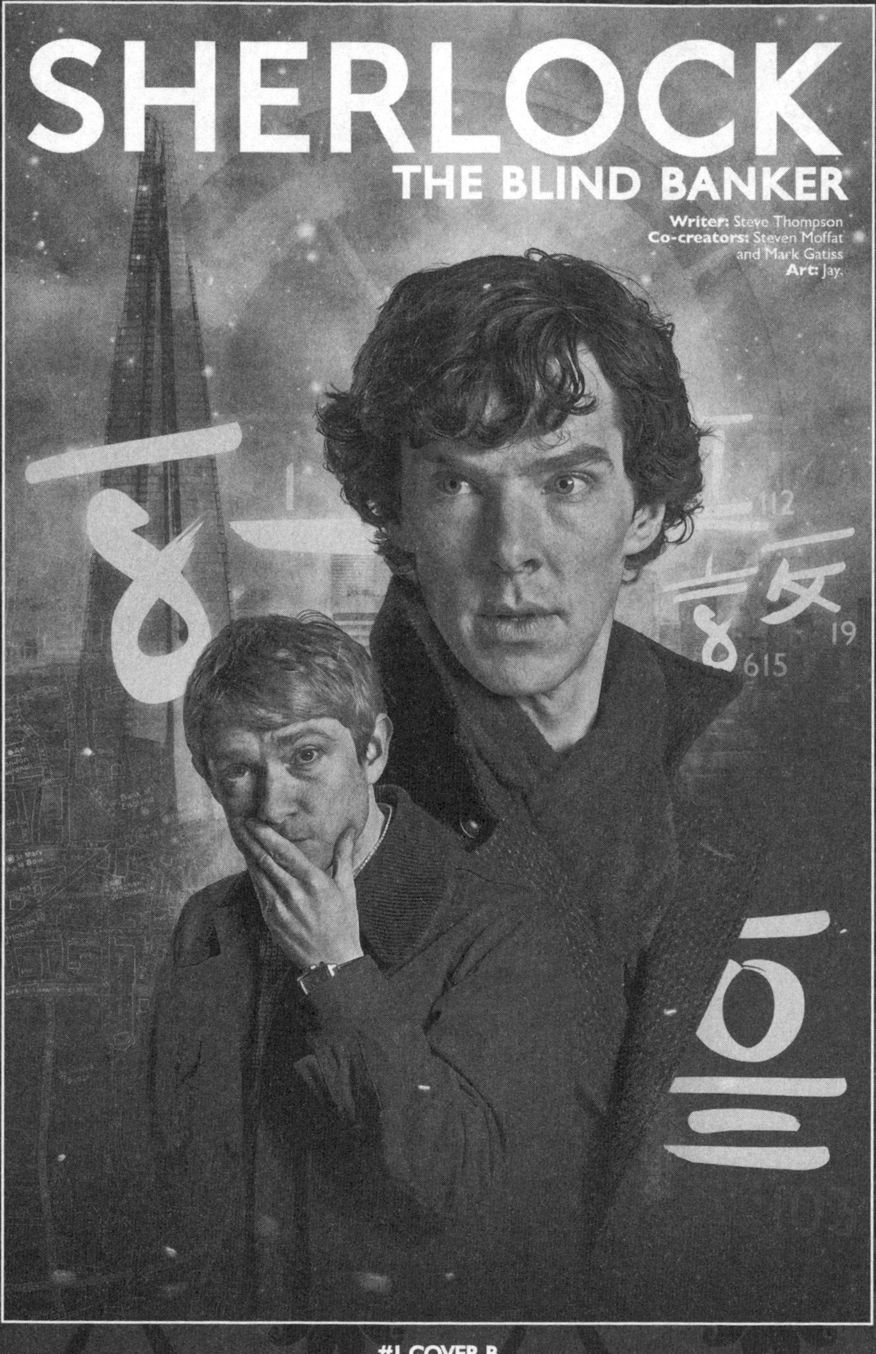
SHERLOCK
THE BLIND BANKER
Writer: Steve Thompson
Co-creators: Steven Moffat and Mark Gatiss
Art: Jay.
112
19
615

#1 COVER B
WILL BROOKS

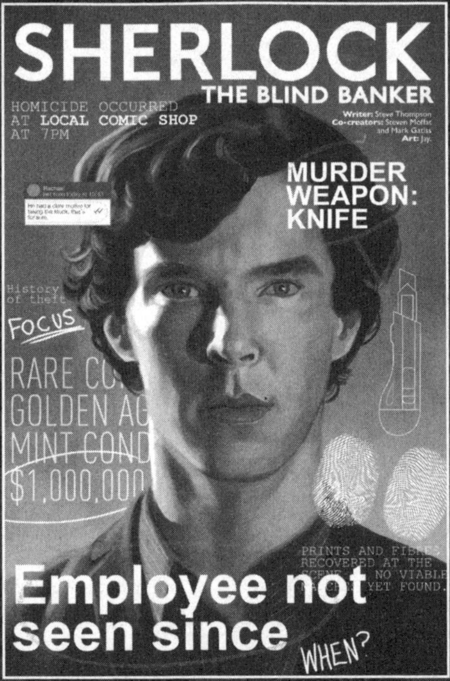
SHERLOCK
THE BLIND BANKER
Writer: Steve Thompson
Co-creators: Steven Moffat and Mark Gatiss
Art: Jay.
HOMICIDE OCCURRED AT LOCAL COMIC SHOP AT 7PM
MURDER WEAPON: KNIFE
FOCUS
RARE CO
GOLDEN AG
MINT COND
$1,000,000
PRINTS AND FIBE
RECOVERED AT THE
SCENE. NO VIABLE
YET FOUND.
Employee not seen since
WHEN?

#1 COVER C
MARIANO LACLAUSTRA

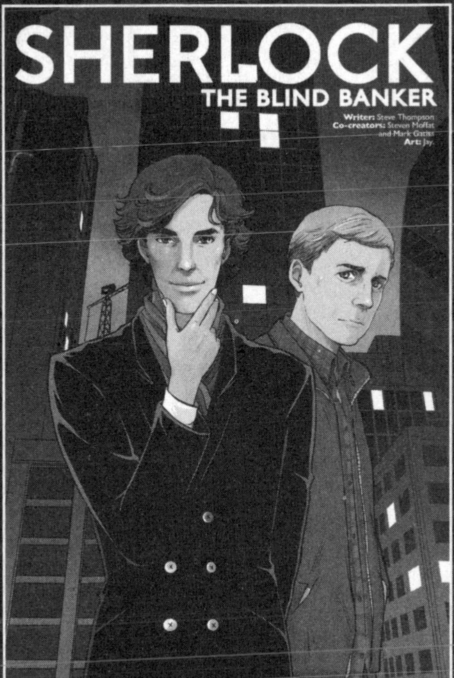
SHERLOCK
THE BLIND BANKER
Writer: Steve Thompson
Co-creators: Steven Moffat and Mark Gatiss
Art: Jay.

#1 COVER E
YISHAN LI

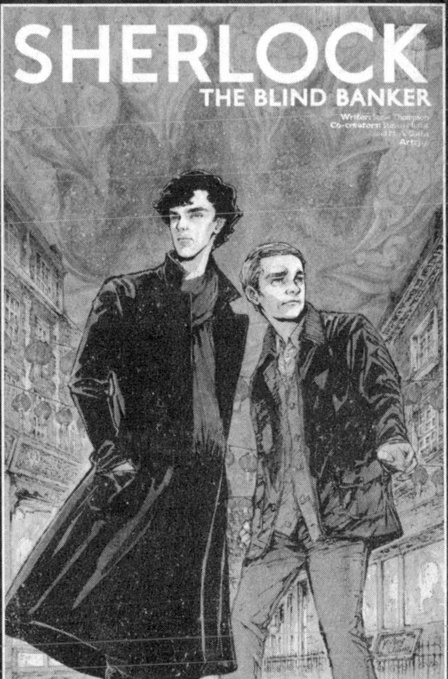
SHERLOCK
THE BLIND BANKER

#1 COVER D
YIFENG JIANG

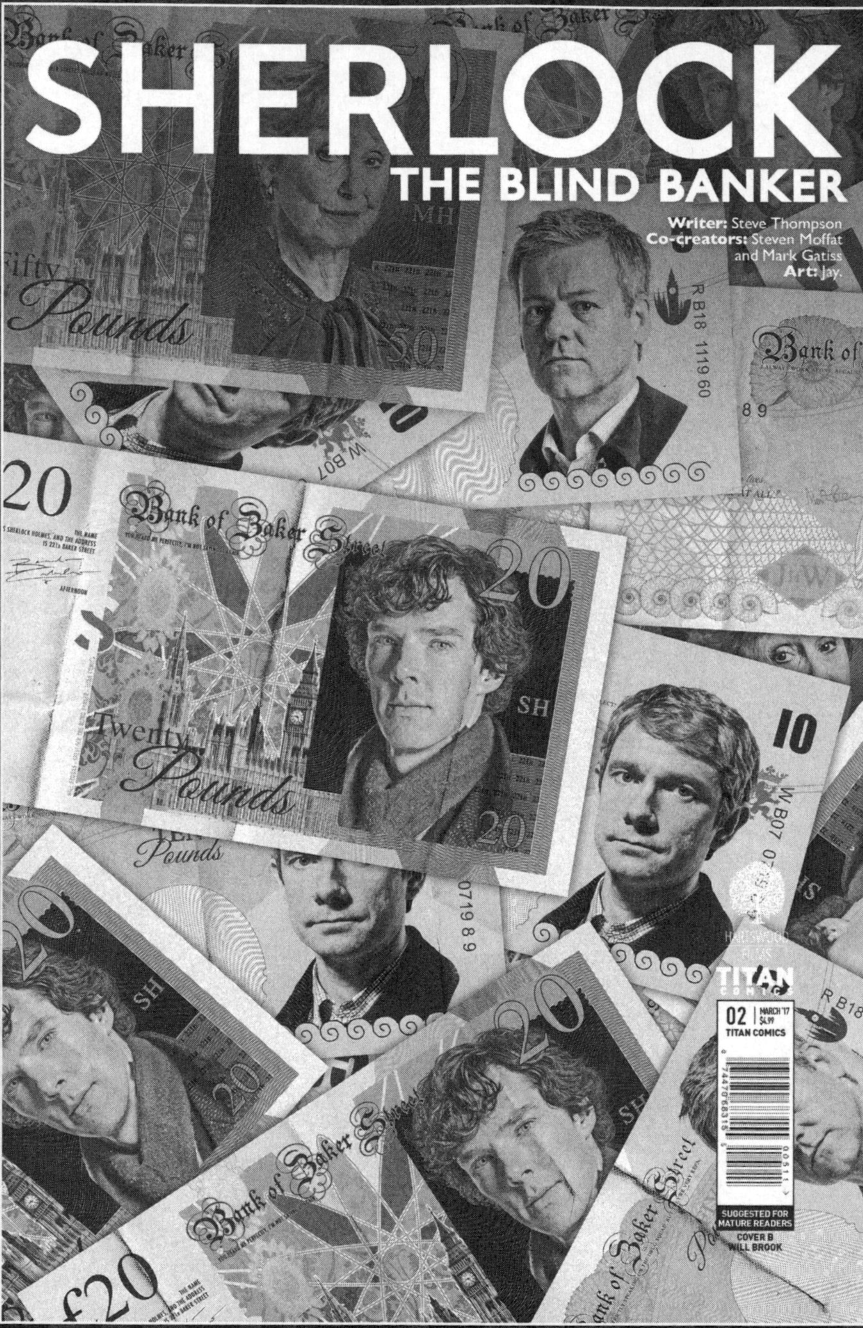
SHERLOCK
THE BLIND BANKER
Writer: Steve Thompson
Co-creators: Steven Moffat and Mark Gatiss
Art: Jay.
Bank of Baker Street
Twenty Pounds
Fifty Pounds
TITAN COMICS
02 | MARCH '17 $4.99
TITAN COMICS
SUGGESTED FOR MATURE READERS
COVER B
WILL BROOK

#2 COVER B
BY WILL BROOKS

#2 COVER C
BY JAY.

#2 COVER D
BY AMOONA SAOHIN

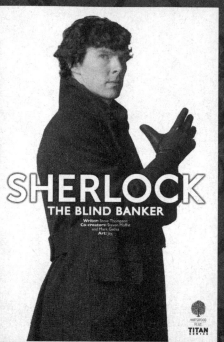

#3 COVER B
PHOTO

#3 COVER C
BY QUESTION NO. 6

#4 COVER B
PHOTO

#4 COVER C
BY YIFENG JIANG

#5 COVER B
PHOTO

#5 COVER C
BY AMOONA SAOHIN

#6 COVER B
BY WILL BROOKS

#6 COVER C
BY SIMON MYERS

STOP!

This manga is presented in its original right-to-left reading format. This is the back page!

Pages, panels, and speech balloons read from top right to bottom left, as shown above. Sound effects are translated in the gutters between the panels.